CLASSIC AND CONTEMPORARY READINGS IN SOCIAL PSYCHOLOGY

THIRD EDITION

Erik J. Coats
Vassar College

Robert S. Feldman
University of Massachusetts at Amherst

Prentice
Hall

Library of Congress Cataloging-in-Publication Data
Classic and contemporary readings in social psychology / [edited by] Erik J. Coats,
Robert S. Feldman.—3rd ed.
     p. cm.
  Includes bibliographical references.
  ISBN 0-13-087366-7
  1. Social psychology. I. Coats, Erik J., II. Feldman, Robert S. (Robert Stephen).

HM1033.C597 2001
302-dc21   00-056536

VP/Editorial Director: Laura Pearson
Executive Editor: Bill Webber
AVP/Director of Production and Manufacturing: Barbara Kittle
Managing Editor: Mary Rottino
Production Editor: Lisa Guidone
Prepress and Manufacturing Manager: Nick Sklitsis
Prepress and Manufacturing Buyer: Tricia Kenny
Director of Marketing: Beth Gillett Mejia
Marketing Manager: Sharon Cosgrove
Cover Design: Jayne Conte

This book was set in 11/13 Garamond by Storm King Publishing Services
and printed and bound by R. R. Donnelley-Harrisonburg. The cover was
printed by Phoenix Color Corp.

Cover art © Julia Lapine. Represented by Carolyn Potts and Associates, Inc.

© 2001, 1998 by Prentice-Hall, Inc.
A Division of Pearson Education
Upper Saddle River, New Jersey 07458

Printed in the United States of America
10 9 8 7 6 5 4 3

0-13-087366-7

Prentice-Hall International (UK) Limited, London
Prentice-Hall of Australia Pty. Limited, Sydney
Prentice-Hall Canada Inc., Toronto
Prentice-Hall Hispanoamericana, S.A., México
Prentice-Hall of India Private Limited, New Delhi
Prentice-Hall of Japan, Inc. Tokyo
Pearson Education Asia Pte. Ltd, Singapore
Editora Prentice-Hall do Brasil, Ltda., Rio de Janeiro

Ψ CONTENTS Ψ

Ψ PREFACE Ψ

Classic and Contemporary Readings in Social Psychology is a unique set of 30 paired selections from articles and books encompassing the breadth of the field of social psychology. Each reading represents either a classic, seminal article or a contemporary work that addresses a topic relevant to social psychology.

The classic articles are written by a "who's who" in the field, including such figures as Leon Festinger, Stanley Milgram, and Edward Jones. In addition, we have included more recent articles that have risen to classic status because of their impact on the field and the frequency with which they are cited.

The contemporary articles are written by a variety of individuals, most of whom are active scholars in the field of social psychology. Each is a recent and provocative report on some fundamental social psychological topic or issue. By pairing classic and contemporary articles, readers can plainly see the contrast between the old and the new, illustrating the progress and advances of the discipline.

In choosing these readings, we have cast our net widely. In addition to traditional journal articles, we examined book chapters, magazine articles, and even presentations at meetings and conventions. Our goal was not just to find articles that were technically sound or ones that revolutionized the field. Rather, we also sought to identify articles that helped to provide a picture of the development of the field, the concerns of its practitioners at a given moment in history, and a sense of the dynamic qualities of a constantly evolving discipline.

In editing the articles, we tried to provide sufficient detail to convey the depth, subtleties, and importance of the work being described. Furthermore, we tried to keep intact the original voice of the researcher who wrote the piece.* At the same time, we avoid including so much technical material that the readers would get mired in detail and miss the forest for the trees.

To meet these editing requirements, we were careful to choose sources that were accessible to students. In some articles, for purposes of clarity, we abridged and condensed the original text. In such cases, we have made clear where material has been dropped by inserting ellipses.

Each article begins with an introduction that provides a broad conceptual orientation to the piece. When appropriate, we have included a historical framework, discussing the import of the article and giving a sense of what social psychology was like at the time the article was written. These introductions not only show how the field has progressed and changed but also point out how the various parts of the field form a cohesive whole.

---

* As a result, the reader may occasionally come across attitudes or language in a classic article that is no longer considered appropriate or acceptable (e.g., regarding racial or sexual matters). Yet, after careful consideration, we have elected to leave unedited the offending text, not because we approve of the sentiments being expressed— we don't— but simply in the interests of historical accuracy.

Each article is followed by a series of questions designed to promote recall of the information that is presented and to consolidate the material. These questions are also meant to raise intriguing issues and challenge assumptions that readers may have developed. Most important, they are designed to make readers think critically about the articles' content.

READING ABOUT EXPERIMENTS IN SOCIAL PSYCHOLOGY

Each year researchers conduct thousands of empirical studies on topics related to social psychology. One of the challenges that face students who are just beginning to learn about the field is how to locate articles, chapters, and other reports of studies that are relevant to their interests. The goal of this section is to introduce you to the many outlets that social psychologists use to present their research findings. We begin by briefly describing five sources of psychological information -- textbooks, professional conferences, empirical articles, academic books and review articles, and the popular press -- and then focus on the most important source: the empirical article. As you will see, each type has its advantages and disadvantages.

Undergraduate textbooks. You are probably reading or have read one or two undergraduate textbooks about psychology. Such texts present a large amount of information in a relatively small amount of space. They are ideal for people who are first learning about psychology or one of its many subareas. However, as a secondary source, texts are somewhat limited. One limitation is that they represent the author(s)'s interpretation of other people's work. Although textbook authors strive to be accurate, occasionally their own biases creep into their work. Additionally, because new discoveries are made every day, you have to read primary sources to stay on top of the field.

Professional conferences. Perhaps the best way to learn about the most current research in psychology is to attend professional conferences. New findings are often presented at professional conferences before they appear anywhere else. If you are unable to attend a conference, you may be able to read a report of the talks that were given. Most psychologists will, upon request, send a paper version of their talk to people who were unable to hear them in person. Additionally, some organizations routinely publish all of the talks presented at their conferences.

Empirical articles. Although data are often presented first at a professional conference, the most important medium for communicating new findings is the empirical article. The empirical article is especially important because it is the only place where research projects are described in complete detail. This makes journals invaluable as primary sources. It is impossible to evaluate a research project fairly without reading the empirical article that describes the work.

Empirical journal articles are an important source of information for another reason. Before a journal will agree to publish an article, the research must pass a rigorous review process. Articles submitted for possible publication are sent to an action editor who is knowledgeable in the field that the article discusses. Action editors read the article themselves and then send it out to two or more experts on the issues raised in the article. Only after the reviewers and action editor are satisfied that an article is methodologically sound and will make an important contribution to the field will they agree to publish it. Many of the top journals reject 80 to 90 percent of the articles that researchers submit for publication. Because of this thorough review process, articles that journals agree to publish are likely to be largely fair and sound.

Unfortunately, empirical articles are somewhat difficult to read if you are not a psychologist yourself. In the next section we outline the typically empirical article. Knowing how empirical articles are organized will help get the most out of reading them. And you will soon get a chance to practice your new skills: Readings 7, 9, 13, 15, 17, 21, and 23 in this volume are reprints of empirical articles from some of the top journals in social psychology.

Academic books and review articles. After a researcher has published several empirical articles on the same general topic, he or she may decide to write a paper that summarizes the most important or interesting of his or her findings. There are two outlets for such reviews: review articles and academic books. Many academic books are collections of edited chapters, with each chapter being written by a different researcher. Some authors of book chapters and review articles focus primarily on one person's research (usually their own). Readings 10, 18, 20, and 22 are examples of articles that primarily review the author's own work. In contrast, some authors of book chapters and review articles focus less on their own work and instead attempt to give a complete picture of all the latest research in a particular area. Readings 11 and 27 are examples of this type of review.

The popular press. Researchers whose work catches the attention of editors of journals and of edited books will also likely catch the attention of journalists writing for the popular press. It may surprise you to know that many of the magazines and newspapers you read each day are extremely interested in following the major developments in psychology. However, not all magazines are careful when selecting what research to report. Like research in any field, not all psychological studies are as valid as others. Some newspapers and magazines ensure that the research they report is of the highest quality; some others are less careful in their choices. The popular magazine articles that are represented in this book, such as those from *The Atlantic Monthly* (Reading 6), *Scientific American* (Reading 8), *Newsweek* (Reading 12) and *Science* (Reading 27), are among those that are usually, although not invariably, trustworthy. Leading newspapers such as the *New York*

Times, *Washington Post*, and *Los Angeles Times* are also respectable sources of information about the field of psychology.

Reading Empirical Articles

As discussed earlier, the empirical article is the most important medium for communicating new information to the larger psychological community. Unfortunately, because their intended audience is other psychologists, empirical articles can be somewhat confusing to budding psychologists such as yourself. In order to aid you when you begin to read the empirical articles included in this volume, we discuss their main features.

Empirical articles have five main sections: Abstract, Introduction, Method, Results, and Discussion. The goal of the Abstract is to give the reader a very brief review of the entire article. The Abstract lets us know what topic the article addresses, what specific hypotheses were tested and how, and whether the hypotheses were supported by the data. Because of strict word limits placed on Abstracts, they can be overly terse. Consequently, you should read Abstracts carefully (and possibly more than once) in order to understand fully what the article is setting out to do.

The Introduction is the beginning of the article proper. The Introduction is typically not explicitly identified by a heading. We know we are reading the Introduction because it comes first; we know the Introduction is over when the Method section begins. (All further sections of the article are identified by headings.) The goal of the Introduction is to introduce the readers to the general problem being studied, to review relevant prior research, and to interest readers in the area being addressed. For example, in the Introduction to Reading 7, the authors tell us that they are interested in how people know when they are experiencing an emotion. After reviewing previous research in this area, the authors explain that the goal of their research is to find support for a new theory of emotion identification. If at this point we find ourselves interested in emotion identification, then one of the goals of the Introduction has been accomplished.

In the Method section, the authors explain in detail how the research was conducted. The goal of the Method section is to give readers sufficient detail so that they could repeat, or *replicate*, the study themselves. Replication is an important part of the scientific process, so the Method section must be complete and exact. If the experimenters used only women as participants in their study, we, the readers, need to know this. If participants' attitudes were surveyed, we need to know the exact wording of the questions. If several types of attitudes were measured, we need to know in what order this was done.

In order to help organize all of this information, the Method section is itself divided into subsections. All articles include what is called a Participant (or what was previously called a Subject) subsection. (The American Psychological Association, which determines the linguistic style for psychological research articles, now recommends that people who participate in experiments be called "participants" rather than the previously employed "subjects." You'll see that both terms are used in the readings in this volume, reflecting when the article was written.)

In the Participant section, the authors describe the people who took part in the study. This typically includes stating how many people participated, as well as their age and gender. If a study made use of a complicated apparatus (e.g., the reel-racing device described in Reading 1), this will be described in an Apparatus subsection. If the study employed a newly developed questionnaire that would not be available to the average reader, selected questions may be reprinted in a Materials subsection.

The final, and most important, Method subsection is Procedure. The Procedure subsection explains how the experiment was conducted in a step-by-step fashion, beginning with the moment the participants arrived for the study. After reading the Procedure subsection, the reader should know what it was like to have been a participant in the study. More important, the reader should be able to replicate the study in exact detail. The Method section also explains what data were collected from participants in the study.

After the data are analyzed, the results of the study are summarized in the next section—Results. The goal of the Results section is to explain the experimenter's findings in two ways: first in English, second in statistics. Reporting statistics is important because it allows readers to decide for themselves whether the author(s) performed the most appropriate analyzes. For now, assume that the journal editors have done their jobs and weeded out articles containing statistical flaws. Concentrate, instead, on the conclusions the author has drawn about the tests that have been carried out. As you become more knowledgeable about statistics, you will probably focus more on the statistics themselves, drawing your own conclusions instead of automatically accepting the authors' interpretations.

After reporting the study's findings in the Results section, the authors will next explain the practical significance of their findings in the Discussion section. The goal of the Discussion section is twofold: to remind the reader of the issues being considered and to explain how the current study has extended our knowledge of these issues. For example, in Reading 9, the authors compared participants' physical health after participating in the study. Reading the Results section we learn that some participants were healthier after being in the study. Yet after spending perhaps 15 to 30 minutes examining and considering the exact methods and findings of the study, readers may have forgotten why this is theoretically interesting. In the Discussion section, the authors remind us that their findings are important because they contribute to our understanding of the Freudian notion of catharsis.

Although empirical articles are written in something like a story format— with a beginning (Introduction), middle (Method and Results), and end (Discussion)— it is not essential that you read them in that order. Some people find it easier to read the Discussion immediately after the Introduction and before the Results. Some even skip the Introduction altogether and begin with the Method. However, we suggest that you first try reading articles as they were intended -- first Abstract, then Introduction, then Method, then Results, and then Discussion. Later you might want to experiment with different strategies.

USING THESE READINGS

These readings can be used in several ways. Some professors may wish their students to focus on classic selections, whereas others may choose to focus on the contemporary readings. Some may wish to assign the questions at the end of each reading. These readings can be used to supplement any social psychology text, but they specifically reflect the 15 chapters of *Social Psychology, Third Edition*, the introduction to social psychology written by Robert S. Feldman.

In sum, *Classic and Contemporary Readings in Social Psychology* provides a worthwhile supplement for students being introduced to the field of social psychology. We welcome any feedback that readers are willing to provide and encourage you to write to us. Erik Coats is at the Dept. of Psychology, Vassar College Box 214, 124 Raymond Ave., Poughkeepsie, NY 12604, email: ercoats@vassar.edu. Robert Feldman is at the Dept. of Psychology, University of Massachusetts, Amherst, MA 01003, email: feldman@psych.umass.edu.

ACKNOWLEDGMENTS

Improvements in the second and third edition of this reader owe a great deal to the editors and production staff at Prentice Hall, especially Bill Webber and Jennifer Blackwell. Their many suggestions have improved the quality of this book in countless ways. We would also like to thank our students at Vassar College and at the University of Massachusetts. Their comments – and those of the three reviewers Glenda J. Sehested, Augustana College, Cheryl Armstrong, Fitchburg State College, and Traci Giuliano, Southwestern University – guided many of our decisions in updating this reader.

Ψ

PART I
INTRODUCTION
TO A DISCIPLINE

$\Psi \ \Psi$

Ψ CHAPTER 1 Ψ

AN INTRODUCTION
TO SOCIAL PSYCHOLOGY

Reading 1: Classic

The Dynamogenic Factors in Pacemaking and Competition

Norman Triplett

Norman Triplett's study of "dynamogenic" factors in competition is widely considered to be the first ever social psychological study. Reviewing speed records in three different types of bicycle races, Triplett noticed that cyclists went much faster when racing with other cyclists than when racing alone. This fact was well known among cyclists, who believed that racing with another increased speeds, on average, by 20 to 30 seconds per mile.

A host of explanations, both mechanical and psychological, had been proposed to explain the observed faster times in competition and "paced" races, some of which we know today to be perfectly accurate. But Triplett believed that another set of factors was operating in addition to those that had already been proposed. His dynamogenic theory held that the physical presence of other riders increased a rider's level of arousal, which released additional energy.

To test this theory, Triplett designed a study similar to cycling, but in which the mechanical and psychological factors other than dynamogenic would not be present. If competition increased performance in this experimental situation, it could only be due to the physical presence of the other competitor.

In the article, Triplett describes the various theories that can account for the benefits of paced races, the apparatus he built to test the dynamogenic theory, and the results he obtained. As expected, the majority of subjects exhibited faster times when competing with another than when performing alone.

Ψ

PART I: THEORIES ACCOUNTING FOR THE FASTER TIME OF PACED AND COMPETITION RACES

Of the seven or eight not wholly distinct theories which have been advanced to account for the faster time made in paced as compared with unpaced competitive races and paced races against time as against unpaced races against time, a number need only be stated very briefly. They are grouped according to their nature and first are given two mechanical theories.

Source: Triplett, N. (1897). The dynamogenic factors in pacemaking and competition. *American Journal of Psychology, 9,* 507-533

Suction Theory

Those holding to this as the explanation assert that the vacuum left behind the pacing machine draws the rider following, along with it. Anderson's ride of a mile a minute at Roodhouse, Ill., with the locomotive as pacemaker, is the strongest argument in its favor. Those maintaining this theory believe that the racer paced by a tandem is at a disadvantage as compared with the racer paced by a quod or a larger machine, as the suction exerted is not so powerful.

The Shelter Theory

This is closely related to the foregoing. Dr. Turner accepts it as a partial explanation of the aid to be gained from a pace, holding that the pacemaker or the leading competitor serves as a shelter from the wind, and that "a much greater amount of exertion, purely muscular, is required from a man to drive a machine when he is leading than when he is following, on account of the resistance of the air, and the greater the amount of wind blowing the greater the exertion, and conversely, the greater the shelter obtained the less the exertion."

This is the theory held, in general, by racers themselves. One of the champion riders of the country recently expressed this common view in a letter, as follows: "It is true that some very strong unpaced riders do not have any sort of success in paced racing. The only reason I can give for this is just simply that they have not studied the way to follow pace so as to be shielded from the wind. No matter which way it blows there is always a place where the man following pace can be out of the wind."

Encouragement Theory

The presence of a friend on the pacing machine to encourage and keep up the spirits of the rider is claimed to be of great help. The mental disposition has been long known to be of importance in racing as in other cases where energy is expended. It is still as true as in Virgil's time that the winners "can because they think they can."

The Brain Worry Theory

This theory shows why it is difficult for the leader in an unpaced competition race to win. For "a much greater amount of brain worry is incurred by making the pace than by waiting" (following). The man leading "is in a fidget the whole time whether he is going fast enough to exhaust his adversary; he is full of worry as to when that adversary means to commence his spurt; his nervous system is generally strung up, and at concert pitch, and his muscular and nervous efforts act and react on each other, producing an ever-increasing exhaustion, which both dulls the impulse-giving power of the brain and the impulse-receiving or contractile power of the muscles."

Theory of Hypnotic Suggestions

A curious theory, lately advanced, suggests the possibility that the strained attention given to the revolving wheel of the pacing machine in front produces a sort of hypnotism and that the accompanying muscular exaltation is the secret of the endurance shown by some long-distance riders in paced races. Notice that Michael was able to make the last mile of his great 30 mile competition race the fastest of all and one of the fastest ever ridden.

The Automatic Theory

This is also a factor which favors the waiting rider, and gives him a marked advantage. The leader, as has been noted, must use his brain to direct every movement of his muscles. As he becomes more distressed it requires a more intense exertion of will power to force his machine through the resisting air. On the other hand, the "waiter" rides automatically. He has nothing to do but hang on. "His brain having inaugurated the movement leaves it to the spinal cord to continue it and only resumes its functions when a change of direction or speed is necessary." – (Lagrange.) When he comes to the final spurt, his brain, assuming control again, imparts to the muscles a winning stimulus, while the continued brain work of the leader has brought great fatigue.

These facts seem to have large foundation in truth. The lesser amount of fatigue incurred in paced trials is a matter of general knowledge. It is a common experience with wheelmen, and within that of the writer, that when following a lead on a long ride the feeling of automatic action becomes very pronounced, giving the sensation of a strong force pushing from behind. Of course the greater the distance ridden the more apparent becomes the saving in energy from automatic riding, as time is required to establish the movement. It may be remembered, in this connection, that while the average gain of the paced over the unpaced record is 34.4 seconds, the difference between them for the first mile is only 23.8 seconds.

As between the pacer and the paced, every advantage seems to rest with the latter. The two mechanical factors of suction and shelter, so far as they are involved, assist the rider who follows. So the psychological theories, the stimulation from encouragement, the peculiar power induced by hypnotism, and the staying qualities of automatic action, if of help at all, directly benefit the paced rider. The element of disadvantage induced by brain action, on the contrary, belongs more especially to the rider who leads.

The Dynamogenic Factors

The remaining factors to be discussed are those which the experiments on competition, detailed in the second part hereof, attempt to explain. No effort is made to weaken the force of the foregoing factors in accounting for the better time of paced races in comparison with unpaced races of the same type, but the facts of this study are given to throw whatever additional light they may.

This theory of competition holds that the bodily presence of another rider is a stimulus to the racer in arousing the competitive instinct; that another can thus be the means of releasing or freeing nervous energy for him that he cannot of himself release; and, further, that the sight of movement in that other by perhaps suggesting a higher rate of speed, is also an inspiration to greater effort. These are the factors that had their counterpart in the experimental study following; and it is along these lines that the facts determined are to find their interpretation.

PART II: THE EXPERIMENTAL STUDY

From the laboratory competitions to be described, abstraction was made of nearly all the forces above outlined. In the 40 seconds the average trial lasted, no shelter from the wind was required, nor was any suction exerted, the only brain worry incident was that of maintaining a sufficiently high rate of speed to defeat the competitors. From the shortness of the time and nature of the case, generally, it is doubtful if any automatic movements could be established. On the other hand, the effort was intensely voluntary. It may be likened to the 100 yard dash— a sprint from beginning to end.

Description of Apparatus

The apparatus for this study consisted of two fishing reels whose cranks turned in circles of one and three-fourths inches diameter. These were arranged on a Y-shaped framework clamped to the top of a heavy table, as shown in Figure 1. The sides of this framework were spread sufficiently far apart to permit of two persons turning side by side. Bands of twisted silk cord ran over the well lacquered axes of the reels and were supported at C and D, two meters distant, by two small pulleys. The records were taken from the course A D. The other course B C was used merely for pacing or competition purposes. The wheel on the side from which the records were taken communicated the movement made to a recorder, the stylus of which traced a curve on the drum of a kymograph. The direction of this curve corresponded to the rate of turning, as the greater the speed the shorter and straighter the resulting line.

Method of Conducting the Experiment

A subject taking the experiment was required to practice turning the reel until he had become accustomed to the machine. After a short period of rest the different trials were made with five-minute intervals between to obviate the possible effects of fatigue.

A trial consisted in turning the reel at the highest rate of speed until a small flag sewed to the silk band had made four circuits of the four-meter course. The time of the trial was

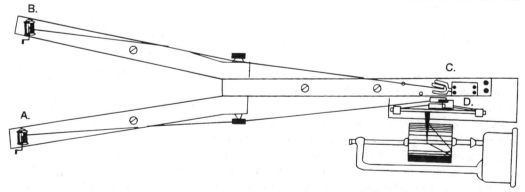

Figure 1
Competition Machine

taken by means of a stop-watch. The direction of the curves made on the drum likewise furnished graphic indications of the difference in time made between trials...

Statement of Results

In the course of the work the records of nearly 225 persons of all ages were taken. However, all the tables given below, and all statements made, unless otherwise specified, are based on the records of 40 children taken in the following manner: After the usual preliminaries of practice, six trials were made by each of 20 subjects in this order: first a trial alone, followed by a trial in competition, then another alone, and thus alternating through the six efforts, giving three trials alone and three in competition. Six trials were taken by 20 other children of about the same age, the order of trials in this case being the first trial alone, second alone, third a competition trial, fourth alone, fifth a competition, and sixth alone.[1] The 20 subjects given in Group A and Group B, of Table I, in nearly all cases make marked reductions in the competition trials. The averages show large gains in these trials and small gains or even losses for the succeeding trials alone. The second trial for Group A is a competition, for Group B a trial alone. The gain between the first and second trials of the first group is 5.6 seconds, between the first and second trials of the second group, 2.52 seconds. The latter represents the practice effect – always greatest in the first trials, the former the element of competition plus the practice. The third trial in Group A – a trial alone – is .72 seconds slower than the preceding race trial. The third trial in Group B – a competition – is 4.48 seconds faster than the preceding trial alone. The fourth trials in these two groups are on an equality, as regards practice, from an equal number of trials of the same kind. In the first case the gain over the preceding trial is 3.32 seconds. In the latter there is a loss of 1.58 seconds from the time of the preceding competition trial. In like manner there is an equality of conditions in regard to the sixth trial of these groups, and again the effect of competition plainly appears, the competition trial gaining 2.12 seconds, and the trial alone losing .82 seconds with respect to the preceding trial. These are decided differences. Curve No. I in Chart I is a graphical representation of them.

The 10 subjects whose records are given in Table II are of interest. With them stimulation brought a loss of control. In one or more of the competition trials of each subject in this group the time is very much slower than that made in the preceding trial alone. Most frequently this is true of the first trial in competition, but with some was characteristic of every race. In all, 14 of the 25 races run by this group were equal to or slower than the preceding trial alone. This seems to be brought about in large measure by the mental attitude of the subject: an intense desire to win, for instance, often resulting in over-stimulation. Accompanying phenomena were labored breathing, flushed faces and a stiffening or contraction of the muscles of the arm. A number of young children of from 5 to 9 years, not included in our group of 40, exhibited the phenomena most strikingly, the rigidity of the arm preventing free movement and in some cases resulting in an almost total inhibition of movement. The effort to continue turning in these cases was by a swaying of the whole body.

---

[1] In the tables, A represents a trial alone, C, a trial in competition.

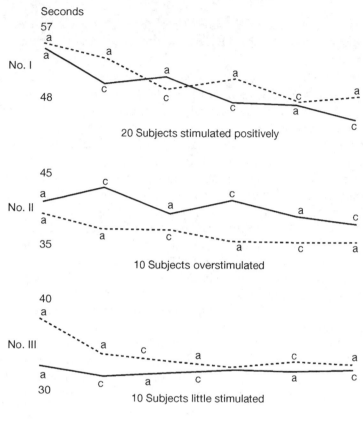

CHART I
Solid line represents Group A. Dotted line represents Group B.

This seems a most interesting fact and confirmatory of the probable order of development of the muscles as given by Dr. Hall and others. In the case of those sufficiently developed to have the fast forearm movement, fatigue or overstimulation seemed to bring a recurrence to the whole arm and shoulder movement of early childhood, and if the fatigue or excitement was sufficiently intense, to the whole body movement, while younger children easily fell into the swaying movement when affected by either of the causes named.

It reminds one of the way in which fatigue of a small muscle used in ergographic work will cause the subject to attempt to draw on his larger muscles, or of the man who moves to the city and acquires the upright carriage and springing step of the city-bred man, who, when greatly fatigued, insensible falls into the old "clodhopper" gait. This tendency to revert to earlier movements and also old manners of speech, as Höpfner has shown in his "Fatigue of School Children," is common, when, for any reason, the centers of control are interfered with. It may be said, therefore, that in the work under consideration the chief difference between this group and the large group in Table I, was a difference in control; the stimulation inhibiting the proper function of the motor centers in the one

TABLE 1
SUBJECTS STIMULATED POSITIVELY

	Group A					
	Age	A	C	A	C	A	C
Violet F.	10	54.4	42.6	45.2	41.	42.	46.
Anna P.	9	67.	57.	55.4	50.4	49.	44.8
Willie H.	12	37.8	38.8	43.	39.	37.2	33.4
Bessie V.	11	46.2	41.	39.	30.2	33.6	32.4
Howard C.	11	42.	36.4	39.	41.	37.8	34.
Mary M.	11	48.	44.8	52.	44.6	43.8	40.
Lois P.	11	53.	45.6	44.	44.	40.6	35.8
Inez K.	13	37.	35.	35.8	34.	34.	32.6
Harvey L.	9	49.	42.6	39.6	37.6	36.	35.
Lora F.	11	40.4	35.	33.	35.	30.2	29.
Average	11	47.48	41.88	42.6	39.28	38.42	36.3
P.E.		6.18	4.45	4.68	3.83	3.74	3.74
Gains			5.6	.72	3.32	.86	2.12

	Group B					
	Age	A	A	C	A	C	A
Stephen M.	13	51.2	50.	43.	41.8	39.8	41.2*
Mary W.	13	56.	53.	45.8	49.4	45.	43.*
Bertha A.	10	56.2	49.	48.	46.8	41.4	44.4
Clara L.	8	52.	44.	46.	45.6	44.	45.2
Helen M.	10	45.	45.6	35.8	46.2	40	40.
Gracie W.	12	56.6	50.	42.	39.	40.2	41.4
Dona R.	15	34.	37.2	36.	41.4	37.	32.8
Pearl C.	13	43.	43.	40.	40.6	33.8	35.
Clyde G.	13	36.	35.	32.4	33.	31.	35.
Lucile W.	10	52.	50.	43.	44.	38.	40.2
Average	11.7	48.2	45.68	41.2	42.78	39.	39.82
P.E.		5.6	4.	3.42	3.17	2.89	2.84
Gains			2.52	4.48	1.58	3.78	.82

*Left-handed
IX-35

case, and reinforcing it in the other. This, at least, seemed apparent from the characteristics exhibited by the two classes. Observation of the subjects of this class under trial, and careful scrutiny of their graphic records show how decided gains were sometimes lost by the subject "going to pieces" at the critical point of the race, not being able to endure the nervous strain. Yet there exists no sharp line of division between subjects stimulated to make faster time and those affected in the opposite way. In some instances the nervous excitement acted adversely in every race trial, while in others, a gain in control enabled the subject to make a material reduction in the last competition. A. B., one of three adults affected adversely, is an athletic young man, a fine tennis and handball

TABLE 2
SUBJECTS STIMULATED ADVERSELY

		Group A					
	Age	A	C	A	C	A	C
Jack R.	9	44.2	44.	41.8	48.	44.2	41.
Helen F.	9	44.	51.	43.8	44.	43.	41.2
Emma P.	11	38.4	42.	37.	39.6	36.6	32.
Warner J.	11	41.6	43.6	43.4	43.	40.	48.
Genevieve M.	12	36.	36.	32.6	32.8	31.2	34.8
Average	10.4	40.84	43.32	39.72	41.48	39.	37.4
P.E.		2.41	3.57	3.25	3.85	3.55	2.52
Gains							

		Group B					
	Age	A	A	C	A	C	A
Hazel M.	11	38.	35.8	38.2	37.2	35.	42.
George B.	12	39.2	36.	37.6	34.2	36.	33.8
Mary B.	11	50.	46.	43.4	42.	48.	36.8
Carlisle B.	14	37.	35.4	35.	33.4	36.4	31.4
Eddie H.	11	31.2	29.2	27.6	27.	26.8	28.8
Average	11.8	39.08	36.48	36.36	34.76	34.4	34.56
P.E.		4.61	4.07	3.89	3.71	5.33	3.45
Gains							

player, and known to be stimulated in contests of these kinds. It was noticed that in his competition trials time was lost because of his attempt to take advantage of the larger muscles of the arm and shoulder. After many trials and injunctions to avoid the movement, he gained sufficient control to enable him to reduce the time in the competitions.

A. V., an adult of nervous organization, went half through his race with a great gain over his trial alone, but seeing his antagonist pushing him closely, broke down and lost the most of the gain made in the first half. The time of the trial alone was 38.6 seconds, that of the competition was 37.2 seconds. A comparison of the time in which the halves of the trials were made was computed in he following way: On the ordinate of the graph is measured the distance the stylus travels across the drum during 150 turns of the reel – the number in a trial. The distance on the abscissa between the ordinates running through he ends of the curve of any trial gives the time of the trial.

Parallel abscissas were drawn at the extremities of the curves, and a third one-half way between them. Half of the turns made in a trial were thus on each side of this middle line, and the times in which these turns were made were proportional to the segments of this line made by the curve intersecting it. By this means it was found that A. V. made the first 75 turns in his competition trial in 15 seconds, the second half in 22.2 seconds. By

TABLE 3
SUBJECTS LITTLE AFFECTED BY COMPETITION

	Age	A	Group A C	A	C	A	C
Albert P.	13	29.	28.	27.	29.	27.	26.8
Milfred V.	17	36.4	29.	29.4	30.2	30.2	32.2
Harry V.	12	32.	32.	32.6	32.6	32.6	31.6
Robt. H.	12	31.4	31.4	32.2	35.4	35.	32.4
John T.	11	30.2	30.8.	32.8	30.6	32.8	31.8
Average	13	31.8	30.24	30.8	31.56	31.5	31.3
P.E.		1.9	1.13	1.71	1.7	2.06	1.05

	Age	A	Group B A	C	A	C	A
Hazel M.	10	45.	37.4	36.8	36.	37.2	38.
George B.	11	42.	39.	38.	37.	37.	38.
Mary B.	13	38.	30.	28.	30.	30.2	29.6
Carlisle B.	11	35.	31.8	32.4	30.	32.	30.4
Eddie H.	14	37.2	30.	29.	27.8	28.4	26.8
Average	11.8	39.44	33.64	32.84	32.16	32.96	32.16
P.E.		3.11	2.88	3.03	2.75	2.69	3.71
Gains							

the same means, each half of the preceding trial alone was 19.3 seconds – an exception to the rule that the last half is slower because of fatigue.

Other curves when worked out in this way gave similar results. The time record, therefore, it must be seen, is not always a true index to the amount of stimulation present. Had the trials consisted of but half as many turns, the effect of competition as it appears in the tables would have been shown much more constantly. Table II would have been a smaller group if indeed any necessity existed for retaining it.

A comparison of the time made by the different groups shows that the subjects of Table I are much slower than those of Table II, and that a still greater difference exists between this group and the subjects found in Table III. It may be said that they are slower because of greater sluggishness of disposition, and that the reductions made are largely a result of the subjects warming up. This, indeed, may be a part of the cause for it, but as the larger reductions coincide with the competition trials this cannot be held to completely account for it. A glance over the individual records discovers some facts which furnish a plausible partial explanation, when taken in connection with the following fact. The age at which children acquire control of the wrist movements, a large factor in turning the reel with speed, was found to be about 11 years in general, although a few of 9 and 10 years had this power. Now, of the 20 subjects composing Table I, 7 are 10 years of age or younger, while two others, age 13, are left-handed and being compelled to use the right hand are slow in consequence. So, here are 9 subjects, a number nearly equal to the group in Table II or Table III, who had a reason for being slow. Were these omitted from the count, the time of the initial trial would be found not to vary materially from that of Table II.

Besides the lack of muscular development of the younger subjects mentioned above, many of the subjects of Table I seemed not to have proper ideals of speed. The desire to beat, if it did nothing else, brought them to a sense of what was possible for them. The arousal of their competitive instincts and the idea of a faster movement, perhaps, in the contestant, induced greater concentration of energy.

The subjects in Table III are a small group who seemed very little affected by competition. They made very fast time, but they are older than the average; their muscular control was good, and they had the forearm movements. Practice gains while somewhat apparent at first in some cases, are, as shown by curve No. 3 of the chart, on the whole, less in amount. Their drum records show fewer fluctuations and irregularities, and less pronounced fatigue curves at the end.

There seems to be a striking analogy between these subjects and those racing men who are fast without a pace, but can do little or no better in a paced or competition race...

CONCLUDING STATEMENT

From the above facts regarding the laboratory races we infer that the bodily presence of another contestant participating simultaneously in the race serves to liberate latent energy not ordinarily available. This inference is further justified by the difference in time between the paced competition races and the paced races against time, amounting to an average of 5.15 seconds per mile up to 25 miles. The factors of shelter from the wind, encouragement, brain worry, hypnotic suggestion, and automatic movement are common to both, while the competitors participate simultaneously in person only in the first.

In the next place the sight of the movements of the pacemakers or leading competitors, and the idea of higher speed, furnished by this or some other means, are probably in themselves dynamogenic factors of some consequence.

QUESTIONS

1. What two mechanical theories are suggested to account for the effects of pacing? How does the influence of the dynamogenic factors differ from other psychological factors?

2. Which factors does Triplett say most cyclists themselves believe are responsible for the benefits of pacing? Which factors does Triplett believe are responsible?

3. Which suggested factors that influence cycle races are also present in the fishing-reel races that Triplett designed?

4. Of the 40 children whose data are discussed, what percentage show marked improvement in the competition phases? What percentage performed equally well?

5. How does Triplett explain his findings? Can the dynamogenic process explain all three different performance patterns observed with only the dynamogenic factor?

Reading 2: Contemporary

A Glance Back at a Quarter Century of Social Psychology

Ellen Berscheid

If social psychology was born at the turn of the century and reached adulthood in the 1940s, its first midlife crisis came in the 1960s. At this time, social psychology was experiencing several crises: a crisis of growth caused by a boom of new Ph.D.s in the field, a crisis of faith as those outside (and inside) the field began to question its ability to discover anything other than temporary social fads, and a crisis of identity as social psychologists struggled to distinguish themselves from other branches of psychology and from other social sciences such as sociology. It was a critical time for the field, and social psychologists were not always sure what new paths the field was taking.

This was the atmosphere when Ellen Berscheid earned her Ph.D. in social psychology in 1965. In the three decades since, she argues, social psychology has matured into a much stronger, more robust field.

In this article, Berscheid takes a personal look back at this period of growth and maturity. Noticing the improved lot of social psychologists today, she suggests a few reasons for how the uncertainty of the 1960s were overcome. Among the reasons are the acceptance and encouragement of women in the field; the guidance of important thinkers such as Kurt Lewin; expansion into new areas of research; and, surprisingly, the inadequacy of federal financial support.

ψ

Twenty-five years ago, social psychology was experiencing growing pains. Hollander (1968) related that the size of APA's Division 8, now the Society of Personality and Social Psychology, had become so large that the convention program had reached "intimidating dimensions" and that "personal contact and communication [had become] unwieldy." Hence, the establishment of the Society of Experimental Social Psychology (SESP) in 1965, which the organizers envisioned as including "a relatively small number of social psychologists whose interests were primarily research-oriented," believing that "the common focus and smaller size of such a group [beginning with about 50 members and growing slowly to a limit of 100] would allow more flexible organization and would permit the group to engage in more intimate and informal dialogue than is possible at the conventions of the larger associations" (p. 280). Those who have attended an SESP

Source: Berscheid, E. (1992) A glance back at a quarter century of social psychology. *Journal of Personality and Social Psychology, 63*, 525-533. Copyright © 1992 by the American Psychological Association. Reprinted with permission.

conference recently and have had to shoehorn themselves into one of the meeting rooms (the "intimate and informal dialogue," where all attendees sat in one room and talked about a common problem of interest, having disappeared years ago) will conclude that the original vision for the society failed miserably in the execution. In retrospect, however, it is clear that, rather than creating a cozy atmosphere in which social psychologists could interact, it was the idea of bringing together social psychologists with a "common focus," specifically, a *research* focus, that was to play an important role in transforming social psychology from a gangly adolescent afflicted with growing pains and facing an uncertain future to the robust and mature discipline it is today. But I am getting ahead of myself.

The remarkable evolution social psychology has undergone over the past quarter century encompasses so many changes in the field's form and content, in the number and nature of its contributors, as well as in the context in which it is embedded, both in psychology and in society, that which of these changes can be singled out for notice in a brief, informal retrospective is necessarily a very personal and impressionistic matter. The comments that follow, which highlight only three of the many changes the field has undergone in the past few decades, meet none of the historian's claims. I hope only to give the flavor of social psychology's evolution over the past 25 years, a period which is clearly demarcated for me, for it was in 1965 that I received my doctorate in social psychology from the University of Minnesota, where I have remained ever since.

What happened to me after I received my degree at Minnesota, and what likely would happen to me today, illustrates with a single brushstroke many of the changes to which social psychologists in my age cohort have been witness. Like many female graduate students of the day, I had expected to retire from academic life after receiving my degree; women were rarely admitted into the academy and none of the three institutions at which I had received my undergraduate and graduate training (including the University of Nevada where I earned a master's degree with Paul Secord) had one female professor on their psychology faculty, although there were a few women "adjunct" professors. The Minnesota psychology department, I was told, once had a woman faculty member but relation of that fact was often followed by a somber pause and then, in sotto voce, the phrase "but it just didn't work out." Unexpectedly, however, my retirement plans were shelved when I was offered a temporary but open-ended, nontenure track assistant professorship in the Department of Marketing of Minnesota's business school. There, I quickly became known as "the lady professor" (as in "Good morning, lady professor!"), being the only female professor in the business school. The student body, both graduate and undergraduate, was overwhelmingly if not exclusively male (I did not set eyes on, and never taught, a single female student there), and, befitting my place in the general scheme of things, these young men called me either Mrs. Berscheid or "Blondie" (as in "Hey, Blondie, what'd I get on the test?"). I look back on my business school job with nostalgia, for it was my good fortune, no doubt the result of my being a temporary alien, that I was left almost entirely alone. I was not invited to attend department meetings, for example, or to serve on college and university committees, or asked to do any of those things for discipline, God, and country that young professors are required to do today, sapping vast quantities of their time and their energy.

Unfortunately, the beginning of the end of my halcyon days at the business school came about a year later when, waiting for the elevator one day, I casually surveyed the business school's employment bulletin board and noticed an advertisement for a "market research analyst" at the company where I briefly had held such a position. I was dismayed to read that the only "qualification" for the job, entered on the appropriate blank on the business school's standard form, was "male." I removed the ad (politely, I thought) for reconsideration of the gender qualification, copying the business school's employment bureau. Moreover, I wrote letters to my Senators, at that time Eugene McCarthy and Hubert Humphrey, telling them that it had become apparent to me that women did not have the same opportunities as men did in the workplace and asking what, if anything, they were doing about it. I then forgot about the whole episode, having discharged my duties as I saw them, and so I was truly surprised when a week or so later, I received a curt summons to appear "immediately" in the office of the associate dean. There, I found an agitated man who, venting his anger with the coarsest of language, told me that my actions had jeopardized scholarships and other monies donated to the school by the company in question and that he intended to bring charges against me. When I asked him what the charge was going to be, he replied, "It is against the law to mutilate University property, and by removing that ad, you mutilated our employment bulletin board."

Fortunately, several things happened to allow me to leave the business school quietly, and each event reflected the times: First, it turned out that the reason the associate dean, rather than the dean, had handled the matter was because the dean had been in Chicago that week attending a national conference addressed to the topic "The Place of Women in Business." That was heartening because it at least assumed that women had a place, although it apparently was taking a great deal of deliberation to figure out exactly where that place might be. Second, several weeks later, a group of black students who were shortcutting through the building lobby (there were no black students at the school either) spied an ad on the employment bulletin board that, under qualifications, listed "Caucasian." Their response was to douse the board with gasoline and set it afire, thereby leaving a rather large black hole where the employment bulletin board used to be for the remainder of the academic year. Third, the senior business school faculty rallied in my support and called a special meeting where impassioned speeches were made decrying the vulgar language and ungentlemanly behavior of the associate dean toward their lady professor and demanding that he apologize. No one mentioned the advertisement. Although an apology was subsequently made, when Elaine Hatfield left her research position with the Student Activities Bureau in the office of the Dean of Students to take a "real" psychology professorship at the University of Rochester, she arranged for me to be offered her job in the Bureau and I accepted it, believing it to be a safer foxhole than the business school. (For one thing, the Dean was a personal friend of Leon Festinger's, who had been Elaine Hatfield's doctoral adviser as well as Elliot Aronson's, who had been my own adviser.) A year or so later, I too, was able to join a psychology department, when John G. Darley, the powerful and wily chair of the Minnesota department, called a faculty meeting for a Saturday morning after a violent snowstorm during spring break and made a motion that I be hired; when he later informed me that I was going to be transferred to the psychology department, Darley professed himself to have been "terribly pleased" that his motion had received the "unanimous" support of all who had attended the faculty meeting.

As all this suggests, in 1965 few people, including myself, and few institutions were aware that the word *sex* had been inserted at the last minute into Title VII of the 1964 Civil Rights Act. Indeed, it may have been the case that even some members of Congress were yet to become aware of what they had voted for, as neither of the replies I received from Senators McCarthy and Humphrey made reference to that piece of legislation, although each man personally assured me that he was laboring mightily to improve working conditions for women. (Because one of the letters was addressed to "Dr. Allen Berscheid" and began "Dear Sir," I wasn't entirely convinced). The word *race* had been noticed, of course, being the focus of the legislation, but as the business schools's employment bulletin board reflected, most employers were still conducting business as usual. Martin Luther King's freedom marches, however, were keeping the issue in the headlines and on our minds. In fact, Elaine Hatfield had the wit to send Rev. King copies of our studies (e.g., "When Does a Harm-Doer Compensate a Victim?" [Berscheid & Walster, 1967]), in the hope that he could make some use of them. To our surprise, he wrote back to express his appreciation for the information, commenting that he was sure that there were many other studies in the social science literature that would be helpful to him if only he knew where they were. In 1965, that was wishful thinking on his part.

But that was then. Now, and just as I was preparing these remarks, my college, Gene Borgida, dropped on my desk a reprint of an article (that has since appeared in the *American Psychologist*; Fiske, Bersoff, Borgida, Deaux, & Heilman, 1991) entitled "Social Science Research on Trial: The Use of Sex Stereotyping Research in *Price Waterhouse v. Hopkins*." As I picked it up and read how social psychological research on the antecedent conditions, indicators, consequences, and remedies of stereotyping played a crucial role at each stage of Hopkins's litigation, a lengthy judicial process that included a Supreme Court decision and ended with Hopkins winning her case of sex discrimination, I unabashedly admit that my eyes dampened with pride in social psychology. Twenty-five years ago, few of us could have imagined that there soon would be an army of social psychologists who would give the problem of stereotypes a full-court press in theory and research and that well within our lifetime, the fruits of our own discipline would be used to strike a landmark legal blow against sex discrimination.

WOMEN IN SOCIAL PSYCHOLOGY

In my personal view, then, one of the biggest changes that has taken place in the past 25 years has been the increase in the number of women social psychologists and the dramatic improvement in our working conditions (improvement but not yet equality, according to Brush, 1991). In fact, my guess is that the proportional increase of women into research positions in social psychology was greater than in any other subarea of psychology. (Unfortunately, the APA does not have the appropriate statistics, identifying researchers and nonresearchers, that would allow documentation of this point.)

There are several possible reasons for the influx of women into social psychology, but one that should be noted on an anniversary occasion is that the men who were influential in social psychology in 1965 – and they were all men, as the identities of the founding fathers of SESP reflects – were far more egalitarian in outlook and values than those in any other area of psychology. The overlap in membership between Divisions 8 (the Society of Personality and Social Psychology) and 9 (the Society for the Psychological Study of Social Issues) of the APA, as well as the pervasive influence of Kurt Lewin, his students, and such other important early social psychologists as Gordon Allport would suggest that women and minorities could expect a warmer reception in social psychology than in other domains of psychology. And, for the most part, we did. Many of these men are still alive and active today, and their extracurricular contribution to social psychology through training their own female students and through the other professional roles they played at the time should be acknowledged. In addition to those who trained us and gave us jobs, one also immediately thinks of such people as Bill McGuire, then editor of *JPSP*, and Bob Krauss, then editor of the *Journal of Experimental Social Psychology*, who made special efforts to include women in the research review and editorial enterprise, as well as the rapidity (1967) with which SESP put women on its program. It is important to note that these efforts to encourage women to join the mainstream of social psychology were made long before such actions were regarded as socially chic, politically correct, or legally mandated. In short, the "culture" of social psychology in 1965 was well ahead of its time.

It can be argued that the relatively rapid entry of women into social psychology had a number of salutary consequences for the development of the field. Perhaps the most important of these was to keep the caliber of talent high while social psychology was undergoing enormous growth. By allowing the other half of the human race to participate in the enterprise – a half equal to the other in what we graduate students used to call "raw g" – the intellectual talent devoted to social psychological problems was not diluted in quality as it expanded in quantity, as appears to have been the case in certain other subareas of psychology that shall remain nameless here but whose graduate student applicants' Graduate Record Examination scores and GPA records at Minnesota over the years tell the tale.

Second, the influx of women into social psychology influenced the approach taken to many traditional research questions in the field. In this regard, it should be noted that because women were admitted into the mainstream and thus worked on research questions central to discipline, there has been less "ghettoization" of women in social psychology than there has been in many other disciplines. Rather than an alternative and "feminist" view of social psychology, one that offers an opposing view of the discipline's dominant knowledge domain, there has evolved, by and large, a single social psychology that has integrated, and has been enriched by, the different experiences and views that female social psychologists have brought to their work. Because examples of such enrichment abound, they perhaps are unnecessary, but one spontaneously remembers the sighs of recognition that greeted the Deaux and Emswiller (1974) article, whose subtitle, "What Is Skill for the Male Is Luck for the Female," said it all for many of us. The work of Alice Eagly and her colleagues also quickly comes to mind, for when I began teaching in 1965, it was a "fact," duly reported in the social psychology texts of the day, that women were more influenceable (read "gullible," "childlike," and "uninformed") than men, a finding that seemed to fit nicely into a constellation of data said to document the submissive and dependent nature of women. Those of us using those texts could only caution our students that not all women were easily influenceable (namely, their very own instructor) and once again drag out our all-purpose and over-used example of Golda Meir – the then Prime Minister of Israel and first female political leader of a major country in modern times, whom the daily news was revealing to be no docile "Mrs. Nice Guy" – as an illustration of the hazards of generalizing to the individual case. Sistrunk and McDavid (1971), of course, dealt the first empirical blow to the idea of women's innate influenceability but it was Eagly's (e.g., Eagly, 1978) work that buried it.

That work, in fact, turned up a subsidiary finding with important implications for the development of the social and behavioral sciences, both then and now. Pursuing the question of women's special influenceability with the then-new technique of meta-analysis, Eagly and Carli (1981) found an association between the sex of the researcher and the outcome of the experiment, such that both male and female researchers were more likely to find results favorable to their own sex. A tendency to produce findings favorable to groups intimately associated with the researcher's own identity, through unintentional and as yet unidentified mechanisms, argues that diversification of the researcher population – apart from moral, legal, and human resource utilization considerations – serves an important scientific goal: Diversification protects against unintended and unidentified bias in any knowledge domain that purports to be applicable to all humans.

Ironically, the concern today seems to be that the discipline of psychology is tilting again but in the other direction. According to the APA newsletter *Advancing the Public Interest* (J. M. Jones, 1991), the profession of psychology currently consists of 60% men and 40% women. That number is likely to reach parity soon, for in 1989 56% of the graduates with doctoral degrees in psychology were women. Curiously, this movement toward gender parity has been popularly termed, not the *demasculinization* nor even the *degenderization* of our discipline but, rather, the *feminization of psychology*. However, in terms of the knowledge domain that we disseminate to the world -- and this surely is where it counts – it is questionable whether psychology will be feminized soon. The critical issue concerns the extent to which the current 60:40 ratio holds in the research arena where psychological knowledge is produced. Only a small fraction of those who receive doctorates ever contribute to the knowledge base of their discipline, and, according to the National Research Council's recent report (Gerstein, Luce, Smelser, & Sperlich, 1988), this figure is not only lower for the social and behavioral sciences than it is for other science and engineering doctorates, but also "even at its highest point, campus strength in behavioral and social sciences research was well short of what one might expect on the basis of the numbers of trained personnel available" (p. 205). My guess is that the percentage of men in the population of researchers in psychology at the present time is higher than 60%. Supporting that hypothesis are figures cited by Bernadine Healy (1992), the new director of the National Institutes of Health. Although women's share of research grant money from the National Institutes of Health has doubled since 1981, and women's success rates for competing research grants is now equal to men's, women submitted and received only 19% of these awards, accounting for "a mere 16% of funds for research project grants" (1992, p. B5).[1]

Women, accounting as they do for half of humankind, constituted the biggest and most obvious boulder to be moved on the road to diversification, but we have become more sophisticated over the past few decades about what true diversification means. And there is yet no reason for celebration. With respect to ethnic minorities, for example, E. E. Jones (1990) recently reported that ethnic minorities account only for about 3%-4% of APA membership and only about 8% of new doctorates. When one considers that these figures include African-Americans, native Americans, Hispanics, and Asian-Americans – people who, collectively, soon will comprise one third of the population in this country – it is clear that no subarea of psychology can claim it has a diversified research arm.

INCREASE IN THE STATUS AND CENTRALITY
OF SOCIAL PSYCHOLOGY WITHIN PSYCHOLOGY

Rivaling in importance the increase in the number of women within social psychology over the past quarter century has been the increase in the status and centrality of social psychology within psychology. As Zimbardo (1992) recently observed, social psychology was "long relegated to a subordinate position within psychology's status hierarchy" (p. xiv), a delicate way of saying that back in 1965, and for many years after, social psychologists were the lowest of the low. When I went off to the business school, social psychologists were having a tough time in departments of psychology. The reigning prima dons were the "experimentalists" in learning psychology, easily recognized as they flapped through the halls in their white lab coats stained with rat urine and pigeon droppings. Searching for universal laws of behavior that would span millions of years of evolutionary time, from earthworms to Homo sapiens, and often using precise mathematical models to represent their hypotheses and findings (many of which later turned out to be much ado about not very much of enduring interest), the experimental psychologists, one much admit, were doing a fine job of imitating their acknowledged betters in the "hard" sciences, especially their much admired colleagues in classical physics (most of whom, ironically, were already dead in 1965 or in a deep funk and paralyzed into inactivity by the epistemological conundrums posed by the new physics; see, for example, Capra, 1982).

It was out from the wings and onto this stage where the experimental psychologists were busily performing their classical scientific ballet, that the new social psychologists

---

[1] Some data relevant to the hypothesis that men are overrepresented in the researcher population was provided by a special breakdown I requested of the APA research office on the 16,194 persons who completed work activity forms in the 1989 APA Directory Survey and 1990-1991 new member updates: Of those who indicated that they performed at least some research activities, over 66% were men. Only those who identified their major field as developmental psychology came close to gender parity, with 44% male researchers (this was also the only area in which there was a gender reversal). The figure for social psychology was 69% male. A better index may be authorship of articles in archival journals: for JPSP and Personality and Social Psychology Bulletin in the years 1989 and 1990, and eliminating the 39 authors whose gender was "hard to tell" by virtue of first name alone, 63% of the 1,263 authors appear to have been men.

came clomping in their concrete overshoes. With live humans as our subjects and complex social phenomena as our focus, some of our early attempts to join in the dance were ungraceful at best and downright ludicrous at worst. One thinks, for example, of George Homans's (1961) treatise, *Social Behavior: Its Elementary Forms*, which, while it proved valuable to social psychology for other reasons, was a textbook illustration of the popular game played in most social psychology parlors of the day: "Let's find the Reinforcer!" (of this or that social behavior). Unfortunately, the dominant learning theories of those times had been developed primarily with animals missing an upper cortex, and their raw application to humans in social situations often had a rather surreal quality to them (e.g., one thinks back to those experiments in which bright college students, treated like rats, would look up puzzled each time they heard a penny come rattling down the chute before them as they performed their laboratory task). But we, too, wanted to be real scientists. And so, looking to our superiors for guidance, we spent time doing things we might not have done had we had more confidence in our unique mission. I recall, for example, the months we spent debating the perfect equation to represent such social phenomena as interpersonal equity (e.g., Walster, Berscheid, & Walster, 1973), and none of us will forget the meticulous precision of the "law of interpersonal attraction" (e.g., Borne, 1971; Borne & Nelson, 1965).

Despite our efforts to ape our betters in the world of psychology, and no doubt sometimes because of them, social psychologists were frequently the objects of laughter and derision; we were regarded as soft-headed and sloppy, an embarrassment, in fact, to "serious" psychologists. No one was immune. For example, even though the Laboratory for Research in Social Relations at Minnesota was among the first and most prestigious training grounds for social psychologists, with the likes of Leon Festinger, Stanley Schachter, Hal Kelley, and Elliot Aronson as psychology faculty in residence in its early years, when we left the lab to attend our psychology classes, we frequently heard social psychology ridiculed from the lectern. As an assistant professor, in fact, the first question the then-president of the local American Association of University Professors (AAUP) asked when we were introduced was "Why do you social psychologists take the abuse?" Embarrassed that word of our pariah status had seeped out of Elliott Hall into the wider world, I retorted, "Because tomorrow belongs to us!" The bravado of that reply owed as much to the fact that I had seen the movie *Cabaret* as it did to my faith in the future, for at that time we social psychologists were haunted by dark nights of the soul and afflicted with wrenching "crises of confidence" (e.g., McGuire, 1973). Now, from the distance of 25 years and a cool look back at the hostile context in which social psychology was developing, it seems no wonder that we were frequently driven to contemplate our collective navel and to question whether we had a place in the scientific universe.

But it wasn't just our hostile academic environment that bedeviled us. We had most of the problems any new field has. We suffered from an identity problem, for example. Though still very much apparent in 1965, that problem at least was beginning to abate. In his review of the three new social psychology texts that had just blossomed (the original Roger Brown, 1965, text; the Secord & Backman, 1964, text; and a text by Newcomb, Turner, & Converse, 1965), Brewster Smith (1966) observed that earlier social psychology texts, reflecting the marginal status of social psychology between the disciplines of psychology and sociology, had devoted much space to the competing claims of each discipline and to trying to resolve, unsuccessfully, the conflicts between them. But Smith could now report that

> None of the [current] books pays attention to the earlier quarrels of sociology and psychology over the lineage and legitimacy of their offspring. Indeed, for two of them (Brown and Secord-Backman), the field that they survey or sample is to be defined only by academic and scientific convention: what social psychologists have been curious and busy about. (p. 110)

These three books broke a 13-year hiatus in social psychology texts (with only the Krech, Crutchfield, & Ballachey, 1962, revision of the 1948 Krech and Crutchfield text appearing in this time). The Brown and the Secord and Backman texts, along with the E. E. Jones and Gerard (1967) classic that was to appear shortly, were signal landmarks in social psychology for several reasons, but especially because they gave shape and direction to the field. They not only finessed questions of genealogy, but also their surveys of "what social psychologists have been curious and busy about" turned out to be mostly what psychological social psychologists were curious and busy about. Moreover, they systematically infused those doings with heavy doses of theory and findings from psychology proper, making useful interpretations and translations to social behavior (e.g., from object perception to social perception). In addition, by this time there were enough concrete findings to report that the empirical quality of the field was emerging clearly, putting armchair philosophizing in retreat. In this regard, and given the blizzards of findings that social psychologists today routinely attempt to assimilate, it is amusing to read Brewster Smith's plaint back in 1966:

> For myself, I am proud of the real gains in the course of the thirteen years since my last comparative review, but I am not too happy about the clogged state of our journals, filled with the products of project-supported busyness, in which fad and fashion, methodological fetishism, and what I remember Gordon Allport to have called 'itsy-bitsy empiricism' make it easy to lose direction and significance. (p. 117)

In bypassing questions of identity, and in moving social psychology toward its psychological and Lewinian heritage, the appearance of these texts also was a godsend to those of us who had to fend off perennial attempts to eject us (all two of us at Minnesota, until 1976) from the psychology department; around budget time, we came to expect that someone would come up with the wonderful idea of creating two new line items for the psychology department by making us the wards of the sociology department and ask us if we didn't think it was a wonderful idea, too. In writing our annual "we shall not be moved" statement, the psychological content and orientation of these texts, which we used in our social psychology classes but which the sociological social psychologists did not, were invaluable.[2]

---

[2] In commenting on this article, Sidney Rosen, an observer of the fortunes of social psychologists within sociology over the past 25 years, noted that Herbert Simon addressed a sociological convention some years ago in which he offered a translation of Homan's (1961) propositions into a set of mathematical equations and wondered whatever

Apart from who we were and where we belonged in the academy, serious questions and allegations were frequently raised about the value of our activities. I shall mention only one of these charges and that because, first, it struck at the heart of our claim to scientific status; second, because we were relatively defenseless against it 25 years ago when the field was young in age and few in number; and third, because it retained its currency long after it should have. Although the allegation was made by many, it perhaps was stated most persuasively and succinctly by my Minnesota colleague, Paul Meehl (1978):

> I consider it unnecessary to persuade you that most so-called "theories" in the soft areas of psychology (clinical, counseling, social, personality, community, and school psychology) are scientifically unimpressive and technologically worthless. ... In the developed sciences, theories tend either to become widely accepted and built into the larger edifice of well-tested human knowledge or else they suffer destruction in the face of recalcitrant facts and are abandoned. ... But in fields like personology and social psychology, this seems not to happen. There is a period of enthusiasm about a new theory, a period of attempted application to several fact domains, a period of disillusionment as the negative data come in, a growing bafflement about inconsistent and inexplicable empirical results, multiple resort to ad hoc excuses, and then finally people just sort of lose interest in the thing and pursue other endeavors. ... It is simply a sad fact that in soft psychology theories rise and decline, come and go, more as a function of baffled boredom than anything else; and the enterprise shows a disturbing absence of that *cumulative* character that is so impressive in disciplines like astronomy, molecular biology, and genetics. (pp. 806-807)

Today, the charge of noncumulativeness against social psychology has a musty odor to it. In his article, "How Hard Is Hard Science, How Soft Is Soft Science? The Empirical Cumulativeness of Research," Hedges (1987) distinguished between *theoretical cumulativeness* and *empirical cumulativeness*; the latter being defined as the "degree of agreement among replicated experiments or the degree to which related experimental results fit into a simple pattern that makes conceptual sense" (p. 443). Comparing the consistency of research results in physics and in psychology using a sample of reviews of empirical findings from each domain, Hedges found that the results of physical experiments were not strikingly more consistent than those of social or behavioral experiments and, thus, that "the 'obvious' conclusion that the results of physical science experiments are more cumulative than those of social science experiments does not have

---

happened to them, a rather telling question. Rosen then made the following fascinating points: "We might add the observation of a cultural lag distinguishing sociology and psychology. One relevant aspect of this lag was that theoretical sociology started to become attracted to formalization at about the time that such a preoccupation began to lose favor in psychology. Another relevant aspect of this lag is that sociological social psychology is still struggling to establish its identity within sociology. In this regard, Felson wrote the following, in the Winter 1992 newsletter of the social psychology section of ASA: 'Why did the status of social psychology in sociology decline in the last 20 years: I believe that one reason is ideological: social psychology is not politically correct' (p. 3). Suffice it to say here that he meant political correctness from the perspective of traditional sociology." It should also be mentioned that sociological social psychologists are still represented in SESP, although their proportion to the total membership has declined radically over the past 25 years, and that sociological social psychologists as well as sociologists concerned with marriage and the family currently are core contributors to the emerging interdisciplinary science of interpersonal relationships.

much empirical support" (p. 443). For social psychology in particular, there is specific evidence of the empirical cumulativeness of the field. In their analysis of "Publication Trend in *JPSP*: A Three-Decade Review," Reis and Stiller (1992) reported that, since 1968, published articles have become progressively longer, they present more procedural information and tables, they cite more prior literature, they report research based on more studies, they use more subjects per study, and they use more complex statistical methods. These changes, the authors persuasively argued, reflect social psychologists' focus on increasingly complex theoretical issues as well as the field's demand for higher and higher standards of evidence as it has matured.

As Hedges (1987) observed, the assessment of empirical cumulativeness, although possessing the virtue of some objectivity, is also a narrower index of the cumulativeness of a discipline than is its theoretical cumulativeness, or the degree to which the field's "empirical laws and theoretical structures build on one another so that later developments extend and unify earlier work" (p. 443). Subjective though such an assessment must be, the evidence that can be mustered for the theoretical cumulativeness of social psychology in the past quarter century could easily pass the eyeball test of social psychology's severest critic.

In 1965 social psychology was already theory rich, but it remained to be seen whether these theories would provide the muscle and sinew the field needed to develop. Festinger (1954, 1957) had offered his theory of social comparison processes a decade earlier (in 1954), and his theory of cognitive dissonance (in 1957) was already turning the field's attention away from "groupy" phenomena (see Steiner, 1974) to matters that today would fall under the general rubric of "social cognition." Heider (1958) had already published *The Psychology of Interpersonal Relations*, which elaborated his balance theory (sketched over a decade earlier in his hard-to-read 1946 article "Attitudes and Cognitive Organization" that had purportedly influenced Festinger's concept of cognitive dissonance, although Asch, 1946, also had started people thinking about consistency as a principle of cognitive organization). In this seminal work, Heider also discussed his observation that people often try to attribute causes to events, and E. E. Jones and Davis (1965) had already begun to flesh out attribution theory. Thibaut and Kelley (1959) already had published the first version of their theory of interdependence; Homans (1961) had presented his idea of "distributive justice" in social relationships, which shortly was to be elaborated in equity theories; Newcomb (1956) already had drawn attention to problems in the prediction of interpersonal attraction in his APA presidential address and had recently published his study of *The Acquaintance Process* (Newcomb, 1961); and Schachter (1959) had presented both *The Psychology of Affiliation* and his article "The Interaction of Cognitive and Physiological Determinants of Emotional State" (Schachter, 1964). Moreover, Asch's (1946) empirical studies of conformity phenomena and of social perception were well-known, and the "Yale school's" work on attitude change (e.g., Hovland, Janis, & Kelley, 1953) had been around for a decade, with its "incentive motivation" view currently dueling with dissonance theory on the pages of the journals. There was much more, of course, but suffice it to say that, today, the names and the content of these theories will not strike even an undergraduate in social psychology as unfamiliar. Although some of these theories and the findings they produced may have been baffling from time to time, they were never boring, and they were never wholly abandoned. All were to prove to be vital building blocks for later theorists and investigators. And all have remained alive in the sense that they have been revised frequently in response to new findings – or they have been incorporated into other theories – or the findings they spawned have remained important in themselves or have played important roles in further theory development.

Perhaps the most impressive example of the cumulative nature of social psychology lies in the attribution area. From the theoretical outlines originally sketched by Heider (1958) to E. E. Jones and Davis's (1965) formulation to Kelley's (1967) rendering of "Attribution Theory in Social Psychology" two years later, the attributionists have patiently and systematically pursued their phenomena along a very long and winding road. A powerful chronicle of attribution theory and research over the past 25 years is presented in E. E. Jones's (1990) book, *Person Perception*. If social psychology is ever again required to defend itself against the charge of noncumulativeness, submission into evidence of this book alone would get the prosecution laughed out of court. And the attributionists aren't done yet; in fact, the best may be just around the bend, for two new and highly integrative theories of person perception recently have been offered, one by Susan Fiske and her colleagues (e.g., Fiske & Neuberg, 1990) and the other by Marilynn Brewer (1988).

Not only have social psychologists not been faddish about their theories, they haven't been flighty in their selection of the social behaviors they've sought to understand. In addition to the previously mentioned work on stereotypes and prejudice, begun in social psychology's infancy with the work of Gordon Allport and Kurt Lewin, and which now constitutes a theoretically impressive and practically useful body of knowledge (e.g., see Hamilton, 1981) that continues to be the subject of much current research (e.g., Swim, Borgida, Maruyama, & Myers, 1989), social comparison is still an active research area (e.g., Wheeler & Miyake, 1992), with its fruits extended over the years to illuminate other social phenomena of interest (e.g., Tesser, Millar, & Moore, 1988). Interpersonal attraction, that rock pile of theory and research on which some of us labored as graduate students, now helps form the core of the burgeoning interpersonal relationships wing of social psychology, where the cumulative and interdisciplinary nature of the work performed in this area over the past 3 decades was traced recently by George Levinger (1990) in his address to the International Society of the Study of Personal Relationships at Oxford University. Progress in this area can be illustrated by the fact that at the University of Minnesota we have graduated from Dr. Gregor Zilstein's (a.k.a. Stanley Schacter) frightening coeds with the prospect of electric shock, from Elaine Hatfield's designing computer dances for the Student Activities Bureau's freshman orientation week, and from Elliot Aronson's engineering pratfalls for otherwise competent people, to the construction of a free-standing doctoral minor in Interpersonal Relationships Research. This new program will join the forces of scholars in psychology, the Institute of Child Development, family social science, sociology, that old business school (now spiffily named the Carlson School of Management), several colleges and departments in the health sciences, and more to train graduate students and facilitate research on interpersonal relationships. As this illustrates, social psychologists not only have burrowed ever more deeply into the social phenomena that were of interest 25 years ago, but another quality of our discipline has been revealed as it's matured: its boundary-spanning nature.

Social psychologists have expanded their knowledge domain in virtually every direction. Surveying the thousands of books submitted to *Contemporary Psychology* for review consideration these past several years for example, we were continually surprised by the number of areas in which social psychologists are currently contributing theory and research. Reflecting this state of affairs, social psychology now often finds itself hyphenated to reflect its alliances with other subareas of psychology: social-developmental, social-clinical, social-personality, social psychology and law, social-health, social-organizational, social-educational, social-environmental, and social-community for examples. Few subareas of psychology interface with and inform so many other scholarly endeavors within psychology as well as in those disciplines located on psychology's perimeter.

It has become apparent, in fact, that social psychology has emerged as a central pivot for much of contemporary psychology. In this regard, it is interesting to note that even those prognosticators of the future of psychology who see it vanishing as a discipline, with many of its current internal domains being absorbed by other disciplines, do not foresee such a fate for social psychology. Scott (1991), for example, who subscribes to the notion that psychology as we know it will disintegrate, predicted that

> Social psychology will continue to expand its strong experimental base, and will increasingly fulfill its promise to address society's most vexing problems. The solutions that emerge from social psychology laboratories will inform gender and racial issues and permeate the workplace, the inner city, and the home. Social psychology will become more practice oriented, affiliating with or creating its own professional schools ... (p. 976)

If Scott is correct, it may fall to social psychologists to carry psychology's banner into the 21st century.

In sum, contemporary social psychology, with its dynamic, ever-changing and expanding, character, is an exemplar of all the social and behavioral sciences as they have been characterized by the National Research Council:

> Taking into consideration the dynamics of specialization, the development of data, theoretical shifts, and interdisciplinary activity – and the interactions of all of these with one another – the behavioral and social sciences resemble not so much a map as a kaleidoscope, with continuous growth, shifting boundaries, and new emphases and highlights (Adams, Smelser & Treiman, 1982, p. 26).

Dynamic. And cumulative. Could anyone have asked more of social psychology 25 years ago?

IF WE'RE SO SMART, WHY AREN'T WE RICH?

Not everything has improved over the past 25 years. We still do not have an epistemology well suited to our endeavors (e.g., see Berscheid, 1986), which makes people uneasy when they think about it, which isn't very often anymore. Good minds have addressed the painful issues here over the years (e.g., Gergen, 1973; Harre & Secord, 1973) but with little practical effect and resolution. Fortunately, the field's momentum is such that we routinely walk on water in the faith that what we are doing is useful and important; it is only when we look down, and are reminded that the philosophy of science that supported classical physics cannot support us, do we sometimes sink and suffer yet another crisis of confidence.

There are other problems, but the most worrisome one, which brings me to the third and last change I wish to highlight, is the decrease in social psychology's funding per capita researcher. In 1965, the social and behavioral sciences were enjoying the "golden age" of research funding, and social psychology shared in the good times. Today, the amount of time talented researchers, both young and old, spend writing grant proposals only to be told that their ideas – through meritorious – must wither for lack of funds, is disheartening. A great many facts and figures have been published documenting our inadequate research support environment, so there is no need to repeat the dreary tale here, except to say that changes in support for all of the behavioral and social sciences have been "starkly different" (as the situation is characterized in Appendix A, "Trends in Support for Research in the Behavioral and Social Sciences," of the National Research Council's 1988 report) from those of other scientific disciplines, whose federal funding increased substantially over the past 15 years.

Ever pragmatic and fleet of foot, however, social psychologists have coped. And it perhaps is not too Panglossian to say that they have done so in ways that have protected the discipline and even strengthened it along several dimensions. As Zimbardo (1992) observed, "social psychologists have become the vanguard of the movement to extend the boundaries of traditional psychology into realms vital to contributing solutions for real-world problems, the areas of health, ecology, education, law, peace and conflict resolution, and much more" (p. xiv). As funding for basic research became more and more scarce, and funding for very specific social problems – such as alcohol and drug abuse, acquired immunodeficiency syndrome (AIDS), aging, and so forth – became available, social psychologists increasingly took their theories and their methodological tools out of the laboratory and into the world of pressing societal problems. In doing so, they have broken down the wall between basic and applied research that was apparent 25 years ago when basic and applied research were seen as parallel, rather than intertwined, research tracks. During the recent funding drought, social psychologists discovered anew the truth of Lewin's dictum that "there is nothing so practical as a good theory!" and have reunited the two faces of social psychology's research coin. We must continue to hope, however, that those who successfully use the tools and theory of social psychology in their applied enterprises never forget their way back home and the necessity for putting something back in the basic theory and research pot during the hard times of inadequate support for the discipline.

Having acknowledged some of the benefits of a harsh environment for the evolutionary development of social psychology, it must also be recognized that in addition to inadequate support for basic research and theory development, funding inadequacies have affected the field in other troubling ways. One of these is our inability to take advantage of the technological marvels that have become available over the past few decades to facilitate our research. A look at our journals today reveals that, just as it was back in 1965, social psychology is very much a pencil-and-paper enterprise. It may be even more of a pencil-and-paper enterprise today than it was then, for the use of self-report questionnaires and written treatments of independent variables seems to have increased; running subjects in large groups and handing out questionnaires is much cheaper, of course, than setting up elaborate treatment scenarios possessing high internal validity and spending one of two hours per subject to collect a single datum, and it is also much less expensive than going out into naturalistic settings to observe behavior.

One of the many unfortunate consequences of our being a pencil-and-paper field is that to those observers who still confuse technology with science – and there are many, both within the academy and without – social psychology still doesn't look like much of a science. In this, however, we are not much different from many of the other social and behavioral sciences. As the National Research Council (Gerstein et al., 1988) observed, "There is a persisting view that behavioral and social sciences research can operate as a virtually equipment-free enterprise, a view that is completely out of date for research in many areas" (p. 214). Needless to say, social psychology is very prominently one of those areas. Even equipment that has been shown to be useful to the exploration of many different social phenomena (e.g., physiological and facial measures of affect) are not routinely available in social psychological laboratories. Moreover, unobtrusive devices to measure important social psychological variables outside of the laboratory, with extremely reactive subjects who range freely over large habitats, still appear only in our dreams. The inability of researchers in social psychology to take advantage of the many technological developments that would facilitate our empirical research and broaden our theoretical horizons currently constitutes a particularly frustrating stumbling block as other, better funded, disciplines increasingly capitalize from rapid technological advances. For now, we can only pray that the lead mines fueling our pencils don't run dry before our funding prospects improve.

In this regard, there now is reason to hope, and hope for the future is always a good place to end a look at the past. As all who keep up with the events that affect the fortunes of psychology now know, a separate directorate for the behavioral and social science disciplines is being formed at the National Science Foundation (e.g., NSF Directorate: Yes!, 1991), the agency social psychologists look to for most of our basic research support. That reorganization, according to knowledgeable observers, should increase funding for all of the social and behavioral sciences and, on that score alone, social psychology's boat should lift along with the others. But beyond that general effect, we surely have reason to be confident that even the most jaundiced observer of social psychology's development and record of contribution over the past 25 years must conclude that social psychology has been faithful to its promise to the society that supports it and that society thus has a vested interest in keeping social psychologists as busy and as curious over the next quarter century as they've been over the last.

REFERENCES

ADAMS, R.Mc, Smelser, D.J. & Trieman, D.J. (1982) *Behavioral and social science research: A national resource (Part I)*. Washington, DC: National Academy Press. p. 30.

ASCH, S. E. (1946). Forming impressions of personality. *Journal of Abnormal and Social Psychology. 41*, 258-290.

BERSCHEID, E. (1986). Mea culpas and lamentations: Sir Francis, Sir Isaac, and 'The slow progress of soft psychology.' In R. Gilmour & S. Duck (Eds.), *The emerging field of personal relationships* (pp. 267-286). Hillsdale, NJ: Erlbaum.

BERSCHEID, E., & WALSTER [HATFIELD], E. (1967). When does a harm-doer compensate a victim? *Journal of Personality and Social Psychology, 6*, 435-441.

BREWER, M. (1988). A dual process model of impression formation. In T. K. Srull & R. S. Wyer (Eds.), *Advances in social cognition* (Vol. 1, pp. 1-36). Hillsdale, NJ: Erlbaum.

BROWN, R. (1965). *Social psychology.* New York: Free Press.

BRUSH, S. G. (1991, September-October). Women in science and engineering. *American Scientist, 79*, 404-419.

BYRNE, D. (1971). *The attraction paradigm.* San Diego, CA: Academic Press

BYRNE, D., & NELSON, D. (1965). Attraction as a linear function of proportion of positive reinforcements. *Journal of Personality and Social Psychology, 1*, 659-663.

CAPRA, F. (1982) *The turning point: Science, society and the rising culture.* New York: Simon & Schuster.

DEAUX, K., & EMSWILLER, T. (1974). Explanation of successful performance on sex-linked tasks: What is skill for the male is luck for the female. *Journal of Personality and Social Psychology, 29*, 80-85.

EAGLY, A. H. (1978). Sex differences in influenceability. *Psychological Bulletin, 85*, 86-116.

EAGLY, A. H. & CARLI, L. L. (1981). Sex of researchers and sex-typed communications as determinants of sex differences in influenceability: a meta-analysis of social influence studies. *Psychological Bulletin, 90*, 1-20.

FESTINGER, L. (1954). A theory of social comparison processes. *Human Relations, 7*, 117-140.

FISKE, S. T., BERSOFF, D. N., BORGIDA, E., DEAUX, K., & HEILMAN, M. E. (1991). Social science research on trial: Use of sex stereotyping research in Price Waterhouse v. Hopkins, *American Psychologist, 46*, 1049-1060.

FISKE, S. T., & NEUBERG, S. L (1990). A continuum of impression formation, from category-based to individuating processes: Influences of information and motivation on attention and interpretation. In M. P. Zanna (Ed.), *Advances in experimental social psychology* (Vol. 23, pp. 1-74). San Diego, CA: Academic Press.

GERGEN, K. J. (1973). Social psychology as history. *Journal of Personality and Social Psychology, 26*, 309-320.

GERSTEIN, D. R., LUCE, R. D., SMELSER, N. J., & SPERLICH, S (Eds.). (1988). *The behavioral and social sciences: Achievements and opportunities.* Washington, DC: National Academy Press.

HAMILTON, D. L. (Ed.). (1981). *Cognitive processes in stereotyping and intergroup behavior.* Hillsdale, NJ: Erlbaum.

HARRE, R., & SECORD, P. F. (1973). *The explanation of social behaviour.* Totowa, NJ: Littlefield Adams.

HEALY, B. (1992, March 25). Quotable: "The astonishing thing is that young women pursue careers in science and medicine at all!" *The Chronicle of Higher Education.* March 25, p. 135.

HEDGES, L. V. (1987). How hard is hard science, how soft is soft science? The empirical cumulativeness of research. *American Psychologist, 42*, 443-455.

HEIDER, F. (1958). *The psychology of interpersonal relations.* New York: Wiley.

HOLLANDER, E. P. (1968). The Society of Experimental Social Psychology: An historical note. *Journal of Personality and Social Psychology, 9*, 280-282.

HOMANS, G. C. (1961). *Social behavior: Its elementary forms.* New York: Harcourt, Brace & World.

HOVLAND, C. I., JANIS, I. L., & KELLEY, H. H. (1953). *Communication and persuasion.* New Haven, CT: Yale University Press.

JONES, E. E. (1990). *Person perception.* Hillsdale, NJ: Erlbaum.

JONES, E. E., & DAVIS, K. E. (1965). From acts to dispositions: The attribution process in person perception. In L. Berkowitz (Ed.), *Advances in experimental social psychology*, Vol. II (pp. 219-266). San Diego, CA: Academic Press.

JONES, E. E., GERARD, H. B. (1967). *Foundations of social psychology.* New York: Wiley.

JONES, J. M. (1991, July). The greening of psychology. *Advancing the Public Interest, 3,* 7-8.

KELLEY, H. H. (1967). Attribution theory in social psychology. In D. Levine (Ed.), *Nebraska Symposium on Motivation* (Vol. 13, pp. 192-214). Lincoln, NE: University of Nebraska Press.

KRECH, D., & CRUTCHFIELD, R. S. (1948). *Theory and problems of social psychology.* New York: McGraw-Hill.

KRECH, D., CRUTCHFIELD, R. S., & BALLACHEY, E. L. (1962). *Individual in society: A textbook of social psychology.* New York: McGraw-Hill.

LEVINGER, G. (1990, July). *Figure versus ground: Micro and macro perspectives on personal relationships.* Invited address to the International Society for the Study of Interpersonal Relationships, Oxford University, Oxford, England.

MCADAMS, R., SMELSER, D. J., & TREIMAN, D. J. (1982). *Behavioral and social science research: A national resource* (Part 1). Washington, DC: National Academy Press.

MCGUIRE, W. J. (1973). The yin and yang of progress in social psychology: Seven Koan. *Journal of Personality and Social Psychology, 26,* 446-456.

MEEHL, P. E. (1978). Theoretical risks and tabular asterisks: Sir Karl, Sir Ronald, and the slow progress of soft psychology. *Journal of Consulting and Clinical Psychology, 46,* 806-834.

NEWCOMB, T. M. (1956). The prediction of interpersonal attraction. *American Psychologist, 11,* 575-586.

NEWCOMB, T. M. (1961). *The acquaintance process.* New York: Holt, Rinehart & Winston.

NEWCOMB, T. M., TURNER, R. H., & CONVERSE, P. E. (1965). *Social psychology: The study of human interaction.* New York: Holt, Rinehart & Winston.

NSF directorate: Yes! (1991, November). *APS Observer, 4,* 1, 28-31.

REIS, H. T., & STILLER, J. (1992). Publication trends in JPSP: A three-decade review. *Personality and Social Psychology Bulletin, 18,* 465-472.

SCHACHTER, S. (1959). *The psychology of affiliation: Experimental studies of the sources of gregariousness.* Stanford, CA: Stanford University Press.

SCHACHTER, S. (1964). The interaction of cognitive and physiological determinants of emotional state. In L. Berkowitz (Ed.), *Advances in experimental social psychology,* (Vol. 1, pp. 49-80). San Diego, CA: Academic Press.

SCOTT, T. R. (1991). A personal view of the future of psychology departments. *American Psychologist, 46,* 975-976.

SECORD, P. F., & BACKMAN, C. W. (1964). *Social psychology.* New York: McGraw-Hill.

SISTRUNK, F., & MCDAVID, J. W. (1971). Sex variable in conformity behavior. *Journal of Personality and Social Psychology, 17,* 200-207.

SMITH M. B. (1966). Three textbooks: A special review. *Journal of Experimental Social Psychology, 2* 109-118.

STEINER, I. D. (1974). Whatever happened to the group in social psychology? *Journal of Experimental Social Psychology, 10,* 93-108.

SWIM, J., BORGIDA, E., MARUYAMA, G., & MYERS, D. G. (1989). Joan McKay versus John McKay: do gender stereotypes bias evaluations? *Psychological Bulletin, 105* 409-429.

TESSER, A., MILLAR, M., & MOORE, J. (1988). Some affective consequences of social comparison and reflection processes: The pain and pleasure of being close. *Journal of Personality and Social Psychology, 54,* 49-61.

THIBAUT, J. W., & KELLEY, H. H. (1959). *The social psychology of groups.* New York: Wiley.

WALSTER, E., BERSCHEID, E., & WALSTER, G. W. (1973). New directions in equity. *Journal of Personality and Social Psychology, 25,* 151-176.

WHEELER, L., & MIYAKE, K. (1992). Social comparison in everyday life. *Journal of Personality and Social Psychology, 62,* 760-773.

ZIMBARDO, P. G. (1992). Foreword. In Brehm, S. S. (Ed.), *Intimate relationships* (pp.xiv-xvi). New York: McGraw-Hill.

QUESTIONS

1. With respect to gender equality, how did social psychology compare to other areas of psychology in the late 1960s? How does Berscheid explain this?

2. Including women within the mainstream of social psychology was obviously morally and legally important. Why does Berscheid believe that it was also scientifically important?

3. Why does Berscheid consider the publication of four new textbooks in 1964-1967 so important to the field? How did this help resolve the identity crisis that social psychology was facing?

4. How does Berscheid respond to charges that social psychology is faddish and flighty? Does she think that the criticism was valid in 1965? Does she feel that it is valid today?

5. Explain how the shrinking availability of funds may have improved the quality of social psychological research.

Ψ

PART II

SOCIAL COGNITION:

PERCEIVING THE SOCIAL WORLD

Ψ Ψ

Ψ CHAPTER 2 Ψ

SOCIAL COGNITION: PERCEIVING AND UNDERSTANDING INDIVIDUALS

Reading 3: Classic

How Do People Perceive the Causes of Behavior?

Edward E. Jones

As Ellen Berscheid mentions in the previous reading, attribution theory is among the most successful social psychological theories developed in recent years. It is also one of the first theories in the field that attempted to explain the mechanisms involved when people think about their social environment. In other words, it is one of the first social cognitive theories.

Attribution theory attempts to explain how people make sense of behavior, both their own and that of others. Interestingly, one major finding in this area is that the types of attributions (i.e., explanations) that people come up with when trying to explain their own behavior differ from those they use when trying to explain the behavior of another. This phenomenon became known as the actor-observer effect.

In this article, Edward Jones, the preeminent researcher in attribution theory, discusses the actor-observer effect. He admits that when he and his colleagues first proposed the phenomenon there was very little empirical support. Over the next few years that quickly changed as dozens of studies in many different labs confirmed Jones's prediction. In a very fundamental way, the same behavior looks very different when we perform it than when someone else does.

Ψ

Finding the causes for behavior is a fundamental enterprise of the psychologist. But it is an enterprise he shares with the man on the street. Our responses to others are affected by the reasons, or *attributes*, we assign for their behavior. At least this is the basic assumption of the attributional approach in social psychology, an approach that concerns itself with phenomenal causality – the conditions affecting how each of us attributes causes for his own and others' behavior. The hope is that if we can better understand how people perceive the causal structure of their social world, we can better predict their responses to that world. If A attributes B's anger to the fact that B has lost his job, A is less likely to reciprocate. If a teacher attributes a student's poor performance to lack of motivation, he is more likely to express open disappointment than if his attribution were

Source: Jones, E. E. (1976, May/June). How do people perceive the causes of behavior? *American Scientist,* 300–305. Reprinted by permission of *American Scientist.*

to lack of ability. A supervisor's appreciation of a subordinate's compliments is more or less alloyed by his attribution of ulterior motives.

The attributional approach (Jones et al. 1972) is essentially a perspective, or a framework, rather than a theory. The perspective owes much of its current prominence to the seminal writings of Fritz Heider. However, propositional statements have been spawned within the framework, and there are some identifiable theoretical positions. Davis and I outlined a theory of *correspondent inferences* in 1965 which is especially concerned with inferences about the dispositions and intentions of a person drawn from observing his behavior in particular contexts. Simply put, the theory states that causal attribution will be made to an actor to the extent that he is not bound by circumstances and is therefore free to choose from a number of behavioral options. If a person has choice, and if his actions depart in any way from expectations, the perceiver-attributor should gain information about his motives and personality. Under these conditions, we might say that the person reveals himself in his actions. We can make a correspondent inference that ties an act to a causal disposition: "He dominated the meeting because he is dominant"; "He cries because he is in pain"; "He voted for ERA because he believes in full civil liberties for women."

Two years later, Kelley proposed a comprehensive theory of *entity attribution* which was the complement of correspondent-inference theory. Whereas Davis and I wanted to explain how attributions to the person can be made by ruling out environmental explanations, Kelley wanted to show how we decide whether an actor's response is caused by the entity to which it is directed rather than by some idiosyncratic bias on his part. Both approaches accepted the division of person and situation as reflecting the terms in which the naive attributor is supposed to make his causal allocations.

In 1971, Nisbett and I rather recklessly proposed that actors and observers make divergent attributions about behavioral causes. Whereas the actor sees his behavior primarily as a response to the situation in which he finds himself, the observer attributes the same behavior to the actor's dispositional characteristics. This proposition had grown out of a number of informal observations as well as a sequence of experiments on attitude attribution. Let me digress for a moment to summarize briefly this line of research.

LABORATORY EXPERIMENTS

Nine separate experiments were run within the same general paradigm with college undergraduates from widely separated universities. Each followed a procedure in which subjects were given a short essay or speech favoring a particular position and were asked to infer the underlying attitude of the target person who produced it. In one experiment the statement was presented as an answer to an examination question; in another it was identified as the preliminary statement of a debater; in still others the statement was attributed to paid volunteers recruited for personality research (cf. Jones and Harris

1967). The statements used in each experiment involved a particular social issue such as the viability of Castro's Cuba, marijuana legalization, desegregation and busing, liberalized abortion, or socialized medicine.

The experimental conditions were created by varying whether the target person could choose which side of the issue to write or speak on, and whether or not the side was the expected or popular position. Some subjects were informed that the target person was assigned to defend a particular side of the issue (by his instructor, the debating coach, or the experimenter). Others were told he had been free to choose either side. The statement itself took one or the other side of the issue. In the typical experiment, then, there were four experimental groups: pro-position with choice, anti-position with choice, pro-position with no choice, and anti-position with no choice. For any given sample of subjects, one of the sides (pro or anti) was more popular or expected than the other.

All of the experiments showed remarkable stability in supporting the predictions one would make from correspondent inference theory. Attitudes in line with behavior were more decisively attributed to the target person in the choice than in the no-choice condition, but degree of choice made a greater difference if the essay or speech ran counter to the expected or normative position. This is illustrated in Figure 2–1, which presents the results from an early study (1967) dealing with attitudes toward Fidel Castro. Subjects read an essay presumably written as an opening statement by a college debater, but actually it was scripted beforehand as an unremarkable pro or anti summary, the kind of thing an undergraduate debater might write after minimal study of the issue. The subject was also told either that the target person had been directed by the team advisor to argue a specific side of the debate or that he was given his choice of sides.

After digesting the essay and noting the context in which it was produced, each subject was instructed to rate the target person's true attitude toward the Castro regime. From Figure 1 it is apparent that choice has an effect, but only in the pro-Castro condition, where the debater's position was not in line with the expected attitude of a college student in the late sixties.

For our present purposes, what is most interesting is a finding that could not have been predicted by correspondent inference theory: even in the no-choice conditions, subjects tended to attribute attitudes in line with the speech. They seemed to attach too little weight to the situation (the no-choice instructions) and too much to the person. Although several alternative explanations quickly suggested themselves, these were effectively ruled out by additional experiments (Jones et al. 1971; Snyder and Jones 1974). I became and remain convinced that we are dealing with a robust phenomenon of attributional bias and that persons as observers are all too ready to infer underlying dispositions, like attitudes, from behaviors, like opinion statements, even when it is obvious that the statements are produced under constraint.

Although these results were compatible with the hypothesis that actors and observers have divergent perspectives, they said nothing, of course, about the actor. But there is abundant evidence from other social psychological experiments that actors do not adjust their attitudes to make them consistent with their behavior if they are required

FIGURE 2-1

In this attitude-attribution experiment, target persons presented short speeches either for or against the Castro regime in Cuba. Some were said to have chosen which side to support (choice condition): others were said to have been required to take the position endorsed (no-choice condition). Observers then rated what they felt was each target person's true attitude toward Castro; the possible range was from 10 (extreme anti) to 70 (extreme pro). Observers rating pro-Castro target persons in the "choice" condition saw their true attitude as more decisively in favor of Castro than observers rating Castro supporters in the no-choice condition. Choice was a negligible factor when the speech opposed the Castro regime. At the time the experiment was conducted, most subjects – both target persons and observers – held anti-Castro views. Data from Jones and Harris (1967).

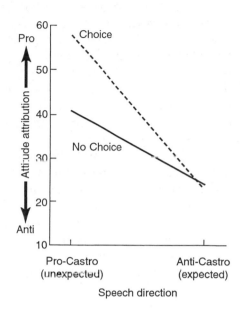

(given little or no choice but) to defend the opposite of their initial position on an issue (cf. Aronson 1969; Bem 1972). Their behavior can be adequately explained by an attribution to the situation.

Nisbett and his associates (1973) set out to test the actor-observer proposition more directly. They found in a questionnaire study that people assign more traits to others than to themselves, a finding quite consistent with the notion that observers see personal dispositions in others but believe their own behavior depends primarily on the situation. Nisbett and his group also conducted an experiment in which some subjects were turned into actors and some into observers. The actors were asked to volunteer to take distinguished visitors around the Yale campus, while observers monitored the actors' responses to the volunteering request. Actors who volunteered were judged by the observers to be more likely to agree to canvass for the United Fund (an instance of response generalization implying a "volunteering trait") than those who did not volunteer. There was a slight reversal in this trend when the actors themselves were asked whether they would volunteer to canvass. By inference, then, the observers assumed that someone who volunteers in one setting will volunteer in others – they attributed a volunteering disposition to the actor.

Nisbett and I (1971) incorporated these data and tried to elucidate some of the reasons why the actor-observer divergence might occur. As a starting point, it may be helpful to consider the observer's orientation. In the attitude-attribution paradigm, and in the volunteering experiments, we confront the observer with a brief sample of behavior produced in a particular setting. The actor is aware of a history of his prior actions in similar settings and is likely to compare the present behavior to previous behavior. Differences in his behavior over time can readily be attributed to the situation. The observer, on the other hand, is typically ignorant about details of the actor's history and is likely to take a cross-sectional, or normative, view, asking himself, "How do this person's reactions differ from those I would expect from others, from the average, from the norm?" Thus the observer's orientation is individuating; he seeks out (and exaggerates?) differences among people, perhaps because this gives him a feeling of control against the unexpected. His error seems to lie in failing to see the situation as a completely sufficient cause of the behavior observed. Heider (1958) must have had something similar in mind when he talked about the tendency for behavior to "engulf the field." Behavior belongs to the person; the "field" acts on everyone.

In addition to the observer's relative poverty of information, it is also true that the same information will be processed differently by actors and observers. For the observer, in general, action is dynamic, changing, unpredictable, and therefore *salient*. In the attitude-attribution paradigm, the essay appears to stand out as the unique product of the writer. It must, since it is the only concrete information the perceiver has about the writer, reflect the writer's characteristics in a number of ways. That is what "the experiment" is about: the subject is in the position of wondering how good he is at estimating a person's true attitudes. The actor who writes a counterattitudinal essay has faced situational pressure and succumbed to it. The observer knows in some intellectual sense that the pressure was there, but he is so drawn to the essay as the focus of his judgment task that he infers too much about the individual and his uniqueness.

There is good evidence, finally, that *perceptual focusing* leads to attribution (Duncker 1938; Wallach 1959). Of special relevance here is a study by Storms (1973). He set out to investigate whether observers and actors could be induced to exchange perspective with the aid of videotape replay. As is the case with most important experiments, the design was elegantly simple. Two experimental subjects (actors) held a brief get-acquainted conversation while two other subjects were each assigned to observe a different actor. Television cameras were pointed at each actor, but after the conversation the experimenter appeared to notice that only one had been working properly.

During the next phase of the experiment, all subjects observed the intact videotape replay of the conversation (focusing on one of the actors) and then made a series of attributional judgments. Thus, one actor had the same orientation toward the other actor that he had in the conversation – he was looking at the other on the video replay. The other actor was looking at himself on the replay. He had become a self-observer. When asked to account for the target person's behavior in terms of the contributions of personal characteristics and characteristics of the situation, the actors observing themselves were much more inclined to attribute their behavior to dispositional influences. Attributions by the two observers varied depending on their new orientation. The original observer of the nontaped actor was asked to account for his target person's behavior after looking at the other actor. In this changed orientation, he attributed his target person's behavior to situational factors. The other observer, who watched the taped subject originally as well as in phase two, assigned much greater dispositional influence to his target person.

To summarize these findings, then, attribution seems to follow along with perceptual focus, or perspective. It appears that we attribute causality to whatever or whomever we look at, at least when we are asked. The implications of this fact for persistent interpersonal misunderstandings are obvious. In a persuasive communication setting, for example, the communicator thinks he is describing reality, whereas the target person thinks he is expressing his personal biases.

The results of Storms' experiment also suggest that seating arrangements might be extremely important in a discussion group. In fact, this has been demonstrated by Taylor and Fiske (1975). In their experiment, subjects observing a two-person "get-acquainted" discussion between two confederates of the experimenter were seated in such a way that some faced one discussant, some faced the other, and some observed both from a 90° angle. These differences in literal perception strongly affected the observer-subjects' attributions of causality for various aspects of the conversation. Specifically, the discussant directly in the observer's line of sight was assigned greater personal causality. When the discussants were both observed from the side, equal personal causality was assigned.

In an even more subtle manipulation of perspective, Hansen et al. (unpublished) presented videotaped shots of a person solving a jigsaw puzzle or playing chess. The shots either viewed the puzzle or chessboard from the point of view of the actor or from an angle perpendicular to that of the actor. Once again, the observer focusing on the actor attributed greater behavioral causality to him. The observer with the same angle of vision as the actor attributed the game outcome to the situation.

These experiments essentially converted observers into actors by letting them literally see what the actor saw. Could the same result be achieved by a shift in *psychological* perspective? Regan and Totten (1975) showed college women a videotaped "getting-acquainted" discussion, telling half of them to empathize with discussant A (the target person) and to try to imagine how A felt as she engaged in the conversation. The remaining subjects were given no such instructions. Using the same measures that Storms had used, Regan and Totten confirmed their hypothesis that empathy-inducing instructions produce a shift toward attributing behavior causation to the situation. This was especially true in a condition where the subject could see only the target person on the tape, though she could hear the other discussant as well. Thus, the authors argue, the divergence of perspective between actors and observers is founded in more than differences in available information. It derives at least in part, from differences in the ways in which the same information is processed.

Arkin and Duval (1975) have also found that the subjects' attention can be manipulated to affect their causal attributions. Actors in a picture-judging experiment attributed their preferences more to various features of the situation than to themselves (whereas observers were more inclined to attribute the preferences to the actor as a person). However, these differences were reversed when actors felt that they were being videotaped. The self-consciousness induced by the presence of a TV camera apparently shifted the causal assignment from the situation to the self. This is quite in line with the Duval and Wicklund (1972) theory of *objective self-awareness*, which suggests that an actor's causal attributions are a function of whether or not his attention is focused on himself.

FIELD STUDIES

It is quite apparent that something interesting is happening here, and the evidence that perceptual perspective influences causal attribution seems reliable and replicable. But, the reader might demur, is this one of those hothouse laboratory phenomena that is overwhelmed by other variables in the more chaotic and complex natural environment? Obviously, we should not expect to find a quick answer to this question, but a recent study by West et al. (1975) shows the predicted basic pattern of actor-observer differences in a dramatic field experiment simulating the Watergate burglary attempt.

Undergraduate criminology majors at a state university were contacted by a man whom they knew as a local private investigator. He arranged a meeting with each subject at which detailed plans of a business burglary were presented. The subject was asked to participate in breaking into the offices of a local firm to microfilm a set of records. In one condition of the experiment, the subjects were told that a competing local firm had offered $8,000 for a copy of designs prepared by the first firm. The subjects were told that they would be paid $2,000 for their participation in the crime. In other conditions, the experimenter presented himself as working for the Internal Revenue Service and said that the records would allegedly show that the firm was trying to defraud the U.S. government. Of the subjects exposed to the IRS cover story, half were told that they would receive immunity from prosecution if caught; the other half were told that there would be no immunity. After an elaborate and convincing presentation of the plan, subjects were asked to come to a final planning meeting. Their assent or refusal was the major dependent measure of the experiment. Once the subjects either agreed or did not agree to participate in the burglary, the experiment was then over and they were given extensive debriefing concerning the deceptions involved and the purpose of the experiment. (Readers interested in the ethical problems of this experiment will find a considered view presented by West and his colleagues, 1975, and comments by Cook, 1975, who tries to place the experiment in the more general framework of ethical problems in psychological research.)

Not surprisingly, whether the subject thought he or she would be granted immunity if caught was a crucial determinant of the frequency of compliance. Nearly half (45 percent) of the subjects in the immunity condition agreed to attend the final planning session. It is somewhat surprising that only 1 out of 20 subjects in the IRS no-immunity condition complied, whereas 4 out of 20 subjects in the reward condition agreed, although this difference was not statistically significant.

In addition to the involved subjects, a large sample of role-playing "observers" were asked to imagine themselves in the situation of the subject They were given a very detailed description of experimental events in the condition to which they were assigned and asked whether they would or would not comply. About 18 percent of these observer-subjects said that they would have agreed, and there was no difference as a function of the various conditions. Of special interest in the present context, all subjects (actors and role-players) were asked to explain *why* they did or did not agree to move closer toward the burglary. Whether the actors were compliers or noncompliers, they attributed their decision to environmental factors more than to personal dispositions. The role-playing observers, on the other hand, were much more likely to attribute the decision to dispositions in the actor. This was true whether they were asked to explain the decision of a complying or a noncomplying actor. Thus the actor-observer divergence in this case is not simply a matter of the actor's being inclined to rationalize his "criminal" behavior by blaming the situation.

In another, less dramatic, field study McGee and Snyder (1975) followed their hunch that there are interesting attributional differences between those who salt before and those who salt after tasting their food. Restaurant patrons were approached after placing themselves in one of these two categories by their salting behavior, and were asked to rate themselves on a series of polar adjectives like realistic-idealistic, cautious-bold, and energetic-relaxed. Each adjective pair was followed by another option, "it depends on the situation." As predicted, the before-tasting salters tended to check more traits as characteristic of themselves than the after-tasting salters, who were much more inclined to check "it depends on the situation." (It should be emphasized that none of the traits made any reference to eating behavior, taste, and so on.) When asked why they salted their food, the two types also diverged: the before-salters explained their behavior in terms of personal characteristics, whereas the after-salters tended to refer to the food.

Snyder and Monson (in press) have also shown that subjects classified as high "self-monitors" expect themselves to behave variably across different hypothetical situations. Low "self-monitors," on the other hand, expect to show greater cross-situational consistency. The authors classified their subjects by means of the score attained on a self-descriptive questionnaire.... On another questionnaire, describing different hypothetical situations, low self-monitors expected their behavior and environment in these different situations to be much more stable than did the high self-monitors. There is some evidence, then, that Nisbett's and my proposition must be qualified: *some* actors tend to attribute their actions to themselves, whereas others – more faithful to the proposition – typically make situational attributions.

There are other experimental results which seem more drastically at odds with our proposition. Most of these studies (e.g. Wolosin et al. 1975) involve the perception of behavioral freedom as the main dependent variable. Under some conditions, at least, actors will rate themselves as freer of situational influence than observers would rate them. Thus, if the attributional question is phrased in terms of whether the situation has *required* the actor to behave in a certain way, or if it strongly implies the giving up of his freedom and control, actors will claim greater freedom and responsibility whereas observers will see them as relatively constrained. If the question is more neutral with regard to relinquishing control, however, actors will see their behavioral decisions as responses appropriate to the opportunities and constraints of the environment (cf. Bell 1973).

There is an important philosophical distinction between "reasons" and "causes" (discussed at length by Beck, 1975) that is relevant here. Apparently, under most conditions, actors do not like to think that their behavior is *caused* by either the environment or the personality. At the less deterministic level of *reasons*, however, they are more likely to attribute their behavior to situational rather than to personal factors, thought to some extent we all realize that both factors are involved.

Monson and Snyder (unpublished) raise a caveat that deserves to be mentioned. They point out that most actor-observer studies have been laboratory experiments in which the actor's behavior is, in fact, "controlled" by a situational manipulation. Thus, Nisbett and his colleagues (1973) induced actors to volunteer to lead sightseeing tours by offering to pay them. In such a case, it is not surprising that the actor – who, most would agree, is more sensitive to situational variations – tends to attribute his behavior to the setting. He is right. The monetary incentive was "responsible" for his behavior. On the other hand, Monson and Snyder point out that in the natural environment people are not placed in situations so much as they choose them. Or, as Wachtel (1973) has argued, the situational forces to which actors respond are often of their own making To the extent that this true, actors may see their behavior, even though it varies from situation to situation, as dispositionally caused, whereas observers who see only the variation with situations may, if anything, underestimate the dispositional role.

This is an intriguing point, and it has some support in empirical data. For example, experimental evidence supports the fact that actors attribute their choice *among* situations to personal, dispositional factors. Once in the situation, however they see their behavior as controlled by its salient cues (cf. Gurwitz and Panciera 1975). It remains true, however, that even in the natural environment we often find ourselves in situations which we may have long ago selected but which we do not control in any detail. We should be wary of an easy translation from the laboratory to real life, but we should be equally careful not to assume that the laboratory is some irrelevant microcosm.

WIDER IMPLICATIONS OF THE THEORY

I think the balance of the evidence provides rather remarkable support for our "reckless" proposition. To say that actors attribute to situations what observers assign to dispositions is obviously not a law of behavioral science. But it is a useful guiding hypothesis that holds under a surprising range of conditions. The proposition can be subverted by special motivational factors (such as wanting to claim personal responsibility for a success) or by special knowledge on the part of the actor that he selected among many situations the one to which he now exposes himself. In the absence of these special conditions, however, our proposition seems to be robust and quite general. The proposition derives its validity in part from differences in perceptual perspective and in part from differences in the information available to actors and observers.

The major implication of the observer bias in attitude-attribution studies is that such a bias sows the seeds for interpersonal misunderstandings. It seems reasonable to assume that the more two people get to know each other, the more capable they become of taking each other's perspective: there should be a gradual merging of actor-observer orientations. In more transient interactions, however, we may all be victims of a tendency to misread role for personality. If our research has any generalization value at all, it is very likely that we assign to another's personality what we should be viewing as a complex interaction between person and situation. Particular roles within society or within an organization may call for certain patterns of behavior that are then used as a clue to what the role player is really like. What the reviewed research shows is that people make some allowance for the determining significance of roles and other situational pressures, but the allowance undershoots the mark. As a consequence, people who may be arbitrarily assigned to a group role, or assigned to a role on the basis of some initial response to strong environmental pressures, may have attributed to them a set of unwarranted personality characteristics to explain the role-induced behavior. Furthermore, once the group members make these attributions, their behavior toward the target person may constrain him to meet their expectations by "taking on" the personality they have assigned him. This is in the nature of a self-fulfilling prophecy: I expect John to behave in a certain way, and I give off subtle cues to ensure that he does.

In recent years a number of social scientists have pointed to and commented on the tendency in the field of psychology toward overattribution to the person. Mischel (1968, 1969) has essentially argued that there is not enough personal consistency across situations to warrant the personality psychologist's confident attribution of traits and attitudes to individual subjects or clients. Anthropologists D'Andrade (1974) and Shweder (1975) have also criticized individual difference psychology, claiming (with supportive evidence) that personality impressions follow the conceptual logic of the perceiver but do not fit the behavior of the persons being judged. The present research results point in the same direction by at least hinting at the pervasiveness of personal overattribution.

One final question might be raised: If such a pervasive attributional bias does exist, how come we get along as well as we do in the world? And how come the tendency doesn't get corrected by feedback and eventually drop out? One answer to the first question is, Maybe we don't get along so well. The Peter Principle (1969) is a striking example of attributional bias. A man gets promoted to his level of incompetence because the manager doesn't realize that a good performer in one setting may be incompetent in another. There may be other human costs incurred by the person who is misread by others, costs associated with the strain of meeting false expectations.

Perhaps one reason the bias persists uncorrected is that predictions from personality often overlap with or converge on predictions from situations. Much of our social life is more highly structured than we realize. Because we often see particular others in a restricted range of settings, cross-situational consistency is not an issue. Furthermore, we as observers are always a constant in the situation, which gives a further impetus to behavioral consistency. In situations restricted to a standard setting it makes no difference whether the prediction of behavioral continuity is based on attributions about personality or perceptions of situational requirements. There is no opportunity for corrective feedback. It is also the case that social behavior is notoriously ambiguous as feedback, and many an observer can tailor his perceptions of behavior to previously made personality attributions. We are probably all rather adept at maintaining trait inferences in the face of disconfirming behavioral evidence. When practiced by some psychoanalytic writers, the maneuvering can be truly breathtaking.

REFERENCES

ARKIN, R. M., AND S. DUVAL. (1975). Focus of attention and causal attributions of actors and observers. *Journal of Experimental Social Psychology*, 11:427–438.

ARONSON, E. (1969). The theory of cognitive dissonance: A current perspective. In Leonard Berkowitz (Ed.), *Advances in experimental social psychology: Vol 4* (pp. 1-34). New York: Academic Press, pp. 1–34.

BECK, L. W. (1975). *The Actor and the Spectator*. New Haven: Yale University Press.

BELL, L. G. (1973). *Influence of need to control on differences in attribution of causality by actors and observers*. Ph.D. dissertation, Duke University.

BEM, D. J. (1972). Self-perception theory. In Leonard Berkowitz (Ed.), *Advances in experimental social psychology: Vol. 6* (pp. 2-62). New York: Academic Press.

COOK, S. W. (1975). A comment on the ethical issues involved in West, Gunn, and Chernicky's "Ubiquitous Watergate: An attributional analysis." *Journal of Personality and Social Psychology*, 32, 66–68.

D'ANDRADE, R. (1974). Memory and the assessment of behavior. In Hubert M. Blalock (Ed.), *Measurement in the social sciences*. Chicago: Aldine.

DUNCKER, K. (1938). Induced motion. In Willis D. Wllis (Ed.), *A sourcebook of Gestalt psychology*, (pp. 161-72). New York: Harcourt, Brace.

DUVAL, S., AND R. A. WICKLUND. (1972). *A theory of objective self-awareness*. New York: Academic Press.

GURWITZ, S. B., AND L. PANCIERA. (1975). Attributions of freedom by actors and observers. *Journal of Personality and Social Psychology*, 32, 531–39.

HANSEN, R. D., D. J. RUHLAND, AND C. L. ELLIS. *Actor versus observer: The effect of perceptual orientation on causal attributions for success and failure*. Unpublished manuscript.

HEIDER, F. (1958). *The psychology of interpersonal relations*. New York: Wiley.

JONES, E. E., AND K. E. DAVIS. (1965). A theory of correspondent inferences: From acts to dispositions. In Leonard Berkowitz (Ed.), *Advances in experimental social psychology, Vol. 2* (pp. 219-66). New York: Academic Press.

JONES, E. E. AND V, A. HARRIS (1967). The attribution of attitudes. *Journal of Experimental Social Psychology, 3,* 1-24.

JONES, E. E., D. E. KANOUSE, H. H. KELLEY, R. E. NISBETT, S. VALINS, AND B. WEINER. (1972). *Attribution: Perceiving the causes of behavior.* Morristown, NJ: General Learning.

JONES, E. E., AND R. E. NISBETT. (1971). *The actor and the observer: Divergent perceptions of the causes of behavior.* New York: General Learning.

JONES, E. E., S. WORCHEL, G. R. GOETHALS, AND J. GRUMET. (1971). Prior expectancy and behavioral extremity as determinants of attitude attribution. *Journal of Experimental Social Psychology, 7,* 59–80.

KELLEY, H. H. (1967). Attribution theory in social psychology. In David Levine (Ed.), *Nebraska Symposia on Motivation,* pp. 192-240. Lincoln: University of Nebraska Press.

MCGEE, M. G., AND M. SNYDER. (1975). Attribution and behavior: Two field studies. *Journal of Personality and Social Psychology, 32,* 185–90.

MISCHEL, W. (1968). *Personality and assessment.* New York: Wiley.

MISCHEL, W. (1969). Continuity and change in personality. *American Psychologist, 24,* 1012–18.

MONSON, T. C., AND M. SNYDER. *Actors, observers and the attribution process: Toward a reconceptualization.* Unpublished manuscript.

NISBETT, R. E., C. CAPUTO, P. LEGANT, AND J. MARACEK. (1973). Behavior as seen by the actor and as seen by the observer. *Journal of Personality and Social Psychology, 27,* 154–165.

PETER, L. J., AND R. HULL. (1969). *The Peter Principle.* New York: Morrow.

REGAN, D. T., AND J. TOTTEN. (1975). Empathy and attribution: Turning observers into actors. *Journal of Personality and Social Psychology, 32,* 850–56.

SNYDER, M., AND E, E. JONES. (1974). Attitude attribution when behavior is constrained. *Journal of Experimental Social Psychology, 10,* 585–600.

SNYDER, M., AND T. C. MONSON. Persons, situations, and the control of social behavior. *Journal of Personality and Social Psychology,* in press.

STORMS, M. D. (1973). Videotape and the attribution process: Reversing actors' and observers' points of view. *Journal of Personality and Social Psychology, 27,* 165–175.

SHWEDER, R. A. (1975). How relevant is an individual difference theory of personality? *Journal of Personality, 43,* 455–84.

TAYLOR, S. E., AND S. T. FISKE. (1975). Point of view and perceptions of causality. *Journal of Personality and Social Psychology, 32,* 439–45.

WACHTEL, P. (1973). Psychodynamics, behavior therapy, and the implacable experimenter: An inquiry into the consistency of personality. *Journal of Abnormal Psychology, 82,* 324–34.

WALLACH, H. (1959). The perception of motion. *Scientific American, 201:*56–60.

WEST, S. G., S. P. GUNN, AND P. CHERNICKY. (1975). Ubiquitous Watergate: An attributional analysis. *Journal of Personality and Social Psychology, 32,* 55–65.

WOLOSIN, R. J., J. ESSER, AND G. A. FIND. (1975). Effects of justification and vocalization on actors' and observers' attributions of freedom. *Journal of Personality, 43,* 612–33.

QUESTIONS

1. What are the two types of attributions that people make to explain behavior? Are the two types mutually exclusive – that is, can people make both types about the same behavior?

2. In general, how do the attributions of actors differ from those of observers? In line with this, should people assign more stable personality traits to themselves or to others?

3. What is the role of salience and perceptual focus on the actor-observer effect? By perspective, does Jones mean just visual perspective?

4. How does the personality trait of self-monitoring influence the attributions of actors? How might it affect the attributions of observers?

5. In a sense, psychologists are the ultimate observers. How might this influence the types of theories that they propose?

Reading 4: Contemporary

Like Goes with Like: The Role of Representativeness in Erroneous and Pseudoscientific Beliefs

Thomas Gilovich and Kenneth Savitsky

The reading we have chosen to represent contemporary research on social cognition may at first seem an odd choice because the kinds of thought processes being explained are not very social. Unlike the previous reading, which sought to understand how we make sense of other people's behavior in social situation, this next reading seeks to understand such diverse but wholly unsocial issues as why people are so often fooled by unproved claims of New Age medicine and why highly trained medical doctors resist or accept theories of disease for very illogical reasons. That social psychologists are writing about non-social cognition demonstrates how far research on social cognition has come and how important it now is No longer are thought processes about social situations seen as being but one part of human cognition; instead more and more psychologists have come to believe that the basic thought processes about social and non-social problems are the same.

One important basic thought process identified by social psychology is the use of heuristics. Heuristics are mental short cuts or generalizations. Like all generalizations they are frequently right but sometimes wrong. One such heuristic, known as the representative heuristic, can be summarized by the familiar expression,"if something looks like a duck and walks like a duck then it is a duck." You can probably see that this heuristic will often lead to sensible decisions. But as the authors of this next reading show, it can also lead to some spectacularly insensible decisions. Social psychologists Thomas Gilovich and Kenneth Savitsky review first how use of the representative heuristic can lead to mistakes in social decisions, for example in deciding what sort of job a person has based on a few facts about their background. They then review how this same heuristic can lead to mistakes in a wide range of non-social decisions.

Ψ

It was in 1983, at an infectious-disease conference in Brussels, that Barry Marshall, an internal-medicine resident from Perth, Australia, first staked his startling claim. He argued that the peptic ulcer, a painful crater in the lining of the stomach or duodenum, was not caused by a stressful lifestyle as everyone had thought. Instead, the malady that afflicts millions of adults in the United States alone was caused by a simple bacterium, and thus

Source: Gilovitch, T. and Savitsky, K. (1996, March/April). Like goes with like: The role of representativeness in erroneous and pseudoscientific beliefs. *The Skeptical Inquirer, 20* (2), 34-40. Reprinted with permission of *The Skeptical Inquirer*.

could be cured using antibiotics (Hunter 1993; Monmaney 1993; Peterson 1991; Wandycz 1993).

Although subsequent investigations have sustained Marshall's claim (e.g., Hentschel et al. 1993), his colleagues initially were highly skeptical. Martin Blaser, director of the Division of Infectious Diseases at the Vanderbilt University School of Medicine, described Marshall's thesis as "the most preposterous thing I'd ever heard" (Monmaney 1993).

What made the idea so preposterous? Why were the experts so resistant to Marshall's suggestions? There were undoubtedly many reasons. For one, the claim contradicted what most physicians, psychiatrists, and psychologists knew (or thought they knew): Ulcers were caused by stress. As one author noted, "No physical ailment has ever been more closely tied to psychological turbulence" (Monmaney 1993, p. 64). In addition, science is necessarily and appropriately a rather conservative enterprise. Although insight, creativity, and even leaps of faith are vital to the endeavor, sound empirical evidence is the true coin of the realm. Much of the medical establishment's hesitation doubtless stemmed from the same healthy skepticism that readers of the SKEPTICAL INQUIRER have learned to treasure. After all, Marshall's results at the time were suggestive at best – no cause-effect relationship had yet been established.

But there may have been a third reason for the reluctance to embrace Marshall's contention, a reason we explore in this article. The belief that ulcers derive from stress is particularly seductive – for physicians and laypersons alike – because it flows from a general tendency of human judgment, a tendency to employ what psychologists Amos Tversky and Daniel Kahneman have called the "representativeness heuristic" (Kahneman and Tversky 1972, 1973; Tversky and Kahneman 1974, 1982). Indeed, we believe that judgment by representativeness plays a role in a host of erroneous beliefs, from beliefs about health and the human body to handwriting analysis and astrology (Gilovich 1991). We consider a sample of these beliefs in this article.

THE REPRESENTATIVENESS HEURISTIC

Representativeness is but one of a number of heuristics that people use to render complex problems manageable. Heuristics are often described as judgmental shortcuts that generally get us where we need to go – and quickly – but at the cost of occasionally sending us off course. Kahneman and Tversky liken them to perceptual cues, which generally enable us to perceive the world accurately, but occasionally give rise to misperception and illusion. Consider their example of using clarity as a cue for distance. The clarity of an object is one cue people use to decide how far away it is. The cue typically works well because the farther away something is, the less distinct it appears. On a particularly clear day, however, objects can appear closer than they are, and on hazy days, they can appear farther away. In some circumstances, then, this normally accurate cue can lead to error.

Representativeness works much the same way. The representativeness heuristic involves a reflexive tendency to assess the similarity of objects and events along salient dimensions and to organize them on the basis of one overarching rule: "Like goes with like." Among other things, the representativeness heuristic reflects the belief that a member of a given category ought to resemble the category prototype, and that an effect ought to resemble the cause that produced it. Thus, the representativeness heuristic is often used to assess whether a given instance belongs to a particular category, such as whether an individual is likely to be an accountant or a comedian. It is also used in assigning causes to effects, as when deciding whether a meal of spicy food caused a case of heartburn or determining whether an assassination was the product of a conspiracy.

Note that judgment by representativeness often works well. Instances often resemble their category prototypes and causes frequently resemble their effects. Members of various occupational groups, for example, frequently do resemble the group prototype. Likewise, "big" effects (such as the development of the atomic bomb) are often brought about by "big" causes (such as the Manhattan Project).

Still, the representativeness heuristic is only that – a heuristic or shortcut. As with all shortcuts, the representativeness heuristic should be used with caution. Although it can help us to make some judgments with accuracy and ease, it can also lead us astray. Not all members fit the category prototype. Some comedians are shy or taciturn, and some accountants are wild and crazy. And although causes are frequently representative of their effects, this relationship does not always hold: Tiny viruses give rise to devastating epidemics like malaria or AIDS; and splitting the nucleus of an atom releases an awesome amount of energy. In some cases, then, representativeness yields inaccuracy and error. Or even superstition. A nice example is provided by craps shooters, who roll the dice gently to coax a low number, and more vigorously to encourage a high one (Hanslin 1967). A small effect (low number) requires a small cause (gentle roll), and a big effect (high number) requires a big cause (vigorous roll).

How might the belief in a stress-ulcer link derive from the conviction that like goes with like? Because the burning feeling of an ulcerated stomach is not unlike the gut-wrenching, stomach-churning feeling of extreme stress (albeit more severe), the link seems natural: Stress is a representative cause of an ulcer.[1] But as Marshall suggested (and subsequent research has borne out), the link may be overblown. Stress alone does not appear to cause ulcers (Glavin and Szabo 1992; Soll 1990).

---

[1] Some theories of the link between stress and ulcers are even more tinged with representativeness. Since the symptoms of an ulcer manifest themselves in the stomach, the cause "should" involve something that is highly characteristic of the stomach as well, such as hunger and nourishment. Thus, one theorist asserts, "The critical factor in the development of ulcers is the frustration associated with the wish to receive love – when this wish is rejected, it is converted into a wish to be fed," leading ultimately "to an ulcer." Echoing such ideas, James Masterson writes in his book *The Search for the Real Self* that ulcers affect those who are "hungering for emotional supplies that were lost in childhood or that were never sufficient to nourish the real self" (both quoted in Monmaney 1993).

REPRESENTATIVENESS AND THE CONJUNCTION FALLACY

One of the most compelling demonstrations of how the representativeness heuristic can interfere with sound judgment comes from a much-discussed experiment in which participants were asked to consider the following description (Tversky and Kahneman 1982, 1983):

> Linda is 31 years old, single, outspoken, and very bright. She majored in philosophy. As a student, she was deeply concerned with issues of discrimination and social justice, and also participated in anti-nuclear demonstrations.
> Now, based on the above description, rank the following statements about Linda, from most to least likely:
>   a.   Linda is an insurance salesperson.
>   b.   Linda is a bank teller.
>   c.   Linda is a bank teller and is active in the feminist movement.

If you are like most people, you probably thought it was more likely that "Linda is a bank teller and is active in the feminist movement" than that "Linda is a bank teller." It is easy to see why: A feminist bank teller is much more representative of the description of Linda than is "just" a bank teller. It reflects the political activism, social-consciousness, and left-of-center politics implied in the description.

It makes sense, but it cannot be. The category "bank teller" subsumes the category "is a bank teller and is active in the feminist movement." The latter therefore cannot be more likely than the former. Anyone who is a bank teller and is active in the feminist movement is automatically also a bank teller. Indeed, even if one thinks it is impossible for someone with Linda's description to be solely a bank teller (that is, one who is not a feminist), being a bank teller is still as likely as being both. This error is referred to as the "conjunction fallacy" because the probability of two events co-occurring (i.e., their conjunction) can never exceed the individual probability of either of the constituents (Tversky and Kahneman 1982, 1983; Dawes and Mulford 1993).

Such is the logic of the situation. The psychology we bring to bear on it is something else. If we start with an unrepresentative outcome (being a bank teller) and then add a representative element (being active in the feminist movement), we create a description that is at once more psychologically compelling but objectively less likely. The rules of representativeness do not follow the laws of probability. A detailed description can seem compelling precisely because of the very details that, objectively speaking, actually make it less likely. Thus, someone may be less concerned about dying during a trip to the Middle East than about dying in a terrorist attack while there, even though the probability of death due to a *particular* cause is obviously lower than the probability of death due to the set of all possible causes. Likewise, the probability of global economic collapse can seem remote until one sketches a detailed scenario in which such a collapse follows, say, the destruction of the oil fields in the Persian Gulf. Once again, the additional details make the outcome less likely at the same time that they make it more psychologically compelling.

REPRESENTATIVENESS AND CAUSAL JUDGMENTS

Most of the empirical research on the representativeness heuristic is similar to the work on the conjunction fallacy in that the judgments people make are compared to a normative standard – in this case, to the laws of probability. The deleterious effect of judgment by representativeness is thereby established by the failure to meet such a standard. Previous work conducted in this fashion has shown, for example, that judgment by representativeness leads people to commit the "gambler's fallacy," to overestimate the reliability of small samples of data, and to be insufficiently "regressive" in making predictions under conditions of uncertainty.

The ulcer example with which we began this article does not have this property of being obviously at variance with a clear-cut normative standard. The same is true of nearly all examples of the impact of representativeness on causal judgments: It can be difficult to establish with certainty that a judgmental error has been made. Partly for this reason, there has been less empirical research on representativeness and causal judgments than on other areas, such as representativeness and the conjunction fallacy. This is not because representativeness is thought to have little impact on causal judgments, but because without a clear-cut normative standard it is simply more difficult to conduct research in this domain. The research that has been conducted, furthermore, is more suggestive than definitive. Nonetheless, the suggestive evidence is rather striking, and it points to the possibility that representativeness may exert at least as much influence over causal judgments as it does over other, more exhaustively researched types of judgments. To see how much, we discuss some examples of representativeness-thinking in medicine, in pseudoscientific systems, and in psychoanalysis.

REPRESENTATIVENESS AND MEDICAL BELIEFS

One area in which the impact of representativeness on causal judgments is particularly striking is the domain of health and medicine. Historically, people have often assumed that the symptoms of a disease should resemble either its cause or its cure (or both). In ancient Chinese medicine, for example, people with vision problems were fed ground bat in the mistaken belief that bats had particularly keen vision and that some of this ability might be transferred to the recipient (Deutsch 1977). ...

Representative-thinking continues to abound in modern "alternative" medicine, a pursuit that appears to be gaining in perceived legitimacy (Cowley, King, Hager, and Rosenberg 1995). An investigation by Congress into health fraud and quackery noted several examples of what appear to be interventions inspired by the superficial appeal of representativeness (U.S. Congress House Subcommittee on Health and Long-Term Care 1984). In one set of suggested treatments, patients are encouraged to eat raw organ concentrates corresponding to the dysfunctional body part: e.g., brain concentrates for mental disorders, heart concentrates for cardiac conditions, and raw stomach lining for ulcers. Similarly, the fingerprints of representativeness are all over the practice of "rebirthing," a New Age therapeutic technique in which individuals attempt to reenact their own births in an effort to correct personality defects caused by having been born in an "unnatural" fashion (Ward 1994). One person who was born breech (i.e., feet first) underwent the rebirthing procedure to cure his sense that his life was always going in the wrong direction and that he could never seem to get things "the right way round." Another, born Caesarian, sought the treatment because of a lifelong difficulty with seeing things to completion, and always relying on others to finish tasks for her. As one author quipped, "God knows what damage forceps might inflict... a lifelong neurosis that you're being dragged where you don't want to go?" (Ward 1994, p. 90).

A more rigorous examination of the kind of erroneous beliefs about health and the human body that can arise from the appeal of representativeness has dealt with the adage, "You are what you eat." Just how far do people take this idea? In certain respects, the saying is undeniably true: Bodies are composed to a large extent of the molecules that were once ingested as food. Quite literally, we are what we have eaten. Indeed, there are times when we take on the character of what we ingest: People gain weight by eating fatty foods, and a person's skin can acquire an orange tint from the carotene found in carrots and tomatoes. But the notion that we develop the characteristics of the food we eat sometimes goes beyond such examples to almost magical extremes. The Hua of Papau New Guinea, for example, believe that individuals will grow quickly if they eat rapidly growing food (Meigs 1984, cited by Nemeroff and Rozin 1989).

But what about a more "scientifically minded" population? Psychologists Carol Nemeroff and Paul Rozin (1989) asked college students to consider a hypothetical culture known as the "Chandorans," who hunt wild boar and marine turtles. Some of the students learned that the Chandorans hunt turtles for their shells, and wild boar for their meat. The others heard the opposite: The tribe hunts turtles for their meat, and boar for their tusks.

After reading one of the two descriptions of the Chandorans, the students were asked to rate the tribe members on numerous characteristics. Their responses reflected a belief that the characteristics of the food that was eaten would "rub off" onto the tribe members. Boar-eaters were thought to be more aggressive and irritable than their counterparts – and more likely to have beards! The turtle-eaters were thought to live longer and be better swimmers.

However educated a person may be (the participants in Nemeroff and Rozin's experiment were University of Pennsylvania undergraduates), it can be difficult to get beyond the assumption that like goes with like. In this case, it leads to the belief that individuals tend to acquire the attributes of the food they ingest. Simple representativeness.

REPRESENTATIVENESS AND PSEUDOSCIENTIFIC BELIEFS

A core tenet of astrology is that an individual's personality is influenced by the astrological sign under which he or she was born (Huntley 1990). A glance at the personality types associated with the various astrological signs reveals an uncanny concordance between the supposed personality of someone with a particular sign and the characteristics associated with the sign's namesake (Huntley 1990; Howe 1970; Zusne and Jones 1982). Those born under the sign of the goat (Capricorn) are said to be tenacious, hardworking, and stubborn; whereas those born under the lion (Leo) are proud, forceful leaders. Likewise, those born under the sign of Cancer (the crab) share with their namesake a tendency to appear hard on the outside; while inside their "shells" they are soft and vulnerable. One treatment of astrology goes so far as to suggest that, like the crab, those born under the sign of Cancer tend to be "deeply attached to their homes" (Read et al. 1978).

What is the origin of these associations? They are not empirically derived, as they have been shown time and time again to lack validity (e.g., Carlson 1985; Dean 1987; for reviews see Abell 1981; Schick and Vaughn 1995; Zusne and Jones 1982). Instead, they are conceptually driven by simple, representativeness-based assessments of the personalities that should be associated with various astrological signs. After all, who is more likely to be retiring and modest than a Virgo (the virgin)? Who better to be well-balanced, harmonious, and fair than a Libra (the scales)? By taking advantage of people's reflexive associations, the system gains plausibility among those disinclined to dig deeper.

And it doesn't stop there. Consider another elaborate "scientific" system designed to assess the "secrets" of an individual's personality – graphology, or handwriting analysis. Corporations pay graphologists sizable fees to help screen job applicants by developing personality profiles of those who apply for jobs (Neter and Ben-Shakhar 1989). Graphologists are also called upon to provide "expert" testimony in trial proceedings, and to help the Secret Service determine if any real danger is posed by threatening letters to government officials (Scanlon and Mauro 1992). How much stock can we put in the work of handwriting analysts?

Unlike astrology, graphology is not worthless. It has been, and continues to be, the subject of careful empirical investigation (Nevo 1986), and it has been shown that people's handwriting can reveal certain things about them. Particularly shaky writing can be a clue that an individual suffers from some neurological disorder that causes hand tremors; whether a person is male or female is often apparent from his or her writing. In general, however, what handwriting analysis can determine most reliably tends to be things that can be more reliably ascertained through other means. As for the "secrets" of an individual's personality, graphology has yet to show that it is any better than astrology.

This has not done much to diminish the popularity of handwriting analysis, however. One reason for this is that graphologists, like astrologers, gain some surface plausibility or "face validity" for their claims by exploring the tendency for people to employ the representative heuristic. Many of their claims have a superficial "sensible" quality, rarely violating the principle that like goes with like. Consider, for instance, the "zonal theory" of graphology, which divides a person's handwriting into the upper, middle, and lower regions. A person's "intellectual," "practical," and "instinctual" qualities supposedly correspond to the different regions (Basil 1989). Can you guess which is which? Could our "lower" instincts be reflected anywhere other than the lower region, or our "higher" intellect anywhere other than the top?

The list of such representativeness-based "connections" goes on and on. Handwriting slants to the left? The person must be holding something back, repressing his or her true emotions. Slants to the right? The person gets carried away by his or her feelings. A signature placed far below a paragraph suggests that the individual wishes to distance himself or herself from what was written (Scanlon and Mauro 1992). Handwriting that stays close to the left margin belongs to individuals attached to the past, whereas writing that hugs the right margin comes from those oriented toward the future.

What is ironic is that the very mechanism that many graphologists rely upon to argue for the persuasive value of their endeavor – that the character of the handwriting resembles the character of the person – is what ultimately betrays them: They call it "common sense;" we call it judgment by representativeness.

REPRESENTATIVENESS AND PSYCHOANALYSIS

Two prominent social psychologists, Richard Nisbett and Lee Ross, have argued that "the enormous popularity of Freudian theory probably lies in the fact that, unlike all its competitors among contemporary views, it encourages the layperson to do what comes naturally in causal explanation, that is, to use the representativeness heuristic" (Nisbett and Ross 1980, p. 244). Although this claim would be difficult to put to empirical test, there can be little doubt that much of the interpretation of symbols that lies at the core of psychoanalytic theory is driven by representativeness. Consider the interpretation of dreams, in which the images a client reports from his or her dreams are considered indicative of underlying motives. An infinite number of potential relationships exist between dream content and underlying psychodynamics, and it is interesting that virtually all of the "meaningful" ones identified by psychodynamically oriented clinicians are ones in which there is an obvious fit or resemblance between the reported image and inner dynamics. A man who dreams of a snake or a cigar is thought to be troubled by his penis or his sexuality. People who dream of policemen are thought to be concerned about their fathers or authority figures. Knowledge of the representativeness heuristic compels one to wonder whether such connections reflect something important about the psyche of the client, or whether they exist primarily in the mind of the therapist.

One area of psychodynamic theorizing in which the validity of such superficially plausible relationships has been tested and found wanting is the use of projective tests. The most widely known projective test is the Rorschach, in which clients report what they "see" in ambiguous blotches of ink on cards. As in all projective tests, the idea is that in responding to such an unstructured stimulus, a person must "project," and thus reveal, some of his or her inner dynamics. Countless studies, however, have failed to produce evidence that the test is valid – that is, that the assessments made about people on the basis of the test correspond to the psychopathological conditions from which they suffer (Burros 1978).[2]

The research notwithstanding, clinicians frequently report the Rorschach to be extremely helpful in clinical practice. Might representativeness contribute to this paradox of strongly held beliefs coexisting with the absence of any real relationship? You be the judge. A person who interprets the whole Rorschach card, and not its specific details, is considered by clinicians to suffer from a need to form a "big picture," and a tendency toward grandiosity, even paranoia. In contrast, a person who refers only to a small detail of the ink blots is considered to have an obsessive personality – someone who attends to detail at the expense of the more important holistic aspects (Dawes 1994). Once again, systematic research has failed to find evidence for these relationships, but the sense of representativeness gives them some superficial plausibility.

CONCLUSION

We have described numerous erroneous beliefs that appear to derive from the overuse of the representativeness heuristic. Many of them arise in domains in which the reach for solutions to important problems exceeds our grasp – such as the attempt to uncover (via astrology or handwriting analysis) simple cues to the complexities of human motivation and personality. In such domains in which no simple solutions exist, and yet the need or desire for such solutions remains strong, people often let down their guard. Dubious cause-effect links are then uncritically accepted because they satisfy the principles of like goes with like.

Representativeness can also have the opposite effect, inhibiting belief in valid claims that violate the expectation of resemblance. People initially scoffed at Walter Reed's suggestions that malaria was carried by the mosquito. From a representativeness standpoint, it is easy to see why: The cause (a tiny mosquito) is not at all representative of the result (a devastating disease). Reed's claim violated the notion that big effects should have big causes, and thus was difficult to accept (Nisbett and Ross 1980). Although skepticism is a vital component of critical thought, it should not be based on an excessive adherence to the principle that like goes with like.

Indeed, it is often those discoveries that violate the expected resemblance between cause and effect that are ultimately hailed as significant breakthroughs, as with the discovery of *Helicobacter pylori*, as the ulcer-causing bacterium is now named. As one

---

[2] Actually, a nonprojective use of the Rorschach, called the Exner System, has been shown to have some validity (Exner 1986). The system is based on the fact that some of the inkblots *do* look like various objects, and a person's responses are scored for the number and proportion that fail to reflect this correspondence. Unlike the usual Rorschach procedure, which is subjectively scored, the Exner system is a standardized test.

author put it, "The discovery of *Helicobacter* is no crummy little shift. It's a mindblower – tangible, reproducible, unexpected, and, yes, revolutionary. Just the fact that a bug causes peptic ulcers, long considered the cardinal example of a psychosomatic illness, is a spear in the breast of New Age medicine" (Monmaney 1993, p. 68). Given these stakes, one might be advised to avoid an overreliance on the shortcut of representativeness, and instead to devote the extra effort needed to make accurate judgments and decisions. (But not too much effort – you wouldn't want to give yourself an ulcer).

REFERENCES

ABELL, G. O. (1981). Astrology. In *Science and the Paranormal: Proving the Existence of the Supernatural*, ed. by G. O. Abell and B. Singer. New York: Charles Scribner's Sons.

BARRETT, S. (1987). Homeopathy: Is it medicine? *Skeptical Inquirer 12* (1) (Fall): 56-62

BASIL, R. 1989 Graphology and personality: Let the buyer beware. *Skeptical Inquirer 13* (3) (Spring): 213-243.

BURROS, O. K. (1978). *Mental Measurement Yearbook*. 8th ed. Highland Park, N.J.: Gryphon Press.

CARLSON, S. (1985). A double-blind test of astrology. *Nature* 318: 419-425.

COWLEY, G., P. KING, M. HAGER, AND D. ROSENBERG. (1995) Going mainstream. *Newseek* June 26: 56-57.

DAVES, R. M. (1994). *House of Cards: Psychology and Psychotherapy Build on Myth*. New York: Free Press.

DAWES, R. M., AND M. MULFORD. (1993). Diagnoses of alien kidnappings that result from conjunction effects in memory. *Skeptical Inquirer 18* (1) (Fall) 50-51.

DEAN, G. (1987). Does astrology need to be true? Part 2: The answer is no. *Skeptical Inquirer 11* (3) (Spring) 257-273.

DEUTSCH, R. M. (1977). *The New Nuts among the Berries: How Nutrition Nonsense Captured America*. Palo Alto, Calif.: Ball Publishing.

EVANS-PRITCHARD, E. E. (1937). *Witchcraft, Oracles and Magic among the Azande*. Oxford: Clarendon.

EXNER, J. E. (1986). *The Rorschach: A Comprehensive System*. 2d ed. New York: John Wiley.

GILOVICH, T. (1991). *How We Know What Isn't So: The Fallibility of Human Reason in Everyday Life*. New York: The Free Press.

GLAVIN, G. B., AND S. SZABO (1992). Experimental gastric mucosal injury: Laboratory models reveal mechanisms of pathogenesis and new therapeutic strategies. *FASEB Journal* 6: 825-831.

HANSLIN, J. M. (1967). Craps and magic. *American Journal of Sociology* 73: 316-330.

HENTSCHEL, E., G. BRANDSTATTER, B. GRAGOSICS, A. M. HIRSCHEL, H. NEMEC, K. SCHUTZE, M. TAUFER, AND H. WURZER. (1993). Effect of ranitidine and amoxicillin plus metronidazole on the eradication of Helicobacter pylori and the recurrence of duodenal ulcer. *New England Journal of Medicine* 328: 308-312.

HOWE, E. (1970). Astrology. In *Man, Myth, and Magic: An Illustrated Encyclopedia of the Supernatural*, ed. by R. Cavendish. New York: Marshall Cavendish.

HUNTER, B. T. (1993). Good news for gastric sufferers. *Consumer's Research* 76 (October): 8-9.

HUNTLEY, J. (1990). *The Elements of Astrology*. Shaftesbury, Dorset, Great Britain: Element Books.

KAHNEMAN, D., AND A. TVERSKY. (1972). Subjective probability: A judgment of representativeness. *Cognitive Psychology* 3: 430-454.

KAHNEMAN, D., AND A. TVERSKY. (1973). On the psychology of prediction. *Psychological Review* 80: 237-251.

MEIGS, A. S. (1984). *Food, Sex and Pollution: A New Guinea Religion*. New Brunswick, N.J.:Rutgers University Press.

MONMANEY, T. (1993). Marshall's hunch. *The New Yorker* 69 (September 20): 64-72.

NEMEROFF, C., AND P. ROZIN. (1989). 'You are what you eat': Applying the demand-free 'impressions' technique to an unacknowledged belief. *Ethos* 17: 50-69

NETER, E., AND G. BEN-SHAKHAR. (1989). The predictive validity of graphological inferences: A meta-analytic approach. *Personality and Individual Differences* (10) 737-745.

NEVO, B. 1986. ed. *Scientific Aspects of Graphology: A Handbook*. Springfield, Ill.: Charles C. Thomas.

NISBETT, R., AND L. ROSS. (1980). *Human Inference: Strategies and Shortcomings of Social Judgment*. Englewood Cliffs, N.J.: Prentice Hall.

PETERSON, W.L. (1991). Heliobacter pylori and peptic ulcer disease. *New England Journal of Medicine* 324: 1043-1048.

READ, A. W. et al. eds. (1978). *Funk and Wagnall's New Comprehensive International Dictionary of the English Language*. New York: Publishers Guild Press.

SCANLON, M., AND J. MAURO. (1992). The lowdown on handwriting analysis: Is it for real? *Psychology Today* (November/December): 46-53; 80.

SCHICK, T., AND L. VAUGHN. (1995). *How to Think about Weird Things: Critical Thinking for a New Age*. Mountain View, Calif.: Mayfield Publishing Company.

SOLL, A. I I. 1990. Pathogenesis of peptic ulcer and implications for therapy. *New England Journal of Medicine*. 322: 909-916.

TVERSKY, A., AND D. KAHNEMAN. (1974). Judgments under uncertainty: Heuristics and Biases. *Science* 185: 1124-1131.

TVERSKY, A., AND D. KAHNEMAN. (1982). Judgments of and by representativeness. In *Judgment under Uncertainty: Heuristics and Biases*, ed. by D. Kahneman, P. Slovic, and A. Tversky. Cambridge: Cambridge University Press.

TVERSKY, A., AND D. KAHNEMAN. (1983). Extensional versus intuitive reasoning: The conjunction fallacy in probability judgment. *Psychological Review* 90: 293-315.

U.S. CONGRESS. (1984). *Quackery: A $10 Billion Scandal: A Report by the Chairman of the (House) Subcommittee on Health and Long-Term Care*. Washington D.C.: United States Government Printing Office.

WANDYCZ, K. (1993). The H. pylori factor. *Forbes* 152 (August 2): 128.

WARD, R. (1994). Maternity Ward. *Mirabella* (February): 89-90.

ZUSNE, L. AND W. H. JONES (1982). *Anomalistic Psychology*. Hillsdale, N.J.: Lawrence Erlbaum Associates.

QUESTIONS

1. In the conjunction problem that described a woman named Linda, why is it incorrect to say that the most likely of the three statements about her is that she is a bank teller who is also a feminist?

2.   How can representative thinking explain the popularity of the New Age rebirthing technique? What is the role of salience and perceptual focus on the actor-observer effect? By perspective, does Jones mean just visual perspective?

3.   This article cites many examples from medicine. Why do the authors believe that medical doctors (and clinical psychologists too) often fall prey to the representative heuristic despite their extensive training in the logic-based scientific method?

4.   Recent medical studies found a people's blood serum cholesterol will increase more if they eat foods high in saturated fat than if they eat foods high in cholesterol.   Will the representative heuristic make such a finding easier or more difficult for people to believe?

5.   The authors argue that astrology is so widely believed in part because the symbols that represent each sign match the presumed characteristics of such people. Can you think of a way to test this hypothesis?

Ψ CHAPTER 3 Ψ

Prejudice, Discrimination, and Stereotypes: Perceiving and Understanding Groups

Reading 5: Classic

The Robber's Cave Experiment: Intergroup Conflict and Cooperation

Muzafer Sherif, O.J. Harvey, B. Jack White, William E. Hood, and Carolyn W. Sherif

The hallmark of social psychology, what separates it from other areas of psychology, is a focus on social groups. For example, some of the earliest research in social psychology investigated the dynamics of individuals when interacting with other group members. On a different level of analysis, social psychologists are also concerned with how entire groups behave when interacting with other groups. Moving to this broader level of analysis enables social psychologists to study intergroup conflict.

The study of intergroup conflict is a complicated matter. Just as the dynamics within two groups are never exactly alike, the dynamics between two groups are also never exactly alike. Not satisfied with simply describing conflict between two particular groups, social psychologist Muzafer Sherif wanted to find the universals of intergroup conflict. To this end, he decided to create two new groups and carefully observe the dynamics of each: first in isolation of each other, later in situations designed to foster hostility between the groups, and finally in situations designed to foster cooperation and to eliminate hostility between the groups. Sherif hoped the results would be the discovery of universal principles for fostering better intergroup relations.

Most social psychologists today believe that Sherif was successful. The following is an overview of his now famous Robber's Cave study outlining the concept of superordinate goals, and how they can be used to reduce tension between any two antagonistic groups.

A. THE PRESENT APPROACH

The word "group" in the phrase "intergroup relations" is not a superfluous label. If our claim is the study of relations between two or more groups or the investigation of intergroup attitudes, we have to bring into the picture the properties of the groups and the consequences of membership for the individuals in question. Otherwise, whatever we may be studying, we are not, properly speaking, studying intergroup problems.

Accordingly, our first concern was an adequate conception of the key word "group" and clarification of the implications of an individual's membership in groups. A definition of the concept improvised just for the sake of research convenience does not carry us far if we are interested in the validity of our conclusions. The actual properties of groups which brought them to the foreground in the study of serious human problems have to be spelled out.

The task of defining groups and intergroup relations can be carried out only through an *interdisciplinary approach*. Problems pertaining to groups and their relations are not studied by psychologists alone. They are studied on various levels of analysis by men in different social sciences. In the extensive literature on relations within and between small groups, we found crucial leads for a realistic conception of groups and their relations.

Abstracting the recurrent properties of actual groups, we attained a definition applicable to small groups of any description. A *group* is a social unit which consists of a number of individuals who, at a given time, stand in more or less definite interdependent status and role relationships with one another, and which explicitly or implicitly possesses a set of norms or values regulating the behavior of the individual members, at least in matters of consequence to the group.

Intergroup relations refer to relations between groups thus defined. Intergroup attitudes (such as prejudice) and intergroup behavior (such as discriminatory practice) refer to the attitudes and the behavior manifested by members of groups collectively or individually. The characteristic of an intergroup attitude or an intergroup behavior is that it is related to the individual's membership in a group. In research the relationship between a given attitude and facts pertaining to the individual's role relative to the groups in question has to be made explicit.

Unrepresentative intergroup attitudes and behavior are, to be sure, important psychological facts. But attitude and behavior unrepresentative of a group do not constitute the focal problem of intergroup relations, nor are they the cases which make the study of intergroup relations crucial in human affairs. The central problem of intergroup relations is not primarily the problem of *deviate behavior*.

In shaping the reciprocal attitudes of members of two groups toward one another, the limiting determinant is the nature of functional relations between the groups. The groups in question may be competing to attain some goal or some vital prize so that the success of one group necessarily means the failure of the other. One group may have claims on another group in the way of managing, controlling or exploiting them, in the way of taking over their actual or assumed rights or possessions. On the other hand, groups may have complementary goals, such that each may attain its goal without hindrance to the achievement of the other and even aiding this achievement.

Even though the nature of relations between groups is the limiting condition, various other factors have to be brought into the picture for an adequate accounting of the resulting intergroup trends and intergroup products (such as norms for positive or negative treatment of the other group, stereotypes of one's own group and the other group, etc.). Among these factors are the kind of leadership, the degree of solidarity, and the kind of norms prevailing within each group. Reciprocal intergroup appraisals of their relative strengths and resources, and the intellectual level attained in assessing their worth and rights in relation to others, need special mention among these factors. The frustrations, deprivations and the gratifications in the life histories of the individual members also have to be considered.

Theories of intergroup relations which posit single factors (such as the kind of leadership, national character, or individual frustrations) as sovereign determinants of intergroup conflict or harmony have, at best, explained only selectively chosen cases.

Of course leadership counts in shaping intergroup behavior; the prevailing norms of social distance count; so do the structure and practices within the groups, and so do the personal frustrations of individual members. But none of these singly determines the trend of intergroup behavior at a given time. They all contribute to the structuring of intergroup behavior, but with different relative weights at different times. Intergroup behavior at a given time can be explained only in terms of the entire frame of reference in which all these various factors function interdependently. This approach, here stated briefly, constituted the starting point of our experiments on intergroup relations. The approach was elaborated fully in our previous work, *Groups in Harmony and Tension*.

The relative weights of various factors contributing to intergroup trends and practices are not fixed quantities. Their relative importance varies according to the particular set of conditions prevailing at the time. For example, in more or less closed, homogeneous or highly organized groups, and in times of greater stability and little change, the prevailing social distance scale and established practices toward out-group which have been standardized in the past for group members will have greater weight in determining the intergroup behavior of individual members. But when groups are in greater functional interdependence with each other and during periods of transition and flux, other factors contribute more heavily. In these latter cases, there is a greater discrepancy between expressed attitude and intergroup behavior in different situations, attributable to situational factors, as insistently noted by some leading investigators in this area of research. Alliances and combinations among groups which seem strange bedfellows are not infrequent in the present world of flux and tension.

Because of their influence in social psychology today, two other approaches to intergroup behavior deserve explicit mention. A brief discussion of them will help clarify the conception of the experiment reported in this book.

One of these approaches advances frustration suffered in the life history of the individual as the main causal factor and constructs a whole explanatory edifice for intergroup aggression on this basis. Certainly aggression is *one* of the possible consequences of frustration experienced by the individual. But, in order that individual frustration may appreciably affect the course of intergroup trends and be conductive to standardization of negative attitudes toward an out-group, the frustration has to be shared by other group members and perceived as an issue in group interaction. Whether interaction focuses on matters *within* a group or between groups, group trends and attitudes of members are not crystallized from thin air. The problem of intergroup behavior, we repeat, is not primarily the problem of the behavior of one or a few deviate individuals. The realistic contribution of frustration as a factor can be studied only within the framework of in-group and intergroup relations.

The other important approach to intergroup relations concentrates primarily on processes within the groups in question. It is assumed that measures introduced to increase cooperativeness and harmony within the groups will be conducive to cooperativeness and harmony in intergroup relations. This assumption amounts to extrapolating the properties of in-group relations to intergroup relations, as if in-group norms and practices were commodities easily transferable. Probably, when friendly relations already prevail between groups, cooperative and harmonious in-group relations do contribute to solutions of joint problems among groups. However there are numerous cases showing that in-group cooperativeness and harmony may contribute effectively to intergroup competitiveness and conflict when interaction between groups is negative and incompatible.

The important generalization to be drawn is that the properties of intergroup relations cannot be extrapolated either (1) from individual experiences and behavior or (2) from the properties of interaction within groups. The limiting factor bounding intergroup attitudes and behavior is the nature of relations between groups. Demonstration of these generalizations has been one of the primary objectives of our experiment.

B. THE EXPERIMENT

The Design in Successive Stages

Experimental Formation of Groups. In order to deal with the essential characteristics of intergroup relations, one prerequisite was the production of two distinct groups, each with a definite hierarchical structure and a set of norms. The formation of groups whose natural histories could thus be ascertained has decided advantage for experimental control and exclusion of other influences. Accordingly, *Stage 1* of the experiment was devoted to the formation of autonomous groups under specified conditions. A major precaution during this initial stage was that group formation proceed independently in each group without contacts between them. This separation was necessary to insure that the specified conditions introduced, and not intergroup relations, were the determining factors in group formation. Independent formation of distinct groups permitted conclusions to be drawn later from observations on the effects of intergroup encounters and engagements upon the group structure.

The distinctive features of our study are *Stages 2* and *3* pertaining to intergroup relations. The main objective of the study was to find effective measures for reducing friction between groups and to discover realistic steps toward harmonious relations between them. If we had attempted to get two groups to cooperate without first bringing about a state of friction between them, there would have been no serious problem to be solved. The great task that social scientists, practitioners and policy-makers face today is the reduction of prevailing intergroup frictions.

Intergroup Conflict. After formation of definite in-groups, we introduced a period of intergroup relations as *Stage 2* of the experiment. During this stage, the two experimentally formed groups came into contact under conditions which were competitive, so that the victory of one group meant loss for the other. This series of encounters was conducive to successive frustrations whose causes were experienced as coming from the other group.

Only after an unmistakable state of friction between the two groups was manifested in hostile acts and derogatory stereotypes was the stage of reducing intergroup friction introduced.

Reduction of Intergroup Hostility. Various measures could have been tried in this experimental attempt toward the reduction of intergroup friction. One possible measure is the introduction of a "common enemy." Exposed to a common enemy, groups may join hands to do away with the common threat. This measure was not resorted to because it implies intergroup conflict on a larger scale.

Another possible approach is through dissemination of specific information designed to correct prevailing group stereotypes. This measure was not seriously considered because of the large body of research showing that discrete information, unrelated to central concerns of a group, is relatively ineffective in changing attitudes. Stereotypes crystallized during the eventful course of competition and conflict with the out-group are usually more real in the experience of the group members than bits of information handed down to them.

The alternative of channeling competition for highly valued rewards and prizes along individualized directions may be effective in reducing intergroup friction by breaking down group action to individual action. This measure may be practicable for small groups and is attempted at times by supervisors in classroom and recreational situations. However frictions and conflicts of significant consequence in life and the problem of their resolution are in terms of group demarcations and alignments.

The initial phase of *Stage 3* was devoted to testing the effects of intergroup contact involving close physical proximity in activities that were satisfying in themselves, such as eating meals or seeing a movie. This initial phase was introduced with the objective of clarifying the blanket term "contact" as applied to intergroup relations.

The alternative chosen as the most effective measure for reducing intergroup friction was the introduction of a series of *superordinate goals*, in line with the hypothesis stated prior to the experiment. Superordinate goals are goals of high appeal value for both groups, which cannot be ignored by the groups in question, but whose attainment is beyond the resources and efforts of any one group alone.

Research Methods

The methods used in this experiment to bring about the formation and subsequent change of attitude and behavior in directions predicted by the hypotheses were neither lecture method nor discussion method. Instead, the procedure was to place the members of respective groups in demanding problem situations, the specifications of which met the criteria established for the experimental state in question. The problem situations concerned activities, objects or materials which we knew, on the basis of the expressed preferences of the individuals or the state of their organisms, were highly appealing to them at the time. Facing a problem situation which is immediate, which must be attended to, which embodies a goal that cannot be ignored, group members do initiate discussion, do plan, do make decisions and do carry through the plans by word and deed until the objective is achieved. In this process, the discussion becomes *their* discussion, the plan becomes *their* plan, the decision becomes *their* decision, and the action becomes *their* action. In this process, discussion has its place, planning has its place, action has its place and when occasion arises, lecture has its place, too. The sequence of these related activities need not be the same in all cases. In many instances, we observed two or three of them carried on simultaneously.

Thus, problem situations introduced in *Stage 1* embodied goals of immediate appeal value to all members within a group, and the goals required their concerted activity or coordinated division of labor for attainment. The problem situations of *Stage 2* offered goals whose attainment by one group necessarily meant failure for the other group. Intergroup conflict was generated in the course of such engagements. The main part of *Stage 3* consisted of introducing a series of situations conducive to superordinate goals requiring joint action by both groups towards common ends. In every stage, changes in attitudes and action were not attempted through a single problem situation, but through the cumulative effect of a series of varied activities which, during each stage, had the distinctive characteristics summarized here.

All problem situations were introduced in a naturalistic setting and were in harmony with activities usually carried out in such a setting. The individuals participating in the study were not aware that each step was especially designed to study a particular phase of group relations. Once the problem situation was introduced under specified conditions and at a specified time, the initiative, discussion and planning were theirs, of course within bounds insuring health, security and well-being of the individuals studied.

Every effort was made that the activities and the flow of interaction in these activities appear natural to the subjects. Yet these activities and the interaction in them were *experimental*: Problem situations were chosen for each stage according to specified criteria . . . and were introduced under specified conditions (including the place, terrain, time, arrangement of facilities, stimulus materials available, etc.). The choice of an isolated site made it possible to restrict interaction situations and the individuals involved in them to those appropriate during each experimental stage.

Techniques of data collection were also determined by the theoretical approach and methodological considerations briefly stated above. The subjects were not aware that behavioral trends reflecting favorable or unfavorable, friendly or hostile intergroup attitudes were being studied. Knowing that one is under constant observation cannot help becoming a factor in structuring experience and behavior, particularly when the observation is related to our status concerns, our acceptance or rejection by others, our good or bad intentions toward others.

To the subjects, the participant observers appeared to be personnel of a usual camp situation. They were introduced as senior counselors. In this capacity they were close to their respective groups in a continuing way. True to their announced roles, the participant observers jotted down relevant observations out of the subjects' sight, and then expended their notes later each day.

When the technique of observation is adapted to the flow of interaction, there is danger of being selective in the choice of events to be recorded. The effective remedy against possible selectivity is using a *combination of methods* to check findings obtained with one method against those obtained by other methods.

The events which revealed stabilization and shifts in statuses, and crystallization of negative and then positive intergroup attitudes, were recurrent and so striking that one could not help observing them. However, in testing our main hypotheses, we supplemented the observational method with sociometric and laboratory-like methods. One distinctive feature of this study was introducing, at choice points, laboratory-like techniques to assess emerging attitudes through indirect, yet precise indices. Such laboratory-like assessment of attitudes is based on the finding that under relevant conditions, simple judgments or perceptions reflect major concerns, attitudes and other motives of man.

Reliability of observation and observer ratings was checked by comparing those of the participant observer with independent observations by others in crucial test situations. One such test situation illustrates the technique. When the status hierarchy in one group became stabilized toward the end of *Stage 1*, a problem situation was introduced which, like other problem situations of this stage, required initiative and coordination of the membership. A staff member who was not with the group regularly and who had not rated the status positions from day to day observed the group interaction in this situation. On this basis he made independent ratings of the status hierarchy, which were significantly correlated with those of the participant observer of that group.

C. MAIN CONCLUSIONS

Individual Characteristics and Intergroup Behavior

In this experiment, the rigorous criteria and painstaking procedures for selecting subjects ruled out explanations of hostile or friendly intergroup attitudes in terms of differences in socioeconomic, ethnic, religious, or family backgrounds. Similarly, the criteria for subject selection insured against explanations on the basis of unusual individual frustrations, failures, maladjustment or instability.

The subjects came from families who were established residents of the same city. They were stable families composed of natural parents and siblings. No subjects came from broken homes. Their religious affiliations were similar. They were from the middle socioeconomic class. They were of the same chronological and educational level. They had all made satisfactory progress academically; none had failed in school. In school and neighborhood, their social adjustment was above average. None was a behavior problem in home, neighborhood or school. In short, they were normal, healthy, socially well-adjusted boys who came from families with the same or closely similar socioeconomic, ethnic, and religious backgrounds.

Since none of the individuals was personally acquainted with others prior to the experiment, pre-existing positive or negative interpersonal relations did not enter into the rise of intergroup attitudes.

The conclusion that explanations of the intergroup trends and attitudes on the basis of individual characteristics are ruled out in this experiment should not be construed to mean that the relative contributions of individuals within their own groups and intergroup relationships are unimportant. Individuals do contribute differentially both in shaping and carrying on the trend of group relationships. This experiment does indicate, however, that intergroup attitudes are not merely products of severe individual frustrations or background differences brought to the situation.

Formation of Group Organization and Norms

When the individuals interacted in a series of situations toward goals with common appeal value which required interdependent activity for their attainment, definite group structures arose. These groups developed stable, but by no means immutable *status hierarchies* and *group norms* regulating experience and behavior of individual members.

More concretely, a pattern of leader-follower relations evolved within each group as members faced compelling problem situations and attained goals through coordinated action. As group structure was stabilized, it was unmistakably delineated as an "in-group." Certain places and objects important in group activities were incorporated as "ours." Ways of doing things, of meeting problems, of behaving under certain conditions were standardized, permitting variation only within limits. Beyond the limits of the group norms, behavior was subject to group sanctions, which ranged from ridicule, through ignoring the offender and his behavior, to threats, and occasionally to physical chastisement.

In-Group Cooperativeness Is Not Directly Transferable

When two groups met in competitive and reciprocally frustrating engagements, in-group solidarity and cooperativeness increased. Toward the end of the intergroup friction (*Stage 2*), in-group solidarity became so strong that when the groups were taken to a public beach crowded with outsiders and affording various distractions, our groups stuck almost exclusively to activities within their respective in-groups. Psychologically, other people did not count as far as they were concerned. In the presence of so many people and distractions, this intensive concentration of interests and activities within the group atmosphere would have been impossible had the groups gone there before attaining such a high degree of solidarity.

This heightened in-group solidarity and cooperativeness were observed at the very time when intergroup hostility was at its peak, during the period when the groups asserted emphatically that they would not have anything more to do with each other. This can only mean that the nature of intergroup relations cannot be extrapolated from the nature of in-group relations. In-group solidarity, in-group cooperativeness and democratic procedures need not necessarily be transferred to the out-group and its members. Intergroup relations cannot be improved simply by developing cooperative and friendly attitudes and habits within groups.

Consequential Intergroup Relations Affect In-Group Relations

Special note should be made of a related finding, namely that consequential intergroup relations have an impact on the in-group organization.

When it became evident that certain members of one group, including the leader, were not living up to the responsibilities expected of them by other members during the eventful course of intergroup competition, leadership changed hands. Those individuals who distinguished themselves by giving a good account for their group rose in the status hierarchy. Internal shifts in status were observed again during the cooperative intergroup activities of *Stage 3*. Functional relations between groups which are of consequence tend to bring about changes in the pattern of in-group relations.

Limiting Conditions for Intergroup Attitude and Behavior

We have seen that the individuals studied in this experiment were selected in ways which rule out explanations for the direction of intergroup behavior on the basis of differences in their backgrounds or on the basis of their individual frustrations, instabilities and the like. In the preceding sections, we have seen evidence that in-group properties were affected by consequential intergroup relations. Thus the intergroup hostility and its reduction cannot be explained merely by the nature of relationships within the groups.

Our findings indicate that the limiting condition determining friendly or hostile attitudes between groups is the nature of functional relations between them, as defined by analysis of their goals. When the groups competed for goals which could be attained by only one group, to the dismay and disappointment of the other, hostile deeds and unflattering labels developed in relation to one another. In time, derogatory stereotypes and negative attitudes toward the out-group were crystallized. These conclusions are based on observations made independently by observers of both groups and other staff members. Sociometric indices pointed to the overwhelming preponderance of friendship choices for in-group members. Experimental assessment of intergroup attitudes showed unmistakable attribution of derogatory stereotypes to the villainous out-group and of favorable qualities to the in-group. Laboratory-type judgments of performance showed the tendency to overestimate the performance attributed to fellow group members and to minimize the performance of members of the out-group.

What Kind of Contact Between Groups is Effective?

The novel step in this experiment was *Stage 3*, in which intergroup friction was reduced. We have already stated why we discarded certain procedures in this stage, such as introducing a "common enemy" or disseminating information. In order to clarify the term "contact," we tried the method of bringing the groups into close proximity in a series of activities. Most of these contact situations involved activities which were satisfying in themselves, such as eating good food in the same room, attending a movie together, or engaging in an exciting activity like shooting fireworks. But none of them created a state of interdependence between the groups. Such contact situations did not prove effective in reducing friction. Instead contact situations not conducive to interdependence were used by our groups for overt acts of hostility and further exchanges of unflattering invectives.

The ineffectiveness of contacts during which hostile groups engaged, while in close physical contiguity, in activities which were themselves satisfying to each individual has obvious implications for psychological theorizing.

The Introduction of Superordinate Goals

During the final period of the experiment, the prevailing friction between groups was reduced. Reduction of the conflict and hostility was observed in reciprocally cooperative and helpful intergroup actions, in friendly exchanges of tools, in developing standard procedures for alternating responsibilities and in meeting problems. The change in behavior and patterns of interaction between the groups was striking to all observers. The reliability of these observations is established by sociometric indices which showed increases of friendship choices for the erstwhile antagonists and also in the sharp decrease of unfavorable stereotypes toward the out-group. Favorable conceptions of the out-group developed, so that ratings of the in-group and out-group were no longer a set of contrasted polarities.

The end result was obtained through introduction of a series of superordinate goals which had compelling appeal value for both groups but which could not be achieved by the efforts and resources of one group alone. When a state of interdependence between groups was produced for the attainment of superordinate goals, the groups realistically faced common problems. They took them up as common problems, jointly moving toward their solution, proceeding to plan and to execute the plans which they had jointly envisaged.

In this experiment, the setting and circumstances for the introduction of superordinate goals were elaborately prepared by the experimenters. But beyond setting the scene, the methods followed, the discussion necessary for the solution, the plans to be made and executed were left to the groups themselves. Faced with superordinate goals, the groups carried on discussion when necessary, listened to the advice and suggestions of members of both groups who were resourceful, made decisions, and even combined discussion, decision and deeds simultaneously when the goal was attained more effectively this way.

Cumulative Effects of Superordinate Goals

If the hostile attitudes generated during intergroup friction had any stability, it could not be expected that one or two situations embodying superordinate goals could wipe them out. Indeed intergroup antagonisms did not disappear in one stroke. At first, cooperative interaction involving both groups developed in specific situations in response to common interaction involving both groups developed in specific situations in response to common problems and goals, only to be followed by a renewal of sharply drawn group lines and intergroup friction after the challenge had been met. Patterns and procedures for intergroup cooperation were laid down at first on a small scale in specific activities. Only during interaction in a series of situations involving superordinate goals did intergroup friction begin to disappear and the procedures for intergroup reciprocity developed in specific situations extend spontaneously to widening areas of activity.

In the sequential events of *Stage 3*, it was abundantly evident that the series of activities conducive to superordinate goals provided opportunities for members of the two groups to work out and develop procedures for cooperation in various spheres of action. Once a cooperative pattern was effective in a specific activity, it was extended by members of both groups to related actions. In the face of successful functioning of such procedures, the occasional dissident member who preferred the old days of intergroup strife or self-imposed separation found it more difficult to make his voice count in his own group.

Some procedures successful in intergroup interaction had previously been used by the groups in meeting problems within their own groups. But their transfer to intergroup interaction involved a significant step: the tacit recognition that the procedures now involved groups of individuals and not merely so many individual members within a group. Each individual within his group had been expected and encouraged by others to contribute to group efforts to the best of his abilities. Now, each group expected the other to contribute its share to meeting intergroup problems. While previously solutions were experienced as equitable or not relative to the individual's expectations and contributions within his group, now justice was also evaluated relative to equitable participation and opportunity for the groups as well.

The Same Tools May Serve Intergroup Conflict or Cooperation

In planning and working towards superordinate goals, there were times when the groups used jointly the tools and techniques which had been used by one or both groups separately in the service of fights during the intergroup conflict. Tools and techniques can be put to the service of harmony and integration as well as of deadly competition and conflict. Tools, in themselves, are not opposed to cooperation among individuals using them. It is the individuals as group members who put the tool to use in their opposition to other groups.

Even the proprietary pride that a place, a technique, a tool is "ours" takes on a different significance when the trend in intergroup relations is cooperation toward superordinate goals. Use of the technique or the tool in intergroup activities now implies a contribution toward a goal common to both groups – a contribution by the group in which members may take personal pride and which can be reciprocated by the other group equally enjoying its benefits through its own contributions at that or future occasions.

Superordinate Goals Alter the Significance of Other Influences

Contacts between groups in the course of actions towards superordinate goals are effective. They are used for developing plans, making decisions, and for pleasant personal exchanges. *Information* about the out-group becomes a matter of interest to group members and is actually sought in the course of interactions between members of the two groups. *Leaders* find that the trend toward intergroup cooperation in activities involving superordinate goals widens the spheres in which they may take positive steps toward working out procedures for joint endeavors and planning future contacts. Mingling with members of the other group and sharing in activities with them is no longer perceived by in-group members as "betrayal" or "treason." Similarly, the out-group member who engages in activities with the in-group is no longer seen by them as a strange and threatening figure in "our midst." On the contrary, intermingling of persons from different groups becomes a joint opportunity to work towards goals shared by both groups.

These are products of interaction towards goals superordinate to all groups, which are genuinely appealing to all, whose attainment requires equitable participation and contributions from all groups in interdependent activities.

QUESTIONS

1. What two methods of reducing intergroup friction did the experimenters choose not to attempt? Why?

2. What two methods did the experimenters use to reduce friction between the two groups? Which method did they expect to be more successful?

3. Briefly describe the methodology of this experiment. How did the experimenters control for possible bias in their observations?

4. What do the authors mean by "in-groups?" How are the dynamics of in-groups affected by the presence of another group? What is the relation between in-group solidarity and intergroup solidarity?

5. Describe the effect on intergroup relations of allowing the two groups to engage in intrinsically satisfying activities. How does this contact differ from that brought about by superordinate goals?

Reading 6: Contemporary

Thin Ice: "Stereotype Threat" and Black College Students

Claude Steele

One of the strengths of social psychology is its focus on everyday social issues and problems. It is not surprising, then, that the study of prejudice and discrimination has received considerable attention from social psychologists for many years. Recall that in the 1960s, social psychology escaped an identity crisis, in part, by focusing more on applied issues. This coincided with an unprecedented awareness in our culture of the social evils of sexism and racism. As a result, social psychologists have given these topics a great deal of attention.

Three decades later, social psychologists continue to grapple with the problems of racial inequity, which have turned out to be more pernicious than many first imagined. Today, after the removal of explicit barriers to educational opportunities and the expenditure of great efforts to recruit and aid black students, as a group they continue to fare poorly at all levels of education.

In the next reading, social psychologist Claude Steele explains why he believes black college students so often fail to thrive. Rejecting the traditional explanations of lack of preparation or motivation, Steele suggests that negative stereotypes about black students' abilities are the primary reason for their less successful academic performance. To demonstrate his point, Steele describes a series of studies showing that the same black students who fail under conditions of stereotype threat perform as strongly as white students when that threat is removed.

Ψ

The buildings had hardly changed in the thirty years since I'd been there. "There" was a small liberal-arts school quite near the college that I attended. In my student days I had visited it many times to see friends. This time I was there to give a speech about how racial and gender stereotypes, floating and abstract though they might seem, can affect concrete things like grades, test scores, and academic identity. My talk was received warmly, and the next morning I met with a small group of African-American students. I have done this on many campuses. But this time, perhaps cued by the familiarity of the place, I had an experience of déjà vu. The students expressed a litany of complaints that could have come straight from the mouths of the black friends I had visited there thirty years earlier: the curriculum was too white, they heard too little black music, they were

Source: Steele, C. (1999). Thin Ice: "Stereotype threat" and black college students, in *The Atlantic Monthly* (August 1999), 44-54. Copyright © 1999 by Claude M. Steele, as first published in *The Atlantic Monthly*. Reprinted by permission of *The Atlantic Monthly*.

ignored in class, and too often they felt slighted by faculty members and other students. Despite the school's recruitment efforts, they were a small minority. The core of their social life was their own group. To relieve the dysphoria, they went home a lot on weekends.

I found myself giving them the same advice my father gave me when I was in college: lighten up on the politics, get the best education you can, and move on. But then I surprised myself by saying, "To do this you have to learn from people who part of yourself tells you are difficult to trust."

Over the past four decades African American college students have been more in the spotlight than any other American students. This is because they aren't just college students; they are a cutting edge in America's effort to integrate itself in the thirty-five years since the passage of the Civil Rights Act. These students have borne much of the burden for our national experiment in racial integration. And to a significant degree the success of the experiment will be determined by their success.

Nonetheless, throughout the 1990s the national college-dropout rate for African-Americans has been 20 to 25 percent higher than for whites. Among those who finish college, the grade-point average of black students is two thirds of a grade below that of whites.

A recent study by William Bowen and Derek Bok, reported in their book *The Shape of the River*, brings some happy news: despite this underachievement in college, black students who attend the most selective schools in the country go on to do just as well in postgraduate programs and professional attainment as other students from those schools. This is a telling fact in support of affirmative action, since only these schools use affirmative action in admissions. Still, the underperformance of black undergraduates is an unsettling problem, one that may alter or hamper career development, especially among blacks not attending the most selective schools.

Attempts to explain the problem can sound like a debate about whether America is a good society, at least by the standard of racial fairness, and maybe even about whether racial integration is possible. It is an uncomfortably finger-pointing debate. Does the problem stem from something about black students themselves, such as poor motivation, a distracting peer culture, lack of family values, or – the unsettling suggestion of *The Bell Curve* – genes? Or does it stem from the conditions of blacks' lives; social and economic deprivation, a society that views blacks through the lens of diminishing stereotypes and low expectations, too much coddling, or too much neglect?

In recent years this debate has acquired a finer focus: the fate of middle-class black students. Americans have come to view the disadvantages associated with being black as disadvantages primarily of social and economic resources and opportunity. This assumption is often taken to imply that if you are black and come from a socioeconomically middle-class home, you no longer suffer a significant disadvantage of race. "Why should the son of a black physician be given an advantage in college admission over the son of a white delivery-truck driver?" This is a standard question in the controversy over affirmative action. And the assumption behind it is that surely in today's society the disadvantages of race are overcome when lower socioeconomic status is overcome.

But virtually all aspects of underperformance – lower standardized-test scores, lower college grades, lower graduation rates – persist among students from the African-American middle class. This situation forces on us an uncomfortable recognition: that beyond class, something racial is depressing the academic performance of these students.

Some time ago I and two colleagues, Joshua Aronson and Steven Spencer, tried to see the world from the standpoint of these students, concerning ourselves less with features of theirs that might explain their troubles than with features of the world they see. A story I was told recently depicts some of these. The storyteller was worried about his friend, a normally energetic black student who had broken up with his longtime girlfriend and had since learned that she, a Hispanic, was now dating a white student. This hit him hard. Not long after hearing about his girlfriend, he sat through an hour's discussion of *The Bell Curve* in his psychology class, during which the possible genetic inferiority of his race was openly considered. Then he overheard students at lunch arguing that affirmative action allowed in too many underqualified blacks. By his own account, this young man had experienced very little of what he thought of as racial discrimination on campus. Still, these were features of his world. Could they have a bearing on his academic life?

My colleagues and I have called such features "stereotype threat" – the threat of being viewed through the lens of a negative stereotype, or the fear of doing something that would inadvertently confirm that stereotype. Everyone experiences stereotype threat. We are all members of some group about which negative stereotypes exist, from white males and Methodists to women and the elderly. And in a situation where one of those stereotypes applies – a man talking to women about pay equity, for example – or an aging faculty member trying to remember a number sequence in the middle of a lecture – we know that we may be judged by it.

Like the young man in the story, we can feel mistrustful and apprehensive in such situations. For him, as for African-American students generally, negative stereotypes apply in many situations, even personal ones. Why was that old roommate unfriendly to him? Did that young white woman who has been so nice to him in class not return his phone call because she's afraid he'll ask her for a date? Is it because of his race or something else about him? He cannot know the answers, but neither can his rational self fully dismiss the questions. Together they raise a deeper question: Will his race be a boundary to his experience, to his emotions, to his relationships?

With time he may weary of the extra vigilance these situations require and of what the psychologists Jennifer Crocker and Brenda Major have called the "attributional ambiguity" of being on the receiving end of negative stereotypes. To reduce this stress he may learn to care less about the situations and activities that bring it about – to realign his self-regard so that it no longer depends on how he does in the situation. We have called this psychic adjustment "disidentification." Pain is lessened by ceasing to identify with the part of life in which the pain occurs. This withdrawal of psychic investment may be supported by other members of the stereotype-threatened group – even to the point of its becoming a group norm. But not caring can mean not being motivated. And this can have real costs. When stereotype threat affects school life, disidentification is a high price to pay for psychic comfort. Still, it is a price that groups contending with powerful negative stereotypes about their abilities – women in advanced math, African-Americans in all academic areas – may too often pay.

MEASURING STEREOTYPE THREAT

Can stereotype threat be shown to affect academic performance? And if so, who would be most affected – stronger or weaker students? Which has a greater influence on academic success among black college students – the degree of threat or the level of preparation with which they enter college? Can the college experience be redesigned to lessen the threat? And if so, would that redesign help these students to succeed academically?

As we confronted these questions in the course of our research, we came in for some surprises. We began with what we took to be the hardest question: Could something as abstract as stereotype threat really affect something as irrepressible as intelligence? Ours is an individualistic culture; forward movement is seen to come from within. Against this cultural faith one needs evidence to argue that something as "sociological" as stereotype threat can repress something as "individualistic" as intelligence.

To acquire such evidence, Joshua Aronson and I (following a procedure developed with Steven Spencer) designed an experiment to test whether the stereotype threat that black students might experience when taking a difficult standardized test could depress their performance on the test to a statistically reliable degree. In this experiment we asked black and white Stanford students into our laboratory and gave them, one at a time, a thirty-minute verbal test made up of items from the advanced Graduate Record Examination in literature. Most of these students were sophomores, which meant that the test was particularly hard for them – precisely the feature, we reasoned, that would make this simple testing situation different for our black participants than for our white participants.

In matters of race we often assume that when a situation is objectively the same for different groups, it is *experienced* in the same way by each group. This assumption might seem especially reasonable in the case of "standardized" cognitive tests. But for black students, difficulty with the test makes the negative stereotype relevant as an interpretation of their performance, and of them. They know that they are especially likely to be seen as having limited ability. Groups not stereotyped in this way don't experience this extra intimidation. And it is a serious intimidation, implying as it does that they may not belong in walks of life where the tested abilities are important – walks of life in which they are heavily invested. Like many pressures, it may not be experienced in a fully conscious way, but it may impair their best thinking.

This is exactly what Aronson and I found. When the difficult verbal test was presented as a test of ability, black students performed dramatically less well than white students, even though we had statistically matched the two groups in ability level. Something other than ability was involved; we believed it was stereotype threat.

But maybe the black students performed less well than the white students because they were less motivated, or because their skills were somehow less applicable to the advanced material of this test. We needed some way to determine if it was indeed stereotype threat that depressed the black students' scores. We reasoned that if stereotype threat had impaired their performance on the test, then reducing this threat would allow their performance to improve. We presented the same test as a laboratory task that was used to study how certain problems were generally solved. We stressed that the task did not measure a person's level of intellectual ability. A simple instruction, yes, but is profoundly changed the meaning of the situation. In one stroke "spotlight anxiety," as the psychologist William Cross once called it, was turned off – and the black students' performance on the test rose to match that of equally qualified whites.

Aronson and I decided that what we needed next was direct evidence of the subjective state we call stereotype threat. To seek this, we looked into whether simply sitting down to take a difficult test of ability was enough to make black students mindful of their race and stereotypes about it. This may seem unlikely. White students I have taught over the years have sometimes said that they have hardly any sense of even having a race. But blacks have many experiences with the majority "other group" that make their race salient to them.

We again brought black and white students in to take a difficult verbal test. But just before the test began, we gave them a long list of words, each of which had two letters missing. They were told to complete the words on this list as fast as they could. We knew from a preliminary survey that twelve of the eighty words we had selected could be completed in such a way as to relate to the stereotype about blacks' intellectual ability. The fragment "__ce," for example, could become "race." If simply taking a difficult test of ability was enough to make black students mindful of stereotypes about their race, these students should complete more fragments with stereotype-related words. That is just what happened. When black students were told that the test would measure ability, they completed the fragments with significantly more stereotype-related words than when they were told that it was not a measure of ability. Whites made few stereotype-related completions in either case.

What kind of worry is signaled by this race consciousness? To find out, we used another probe. We asked participants on the brink of the difficult test to tell us their preferences in sports and music. Some of these, such as basketball, jazz, and hip-hop, are associated with African-American imagery, whereas others, such as tennis, swimming, and classical music, are not. Something striking emerged: when black students expected to take a test of ability, they spurned things African-American, reporting less interest in, for instance, basketball, jazz, and hip-hop than whites did. When the test was presented as unrelated to ability, black students strongly preferred things African-American. They eschewed these things only when preferring them would encourage a stereotypic view of themselves. It was the spotlight that they were trying to avoid.

STEREOTYPE THREAT VERSUS SELF-FULFILLING PROPHECY

Another question arises: Do the effects of stereotype threat come entirely from the fear of being stereotyped, or do they come from something internal to black students – self-doubt, for example?

Beginning with George Herbert Mead's idea of the "looking-glass self," social psychology has assumed that one's self-image derives in large part from how one is viewed by others – family, school, and the broader society. When those views are negative, people may internalize them, resulting in lower self-esteem – or self-hatred, as it has been called. This theory was first applied to the experience of Jews, by Sigmund Freud and Bruno Bettelheim, but it was also soon applied to the experience of African-Americans by Gordon Allport, Frantz Fanon, Kenneth Clark, and others. According to the theory, black students internalize negative stereotypes as performance anxiety and low expectations for achievement, which they then fulfill. The "self-fulfilling prophecy" has become a commonplace about these students. Stereotype threat, however, is something different, something external: the situational threat of being negatively stereotyped. Which of these two processes, then, caused the results of our experiments?

Joshua Aronson, Michael Lustina, Kelli Keogh, Joseph Brown, Catherine Good, and I devised a way to find out. Suppose we told white male students who were strong in math that a difficult math test they were about to take was one on which Asians generally did better than whites. White males should not have a sense of group inferiority about math, since no societal stereotype alleges such an inferiority. Yet this comment would put them under a form of stereotype threat: any faltering on the test could cause them to be seen negatively from the standpoint of the positive stereotype about Asians and math ability. If stereotype threat alone – in the absence of any internalized self-doubt – was capable of disrupting test performance, then white males taking the test after this comment should perform less well than white males taking the test without hearing the comment. That is just what happened. Stereotype threat impaired intellectual functioning in a group unlikely to have any sense of group inferiority.

In science, as in the rest of life, few things are definitive. But these results are pretty good evidence that stereotype threat's impairment of standardized-test performance does not depend on cueing a pre-existing anxiety. Steven Spencer, Diane Quinn, and I have shown how stereotype threat depresses the performance of accomplished female math students on a difficult math test, and how that performance improves dramatically when the threat is lifted. Jean-Claude Croizet, working in France with a stereotype that links poor verbal skills with lower-class status, found analogous results: lower-class college students performed less well than upper-class college students under the threat of a stereotype-based judgment, but performed as well when the threat was removed.

Is everyone equally threatened by a stereotype? One might expect, for example, that it would affect the weakest students most. But in all our research the most achievement-oriented students, who were also the most skilled, motivated, and confident, were the most impaired by stereotype threat. This fact had been under our noses all along – in our data and even in our theory. A person has to care about a domain in order to be disturbed by the prospect of being stereotyped in it. That is the whole idea of disidentification – protecting against stereotype threat by ceasing to care about the domain in which the stereotype applies. Our earlier experiments had selected black students who identified with verbal skills and women who identified with math. But when we tested participants who identified less with these domains, what has been under our noses hit us in the face. None of them showed any effect of stereotype threat whatsoever.

These weakly identified students did not perform well on the test: once they discovered its difficulty, they stopped trying very hard and got a low score. But their performance did not differ depending on whether they felt they were at risk of being judged stereotypically.

WHY STRONG STUDENTS ARE STEREOTYPE-THREATENED

This finding, I believe, tells us two important things. The first is that the poorer college performance of black students may have another source in addition to the one – lack of good preparation and, perhaps, of identification with school achievement – that is commonly understood. This additional source – the threat of being negatively stereotyped in the environment – has not been well understood. The distinction has important policy implications: different kinds of students may require different pedagogies of improvement.

The second thing is poignant: what exposes students to the pressure of stereotype threat is not weaker academic identity and skills but stronger academic identity and skills. They may have long seen themselves as good students – better than most. But led into the domain by their strengths, they pay an extra tax on their investment – vigilant worry that their future will be compromised by society's perception and treatment of their group.

This tax has a long tradition in the black community. The Jackie Robinson story is a central narrative of black life, literature, and journalism. *Ebony* magazine has run a page for fifty years featuring people who have broken down one or another racial barrier. Surely the academic vanguard among black college students today knows this tradition – and knows, therefore, that the thing to do, as my father told me, is to buckle down, pay whatever tax is required, and disprove the damn stereotype.

That, however, seems to be precisely what these students are trying to do. In some of our experiments we administered the test of ability by computer, so that we could see how long participants spent looking at different parts of the test questions. Black students taking the test under stereotype threat seemed to be trying too hard rather than not hard enough. They reread the questions, reread the multiple choices, rechecked their answers, more than when they were not under stereotype threat. The threat made them inefficient on a test that, like most standardized tests, is set up so that thinking long often means thinking wrong, especially on difficult items like the ones we used.

Philip Uri Treisman, an innovator in math workshops for minority students, who is based at the University of Texas, saw something similar in his black calculus students at the University of California at Berkeley: they worked long hours alone but they worked inefficiently – for example, checking and rechecking their calculations against the correct answers at the back of the book, rather than focusing on the concepts involved. Of course, trying extra hard helps with some school tasks. But under stereotype threat this effort may be misdirected. Achievement at the frontier of one's skills may be furthered more by a relaxed, open concentration than by a strong desire to disprove a stereotype by not making mistakes.

Sadly, the effort that accompanies stereotype threat exacts an additional price. Led by James Blascovich, of the University of California at Santa Barbara, we found that the blood pressure of black students performing a difficult cognitive task under stereotype threat was elevated compared with that of black students not under stereotype threat or white students in either situation.

In the old song about the "steel-drivin' man," John Henry races the new steam-driven drill to see who can dig the hole faster. When the race is over, John Henry has prevailed by digging the deeper hole – only to drop dead. The social psychologist Sherman James uses the term "John Henryism" to describe a psychological syndrome that he found to be associated with hypertension in several samples of North Carolina blacks: holding too rigidly to the faith that discrimination and disadvantage can be overcome with hard work and persistence. Certainly this is the right attitude. But taken to extremes, it can backfire. A deterioration of performance under stereotype threat by the skilled, confident black students in our experiments may be rooted in John Henryism.

This last point can be disheartening. Our research, however, offers an interesting suggestion about what can be done to overcome stereotype threat and its detrimental effects. The success of black students may depend less on expectations and motivation – things that are thought to drive academic performance – than on trust that stereotypes about their group will not have a limiting effect in their school world.

HOW TO REDUCE STEREOTYPE THREAT

Putting this idea to the test, Joseph Brown and I asked, How can the usual detrimental effect of stereotype threat on the standardized-test performance of these students be reduced? By strengthening students' expectations and confidence, or by strengthening their trust that they are not at risk of being judged on the basis of stereotypes? In the ensuing experiment we strengthened or weakened participants' confidence in their verbal skills, by arranging for them to have either an impressive success or an impressive failure on a test of verbal skills, just before they took the same difficult verbal test we had used in our earlier research. When the second test was presented as a test of ability, the boosting or weakening of confidence in their verbal skills had no effect on performance: black participants performed less well than equally skilled white participants. What does this say about the commonsense idea that black students' academic problems are rooted in lack of self-confidence?

What did raise the level of black students' performance to that of equally qualified whites was reducing stereotype threat – in this case by explicitly presenting the test as racially fair. When this was done, blacks performed at the same high level as whites even if their self-confidence had been weakened by a prior failure.

These results suggest something that I think has not been made clear elsewhere: when strong black students sit down to take a difficult standardized test, the extra apprehension they feel in comparison with whites is less about their own ability than it is about having to perform on a test and in a situation that may be primed to treat them stereotypically. We discovered the extent of this apprehension when we tried to develop procedures that would make our black participants see the test as "race-fair." It wasn't easy. African-Americans have endured so much bad press about test scores for so long that, in our experience, they are instinctively wary about the tests' fairness. We were able to convince them that our test was race-fair only when we implied that the research generating the test had been done by blacks. When they felt trust, they performed well regardless of whether we had weakened their self-confidence beforehand. And when they didn't feel trust, no amount of bolstering of self-confidence helped.

Policies for helping black students rest in significant part on assumptions about their psychology. As noted, they are typically assumed to lack confidence, which spawns a policy of confidence-building. This may be useful for students at the academic rearguard of the group. But the psychology of the academic vanguard appears different – underperformance appears to be rooted less in self-doubt than in social mistrust. ...

My colleagues and I believed that our laboratory experiments had brought to light an overlooked cause of poor college performance among non-Asian minorities: the threat to social trust brought about by the stereotypes of the larger society. But to know the real-life importance of this threat would require testing *in situ*, in the buzz of everyday life.

To this end, Steven Spencer, Richard Nisbett, Kent Harber, Mary Hummel, and I undertook a program aimed at incoming first-year students at the University of Michigan. Like virtually all other institutions of higher learning, Michigan had evidence of black students' underachievement. Our mission was clear: to see if we could improve their achievement by focusing on their transition into college life.

We also wanted to see how little we could get away with – that is, to develop a program that would succeed broadly without special efforts. The program (which started in 1991 and is ongoing) created a racially integrated "living and learning" community in a 250-student wing of a large dormitory. It focused students on academic work (through weekly "challenge" workshops), provided an outlet for discussing the personal side of college life (through weekly rap sessions), and affirmed the students' abilities (through, for example, reminding them that their admission was a vote of confidence). The program lasted just one semester, although most students remained in the dormitory wing for the rest of their first year.

Still, it worked: it gave black students a significant academic jump start. Those in the program (about 15 percent of the entering class) got better first-year grades than black students outside the program, even after controlling for differences between these groups in the skills with which they entered college. Equally important, the program greatly reduced underperformance: black students in the program got first-year grades almost as high as those of white students in the general Michigan population who entered with comparable test scores. This result signaled the achievement of an academic climate nearly as favorable to black students as to white students. And it was achieved through a concert of simple things that enabled black students to feel racially secure.

One tactic that worked surprisingly well was the weekly rap sessions – black and white students talking to one another in an informal dormitory setting, over pizza, about the personal side of their new lives in college. Participation in these sessions reduced students' feelings of stereotype threat and improved grades. Why? Perhaps when members of one racial group hear members of another racial group express the same concerns they have, the concerns seem less racial. Students may also learn that racial and gender stereotypes are either less at play than they might have feared or don't reflect the worst-feared prejudicial intent. Talking at a personal level across group lines can thus build trust in the larger campus community. The racial segregation besetting most college campuses can block this experience, allowing mistrust to build where cross-group communication would discourage it.

Our research bears a practical message: even though the stereotypes held by the larger society may be difficult to change, it is possible to create niches in which negative stereotypes are not felt to apply. In specific classrooms, within specific programs, even in the climate of entire schools, it is possible to weaken a group's sense of being threatened by negative stereotypes, to allow its members a trust that would otherwise be difficult to sustain. Thus when schools try to decide how important black-white test-score gaps are in determining the fate of black students on their campuses, they should keep something in mind: for the greatest portion of black students – those with strong academic identities – the degree of racial trust they feel in their campus life, rather than a few ticks on a standardized test, may be the key to their success.

QUESTIONS

1. Why does Steele believe that high SES blacks should be given more of an advantage in school admissions decisions than low SES whites?

2. What evidence does Steele provide that stereotype threat causes negatively affect black students' school performance? Does he believe that stereotype threat can have similar affects on other types of students as well?

3. Briefly explain the concept of "attributional ambiguity." How, according to Steele, can this ambiguity impact students' performance?

4. Why are the strongest students more affected by stereotype threat?

5. Steele describes the success of a comprehensive program for minority students at the University of Michigan. From his description of that program, what aspect do you think is most responsible for the success of the program? Might such a program help non-minority students as well?

Ψ

PART III
THE SELF
Ψ Ψ

THE SELF: PERCEIVING AND UNDERSTANDING OTHERS

Reading 7: Classic

Cognitive, Social, and Physiological Determinants of Emotional State

Stanley Schacter and Jerome E. Singer

Emotions are unquestionably among the most important phenomena in human life. Although it is our ability for abstract thought that distinguishes us from other animals, it is emotions that give meaning to our lives. You may wonder what business social psychologists have in studying emotions. After all, emotions are a deeply personal experience – an individual experience, not a social experience.

On the contrary, many psychologists believe that the functions of emotions are primarily social. People don't just get angry, they get angry at someone. We don't just like and love, we like and love other people. As these examples suggest, emotional responses serve to inform us about our social environment.

Yet the specific processes that lead to emotions are not clearly understood. Although experienced as a simple experiential reaction, emotions involve physiological components (arousal), cognitive components (perceptions of the situation), and social components (facial expressions). The interplay between these many parts creates a complex and confusing situation for psychologists.

Despite the complexity of emotions, social psychologists have made important steps in understanding them. One classic study, conducted by Stanley Schachter and Jerome Singer, is reported in the following article. To try to understand how arousal, cognitions, and social environment interact to produce emotions, Schachter and Singer manipulated each element independently of the other. Their results may surprise you.

Ψ

The problem of which cues, internal or external, permit a person to label and identify his own emotional state has been with us since the days that James (1890) first tendered his doctrine that "the bodily changes follow directly the perception of the exciting fact, and that our feeling of the same changes as they occur is the emotion" (p. 449). Since we are aware of a variety of feeling and emotion states, it should follow from James' proposition that the various emotions will be accompanied by a variety of differentiable bodily states.

Source: Schachter, S., & Singer, J. E. (1962). Cognitive, social, and physiological determinants of emotional state. *Psychological Review, 69*, 379–399.

Following James' pronouncement, a formidable number of studies were undertaken in search of physiological differentiators of the emotions. The results, in these early days, were almost uniformly negative. All of the emotional states experimentally manipulated were characterized by a general pattern of excitation of the sympathetic nervous system, but there appeared to be no clear-cut physiological discriminators of the various emotions. This pattern of results was so consistent from experiment to experiment that Cannon (1929) offered, as one of the crucial criticisms of the James-Lange theory, the fact that "the same visceral changes occur in very different emotional states and in nonemotional states" (p. 351).

More recent work, however, has given some indication that there may be differentiators. Ax (1953) and Schachter (1957) studied fear and anger. On a large number of indices both of these states were characterized by a similarly high level of autonomic activation, but on several indices they did differ in the degree of activation. Wolf and Wolff (1947) studied a subject with a gastric fistula and were able to distinguish two patterns in the physiological responses of the stomach wall. It should be noted, though, that for many months they studied their subject during and following a great variety of moods and emotions and were able to distinguish only two patterns.

Whether or not there are physiological distinctions among the various emotional states must be considered an open question. Recent work might be taken to indicate that such differences are at best rather subtle and that the variety of emotion, mood, and feeling states are by no means matched by an equal variety of visceral patterns.

This rather ambiguous situation has led Ruckmick (1936), Hunt, Cole, and Reis (1958), Schachter (1959) and others to suggest that cognitive factors may be major determinants of emotional states. Granted a general pattern of sympathetic excitation as characteristic of emotional states, granted that there may be some differences in pattern from state to state, it is suggested that one labels, interprets, and identifies this stirred-up state in terms of the characteristics of the precipitating situation and one's apperceptive mass. This suggests, then, that an emotional state may be considered a function of a state of physiological arousal and of a cognition appropriate to this state of arousal. The cognition, in a sense, exerts a steering function. Cognitions arising from the immediate situation as interpreted by past experience provide the framework within which one understands and labels his feelings. It is the cognition which determines whether the state of physiological arousal will be labeled as "anger," "joy," "fear," or whatever.

In order to examine the implications of this formulation let us consider the fashion in which these two elements, a state of physiological arousal and cognitive factors, would interact in a variety of situations. In most emotion-inducing situations, of course, the two factors are completely interrelated. Imagine a man walking alone down a dark alley; a figure with a gun suddenly appears. The perception-cognition "figure with a gun" in some fashion initiates a state of physiological arousal; this state of arousal is interpreted in terms of knowledge about dark alleys and guns and the state of arousal is labeled "fear." Similarly a student who unexpectedly learns that he has made Phi Beta Kappa may experience a state of arousal which he will label "joy."

Let us now consider circumstances in which these two elements, the physiological and the cognitive, are, to some extent, independent. First, is the state of physiological arousal alone sufficient to induce an emotion? Best evidence indicates that it is not. Marañon (1924), in a fascinating study, (which was replicated by Cantril & Hunt, 1932, and Landis & Hunt, 1932) injected 210 of his patients with the sympathomimetic agent adrenaline and then simply asked them to introspect. Seventy-one percent of his subjects simply reported physical symptoms with no emotional overtones; 29% of the subjects responded in an apparently emotional fashion. Of these the great majority described their feelings in a fashion that Marañon labeled "cold" or "as if" emotions, that is they made statements such as "I feel *as if* I were afraid" or "*as if* I were awaiting a great happiness." This is a sort of emotional "déjà vu" experience; these subjects are neither happy nor afraid, they feel "as if" they were. Finally a very few cases apparently reported a genuine emotional experience. However, in order to produce this reaction in most of these few cases, Marañon (1924) points out:

> One must suggest a memory with strong affective force but not so strong as to produce an emotion in the normal state. For example, in several cases we spoke to our patients before the injection about their sick children or dead parents and they responded calmly to this topic. The same topic presented later, during the adrenal commotion, was sufficient to trigger emotion. This adrenal commotion places the subject in a situation of "affective imminence" (pp. 307–308).

Apparently, then, to produce a genuinely emotional reaction to adrenaline, Marañon was forced to provide such subjects with appropriate cognition.

Though Marañon (1924) is not explicit on his procedure, it is clear that his subjects knew that they were receiving an injection and in all likelihood knew that they were receiving adrenaline and probably had some order of familiarity with its effects. In short, though they underwent the pattern of sympathetic discharge common to strong emotional states, at the same time they had a completely appropriate cognition or explanation as to why they felt this way. This, we would suggest, is the reason so few of Marañon's subjects reported any emotional experience.

Consider now a person in a state of physiological arousal for which no immediately explanatory or appropriate cognitions are available. Such a state could result were one covertly to inject a subject with adrenaline or, unknown to him, feed the subject a sympathomimetic drug such as ephedrine. Under such conditions a subject would be aware of palpitations, tremor, face flushing, and most of the battery of symptoms associated with a discharge of the sympathetic nervous system. In contrast to Marañon's (1924) subjects he would, at the same time, be utterly unaware of why he felt this way. What would be the consequence of such a state?

Schachter (1959) has suggested that precisely such a state would lead to the arousal of "evaluative needs" (Festinger, 1954); that is, pressures would act on an individual in such a state to understand and label his bodily feelings. His bodily state grossly resembles the condition in which it has been at times of emotional excitement. How would he label his present feelings? It is suggested, of course, that he will label his feelings in terms of his knowledge of the immediate situation. Should he at the time be with a beautiful woman he might decide that he was wildly in love or sexually excited. Should he be at a gay party, he might, by comparing himself to others, decide that he was extremely happy and euphoric. Should he be arguing with his wife, he might explode in fury and hatred. Or, should the situation be completely inappropriate he could decide that he was excited about something that had recently happened to him or, simply, that he was sick. In any case, it is our basic assumption that emotional states are a function of the interaction of such cognitive factors with a state of physiological arousal.

This line of thought, then, leads to the following propositions:

1. Given a state of physiological arousal for which an individual has no immediate explanation, he will "label" this state and describe his feelings in terms of the cognitions available to him. To the extent that cognitive factors are potent determiners of emotional states, it could be anticipated that precisely the same state of physiological arousal could be labeled "joy" or "fury" or "jealousy" or any of a great diversity of emotional labels depending on the cognitive aspects of the situation.

2. Given a state of physiological arousal for which an individual has a completely appropriate explanation (e.g., "I feel this way because I have just received an injection of adrenaline") no evaluative needs will arise and the individual is unlikely to label his feelings in terms of the alternative cognitions available.

    Finally, consider a condition in which emotion inducing cognitions are present but there is no state of physiological arousal. For example, an individual might be completely aware that he is in great danger but for some reason (drug or surgical) remain in a state of physiological quiescence. Does he experience the emotion "fear"? Our formulation of emotion as a joint function of a state of physiological arousal and an appropriate cognition, would, of course, suggest that he does not, which leads to our final proposition.

3. Given the same cognitive circumstances, the individual will react emotionally or describe his feelings as emotions only to the extent that he experiences a state of physiological arousal.

PROCEDURE

The experimental test of these propositions requires (a) the experimental manipulation of a state of physiological arousal, (b) the manipulation of the extent to which the subject has an appropriate or proper explanation of his bodily state, and (c) the creation of situations from which explanatory cognitions may be derived.

Manipulating Arousal

In order to manipulate physiological arousal, subjects were given one of two injections. Some subjects were given epinephrine, a type of adrenaline, which increases autonomic arousal. Other subjects were given a placebo...

Manipulating an Appropriate Explanation

By "appropriate" we refer to the extent to which the subject has an authoritative, unequivocal explanation of his bodily condition. Thus, a subject who had been informed by the physician that as a direct consequence of the injection he would feel palpitations, tremor, etc. would be considered to have a completely appropriate explanation. A subject who had been informed only that the injection would have no side effects would have no appropriate explanation of his state. This dimension of appropriateness was manipulated in three experimental conditions which shall be called: Epinephrine Informed (Epi Inf), Epinephrine Ignorant (Epi Ign), and Epinephrine Misinformed (Epi Mis)...

Producing an Emotion Inducing Cognition

Our initial hypothesis has suggested that given a state of physiological arousal for which the individual has no adequate explanation, cognitive factors can lead the individual to describe his feelings with any of a diversity of emotional labels. In order to test this hypothesis, it was decided to manipulate emotional states which can be considered quite different – euphoria and anger.

There are, of course, many ways to induce such states. In our own program of research, we have concentrated on social determinants of emotional states and have been able to demonstrate in other studies that people do evaluate their own feelings by comparing themselves with others around them (Schachter 1959; Wrightsman 1960). In this experiment we have attempted again to manipulate emotional state by social means. In one set of conditions, the subject is placed together with a stooge who has been trained to act euphorically. In a second set of conditions the subject is with a stooge trained to act in an angry fashion...

In summary, this is a seven-condition experiment which, for two different emotional states, allows us (a) to evaluate the effects of "appropriateness" on emotional inducibility and (b) to begin to evaluate the effects of sympathetic activation on emotional inducibility. In schematic form the conditions are the following:

Euphoria	*Anger*
Epi Inf	Epi Inf
Epi Ign	Epi Ign
Epi Mis	Placebo
Placebo	

The Epi Mis condition was not run in the Anger sequence. This was originally conceived as a control condition and it was felt that its inclusion in the Euphoria conditions alone would suffice as a means of evaluating the possible artifactual effect of the Epi Inf instructions.

Measurement

Two types of measures of emotional state were obtained. Standardized observation through a one-way mirror was the technique used to assess the subject's behavior. To what extent did he act euphoric or angry? Such behavior can be considered in a way as a "semiprivate" index of mood, for as far as the subject was concerned, his emotional behavior could be known only to the other person in the room – presumably another student. The second type of measure was self-report in which, on a variety of scales, the subject indicated his mood of the moment. Such measures can be considered "public" indices of mood for they would, of course, be available to the experimenter and his associates...

Subjects

The subjects were all male, college students taking classes in introductory psychology at the University of Minnesota. Some 90% of the students in these classes volunteer for a subject pool for which they receive two extra points on their final exam for every hour that they serve as experimental subjects. For this study the records of all potential subjects were cleared with the Student Health Service in order to insure that no harmful effects would result from the injections.

Evaluation of the Experimental Design

The ideal test of our propositions would require circumstances which our experiment is far from realizing. First, the proposition that: "A state of physiological arousal for which an individual has no immediate explanation will lead him to label this state in terms of the cognitions available to him" obviously requires conditions under which the subject does not and cannot have a proper explanation of his bodily state. Though we toyed with such fantasies as ventilating the experimental room with vaporized adrenaline, reality forced us to rely on the disguised injection of Suproxin – a technique which was far from ideal for no matter what the experimenter told them, some subjects would inevitably attribute their feelings to the injection. To the extent that subjects did so, differences between the several appropriateness conditions should be attenuated.

Second, the proposition that: "Given the same cognitive circumstances the individual will react emotionally only to the extent that he experiences a state of physiological arousal" requires for its ideal test the manipulation of states of physiological arousal and of physiological quiescence. Though there is no question that epinephrine effectively produces a state of arousal, there is also no question that a placebo does not prevent physiological arousal. To the extent that the experimental situation effectively produces sympathetic stimulation in placebo subjects, the proposition is difficult to test, for such a factor would attenuate differences between epinephrine and placebo subjects.

Both of these factors, then, can be expected to interfere with the test of our several propositions. In presenting the results of this study, we shall first present condition by

**TABLE 1   SELF-REPORT OF EMOTIONAL STATE
IN THE EUPHORIA CONDITIONS**

Condition	N	Self-Report Scales	Comparison	p
Epi Inf	25	0.98	Epi Inf vs. Epi Mis	<.01
Epi Ign	25	1.78	Epi Inf vs. Epi Ign	.02
Epi Mis	25	1.90	Placebo vs. Epi Mis, Ign, or Inf	*ns*
Placebo	26	1.61		

All *p* values reported throughout paper are two-tailed.

condition results and then evaluate the effect of these two factors on experimental differences...

Effects of the Manipulations on Emotional State

Euphoria. Self-report. The effects of the several manipulations on emotional state in the euphoria conditions are presented in Table 1. The scores recorded in this table are derived, for each subject, by subtracting the value of the point he checks on the irritation scale from the value of the point he checks on the happiness scale. Thus, if a subject were to check the point "I feel a little irritated and angry" on the irritation scale and the point "I feel very happy and good" on the happiness scale, his score would be + 2. The higher the positive value, the happier and better the subject reports himself as feeling. Though we employ an index for expositional simplicity, it should be noted that the two components of the index each yield results completely consistent with those obtained by use of this index.

Let us examine first the effects of the appropriateness instructions. Comparison of the scores for the Epi Mis and Epi Inf conditions makes it immediately clear that the experimental differences are not due to artifacts resulting from the informed instructions. In both conditions the subject was warned to expect a variety of symptoms as a consequence of the injection. In the Epi Mis condition, where the symptoms were inappropriate to the subject's bodily state, the self-report score is almost twice that in the Epi Inf condition, where the symptoms were completely appropriate to the subject's bodily state. It is reasonable, then, to attribute differences between informed subjects and those in other conditions to differences in manipulated appropriateness rather than to artifacts such as introspectiveness or self-examination.

It is clear that, consistent with expectations, subjects were more susceptible to the stooge's mood and consequently more euphoric when they had no explanation of their own bodily states than when they did. The means of both the Epi Ign and Epi Mis conditions are considerably greater than the mean of the Epi Inf condition.

It is of interest to note that Epi Mis subjects are somewhat more euphoric than are Epi Ign subjects. This pattern repeats itself in other data shortly to be presented. We would attribute this difference to differences in the appropriateness dimension. Though, as in the Epi Ign condition, a subject is not provided with an explanation of his bodily state, it is, of course, possible that he will provide one for himself which is not derived from his interaction with the stooge. Most reasonably he could decide for himself that he feels this way because of the injection. To the extent that he does so he should be less susceptible to the stooge. It seems probable that he would be less likely to hit on such an explanation in the Epi Mis condition than in the Epi Ign condition, for in the Epi Mis condition both the experimenter and the doctor have told him that the effects of the injection would be quite different from what he actually feels. The effect of such instructions is probably to make it more difficult for the subject himself to hit on the alternative explanation described above. There is some evidence to support this analysis. In open-end questions in which subjects described their own mood and state, 28% of the subjects in the Epi Ign condition made some connection between the injection and their bodily state compared with the 16% of subjects in the Epi Mis condition who did so. It could be considered, then, that these three conditions fall along a dimension of appropriateness, with the Epi Inf condition at one extreme and the Epi Mis condition at the other.

Comparing the placebo to the epinephrine conditions, we note a pattern which will repeat itself throughout the data. Placebo subjects are less euphoric than either Epi Mis or Epi Ign subjects but somewhat more euphoric the Epi Inf subjects. These differences are not, however, statistically significant. We shall consider the epinephrine-placebo comparisons in detail in a later section of this paper following the presentation of additional relevant data. For the moment, it is clear that by self-report, manipulating appropriateness has had a very strong effect on euphoria

Behavior. Let us next examine the extent to which the subject's behavior was affected by the experimental manipulations. To the extent that his mind has been affected, one should expect that the subject will join in the stooge's whirl of manic activity and initiate

TABLE 2   BEHAVIORAL INDICATIONS OF EMOTIONAL STATE IN THE EUPHORIAL CONDITIONS

Condition	N	Activity Index	Mean Number of Acts Initiated
Epi Inf	25	12.72	.20
Epi Ign	25	18.28	.56
Epi Mis	25	22.56	.84
Placebo	26	16.00	.54

p Value		
Comparison	Activity Index	Initiates
Epi Inf vs. Epi Mis	.05	.03
Epi Inf vs. Epi Ign	*ns*	.08
Plac vs. Epi Mis, Ign, or Inf	*ns*	*Ns*

Tested by x^2 comparison of the proportion of subjects in each condition initiating new acts.

similar activities of his own. The relevant data are presented in Table 2. The column labeled "Activity Index" presents summary figures on the extent to which the subject joined in the stooge's activity. This is a weighted index which reflects both the nature of the activities in which the subject engaged and the amount of time he was active. The index was devised by assigning the following weights to the subject's activities: 5–hula hooping; 4–shooting with slingshot; 3–paper airplanes; 2–paper basketballs; 1–doodling; 0– does nothing. Pretest scaling on 15 college students ordered these activities with respect to the degree of euphoria they represented. Arbitrary weights were assigned so that the wilder the activity, the heavier the weight. These weights are multiplied by an estimate of the amount of time the subject spent in each activity, and the summed products make up the activity index for each subject. This index may be considered a measure of behavioral euphoria. It should be noted that the same between-condition relationships hold for the two components of this index as for the index itself.

The column labeled "Mean Number of Acts Initiated" presents the data on the extent to which the subject deviates from the stooge's routine and initiates euphoric activities of his own.

On both behavioral indices, we find precisely the same pattern of relationships as those obtained with self-reports. Epi Mis subjects behave somewhat more euphorically than do Epi Ign subjects, who in turn behave more euphorically than do Epi Inf subjects. On all measures, then there is consistent evidence that a subject will take over the stooge's euphoric mood to the extent that he has no other explanation of his bodily state.

Again it should be noted that on these behavioral indices, Epi Ign and Epi Mis subjects are somewhat more euphoric than placebo subjects but not significantly so.

Anger. *Self-Report*. Before presenting data for the anger conditions, one point must be made about the anger manipulation. In the situation devised, anger, if manifested, is most likely to be directed at the experimenter and his annoyingly personal questionnaire. As we subsequently discovered, this was rather unfortunate, for the subjects, who had volunteered for the experiment for extra points on their final exam, simply refused to endanger these points by publicly blowing up, admitting their irritation to the experimenter's face or spoiling the questionnaire. Though as the reader will see, the subjects were quite willing to manifest anger when they were alone with the stooge, they

TABLE 3   SELF-REPORT OF EMOTIONAL STATE IN THE ANGER CONDITIONS

Condition	N	Self-Report Scales	Comparison	p
Epi Inf	22	1.91	Epi Inf vs. Epi Ign	.08
Epi Ign	23	1.39	Placebo vs. Epi Ign or Inf	*ns*
Placebo	23	1.63		

hesitated to do so on material (self-ratings of mood and questionnaire) that the experimenter might see and only after the purposes of the experiment had been revealed were many of these subjects willing to admit to the experimenter that they had been irked or irritated.

This experimentally unfortunate situation pretty much forces us to rely on the behavioral indices derived from observation of the subject's presumably private interaction with the stooge. We do, however, present data on the self-report scales in Table 3. These figures are derived in the same way as the figures presented in Table 1 for the euphoria conditions, that is, the value checked on the irritation scale is subtracted from the value checked on the happiness scale. Though, for the reasons stated above, the absolute magnitude of these figures (all positive) is relatively meaningless, we can, of course, compare condition means within the set of anger conditions. With the happiness-irritation index employed, we should, of course, anticipate precisely the reverse results from those obtained in the euphoria conditions; that is, the Epi Inf subjects in the anger conditions should again be less susceptible to the stooge's mood and should, therefore, describe themselves as in a somewhat happier frame of mind than subjects in the Epi Ign condition. This is the case; the Epi Inf subjects average 1.91 on the self-report scales while the Epi Ign subjects average 1.39.

Evaluating the effects of the injections, we note again that, as anticipated, Epi Ign subjects are somewhat less happy than Placebo subjects but, once more, this is not a significant difference.

Behavior. The subject's responses to the stooge during the period when both were filling out their questionnaires, were systematically coded to provide a behavioral index of anger. The coding scheme and the numerical values attached to each of the categories have been described in the methodology section. To arrive at an "Anger index" the numerical value assigned to a subject's responses to the stooge is summed together for the several units of stooge behavior. In the coding scheme used, a positive value to this

TABLE 4   BEHAVIORAL INDICATIONS OF EMOTIONAL STATE IN THE ANGER CONDITIONS

Condition	N	Anger Units
Epi Inf	22	-0.18
Epi Ign	23	+2.28
Placebo	22[a]	+0.79

Comparison For Anger Units	p
Epi Inf vs. Epi Ign	<.01
Epi Ign vs. Placebo	<.05
Placebo vs. Epi Inf	*ns*

[a] For one subject in this condition the sound system went dead and the observer could not, of course, code the reactions.

index indicates that the subject agrees with the stooge's comment and is growing angry. A negative value indicates that the subject either disagrees with the stooge or ignores him.

The relevant data are presented in Table 4. . . . We must, of course, anticipate that subjects in the Epi Ign condition will be angrier than subjects in the Epi Inf condition. This is indeed the case. The anger index for the Epi Ign condition is positive and large, indicating that these subjects have become angry, while in the Epi Inf condition the Anger index is slightly negative in value, indicating that these subjects have failed to catch the stooge's mood at all. It seems clear that providing the subject with an appropriate explanation of his bodily state greatly reduces his tendency to interpret his state in terms of the cognitions provided by the stooge's angry behavior.

Finally, on this behavioral index, it can be seen that subjects in the Epi Ign condition are significantly angrier than subjects in the Placebo condition. Behaviorally, at least, the injection of epinephrine appears to have led subjects to an angrier state than comparable subjects who received placebo shots.

DISCUSSION

Let us summarize the major findings of this experiment and examine the extent to which they support the propositions offered in the introduction of this paper. It has been suggested, first, that given a state of physiological arousal for which an individual has no explanation, he will label this state in terms of the cognitions available to him. This implies, of course, that by manipulating the cognitions of an individual in such a state we can manipulate his feelings in diverse directions. Experimental results support this proposition, for following the injection of epinephrine, those subjects who had no explanation for the bodily state thus produced gave behavioral and self-report indications that they had been readily manipulable into the disparate feeling states of euphoria and anger.

From this first proposition, it must follow that given a state of physiological arousal for which the individual has a completely satisfactory explanation, he will not label this state in terms of the alternative cognitions available. Experimental evidence strongly supports this expectation. In those conditions in which subjects were injected with epinephrine and told precisely what they would feel and why, they proved relatively immune to any effects of the manipulated cognitions. In the anger condition, such subjects did not report or show anger; in the euphoria condition, such subjects reported themselves as far less happy than subjects with an identical bodily state but no adequate knowledge of why they felt the way they did.

Finally, it has been suggested that given constant cognitive circumstances, an individual will react emotionally only to the extent that he experiences a state of physiological arousal. Without taking account of experimental artifacts, the evidence in support of this proposition is consistent but tentative. When the effects of "self-informing" tendencies in placebo subjects are partialed out, the evidence strongly supports the proposition.

The pattern of data, then, falls neatly in line with theoretical expectations...

REFERENCES

Ax, A. F. (1953). Physiological differentiation of emotional states. *Psychosomatic Medicine, 15* 433–442.

Cannon, W. B. (1929). *Bodily changes in pain, hunger, fear and rage.* (2nd ed.) New York: Appleton.

Cantril, H., & Hunt, W. A. (1932) Emotional effects produced by the injection of adrenaline. *American Journal of Psychology 44,* 300–307.

Festinger, L. (1954). A theory of social comparison processes. *Human Relations 7,* 114–140.

Hunt, J. McV., Cole, M. W., & Reis, E. E. (1958). Situational cues distinguishing anger, fear, and sorrow. *American Journal of Psychology., 71,* 136–151.

James, W. (1890). *The principles of psychology.* New York: Holt.

Landis, C., & Hunt, W. A. (1932). Adrenaline and emotion. *Psychological Review, 39,* 467–485.

Marañon, G. (1924). Contribution à l'étude de l'action émotive de l'adrénaline. *Revue Française d'Endocrinologie,2,* 301–325.

Ruckmick, C. A. (1936). *The psychology of feeling and emotion.* New York: McGraw-Hill.

Schachter, J. (1957). Pain, fear, and anger in hypertensives and normotensives: A psychophysiologic study. *Psychosomatic Medicine, 19,* 17–29.

Schachter, S. (1959). *The psychology of affiliation.* Stanford, Calif.: Stanford University. Press.

Wolf, S., & Wolff, H. G. (1947). *Human gastric function.* New York: Oxford University Press.

Wrightsman, L. S. (1960). Effects of waiting with others on changes in level of felt anxiety. *Journal of Abnormal and Social Psychology, 61,* 216–222.

QUESTIONS

1. Briefly describe the James-Lange theory of emotion. On what grounds did Cannon criticize this theory?

2. Outline the process by which the authors believe emotions are felt. What similarities does this theory share with the James-Lange theory?

3. What physiological, cognitive, and social manipulations were required to test the experimental hypotheses?

4. How did the authors measure subjects' angry responses? Which measure did not produce the expected results?

5. How did subjects in the placebo condition behave in this study? Like which other group were they predicted to behave? Which other group does their behavior most resemble?

Reading 8: Contemporary

The Pursuit of Happiness

David G. Myers and Ed Diener

Many people believe that the job of health professionals is to fix problems. Just as medical doctors are trained to understand illness, psychologists have devoted considerable attention to understanding psychological disorders such as depression and anxiety. The logic of studying medical and psychological problems is straightforward: If you understand the problem, you can fix it. However, in recent years social psychologists, as well as practitioners in a new branch of psychology known as "health psychology," have suggested an alternative approach that focuses on health rather than illness.

For social psychologists, one important aspect of health is subjective well-being. As you will see in this next reading, subjective well-being is a combination of happiness and satisfaction. The authors of this article are not concerned with temporary states of happiness, such as joy after accomplishing an important goal. Instead, they are interested in understanding a form of happiness that is more global and stable – the kind of happiness people use to describe how they feel about their life as a whole.

In the following reading, social psychologists David Myers and Ed Diener review the findings of many recent studies of subjective well-being. They find that most people are reasonably happy about their lives. When they next try to uncover why some people are happier than others, they make some surprising discoveries. After reading their report, you may discover that many of your intuitions about the secrets of happiness are wrong.

Ψ

Compared with misery, happiness is relatively unexplored terrain for social scientists. Between 1967 and 1994, 46,380 articles indexed in *Psychological Abstracts* mentioned depression, 36,851 anxiety, and 5,099 anger. Only 2,389 spoke of happiness, 2,340 life satisfaction, and 405 joy.

Recently we and other researchers have begun a systematic study of happiness. During the past two decades, dozens of investigators throughout the world have asked several hundred thousand representatively sampled people to reflect on their happiness and satisfaction with life – or what psychologists call "subjective well-being." In the U.S. the National Opinion Research Center at the University of Chicago has surveyed a representative sample of roughly 1,500 people a year since 1957; the Institute for Social

Source: Myers, D.G., and Diener, E. (1996, May). The pursuit of happiness. *Scientific American,* 70-72. Copyright © 1996 by Scientific American, Inc. All rights reserved. Reprinted by permission of the publisher.

Research at the University of Michigan has carried out similar studies on a less regular basis, as has the Gallup Organization. Government-funded efforts have also probed the moods of European countries.

We have uncovered some surprising findings. People are happier than one might expect, and happiness does not appear to depend significantly on external circumstances. Although viewing life as a tragedy has a long and honorable history, the responses of random samples of people around the world about their happiness paint a much rosier picture.

In the University of Chicago surveys, three in 10 Americans say they are very happy, for example. Only one in 10 chooses the most negative description, "not too happy." The majority describe themselves as "pretty happy." (The few exceptions to global reports of reasonable happiness include hospitalized alcoholics, new inmates, new psychotherapy clients, South African blacks during apartheid, and students living under conditions of economic and political oppression.)

How can social scientists measure something as hard to pin down as happiness? Most researchers simply ask people to report their feelings of happiness or unhappiness and to assess how satisfying their lives are. Such self-reported well-being is moderately consistent over years of retesting. Furthermore, those who say they are happy and satisfied seem happy to their close friends and family members and to a psychologist-interviewer. Their daily mood ratings reveal more positive emotions, and they smile more than those who call themselves unhappy. Self-reported happiness also predicts other indicators of well-being. Compared with the depressed, happy people are less self-focused, less hostile and abusive, and less susceptible to disease.

We have found that the even distribution of happiness cuts across almost all demographic classifications of age, economic class, race and educational level. In addition, almost all strategies for assessing subjective well-being – including those that sample people's experience by polling them at random times with beepers – turn up similar findings.

Interviews with representative samples of people of all ages, for example, reveal that no time of life is notably happier or unhappier. Similarly, men and women are equally likely to declare themselves "very happy" and "satisfied" with life, according to a statistical digest of 146 studies by Marilyn J. Haring, William Stock and Morris A. Okun, all then at Arizona State University. Alex Michalos of the University of Northern British Columbia and Ronald Inglehart of the University of Michigan, summarizing newer surveys of 18,000 university students in 39 countries and 170,000 adults in 16 countries, corroborate these findings.

Knowing someone's ethnicity also gives little clue to subjective well-being. African-Americans are only slightly less likely than European-Americans to feel very happy. The National Institute of Mental Health found that rates of depression and alcoholism among blacks and whites are roughly equal. Social psychologists Jennifer K. Crocker of the University of Michigan and Brenda Major of the University of California at Santa Barbara assert that people in disadvantaged groups maintain self-esteem by valuing things at which they excel, by making comparisons within their own groups and by blaming problems on external sources such as prejudice.

WHAT MONEY CAN'T BUY

Wealth is also a poor predictor of happiness. People have not become happier over time as their cultures have become more affluent. Even though Americans earn twice as much in today's dollars as they did in 1957, the proportion of those telling surveyors from the National Opinion Research Center that they are "very happy" has declined from 35 to 29 percent.

Even very rich people – those surveyed among *Forbes* magazine's 100 wealthiest Americans – are only slightly happier than the average American. Those whose income has increased over a 10-year period are not happier than those whose income is stagnant. Indeed, in most nations the correlation between income and happiness is negligible – only in the poorest countries, such as Bangladesh and India, is income a good measure of emotional well-being.

Are people in rich countries happier, by and large, than people in not so rich countries? It appears in general that they are, but the margin may be slim. In Portugal, for example, only one in 10 people reports being very happy, whereas in the much more prosperous Netherlands the proportion of very happy is four in 10. Yet there are curious reversals in this correlation between national wealth and well-being – the Irish during the 1980s consistently reported greater life satisfaction than the wealthier West Germans. Furthermore, other factors, such as civil rights, literacy and duration of democratic government, all of which also promote reported life satisfaction, tend to go hand in hand with national wealth. As a result, it is impossible to tell whether the happiness of people in wealthier nations is based on money or is a by-product of other felicities.

HABITS OF HAPPY PEOPLE

Although happiness is not easy to predict from material circumstances, it seems consistent for those who have it. In one National Institute on Aging study of 5,000 adults, the happiest people in 1973 were still relatively happy a decade later, despite changes in work, residence and family status.

In study after study, four traits characterize happy people. First, especially in individualistic Western cultures, they like themselves. They have high self-esteem and usually believe themselves to be more ethical, more intelligent, less prejudiced, better able to get along with others, and healthier than the average person. (Such findings bring to mind Sigmund Freud's joke about the man who told his wife, "If one of us should die, I think I would go live in Paris.")

Second, happy people typically feel personal control. Those with little or no control over their lives – such as prisoners, nursing home patients, severely impoverished groups or individuals, and citizens of totalitarian regimes – suffer lower morale and worse health. Third, happy people are usually optimistic. Fourth, most happy people are extroverted. Although one might expect that introverts would live more happily in the serenity of their less stressed, contemplative lives, extroverts are happier – whether alone or with others.

The causal arrows for these correlations are uncertain. Does happiness make people more outgoing, or are outgoing people more likely to be happy, perhaps explaining why they marry sooner, get better jobs and make more friends? If these traits indeed predispose their carriers to happiness, people might become happier by acting in certain ways. In experiments, people who feign high self-esteem report feeling more positively about themselves, for example.

Whatever the reason, the close personal relationships that characterize happy lives are also correlated with health. Compared with loners, those who can name several intimate friends are healthier and less likely to die prematurely. For more than nine out of 10 people, the most significant alternative to aloneness is marriage. Although broken marital relationships can cause much misery, a good marriage apparently is a strong source of support. During the 1970s and 1980s, 39 percent of married adults told the National Opinion Research Center they were "very happy," as compared with 24 percent of those who had never married. In other surveys, only 12 percent of those who had divorced perceived themselves to be "very happy." The happiness gap between the married and the never-married was similar for women and men.

Religiously active people also report greater happiness. One Gallup survey found that highly religious people were twice as likely as those lowest in spiritual commitment to declare themselves very happy. Other surveys, including a 16-nation collaborative study of 166,000 people in 14 nations, have found that reported happiness and life satisfaction rise with strength of religious affiliation and frequency of attendance at worship services. Some researchers believe that religious affiliation entails greater social support and hopefulness.

Students of happiness are now beginning to examine happy people's exercise patterns, world views and goals. It is possible that some of the patterns discovered in the research may offer clues for transforming circumstances and behaviors that work against well-being into ones that promote it. Ultimately, then, the scientific study of happiness could help us understand how to build a world that enhances human well-being and to aid people in getting the most satisfaction from their circumstances.

QUESTIONS

1. According to psychologists Jennifer Crocker and Brenda Major, why may members of advantaged and disadvantaged groups report similar levels of happiness?

2. How does happiness change over the life span? How is this change different for people who become increasingly wealthy over time? What two explanations have been given for the finding that people in wealthier countries tend to be happier than people in not so wealthy countries?

3. What four traits characterize happy people in Western cultures? Do you think that extroversion causes happiness or that happiness leads to extroversion?

4. What role does self-efficacy have in happiness? Based on your reading of this article, who would be happier – people who are high self-monitors or those who are low self-monitors?

5. After reading this article, what advice could you give to help someone become happier?

WELL-BEING AND HEALTH: CARING FOR THE SELF

Reading 9: Classic

Confronting a Traumatic Event: Toward an Understanding of Inhibition and Disease

James W. Pennebaker and Sandra Klihr Beall

The next reading is not a classic in terms of when it was published in 1986. But in a very short period of time, it has become a modern classic. It has achieved this status because it addresses an issue that has interested psychologists for over 100 years. Freud's first major work in psychology investigated the physical consequences of traumatic events. In this article, James Pennebaker and Sandra Beall breathe new life into Freud's well-known notion of catharsis.

In the following article, Pennebaker and Beall describe a study they conducted over four consecutive days in which subjects wrote about either a traumatic event or a trivial one. Subjects who noted traumatic events wrote about either the facts of the event, the emotions they felt during the event, or about both facts and emotions. Although important differences were observed in how the subjects in each group felt immediately following the essay sessions, more impressive was how they felt six months later.

The following empirical article is divided into four main sections. In the introduction, the authors discuss the previous literature, going all the way back to Freud, and the psychology of confronting trauma. In the second section, a brief overview of the experimental method is provided. In the third section, the authors discuss in detail the results of the study. (Don't worry too much about deciphering the statistical analysis reported.) Finally, the authors discuss the implications of this work.

Ψ

Individuals seek to understand major upheavals in their lives. Although a natural way of understanding traumas is by talking with others, many upsetting events cannot easily be discussed. For example, victims of family or sexual abuse, or perpetrators of illegal or illicit acts are often reticent to divulge these experiences because of guilt or fear of punishment. In order not to betray their true feelings or experiences, they must inhibit their overt behaviors, facial expressions and language. In addition to the work of

Source: Pennebaker, J. W., & Beall, S. K. (1986). Confronting a traumatic event: Toward an understanding of inhibition and disease. *Journal of Abnormal Psychology, 95*, 274–281. Copyright © 1986 American Psychological Association. Reprinted by permission.

inhibiting behavior following a trauma, individuals may actively attempt not to think about aspects of the concealed information because of its aversive and unresolved nature. In short, individuals who are unable to confide in others about extremely upsetting events must work to inhibit their behaviors, thoughts and feelings.

In recent years, evidence has accumulated indicating that not disclosing extremely personal and traumatic experiences to others over a long period of time may be related to disease processes. For example, across several surveys, college students and adults who reported having experienced one of several types of childhood traumatic events (e.g., sexual or physical abuse, death or divorce of parents) were more likely to report current health problems if they had not disclosed the trauma to others than if they had divulged it (Pennebaker & Hoover, 1986; Susman, 1986). These results were obtained independent of measures of social support (see Pennebaker, 1985, for review). Similarly, a survey of spouses of suicide and accidental-death victims revealed that those individuals most likely to become ill in the year following the death were the ones who had not confided in others about their experiences (Pennebaker & O'Heeron, 1984). Survey results indicate that the less individuals confided, the more they ruminated about the death.

A question that emerges from these studies is, What aspects of confiding a traumatic event reduce physiological levels and disease rates? On a strict interpersonal level, discussing a trauma allows for social comparison (e.g., Wortman & Dunkel-Schetter, 1979) and coping information from others (e.g., Lazarus, 1966). From a cognitive perspective, talking about or in some way confronting a traumatic event may help the individual to organize (Meichenbaum, 1977), assimilate (Horowitz, 1976), or give meaning to (Silver & Wortman, 1980) the trauma. These approaches assume that a major upheaval undermines the world view of the person. Confronting the event, then, should help the individual categorize the experience into a meaningful frame work.

Many investigators have argued that discussing an event may also serve a cathartic function (e.g., Scheff, 1979). In one of the few well-controlled clinical studies examining catharsis, Nichols (1974) found that patients undergoing somatic–emotional discharge therapy (in which subjects actively express emotions) were more likely to achieve their therapeutic goals than were matched control subjects who received traditional insight therapy. Other studies that have employed venting, in which subjects hit a pillow or write about fantasies associated with aggression, have produced mixed results in subsequent reports of anger (see Nichols & Zax, 1977, for review).

Catharsis and the cathartic method, as developed by Freud (1904/1954) and Breuer and Freud (1895/1966), stress the fundamental links between cognition and affect surrounding a significant or threatening experience. If the experience is particularly disturbing, the memory or ideation may be suppressed, whereas the emotion or affect associated with the event continues to exist in consciousness in the form of anxiety. The cathartic method, or talking cure, was effective in that the forgotten memories were recalled and linked to the anxiety. Breuer and Freud (1895/1966) noted that hysterical symptoms were most likely to disappear after the patient had described the event in fine detail. Although very few studies have directly tested the original catharsis ideas, some recent work suggests that the linking of the cognitive and affective components of a given phobia helps to reduce the magnitude of the phobia (Tesser, Leone, & Clary, 1978).

Our own views assume that to inhibit one's behavior requires physiological work. To not talk about or otherwise confront major upheavals that have occurred in one's life is viewed as a form of inhibition. Actively inhibiting one's behavior, thoughts, and/or feelings over time places cumulative stress on the body and thus increases the probability of stress-related diseases (cf. Selye, 1976). It would follow that if individuals actively inhibit divulging personal or traumatic events, or both, allowing them to do so in a benign setting could have the positive effect of reducing long-term stress and stress-related disease. The original purpose of the present project was to learn if merely writing about a given traumatic event would reduce stress associated with inhibition in both the short run and over time. Our second purpose was to attempt to evaluate the aspects of dealing with a past trauma that were most effective in reducing stress.

Because we were interested in examining the effects of divulging traumatic events independent of social feedback, subjects in the present experiment were required to write rather than talk about upsetting experiences. On 4 consecutive nights, subjects wrote about either a trivial preassigned topic (control condition) or a traumatic experience in their own life from one of three perspectives. Analogous to the venting view of catharsis, trauma–emotion subjects were instructed to write each night about their feelings concerning their traumatic experiences without discussing the precipitating event. In line with a strict cognitive approach, the trauma–fact subjects were required to write about traumatic events without discussing their feelings. Similar to the cathartic method, the trauma–combination subjects wrote about both the traumatic events and their feelings about them. Heart rate, blood pressure, and self-reports were collected during each session. Finally, health center records and mail-back surveys were collected from 4 to 6 months following the experiment in order to determine long-term health consequences of the study.

METHOD

Overview

Within the 4 X 4 (Condition X Session) between–within design, 46 undergraduates were randomly assigned to write one of four types of essays for 15 minutes each night for 4 consecutive evenings. Those in the control condition ($n = 12$) were assigned different trivial topics each night; those in the trauma-emotion cell ($n = 12$) wrote about their feeling associated with one or more traumas in their life; trauma–fact subjects ($n = 11$) wrote about the facts surrounding traumatic events; and trauma–combination subjects ($n = 11$) wrote about both their feeling and the facts surrounding the traumas. Before and following the writing of each essay, subjects had their blood pressure, heart rate, and self-reported moods and physical symptoms collected. Four months after completion of the study, subjects completed questionnaires about their health and general views of the experiment. In addition, records for both prior to and 6 months following the experiment were collected from the health and counseling centers.....

RESULTS

Overall, the study has four general classes of variables. The first class dealt with the essays themselves, including what the subjects wrote about, the way they approached the essays, and their perceptions of the essays. The second type of variable relates to the subjects' responses to the essays. That is, we sought to learn about changes in the subjects' physiological levels, moods, and symptom reports from before to after writing each essay across the 4 days. The third broad issue concerned the long-term effects of the experiment. For example, did the study influence the various health-related variables or have any lasting psychological or behavioral impact, or both? A final group of variables of interest includes several individual difference factors, such as sex of subject, and measures of anxiety, symptom-reporting, and so forth. Specifically, we sought to learn if any of these variables relate to any of our manipulated factors... .

Content of Essays

... .Of the 127 trauma essays, 27% dealt with the death of a close friend, family member, or pet; 20% involved boyfriend/girlfriend problems (usually the breaking of a relationship); and 16% centered on fights among or with parents or friends. Other percentages of topics were, major failure, such as not being elected cheerleader (8%); public humiliation, such as overhearing friends laughing about them (8%); leaving home to go to college (7%); being involved in car accident (5%); their own health problems (4%); sexual abuse, such as incest or rape (3%); and other, or unclassifiable (13%). The percentages total more than 100% because some of the topics could be classified in two separate categories. One-way ANOVAs [ANOVAs stands for analysis of variance] comparing the three trauma conditions indicated no consistent differences in type of topics written about. Note, however, that a significantly higher percentage of trauma-emotion essays could not be categorized ($p = .03$). The only individual difference variable related to essay topic was sex of subject: women were more likely to write about losing a boyfriend/girlfriend; men were more likely to focus on the death of a pet (both $ps < .05$).

It is difficult to convey the powerful and personal nature of the majority of trauma condition essays with statistical analyses. One woman wrote about teaching her brother to sail; on his first solo outing, he drowned. The father of a male subject separated from his mother when the subject was about 9 years old. Prior to leaving home, the father told the subject that the divorce was the subject's fault (because his birth had disrupted the family). When she was 10 years old, one female subject had been asked to clean her room because her grandmother was to be visiting that night. The girl did not do so. That night, the grandmother tripped on one of the girl's toys, broke her hip, and died of complications during surgery a week later. Another subject depicted her seduction by her grandfather when she was about 12 years old. Another, who had written abut relatively trivial topics during the first sessions, admitted during the last evening that she was gay. A male subject reported that he had considered suicide because he thought that he had disappointed his parents.

Two additional observations are in order. First, there was no discernible pattern about the depth or emotionality of the subject's topic from one night to another. For some subjects, the first session produced the most profound essay, whereas for others the final session did. Often a particularly emotional essay would be followed by a startlingly superficial one. No individual difference measures were related to the patterning or overall depth of essay topic. Second, a mere reading of the topics by each subject overlooks the person's reaction to it. For example, approximately one third of the essays dealing with the death of a close friend or family member indicated that the subjects were not particularly upset by the loss of the person. Rather, the death made them aware of their own mortality.

Responses to Essays

Before and after each day's essay writing, the heart rate and blood pressure of each of the subjects were measured by the experimenter. Also before and after writing the essay, subjects completed a brief questionnaire that assessed the degree to which they were experiencing each of nine physical symptoms and eight moods.

Physiological Measures. Because heart rate and systolic and diastolic blood pressure reflect a general cardiovascular response, all three measures were simultaneously subjected to a 4 X 4 X 2 X 3 (Condition X Session X Pre-versus Post-Essay Reading X Physiological Index [heart rate, systolic and diastolic blood pressure]) between–within repeated measures multivariate analysis of variance (MANOVA). Across all three physiological indexes, a Condition X Session X Pre-Post interaction attained significance, $F(9, 116) = 1.99$, $p = .046$. In addition, the type of physiological index interacted with both session, $F(6, 37) = 11.7$, $p < .001$, and Condition X Pre-Post, $F(6, 80) = 2.26$, $p < .046$. No other main effects or interactions were significant.

Separate repeated measures ANOVAs on each of the physiological measures indicated that all of the above effects were attributable to changes in systolic blood pressure. That is, a 4 X 4 X 2 (Condition X Session X Pre–Post) between–within ANOVA yielded a significant session main effect indicating a general lowering of blood pressures over the course of the experiment for subjects in all conditions, $F(3, 40) = 16.6$, $p < .001$. In addition, a marginally significant Condition X Pre–Post interaction, $F(3, 42) = 2.56$, $p = .068$, and a Condition X Session X Pre-Post interaction, $F(9, 116) = 2.23$, $p = .025$, were obtained. As depicted in Table 1, the Condition X Pre–Post interaction reflects the fact that subjects in the control and trauma–fact cells demonstrated significantly larger decreases in blood pressure following the writing sessions. The triple interaction is primarily attributable to the trauma–combination condition subjects, who initially evidenced a large increase in blood pressure from before to after the essay. After the first session, however, the trauma–combination subjects demonstrated moderate decreases in blood pressure from before to after the writing session. Separate repeated measures ANOVAs on heart rate and diastolic blood pressure yielded no significant condition main effects or interactions.

TABLE 1   MEANS OF ESSAY-RELATED VARIABLES BY CONDITION

		CONDITION		
Variables	Control	Trauma-Emotion	Trauma-Fact	Trauma-Combination
Essay-related dimensions				
Personal	2.8_a	5.2_b	4.4_b	4.9_b
Reveal emotion	2.5_a	5.3_b	2.5_a	5.4_b
Subjects writing personal essay previously not discussed (%)	16.6_a	75.0_b	63.6_b	54.6_b
Words per essay	252_a	301_{ab}	296_{ab}	340_{ab}
Self-references per essay(%)	2.4_a	11.3_b	7.1_c	8.4_c
Self-report and physiological measures				
Systolic blood pressure change	-3.9_a	-0.8_{ab}	-3.0_a	$+0.4_b$
Negative moods change	-1.0_a	$+1.7_{bc}$	$+0.6_{ab}$	$+3.8_c$
N	12	12	11	11

Note: The personal and reveal emotion means are based on subjects' self-reports of their own essays averages all four sessions. Ratings were based on 7-point scales, where 7 = *essay was personal or revealed emotion to a great extent.* Change scores are computed by subtracting the pre-essay score from the post-essay score. A positive number, then, indicates an increase in blood pressure or negative emotion following the essay. For none of the above variables are there significant initial differences. Means with different subscripts are different at $p \leq .05$.

Self-Reports. Before and after each essay, subjects responded to a questionnaire asking them to rate the degree to which they were currently experiencing each of nine symptoms and eight moods – ranging from *not at all* (1) to *a great deal* (7). Because previous research has indicated that the symptoms (racing heart, upset stomach, headache, backache, dizziness, shortness of breath, cold hands, sweaty hands, pounding heart) such as these are correlated, the items were summed to yield an overall symptom index (see Pennebaker, 1982, for scalar properties of comparable symptom and mood indexes). Similarly, the summed mood items (nervous, sad, guilty, not happy, not contented, fatigued, anxious) composed a general negative mood index.

A 4 X 4 X 2 (Condition X Session X Pre- versus Post-Essay) repeated measures ANOVA on the self-reported symptom index yielded no main effects or interactions. A comparable analysis on the negative mood index resulted in a significant pre–post main effect, $F(1, 42) = 4.49, p = .04$, such that subjects tended to report more negative moods after writing each day's essay. In addition, a significant Pre–Post X Session interaction emerged, $F(3, 40) = 3.07, p = .04$, such that over time, subjects' negative moods increased after writing each essay. Finally, the Condition X Pre–Post interaction attained significance, $F(3, 42) = 2.83, p = .05$. As seen in Table 1, these effects reflect the fact that subjects in the trauma conditions reported more negative moods after writing the essays, whereas control subjects typically felt more positive.

The means presented in Table 1 depict the general changes in blood pressure and self-reported negative moods from before to after writing each day's essay. It is of interest that across each of these measures the means of the trauma–emotion and trauma–combination conditions are similar, as are the trauma–fact and control cells. Indeed, contrasts using the mean-square error term comparing these two sets of cells indicate that they are all significantly different. Further, in referring back to Table 1, this general pattern holds for the degree to which subjects revealed emotions and the percentage of self-references used in their essays. The implications of these similarities in response to a relatively brief stimulus are discussed later.

Long-Term Effects

At the conclusion of the school year, Student Health Center personnel recorded the number of times that each subject had visited the health center for each of the following reasons: illness, injury, check-up, psychiatric, or other. The number of visits were recorded separately for number of visits prior to the experiment (i.e., from the beginning of the school year in late August to mid-November) and following the experiment (mid-November through mid-May). Counseling center records were recorded for number of visits for psychological versus other reasons (e.g., vocational) for both prior to and following the experiment. Approximately 4 months following the completion of the laboratory study, subjects were mailed a questionnaire that included a number of health and health-related items that had been assessed on the beginning day of the experiment. The items on the follow-up survey asked subjects about health problems that had occurred since the completion of the laboratory study. Finally, two additional questions were included that asked subjects how much they had thought about and had been affected by their participation in the study. Further, subjects were encouraged to write, in their own words, their perceptions of the experiment. All but four of the subjects completed and returned the questionnaire.

Health and Counseling Center Visits. The number of visits to the health center for illness was subjected to a 4 X 2 (Condition X Before versus After the Experiment) repeated measures ANOVA. Although neither main effect approached significance, the predicted Condition X Before–After interaction was obtained, $F(3, 42) = 2.74$, $p = .055$. As can be seen in Table 2, the change in health center visits for illness was due to an overall increase in all conditions except the trauma–combination cell. Separate repeated measures ANOVA for the number of health center visits due to injury, psychiatric, or other reasons yielded no significant effects. Over the course of the year, only 1 subject visited the counseling center for psychological reasons and 2 for vocational help. Analyses of variance on these data produced no significant effects.

Follow-up Questionnaire Data. Although only 42 of the original 46 subjects returned the follow-up questionnaires, their health data were similar to the health center findings. Subjects were asked at the beginning of the experiment in November and on the follow-up questionnaire to report the number of days their activities had been restricted due to illness (since the beginning of school, during the November administration, and since the experiment for the follow-up questionnaire). A repeated measures ANOVA yielded a trend for the Condition X Time interaction, $F(3,38) = 2.19$, $p = .10$, suggesting

TABLE 2   MEANS OF ESSAY-RELATED VARIABLES BY CONDITION

Variables	Control	CONDITION Trauma-Emotion	Trauma-Fact	Trauma-Combination
No. of health center visits				
Prior to study	0.33	0.33	0.27	0.54
Following study	1.33_{ab}	1.58_a	1.45_{ab}	0.54_b
Change in visits	1.00_a	1.25_a	1.18_a	0.00_b
Self-reported health measures				
Change in No. of days restricted activity for illness	4.00_a	1.18_{ab}	1.90_{ab}	0.70_b
Change in No. of illnesses	0.18_a	-0.73_b	0.10_a	-0.60_b
Amount of thought about study	1.82_a	2.73_b	1.40_a	2.70_b
Degree of long-lasting effects	1.36	2.45	1.70	2.40

Note: The health center visit means are based on all subjects ($N = 46$). All other variables are based on follow-up self-reports ($n = 42$). See text for significance levels of one-way analyses of variance. Means with different subscripts are significantly different, $p \leq .05$. No significant initial differences by condition were obtained for any of the above variables.

that those in the control condition reported the most days and those in the trauma–combination the fewest (see Table 2). On both administrations of the questionnaire, subjects were asked to check if they had experienced each of eight specific health problems (ulcers, high blood pressure, constipation/diarrhea, colds or flu, migraine headaches, acne or skin disorders, heart problems, or other major difficulties). The summed health problem index was then subjected to a repeated measures ANOVA. Overall, subjects in the trauma–combination and trauma–emotion conditions reported reductions in health problems relative to those in the control and trauma–fact cells, $F(3, 38) = 3.05$, $p = .04$. For none of the above measures were there significant condition effects at Time 1. In addition, subjects were asked about several health-related behaviors, such as aspirin consumption, and alcohol, tobacco, and caffeine use for both prior to and following the experiment. No significant differences were obtained on any measure.

All of the subjects were asked to rate the degree to which they had thought about or had been affected by the experiment. In response to the question, "Since the end of the experiment back in November, how much have you thought about what you wrote," on a scale ranging from *not at all* (1) to *a great deal* (7), a marginally significant condition main effect was obtained, $F(3, 38) = 2.58$, $p = .06$. As seen in Table 2, those in the trauma–emotion and trauma–combination conditions were more likely to have thought about their essays than those in the trauma–facts or control cells.

Finally, subjects responded to the question, "Looking back on the experiment, do you feel as if it has had any long-lasting effects? Please answer this in your own words as well as rating it on a 1 to 7 scale." Although the overall one-way ANOVA was not statistically significant, $F(3, 38) = 1.43$, $p = .25$, the Means X Condition interaction is presented in the table. Overall, 7 of the 31 trauma subjects rated the long-lasting effect as 4 or higher along the 7-point scale. The responses to the open-ended question were uniformly positive. Because of the potentially sensitive nature of this paradigm, we feel that it is useful to present the responses of each of these subjects:

Trauma–emotion subjects. It helped me think about what I felt during those times. I never realized how it affected me before.

It helped to write things out when I was tense, so now when I'm worried I sit and write it out . . . later I feel better.

I had to think and resolve past experiences . . . One result of the experiment is peace of mind, and a method to relieve emotional experiences. To have to write emotions and feelings helped me understand how I felt and why.

Trauma–fact subject. It made me think a little deeper about some of the important parts of my life.

Trauma–combination subjects. It made me think a lot – But I'm still in the same situation.

If one writes down things that worry one, there is a tendency to feel better.

Although I have not talked with any one about what I wrote, I was finally able to deal with it, work through the pain instead of trying to block it out. Now it doesn't hurt to think about it...

DISCUSSION

The results of the experiment should be viewed as promising rather than definitive. Writing about earlier traumatic experience was associated with both short-term increases in physiological arousal and long-term decreases in health problems. Although these effects were most pronounced among subjects who wrote about both the trauma and their emotions associated with the trauma, there was substantial overlap in effects with those subjects who wrote only about their emotions associated with traumatic events. Subjects who were instructed to write only about previous traumatic events – without referring to their own emotions – were similar to control condition subjects on most physiological, health, and self-report measures.

Despite the general pattern of results, several weaknesses underscore the importance of future replication. Some of the measures yielded contradictory or only marginally significant effects. The number of subjects was quite small. Subjects were not selected in any way for having a debilitating undisclosed past trauma: therefore, it was impossible to evaluate the degree to which such subjects carried the results. In addition, two possible confounds associated with demand characteristics and changes in coping strategies may have influenced the health center data. These alternative explanations, as well as a number of issues surrounding catharsis, self-disclosure, coping strategies, and behavioral inhibition, are discussed next.

Recall that subjects were debriefed following the final essay-writing session. Although subjects were told about the experimental design, we were honest in admitting that we had no idea which, if any, condition would be most related to health. It is possible that subjects regulated their health center visits and follow-up questionnaire reports to some degree on the basis of our debriefing information.

One unforeseen mechanism that may also have affected the results was that we apparently provided some subjects with a new strategy for coping with both traumatic and significant daily events. It was clear that among those subjects who responded in writing to our follow-up questionnaire, some had begun writing about their experiences on their own after having participated in the experiment. Although we suspect that this behavior occurred with greater frequency in the trauma–emotion and trauma–combination cells, we cannot evaluate its direct impact on health.

Although these alternative explanations must be considered seriously, several of the experimental findings offer important directions for future research. For all but the objective health center data, the trauma–emotion and trauma–combination subjects were strikingly similar. Both groups evidenced higher blood pressure and more negative moods, relative to the other groups, each day after writing the essay; and both groups thought a great deal about the study in the months following the study. The results from both of these conditions cause one to argue against a simple venting or discharge theory of catharsis, which would predict that the expression of emotion should make the person more relaxed or happy, or both. Despite these relatively brief negative effects, both groups showed some long-term benefits. For example, self-reports concerning the change in number of different illnesses reported indicated an improvement in health for both groups. Similar trends emerged for self-reported days of restricted activity due to illness. Unfortunately, we cannot evaluate whether the long-term similarity between the two groups for these self-report measures reflects expectancy effects or true self-perceptions. Clearly, writing about the emotional side of a traumatic event was upsetting and physiologically arousing. However, the arousal per se may not have produced any long-term changes.

Perhaps one of the more unexpected findings was that having subjects write about the objective aspects of the traumatic events alone was neither arousing nor particularly upsetting. Indeed, this is reminiscent of the finding with subjects in studies by Lazarus and colleagues (e.g., Lazarus, Opton, Nomikos, & Rankin, 1965), in which hearing a nonemotional and/or intellectual description of an upsetting scene greatly reduced physiological responses to that event. Despite the fact that there were no short-term adverse effects from writing the nonemotional description of one's own traumatic experiences, there appear to be few, if any, long-term benefits in any objective or subjective indexes of health. It should be emphasized that these results are not necessarily inconsistent with the views of theorists who argue that the resolution of a trauma is associated with the cognitive work of organizing, assimilating, or finding meaning to the events surrounding the trauma (e.g., Horowitz, 1976; Silver, Boon, & Stones, 1983; Swann & Predmore, 1985). Rather, our findings point to the importance of emphasizing the emotions that coincide with the objective (or, at least, perceived) trauma.

Although the results of the experiment support what has been hypothesized by theorists in psychology and psychosomatics for decades, the exact mechanisms linking confiding and disease have not been sufficiently identified. The early ideas of Freud and Breuer were partially confirmed, in that tying both the cognitions and affect surrounding traumatic events was optimally effective in maintaining long-term health. Unlike their early claims, however, these effects were not immediate. It must be admitted, however, that subjects wrote only briefly each night. Either longer writing times or collecting our self-reports and physiological measures several minutes or hours after each night's essay, or both, may have demonstrated different results.

An interesting variation on this idea, posited by Jourard (1971), argues that self-disclosure allows for one's feelings and thoughts to become more concrete, which ultimately results in greater self-knowledge. Disease results, according to Jourard, when the motive toward self-understanding is blocked. Although we cannot evaluate the role of a possible blocked motive related to understanding, the concept of making thoughts and feelings concrete may be critically important. In this study, subjects did not receive social support or social comparison information. In none of the essays did subjects write about developing some type of coping strategies for the future. No love, positive feedback, or other mechanism commonly used to explain psychotherapy was at work.

The ideas of Jourard closely parallel many of our ideas about behavioral inhibition. We have argued that the act of inhibiting behavior is physiologically stressful (cf. Pennebaker & Chew, 1985). Previous surveys indicate that not confiding in others about a traumatic event – which we view as a form of behavioral inhibition – is associated with disease. As our study has indicated, one need not orally confide to another. Rather, the mere act of writing about an event and the emotions surrounding it is sufficient to reduce the long-term work of inhibition.

We have raised more questions than we have answered. The general pattern of results – although promising – must be replicated under more stringent conditions. Further, the role of inhibition must be demonstrated more precisely. Although writing about traumas appears to have positive long-term health effects, we must pinpoint the aspect of this exercise that is beneficial. Possibilities include making an event concrete, linking the affective and cognitive aspects, the reduction of forces associated with behavioral inhibition over time, and so forth. The ultimate resolution of these issues should have direct bearing on our understanding of social, cognitive, and psychosomatic processes.

REFERENCES

BREUER, J., & FREUD, S. (1966). *Studies on hysteria.* New York: Avon. (Original work published 1895)

FREUD, S. (1954). *The origins of psychoanalysis.* New York: Basic Books. (Original work published 1904)

HOROWITZ, M. J. (1976). *Stress response syndromes.* New York: Jacob Aronson.

JOURARD, S. M. (1971) *Self-disclosure: An experimental analysis of the transparent self.* New York: Wiley.

LAZARUS, R. (1966). *Psychological stress and the coping process.* New York: McGraw-Hill.

LAZARUS, R., OPTON, E., NOMIKOS, M., & RANKIN, N. (1965). The principle of short-circuiting of threat: Further evidence. *Journal of Personality, 33,* 622–635.

MEICHENBAUM, D. (1977). *Cognitive–behavior modification: an integrative approach.* New York: Plenum Press.

NICHOLS, M. P. (1974). Outcome of brief cathartic psychotherapy. *Journal of Consulting and Clinical Psychology, 42*, 403–410.

NICHOLS, M. P., & ZAX, M. (1977). *Catharsis in psychotherapy.* New York: Gardner Press.

PENNEBAKER, J. W. (1985). Traumatic experience and psychosomatic disease: Exploring the roles of behavioral inhibition, obsession, and confiding. *Canadian Psychology, 26*, 82–95.

PENNEBAKER, J. W., & CHEW, C. H. (1985). Deception, electrodermal activity, and inhibition of behavior. *Journal of Personality and Social Psychology, 49*, 1427–1433.

PENNEBAKER, J. W., & HOOVER, C. W. (1986). Inhibition and cognition: Toward an understanding of trauma and disease. In R. J. Davidson, G. E. Schwartz & D. Shapiro (Eds.), *Consciousness and self-regulation* (Vol. 4, pp. 107–136). New York: Plenum Press.

PENNEBAKER, J. W., & O'HEERON, R. C. (1984). Confiding in others and illness rates among spouses of suicide and accidental-death victims. *Journal of Abnormal Psychology, 93*, 473–476.

SCHEFF, T. J. (1979). *Catharsis in healing, ritual, and drama.* Berkeley: University of California Press.

SELYE, H. (1976). *The stress of life.* New York: McGraw-Hill.

SILVER, R. L., BOON, C., & STONES, M. H. (1983) Searching for meaning in misfortune: Making sense of incest. *Journal of Social Issues, 39*, 81–102.

SILVER, R. L., & WORTMAN, C. B. (1980). Coping with undesirable life events. In J. Garber & M. E. P. Seligman (Eds.), *Human helplessness: Theory and applications* (pp. 279–375). New York: Academic Press.

SUSMAN, J. R. (1986). *The relationship of expressiveness styles and elements of traumatic experience to self-reported illness.* Unpublished master's thesis, Southern Methodist University.

SWANN, W. B., & PREDMORE, S. C. (1985). Intimates as agents of social support: Sources of consolation or despair? *Journal of Personality and Social Psychology, 49*, 1609–1617.

TESSER, A., LEONE, C., & CLARY, E. G. (1978). Affect control: process constraints versus catharsis. *Cognitive Therapy and Research, 2*, 265–274.

WORTMAN, C. B., & DUNKEL-SCHETTER, C. (1979). Interpersonal relationships and cancer: A theoretical analysis. *Journal of Social Issues, 35*, 120–155.

QUESTIONS

1. According to Pennebaker and Beall, what are the health consequences of not confiding traumatic events? Briefly list a social, cognitive, and emotional explanation that has been given for this relationship. Where does the cathartic explanation fit in?

2. What are the authors' own views about the relationship between confiding traumatic events and health? Which of the three types of traditional explanations does this study investigate?

3. According to the physiological measure taken immediately before and after subjects wrote essays, which group seems to benefit the most from the essay writing?

4. Which group showed the best overall health in the six months following the study? Did these subjects also feel better immediately after the essay sessions?

5. Considering all of the data discussed in this article, which of the four original hypotheses (social, cognitive, emotional, cathartic) were supported?

Reading 10: Contemporary

Psychological Stress, Immunity, and Upper Respiratory Infections

Sheldon Cohen

In the previous reading, Pennebaker and Beall found that writing about a traumatic event reduced people's subsequent visits to the health center. The next reading helps to explain why writing about a past trauma might lead to better health: by lowering stress. Although our culture is often reluctant to believe that mental health can affect physical health, the idea that psychological stress might affect disease has gained increasing acceptance in recent years. As Sheldon Cohen reports below, there is now a standard model for the believed route from stressful life events to poorer health.

But how convinced should we be that this model is correct? What is the quality of the research on which it is based? Cohen begins the following reading by explaining the difficulty of conducting research on the stress-health link and the concomitant reasons to be skeptical. Undaunted, Cohen then describes his own attempts to find more conclusive evidence that stress affects the ability of our immune systems to fight off disease. As you will see, his results confirm a general link between stress and health, but also show that the causal pathways from the stressful life events to illness may not be exactly what we previously thought.

Ψ

The belief that when we are under stress we are more susceptible to the common cold, influenza, and other infectious diseases is widely accepted in our culture. It is the topic of numerous contemporary newspaper and magazine articles and has even been addressed in the lyrics of a popular song ("Adeline's Lament" from *Guys and Dolls*). The wide acceptance of this belief is also supported by data collected from participants in my studies. Sixty percent report that they are more likely to catch a cold during stressful than nonstressful periods of their lives. In this article, I review the scientific evidence that addresses this belief. How could psychological stress influence susceptibility to infectious disease? Is such a relation biologically and psychologically plausible? Is there convincing evidence that psychological stress influences susceptibility to upper respiratory infections?

Source: Cohen, S. (1996, June). Psychological stress, immunity, and upper respiratory infections. *Current Directions in Psychological Science, 5*, 86-90. Copyright © 1996 by Sheldon Cohen. Reprinted by permission of Blackwell Publishers.

HOW COULD STRESS INFLUENCE SUSCEPTIBILITY TO INFECTIOUS DISEASE?

Although constantly exposed to bacteria, viruses, fungi, and parasites that can cause infectious disease, we only periodically develop infectious illnesses. This is because our immune system protects us from infectious microorganisms. This defensive function is performed by the white blood cells and a number of accessory cells, which are distributed throughout the organs of the body. Stress is thought to influence susceptibility to infectious disease by compromising the effectiveness of the immune system. Persons with suppressed immune function are less able to fight off infectious agents and hence, given exposure to an agent, more likely to develop an infectious disease.

A simplified view of how stressful events in our lives might alter immunity is presented in Figure 1. When our demands are perceived to exceed our ability to cope, we label ourselves as stressed and experience a negative emotional response (Lazarus and Folkman, 1984). In turn, negative emotional responses could alter immune function through three different pathways (Rabin, Cohen, Ganguli, Lyle and Cunnick, 1989). Nerve fibers connecting the central nervous system and immune tissue provide one path by which emotional responses may influence immunity. These nerves terminate in immune tissue, where they release chemicals that are thought to suppress the function of

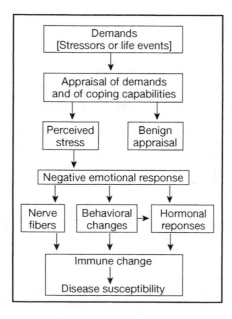

Figure 1.
Pathways through which stressful life events might influence the onset and progression of infectious disease. For simplicity, arrows are drawn in only one direction, from psychological characteristics to disease. This convention does not imply any assumptions about the existence of alternative paths.

immune cells. Stress-induced emotions may also act through their influence on the central nervous system's production and release of hormones, such as epinephrine and cortisol. These hormones circulate in the blood and can attach to receptors on immune cells, resulting in the cells' protective functions "turning off." The third mechanism by which stress may affect health derives from the role of behavioral patterns that reflect attempts to cope with negative emotional responses. For example, persons experiencing psychological stress often engage in unhealthy practices such as smoking, and not eating or sleeping properly, and such behavioral changes may suppress the activity of the immune system. They may affect immune responses directly or may influence immune function by altering hormonal responses.

DOES STRESS INFLUENCE IMMUNE FUNCTION?

As just discussed, the key link between psychological stress and susceptibility to infectious agents is thought to be the immune system. There is substantial evidence supporting the role of stress in the regulation of the immune system. Suppression of immune function has been found among persons taking important examinations (e.g., Kiecolt-Glaser et al., 1984); caring for relatives with chronic diseases (Kiecolt-Glaser, Glaser, et al., 1987); living near the site of a serious nuclear-power-plant accident (McKinnon, Weisse, Reynolds, Bowles, and Baum, 1989); suffering marital conflict (Kiecolt-Glaser, Fisher, et al., 1987); and reporting relatively high levels of unpleasant daily events (Stone et al., 1994), negative moods (Stone, Cox, Valdimarsdottir, Jandorf, and Neale, 1987), or perceived stress (e.g., Jabaaji et al., 1993). Suppression of immune function (called immunosuppression) has also been found in response to acute laboratory stressors, including working on challenging cognitive tasks, such as mental arithmetic, and delivering public speeches (e.g., Manuck, Cohen, Rabin, Muldoon, and Bachen, 1991). Clinical depression has also been associated with decreased immune response (Herbert and Cohen, 1993).

DOES STRESS INFLUENCE SUSCEPTIBILITY TO UPPER RESPIRATORY INFECTIONS?

Do studies that demonstrate induced immunosuppression under stressful conditions provide compelling evidence for stress-induced susceptibility to infectious disease? In general, these data are thought to be consistent with, but not definitively supportive of, the hypothesis that stress results in increased susceptibility to disease. The immune response involves a complex cascading series of events. Because studies of stress and immunity are limited to assessing very few markers of immune function in a limited time span, they can provide only a very rough estimate of the body's ability to mount such a defense (Cohen and Williamson, 1991).

Naturalistic Studies of Stress and Upper Respiratory Infection

A more direct approach to addressing the role of psychological stress in susceptibility to infection is examining the correlation between stress and infectious disease in natural settings. Because upper respiratory infections are by far the most prevalent of infectious diseases, the common cold and influenza have been adopted as the primary models for studying how stress might influence susceptibility. A large group of studies has found correlations between psychological stress and self-reported colds and influenza (reviewed in Cohen and Williamson, 1991). This work, however, is generally difficult to interpret. In many cases, third factors such as social class, age, or ethnic background might be responsible directly for increases in both stress and disease. Moreover, because this work is primarily retrospective, being ill may have caused stress rather than vice versa. Another problem is that unverified self-reports of illness are difficult to interpret. Although they may indicate underlying disease pathology, they may also reflect stress-induced biases to view ambiguous physical sensations as symptoms, and to interpret symptoms as indicating the onset of disease (e.g., Cohen et al., 1995).

There are a few investigations that have associated psychological stress and biologically verified (as opposed to self-reported) upper respiratory disease (e.g., Graham, Douglas, and Ryan, 1986; Meyer and Haggerty, 1962). Verification was accomplished by establishing the presence of a responsible bacterium or virus in nasal secretion or of an elevated level of antibody to the infectious agent in blood (serum). In these studies, measures of psychological stress were administered to healthy subjects who were subsequently monitored for up to 12 months for the development of upper respiratory infections. For those reporting infections, nasal secretions or blood samples were used to biologically verify the disease. These studies have found links between psychological stress and the subsequent development of colds and influenza. These results, however, may be attributable to stress-induced increases in exposure to infectious agents, rather than stress-induced immunosuppression. For example, persons under stress often seek out other people, consequently increasing the probability of exposure. The studies also fail to provide evidence about behavioral and biological mechanisms through which stress might influence a person's susceptibility in infection.

Viral-Challenge Studies

In my own work, I have adopted a procedure in which after completing stress questionnaires, volunteers are intentionally exposed to a common cold virus (in nasal drops) and then quarantined and monitored for 5 or more days for the development of disease. Approximately one third of the volunteers exposed to a virus develop a biologically verified clinical cold. The viral-challenge procedure has a number of advantages over naturalistic studies. By experimentally exposing persons to a virus and limiting their contact with other people, I eliminate the possibility that the results are attributable to stress increasing social contact and hence exposure to infectious agents. Moreover, because participants are closely monitored after exposure, it is easier to verify disease onset and to assess the roles of behavioral and biological pathways that might link stress to disease susceptibility. Finally, this methodology allows for a more refined assessment of the body's response to a virus. Specifically, after exposure to a virus, persons can become infected (i.e., their cells replicate the virus) without developing symptoms. In the viral-challenge trials, bodily fluids used to determine infection are drawn from subjects both with and without upper respiratory symptoms, allowing the identification of sub-clinical (i.e., with few if any symptoms) as well as clinical infections.

In an attempt to take advantage of the strengths of this methodology, my colleagues and I conducted a viral-challenge study addressing the role of stress in susceptibility to the common cold (Cohen, Tyrrell, and Smith, 1991, 1993). By using a prospective design in which psychological stress is assessed before participants are exposed to a virus, we were able to eliminate the possibility that illness causes stress as an interpretation of our results. Because the primary outcome in viral-challenge studies is categorical (sick or not), large sample sizes are required to maximize study sensitivity. Hence, we accumulated data from 420 healthy volunteers. Collection of these data required more than 40 separate 1-week trials conducted over 4 years. Our main hypothesis was that the higher the level of psychological stress, the higher the risk of developing the upper respiratory illness caused by the virus.

Each participant completed psychological stress questionnaires just prior to being exposed to one of five viruses known to cause common colds. A group of control participants received saline in nasal drops instead of a virus. After 7 days of quarantine, each participant was classified as not infected, infected but not ill, or infected and ill (clinical cold). As expected, none of the participants exposed to saline developed clinical colds, so this control group was not included in subsequent analyses.

The model in Figure 1 suggests that when demands imposed by events in someone's life exceed that person's ability to cope, he or she makes a stress appraisal (perceives stress), and in turn experiences a negative emotional response. In this work, we employed instruments to assess each phase of the stress response: a stressful-life-event scale to measure the cumulative event load, a perceived-stress scale to assess perceptions of overload-induced stress, and a measure of negative emotional response. Figure 2 presents the relations we found between stress (high or low, split at the median response) as assessed by each measure and the probability of developing a clinical cold. For all three stress measures, participants reporting high stress were more likely than those reporting low stress to develop a viral disease. These relations were found consistently for all five viruses. Moreover, these results could not be explained by stress-elicited differences in health practices, including smoking, alcohol consumption, exercise, eating, or sleeping habits. They also could not be explained by stress-induced changes in a series of relatively basic measures of immune status – the numbers of various white blood cell populations or total (nonspecific) antibody levels. A large group of plausible alternative factors that might be correlated with both stress and disease (e.g., age, sex, education, and personality characteristics such as self-esteem and personal control) were also unable to account for the relation between stress and susceptibility. In sum, the results provided strong support for a relation between psychological stress and susceptibility to developing a clinical cold, but did not provide confirming evidence for either a biological or a behavioral pathway responsible for the association.

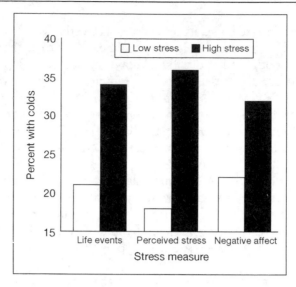

Figure 2.
Percentage of persons developing biologically verified clinical illness as a function of stressful life events, perceived stress, and negative affect. Each participant was exposed to one of five upper respiratory viruses. For each measure, scores were categorized as indicating high or low stress according to whether they were above or below the median score. Adapted from Cohen, Tyrrell, and Smith (1993), with permission of the American Psychological Association.

This study also addressed the validity of the hypothesis that stressful life events influence disease susceptibility by eliciting perceptions of stress and consequent negative emotional responses. However, the data did not totally support this perspective. First, the relation between stressful life events and risk of developing a cold was independent of the relations between perceived stress and colds and between negative affect and colds. That is, more stressful events were associated with greater susceptibility to disease irrespective of whether those events elicited perceptions of stress and negative affect. Second, the association of life events with illness was attributable to different biological processes than the associations of perceived stress and negative affect with illness. Increased risk for developing clinical colds could occur because stress increases the probability of the infectious agent replicating (infection), or because stress increases the production of histamines, bradykinins, or other chemicals that trigger symptoms after infection. In this study, becoming biologically infected was associated with high levels of perceived stress and negative affect, but developing clinical symptoms after infection was associated with high numbers of stressful life events. The fact that these scales have independent relations with clinical illness and that these relations are mediated by different biological processes challenges the assumption that perceptions of stress and negative affect are necessary for stressful life events to influence disease risk. A subsequent viral-challenge study conducted in another laboratory also found that life events and increased susceptibility had a relation independent of perceived stress and negative affect (Stone et al., 1993). As in our data, higher numbers of stressful events were associated with increased symptoms after infection.

A plausible explanation for the direct association between stressful life events and susceptibility is that the effort of coping with events, whether or not successful, results in hormonal responses that modulate immunity (Cohen, Evans, Stokols, and Krantz, 1986). In short, self-perceived negative emotional response may not be the only psychological pathway able to trigger hormonal responses critical to influencing immune function and disease susceptibility.

In sum, there is substantial evidence that both stressful life events and psychological stress (perceptions and negative affect) influence susceptibility to upper respiratory infections. These effects are not a consequence of unhealthy behaviors elicited by stress. We also lack direct evidence that increased susceptibility is attributable to stress-induced immunosuppression. The immune system, however, is terribly complex, and the measures used in human studies may not adequately assess the components most relevant to resisting upper respiratory infections. Finally, contrary to accepted stress and coping theory, the relation between stressful events and susceptibility to infectious disease does not depend on elevated perceptions of stress and negative emotional response.

CONCLUSIONS

The literature linking stress, immunity, and upper respiratory infection is in many ways impressive. First, it provides psychologically and biologically plausible hypotheses for how psychological factors might influence immunity and infectious disease. Second, it provides substantial evidence that psychological factors can influence indicators of immune status and function. Third, it includes consistent and convincing evidence of links between stress and the onset of upper respiratory infections. Where it fails is in identifying the behavioral, hormonal, or immune system pathways that are responsible for the link between stress and disease susceptibility. Only by identifying these pathways will researchers be able to evaluate the extent to which work with upper respiratory viruses provides a generic model that will allow generalization to other infectious agents.

REFERENCES

COHEN, S., DOYLE, W.J., SKONER, D.P., FIREMAN, P., SWALTNEY, J., AND NEWSOM, J. (1995). State and trait negative affect as predictors of objective and subjective symptoms of respiratory viral infections. *Journal of Personality and Social Psychology, 68,* 159-169.

COHEN, S., EVANS, G.W., STOKOLS, D., AND KRANTZ, D.S. (1986). *Behavior, health and environmental stress.* New York: Plenum Press.

COHEN, S., TYRRELL, D.A.J., AND SMITH, A.P. (1991). Psychological stress and susceptibility to the common cold. *New England Journal of Medicine, 325,* 606-612.

COHEN, S., TYRRELL, D.A.J., AND SMITH, A.P. (1993). Life events, perceived stress, negative affect and susceptibility to the common cold. *Journal of Personality and Social Psychology*, *64*, 131-140.

COHEN, S., AND WILLIAMSON, G.M. (1991). Stress and infectious disease in humans. *Psychological Bulletin*, *109*, 5-24.

GRAHAM, N.M.H., DOUGLAS, R.B., AND RYAN, P. (1986). Stress and acute respiratory infection. *American Journal of Epidemiology*, *124*, 389-401.

HERBERT, T.B., AND COHEN, S. (1993). Depression and immunity: A meta-analytic review. *Psychological Bulletin*, *113*, 472-486.

JABAAJI, L., GROSHEIDE, P.M., HEITTINK, R.A., DUIVENVOORDEN, H.J., BALLIEUX, R.E., AND VINGERGOETS, A.J.J.M. (1993). Influence of perceived psychological stress and distress on antibody response to low dose rDNA hepatitis B vaccine. *Journal of Psychosomatic Research*, 37, 361-369.

KIECOLT-GLASER, J.K., FISHER, L.D., OGROCKI, P., STOUT, J.C., SPEICHER, C.E., AND GLASER, R. (1987). Marital quality, marital disruption, and immune function. *Psychosomatic Medicine*, *49*, 13-34.

KIECOLT-GLASER, J.K., GARNER, W., SPEICHER, C.E., PENN, G.M., HOLLIDAY, J., AND GLASER, R. (1984). Psychosocial modifiers of immunocompetence in medical students. *Psychosomatic Medicine*, *46*, 7-14.

KIECOLT-GLASER, J.K., GLASER, R., SHUTTLEWORTH, E.C., DYER, C.S., OGROCKI, P., AND SPEICHER, E. (1987). Chronic stress and immunity in family caregivers of Alzheimer's disease victims. *Psychosomatic Medicine*, *49*, 523-535.

LAZARUS, R.S., AND FOLKMAN, S. (1984). *Stress appraisal and coping.* New York: Springer.

MANUCK, S.B., COHEN, S., RABIN, B.S., MULDOON, M., AND BACHEN, E. (1991). Individual differences in cellular immune response to stress. *Psychological Science*, *1*, 111-115.

MACKINNON, W., WEISSE, C.S., REYNOLDS, C.P., BOWLES, C.A., AND BAUM, A. (1989). Chronic stress, leukocyte subpopulations, and humoral response to latent viruses. *Health Psychology*, *8*, 389-402.

MEYER, R.J., AND HAGGERTY, R.J (1962). Streptococcal infections in families. *Pediatrics*, *29*, 539-549.

RABIN, B.S., COHEN, S., GANGULI, R., LYLE, D.T., AND CUNNICK, J.E. (1989). Bidirectional interaction between the central nervous system and immune system. *CRC Critical Reviews in Immunology*, *9*, 279-312.

STONE, A.A., BOVBJERG, D.H., NEALE, J.M., NAPOLI, A., VALDIMARSDOTTIR, H., COX, D., HAYDEN, F.G., AND GWALTNEY, J.M. (1993) Development of common cold symptoms following experimental rhinovirus infection is related to prior stressful life events. *Behavioral Medicine*, *8*, 115-120.

STONE, A.A., NEALE, J.M., COX, D.S., NAPOLI, AL., VALDIMARSDOTTIR, H., AND KENNEDY-MOORE, F. (1994). Daily events are associated with a secretory immune response to an oral antigen in men. *Health Psychology*, *13*, 140-146.

QUESTIONS

1. What three factors make it difficult to interpret self-report data showing a positive correlation between stress and colds and flu?

2. Cohen argues that stressful life events cause cold symptoms without affecting biological infection. How is this possible?

3. How should the standard stress-health model, shown in Figure 1, be changed to account for the findings reported in this study? What additional causal pathways should be added?

4. Consider the three paths by which stress might affect health (shown at the bottom of Figure 1) in relation to a person who finds that they can relieve stress by smoking. Would stress-reducing smoking increase or decrease the likelihood of developing a cold in each of the three separate pathways?

5. The stringent methodology of Cohen's study eliminated the possibility that behavior following exposure to the cold virus explains the stress-heath link. Could behavior *prior to* exposure to the cold virus account for this link?

Ψ

PART IV
RELATIONSHIPS
Ψ Ψ

Ψ CHAPTER 6 Ψ

INTERPERSONAL ATTRACTION:
OUR LIKING FOR OTHERS

Reading 11: Classic

Physical Attractiveness

Ellen Berscheid and Elaine Hatfield

Romantic love is considered by most contemporary Western cultures to be one of the most meaningful aspects of life. Yet surprisingly, it is an issue that social scientists have largely ignored this century. Social psychologists were no exception and paid love only minor attention until the late 1960s.

Interestingly, the first theories of "mate selection" tended to downplay the importance of physical attractiveness. Discussing the absence of this intuitively important construct, Elliot Aronson, a prominent social psychologist, suggested that psychologists were afraid of what they might find. We would all like to believe that people are judged by others on the basis of their character, not superficial looks. Perhaps psychology's omission of this construct in its research was motivated by the desire not to discover that physical attractiveness does, in fact, greatly influence how others perceive us.

As Ellen Berscheid and Elaine Hatfield discuss in the following reading, Aronson may have been correct. Subsequent research indicates that physical attractiveness has an enormous impact on dating choices. Although both men and women typically report that physical attractiveness is only moderately important to them in selecting dating partners, their behavior suggest otherwise. This reading begins by describing a seminal study in computer dating conducted by Elaine Hatfield (at the time of that study Hatfield was using the name Walster; you'll notice that the study is attributed to this previous name).

Ψ

PHYSICAL ATTRACTIVENESS AND HETEROSEXUAL ATTRACTION: THE LURE OF THE PHYSICALLY ATTRACTIVE

Despite democratic notions of fairness and equal opportunity, and the taint of the morphological, those interested in the antecedents of opposite-sex attraction could not

Source: Berscheid, E., & Hatfield, E. (1974). Physical attractiveness. In L. Berkowitz (Ed.), *Advances in Experimental Social Psychology*. (Vol 7, pp. 157–215). New York: Academic Press. Copyright © 1974 by Academic Press. Reprinted by permission of the publisher.

long ignore the demand to recognize the physical attractiveness variable. Insight into the potency of physical attractiveness initially emerged from experiments designed to test the hypothesis that men and women of similar levels of social desirability tend to "pair off" in courtship and marriage.

A. The Matching Hypothesis

The "matching hypothesis" was first suggested by the sociologist Erving Goffman, who said, "A proposal of marriage in our society tends to be a way in which a man sums up his social attributes and suggests to a woman that hers are not so much better as to preclude a merger or a partnership in these matters [1952, p. 456]." The sum of a person's social attributes is presumably determined by his level of social skills, his intelligence, his access to such material resources as money and prestige, his physical attractiveness, and his possession of other socially valued characteristics.

The hypothesis of matching in social choice was initially tested by Walster, Aronson, Abrahams, and Rottmann (1966), who formally derived their prediction from Level of Aspiration Theory (cf. Lewin, Dembo, Festinger, & Sears, 1944). They reasoned that one's romantic aspirations are influenced by the same factors that influence one's level of aspiration in other areas – the desirability of the goal and the perceived probability of attaining it. While socially desirable people ought to be preferred by everyone, the perceived probability of obtaining their attention and esteem ought to vary with the person's own social desirability. Thus, for romantic liaisons people should select, and like best, those of their own social desirability level.

To test their hypothesis, Walster et al. conducted a "computer dance" for college freshmen, where purchase of a ticket ensured a date for the dance. It was impossible for the investigators to make a precise determination of the "sum" of each student's social attributes, but they reasoned that scores on personality, intelligence, social skill, and physical attractiveness measures would provide an index. (Each student's physical attractiveness level was quickly and roughly assessed at the box office as he or she purchased a ticket to the dance.)

All the men and women who signed up for the dance were paired on a random basis with but one restriction. The informal but apparently cardinal rule of dating, that the man be taller than the woman, was never violated. It was hypothesized that those students who obtained, by chance, dates of their own social desirability levels (whether high or low) would like each other more than those who received dates whose social desirability levels were inferior or superior to their own.

It was fortunate that the investigators suspected that a student's physical attractiveness level might be an important component of each student's social desirability. Questionnaires which were administered at the intermission of the dance to determine how well the partners had hit it off revealed that the only apparent determinant of how much each person liked his or her date, how much he or she wanted to see the partner again, and (it was determined later) how often the man actually did ask his partner for subsequent dates, was simply how physically attractive the partner was. The more physically attractive the date, the more he or she was liked. Every effort to find additional factors which might possibly predict attraction failed. Students with exceptional social skills and intelligence levels, for example, were not liked any better than those less fortunately endowed.

The apparently inordinate importance of physical attractiveness as a determinant of attraction, at least in blind date settings, has been substantiated by other investigators. Brislin and Lewis (1968) found a correlation of .89 between the perceived physical attractiveness of a computer dance date and a desire to date the partner again; Tesser and Brodie (1971) found a correlation of .69 between these two variables. In both studies the partner's perception of the physical attractiveness of the date (physical attractiveness was not independently assessed) correlated higher with the "desire to date again" response than did any of the other perceived characteristics of the partner, including perception of "similar interests," "character," etc.

Although Walster *et al.* failed to find support for the matching principle – everyone seemed to prefer the highly attractive man or woman – subsequent investigators argued that the computer dance situation was not an optimal setting for the test of the hypothesis. The matching hypothesis as derived from Level of Aspiration Theory predicts that an individual will choose a date of approximately his own level of social desirability when making a *realistic*, as opposed to *idealistic*, social choice. Realistic choices, according to Level of Aspiration Theory, are influenced not only by the objective desirability of the choice alternative (as in idealistic choices), but also by the individual's perception of his probability of attaining the goal. An underlying assumption of the matching hypothesis, then, is that people of lesser social desirability feel that they are likely to meet with rejection when they attempt to contact a person of higher social desirability.

Berscheid, Dion, Walster, and Walster (1971) reasoned that the salience of the possibility of social rejection by one's choice, while ever-present in most informal dating situations, was minimized in the Walster *et al.* computer dance setting. Dates had been assigned, and those who by chance secured more attractive dates than themselves were assured not only of social contact, but of the fruits of social courtesy norms for the duration of the dance. In addition, those who had achieved their ideal goal of a physically attractive partner may have shown more interest in *retaining* it than they might have shown in trying to *attain* it initially.

Berscheid *et al.* conducted two experiments to determine if the matching principle would reveal itself when the individual was required to actively *choose* a dating partner (rather than evaluate one already secured) and to discover if matching was especially likely when the salience of possible rejection by the chosen date was emphasized. In both experiments, the physical attractiveness of each S was independently assessed by judges, the salience of possible rejection by the dating choice was varied, and the physical attractiveness level of the date S desired was examined.

The results of both experiments found support for the matching principle. As in Walster *et al.*, physically attractive dates were markedly preferred by everyone. *Within* this general trend, however, it was clear that men and women of lesser attractiveness did tend to choose less attractive dates than did highly attractive individuals.

Both experimental attempts to ascertain whether the degree of matching would vary with the probability of acceptance or rejection by the chosen date failed. Ss in these experiments appeared to operate on the matching principle equally whether the possibility of acceptance or rejection by the chosen person was salient. Thus, although a matching effect was found, there was no evidence of its presumed mediator – high probability of rejection by those of higher social desirabilities.

A recent study conducted by Huston (1973), however, does demonstrate that men do perceive their chances of social acceptance to be less with attractive women and, further, that their subjective probability of rejection may influence attempts to approach them. Huston's Ss were asked to choose a date from an array of women representing three levels of physical attractiveness. Half of the men were assured that each of the women had previously indicated that she would accept a date with him; to the remainder, it was left unclear whether their chosen date would accept or reject them. As well as making their choices, the latter group was asked to indicate the likelihood that each woman would accept them as a date.

Huston found the ubiquitous effect that, overall, the men generally preferred to date the most physically attractive women. This was most pronounced, however, when they were assured of acceptance by them. Ss who were not guaranteed acceptance believed that the highly physically attractive women would be significantly less likely to want them as a date than would either the moderately attractive or the unattractive women. In addition, each man's rating of his own physical attractiveness level was related to perceived chance of acceptance by each of the potential dates. Those men who believed themselves to be highly attractive estimated their chances of acceptance as better than did those who considered themselves relatively unattractive.

Although Huston found no evidence that self-ratings of physical attractiveness corresponded to the chosen date's physical attractiveness level, others have demonstrated a positive relationship. Stroebe, Insko, Thompson, and Layton (1971), for example, found that men and women who believed themselves to be unattractive were more likely to consider dating unattractive others, and less likely to consider attractive others, than were people who had a more favorable opinion of their physical attractiveness.

These studies indicate that while physically attractive men and women are strongly preferred in heterosexual dating relationships, within this overall tendency, a person's own physical attractiveness level acts as a moderating influence on date selection. Further, there is suggestive evidence that differential probabilities of rejection associated with attractive and unattractive dates mediate the matching effect.

B. Matching, *FAIT ACCOMPLI*

If it is true that men and women of equal levels of social desirability tend to pair off in courtship and marriage, and if it is also true that one's degree of physical attractiveness plays an extremely important role in determining both a man's and a woman's social desirability level, then couples who have formed viable affectional relationships should appear to outside observers to be of approximately equal levels of physical attractiveness.

The question of *fait accompli* matching was addressed by Silverman (1971), who examined the degree of similarity in attractiveness exhibited by couples observed in naturalistic dating settings. Teams of observers (two males and two females each) went to such dating habitats as bars, social events, and theater lobbies where they could watch couples unobtrusively. The couples, according to Silverman, were predominantly in the 18- to 22-year range and were unmarried. Each observer rated the dating partner of the opposite sex on a 5–point scale, independently and without knowledge of the ratings made by the other observers.

Silverman and his associates found an extraordinarily high degree of similarity in physical attractiveness between the dating partners. While the distribution of attractiveness scores of the men and women ranged from 1 to 5 in intervals of .5, Silverman found that for 60% of the couples, partners were not separated by more than half a scale point, and no couple was disparate by more than 2.5 scale points.

In addition to rating the physical attractiveness level of the dating partners, the observers recorded whether the couples engaged in intimate touching (such as holding hands, walking arm-in-arm, etc.) during the period of observation. Silverman hypothesized that couples more similar in attractiveness would seem to be happier with each other as reflected by their degree of physical intimacy. The data revealed that 60% of the couples who were highly similar in physical attractiveness level were engaged in intimate physical contact of some kind, as compared to 46% of the moderately similar couples and 22% of those in the lowest similarity group.

Silverman's evidence of *fait accompli* matching along the physical attractiveness dimension is not as unequivocal as one would like. Despite the fact that observers did not know how the other observers rated the attractiveness of the other member of the dating pair, they did, of course, see the dating partners. Thus, it is possible that a "halo" emanating from one dating partner and influencing perception of the other may have produced artifactually similar ratings of dating pairs. This possibility seems especially cogent, since Sigall and Landy (in press) have recently demonstrated that the favorability of the overall impression a man makes on outside observers is affected by the physical attractiveness level of a woman with whom he is romantically associated. Although knowledge of romantic association did not specifically appear to affect the rating of the man's physical attractiveness level, the pervasiveness of its effect along a number of other dimensions suggests that the *fait accompli* matching hypothesis might be best tested under conditions in which attractiveness judges are not aware of who is paired with whom.

A further problem with Silverman's data is that no analyses were undertaken to determine whether the degree of matching observed was significantly above that which might be expected by chance. As Udry (1971) points out, "the frequency of distribution of individual ratings indicates that most individuals were rated between 2 and 4, with two out of three females and half of the men receiving ratings between 2.5 and 3.5. Under these circumstances, random matings would produce most similarly rated couples [p. 23]."

Murstein (1972), avoiding both these difficulties, examined the correspondence between the physical attractiveness levels of 99 couples who were engaged or going steady. The degree of matching exhibited by the dating couples was compared to that of a control group of couples which was formed by randomly paring the physical attractiveness scores of the 99 men and women with each other. Photographs were taken of each of the dating couples, and ratings of the physical attractiveness of each member of each couple were made. According to Murstein, judges did not know which partner belonged to whom when they made their attractiveness judgments.

Murstein found evidence of matching along the physical attractiveness dimension; the physical attractiveness level of the engaged or steadily dating couples was significantly less discrepant than those of the artificially paired couples. Murstein concluded, "Individuals with equal market value for physical attractiveness are more likely to associate in an intimate relationship such as premarital engagement than individuals with disparate values. [p. 11]."

C. Sex Differences in the Importance of Physical Attractiveness in Heterosexual Choice

The data provided by the preceding studies not only tend to support the matching hypothesis but indicate that physical attractiveness is of major significance for both sexes' dating choices. They also suggest that physical attractiveness may be of even more importance to men in making their dating choices than it is to women. Walster *et al.* (1966) devised a Self-Report Popularity index which included the questions "How popular are you with the opposite sex?" and "How many dates have you had in the last six months?" Physical attractiveness and popularity correlated .46 for women and .31 for men. Both coefficients are significantly different from each other, and both are significantly different from 0. Berscheid *et al.* (1971) also found a significant difference between men and women in the strength of correspondence between physical attractiveness and dating popularity. Physical attractiveness and number of dates within the past year correlated .61 for females; the correspondence for males was only .25.

These findings, which indicate that physical attractiveness is more strongly related to a woman's dating popularity than to a man's, are compatible with the results of several studies which have examined the factors college students report to be important in making dating choices (e.g., Coombs & Kenkel, 1966; Hewitt, 1958; Williamson, 1966; Vail & Staudt, 1950). Males, in comparison with females, consistently report that they place more importance on physical attractiveness in making dating choices. Whether these stated preferences are translated into action may be another matter. Byrne, Ervin, and Lamberth (1970) found that, although men reported that the physical attractiveness of their assigned date was a more important factor in determining their attraction for the date than women did, the date's physical attractiveness correlated .60 with the attraction responses of female *Ss* and only .39 for male *Ss*.

D. Summary

The investigators who went hunting for evidence of matching in social choice not only caught their quarry but found the imposing tracks of bigger game. If the "sum" of a person's social desirability in the dating and mating market were composed of a wide variety of components, each with its individual weight and unique mode of interaction with the other components, life would have been much more complex for the matching researchers. The discovery that matching could be observed considering only the physical attractiveness component, as well as the repeated observance of large main effects in choice along the physical attractiveness dimension, provides consistent and convincing evidence that physical attractiveness is a factor which cannot be ignored in the prediction of date and mate selection.

REFERENCES

BERSCHEID, E., DION, K.K., WASLTER, E., AND WALSTER, G.W. (1971) Physical attractiveness and dating choice: A test of the matching hypothesis. *Journal of Experimental Social Psychology, 7,* 173-189.

BRISLIN, R.W., AND LEWIS, S.A. (1968) Dating and physical attractiveness: Replication. *Psychological Reports, 22,* 976.

BYRNE, D., ERVIN, C.R., AND LAMBERTH, J. (1970) Continuity between the experimental study of attraction and real-life computer dating. *Journal of Personality and Social Psychology, 16,* 157-165.

COOMBS, R.H., AND KENKEL, W.F. (1966) Sex differences in dating aspirations and satisfaction with computer-selected partners. *Journal of Marriage and Family, 28(1),* 62-66.

GOFFMAN, E. (1952) On cooling the mark out: Some aspects of adaptation to failure. *Psychiatry, 15,* 451-463.

HEWITT, L.E. (1958). Student perceptions of traits desired in themselves as dating and marriage partners. *Marriage and Family Living, 20,* 344-349.

HUSTON, T.L. (1973) Ambiguity of acceptance, social desirability, and dating choice. *Journal of Experimental Social Psychology, 9(1),* 32-42.

LEWIN, K., DEMBO, T., FESTINGER, L., AND SEARS, P. (1944) Level of aspiration. In J. McV. Hunt (Ed.), *Personality and the behavior disorders.* Vol. 1. New York: Ronald Press.

MURSTEIN, B.I. (1972) Physical attractiveness and marital choice. *Journal of Personality and Social Psychology, 22(1),* 8-12.

SIGALL, H., AND LANDY, D. (in press) Radiating beauty: The effects of having a physical attractive partner on person perception. *Journal of Personality and Social Psychology.*

SILVERMAN, I. (1971, September). Physical attractivenss and courtship. *Sexual Behavior,* 22-25.

STROEBE, W., INSKO, C.A., THOMPSON, V.D., AND LAYTON, B.D. (1971) Effects of physical attractiveness, attitude similarity, and sex on various aspects of interpersonal attraction. *Journal of Personality and Social Psychology, 18,* 79-91.

TESSER, A., AND BRODIE, M. (1971) A note on the evaluation of a "computer date." *Psychnomic Science, 23,* 300.

UDRY, J.R. (1971, September) Commentary. *Sexual Behavior, 23.*

VAIL, J.P., AND STAUDT, V.M. (1950) Attitudes of college students toward marriage and related problems: I. Dating and mate selection. *Journal of Psychology, 30,* 171-182.

WALSTER, E., ARONSON, V., ABRAHAMS, D., AND ROTTMANN, L. (1966) Importance of physical attractiveness in dating behavior. *Journal of Personality and Social Psychology 4(5),* 508-516.

WILLIAMSON, R.L. (1966) *Marriage and family relations.* New York: Wiley.

QUESTIONS

1. Explain the matching hypothesis. What is being "matched?"   What role does physical attractiveness play according to this hypothesis?

2. Did the "computer dance" study done by Walster et al. confirm the predictions of the matching hypothesis? How do Berscheid and Hatfield explain this?

3. What do Silverman's "fait accompli" data suggest about the matching hypothesis? Why are Berscheid and Hatfield hesitant to accept these data?

4. What differences have been found in the importance that men and women place on their partners' attractiveness?

5. Contrary to Goffman's prediction, it appears that people tend to try to date the most attractive person they can. Can you reconcile this with Silverman's evidence of "fait accompli" matching?

Reading 12: Contemporary

The Biology of Beauty

Geoffrey Cowley

In the previous reading, Berscheid and Hatfield convincingly argued for the importance of physical attraction in dating choices. They were less able, however, to explain why people are so influenced by attractiveness. Further, they were unable to specify precisely what features people considered attractive. Both of these issues are addressed in the next reading by Geoffrey Cowley, who writes about psychology for Newsweek *magazine.*

It is obvious to anyone who has ever seen the standards of beauty portrayed in classic works of art from previous centuries that these standards have changed. For example, women in the paintings of the Flemish master Rubens bear little resemblance to contemporary supermodels. Clearly, what people consider beautiful is not universal. But, according to some researchers, beautiful people from all ages, including Rubens and our own, do share some important qualities in common. These commonalties may point to universal features of beauty, features that have their basis in human biology.

Ψ

When it comes to choosing a mate, a female penguin knows better than to fall for the first creep who pulls up and honks. She holds out for the fittest suitor available – which in Antarctica means one chubby enough to spend several weeks sitting on newly hatched eggs without starving to death. The Asian jungle bird *Gallus gallus* is just as choosy. Males in that species sport gaily colored head combs and feathers, which lose their luster if the bird is invaded by parasites. By favoring males with bright ornaments, a hen improves her odds of securing a mate (and bearing offspring) with strong resistance to disease. For female scorpion flies, beauty is less about size or color than about symmetry. Females favor suitors who have well-matched wings – and with good reason. Studies show they're the most adept at killing prey and at defending their catch from competitors. There's no reason to think that any of these creatures understands its motivations, but there's a clear pattern to their preferences. "Throughout the animal world," says University of New Mexico ecologist Randy Thornhill, "attractiveness certifies biological quality."

Is our corner of the animal world different? That looks count in human affairs is beyond dispute. Studies have shown that people considered attractive fare better with parents and teachers, make more friends and more money, and have better sex with more

Source: Cowley, G. (1996, June 3). The biology of beauty. *Newsweek, 127,* 61-66. Copyright © 1996 Newsweek, Inc. All rights reserved. Reprinted by permission of the publisher.

(and more beautiful) partners. Every year, 400,000 Americans, including 48,000 men, flock to cosmetic surgeons. In other lands, people bedeck themselves with scars, lip plugs or bright feathers. "Every culture is a 'beauty culture'," says Nancy Etcoff, a neuroscientist who is studying human attraction at the MIT Media Lab and writing a book on the subject. "I defy anyone to point to a society, any time in history or any place in the world, that wasn't preoccupied with beauty." The high-minded may dismiss our preening and ogling as distractions from things that matter, but the stakes can be enormous. "Judging beauty involves looking at another person," says University of Texas psychologist Devendra Singh, "and figuring out whether you want your children to carry that person's genes."

It's widely assumed that ideals of beauty vary from era to era and from culture to culture. But a harvest of new research is confounding that idea. Studies have established that people everywhere – regardless of race, class or age – share a sense of what's attractive. And though no one knows just how our minds translate the sight of a face or a body into rapture, new studies suggest that we judge each other by rules we're not even aware of. We may consciously admire Kate Moss's legs or Arnold's biceps, but we're also viscerally attuned to small variations in the size and symmetry of facial bones and the placement of weight on the body.

This isn't to say that our preferences are purely innate – or that beauty is all that matters in life. Most of us manage to find jobs, attract mates and bear offspring despite our physical imperfections. Nor should anyone assume that the new beauty research justifies the biases it illuminates. Our beautylust is often better suited to the Stone Age than to the Information Age; the qualities we find alluring may be powerful emblems of health, fertility and resistance to disease, but they say nothing about people's moral worth. The human weakness for what Thornhill calls "biological quality" causes no end of pain and injustice. Unfortunately, that doesn't make it any less real.

No one suggests that points of attraction never vary. Rolls of fat can signal high status in a poor society or low status in a rich one, and lip plugs go over better in the Kalahari than they do in Kansas. But local fashions seem to rest on a bedrock of shared preferences. You don't have to be Italian to find Michelangelo's David better looking than, say, Alfonse D'Amato. When British researchers asked women from England, China and India to rate pictures of Greek men, the women responded as if working from the same crib sheet. And when researchers at the University of Louisville showed a diverse collection of faces to whites, Asians and Latinos from 13 countries, the subjects' ethnic background scarcely affected their preferences.

To a skeptic, those findings suggest only that Western movies and magazines have overrun the world. But scientists have found at least one group that hasn't been exposed to this bias. In a series of groundbreaking experiments, psychologist Judith Langlois of the University of Texas, Austin, has shown that even infants share a sense of what's attractive. In the late '80s, Langlois started placing 3- and 6-month-old babies in front of a screen and showing them pairs of facial photographs. Each pair included one considered attractive by adult judges and one considered unattractive. In the first study, she found that the infants gazed significantly longer at "attractive" white female faces than at "unattractive" ones. Since then, she has repeated the drill using white male faces, black female faces, even the faces of other babies, and the same pattern always emerges. "These kids don't read *Vogue* or watch TV," Langlois says. "They haven't been touched by the media. Yet they make the same judgments as adults."

What, then, is beauty made of? What are the innate rules we follow in sizing each other up? We're obviously wired to find robust health a prettier sight than infirmity. "All animals are attracted to other animals that are healthy, that are clean by their standards and that show signs of competence," says Rutgers University anthropologist Helen Fisher. As far as anyone knows, there isn't a village on earth where skin lesions, head lice and rotting teeth count as beauty aids. But the rules get subtler than that. Like scorpion flies, we love symmetry. And though we generally favor average features over unusual ones, the people we find extremely beautiful share certain exceptional qualities.

When Randy Thornhill started measuring the wings of Japanese scorpion flies six years ago, he wasn't much concerned with the orgasms and infidelities of college students. But sometimes one thing leads to another. Biologists have long used bilateral symmetry – the extent to which a creature's right and left sides match – to gauge what's known as developmental stability. Given ideal growing conditions, paired features such as wings, ears, eyes, and feet would come out matching perfectly. But pollution, disease and other hazards can disrupt development. As a result, the least resilient individuals tend to be the most lopsided. In chronicling the scorpion flies' daily struggles, Thornhill found that the bugs with the most symmetrical wings fared best in the competition for food and mates. To his amazement, females preferred symmetrical males even when they were hidden from view; evidently, their smells are more attractive. And when researchers started noting similar trends in other species, Thornhill turned his attention to our own.

Working with psychologist Steven Gangestad, he set about measuring the body symmetry of hundreds of college-age men and women. By adding up right-left disparities in seven measurements – the breadth of the feet, ankles, hands, wrists and elbows, as well as the breadth and length of the ears – the researchers scored each subject's overall body asymmetry. Then they had the person fill out a confidential questionnaire covering everything from temperament to sexual behavior, and set about looking for connections. They weren't disappointed. In a 1994 study, they found that the most symmetrical males had started having sex three to four years earlier than their most lopsided brethren. For both men and women, greater symmetry predicted a larger number of past sex partners.

That was just the beginning. From what they knew about other species, Thornhill and Gangestad predicted that women would be more sexually responsive to symmetrical men, and that men would exploit that advantage. To date, their findings support both suspicions. Last year they surveyed 86 couples and found that women with highly symmetrical partners were more than twice as likely to climax during intercourse (an event that may foster conception by ushering sperm into the uterus) than those with low-symmetry partners. And in separate surveys, Gangestad and Thornhill have found that, compared with regular Joes, extremely symmetrical men are less attentive to their partners and more likely to cheat on them. Women showed no such tendency.

It's hard to imagine that we even notice the differences between people's elbows, let alone stake our love lives on them. No one carries calipers into a singles bar. So why do these measurements predict so much? Because, says Thornhill, people with symmetrical elbows tend to have "a whole suite of attractive features." His findings suggest that besides having attractive (and symmetrical) faces, men with symmetrical bodies are typically larger, more muscular and more athletic than their peers, and more dominant in personality. In a forthcoming study, researchers at the University of Michigan find evidence that facial symmetry is also associated with health. In analyzing diaries kept by 100 students over a two-month period, they found that the least symmetrical had the most physical complaints, from insomnia to nasal congestion, and reported more anger, jealously and withdrawal. In light of all Thornhill and Gangestad's findings, you can hardly blame them.

If we did go courting with calipers, symmetry isn't all we would measure. As we study each other in the street, the office or the gym, our beauty radars pick up a range of signals. Oddly enough, one of the qualities shared by attractive people is their averageness. Researchers discovered more than a century ago that if they superimposed photographs of several faces, the resulting composite was usually better looking than any of the images that went into it. Scientists can now average faces digitally, and it's still one of the surest ways to make them more attractive. From an evolutionary perspective, a preference for extreme normality makes sense. As Langlois has written, "Individuals with average population characteristics should be less likely to carry harmful genetic mutations."

So far, so good. But here's the catch: while we may find average faces attractive, the faces we find most beautiful are not average. As New Mexico State University psychologist Victor Johnston has shown, they're extreme. To track people's preferences, Johnston uses a computer program called FacePrints. Turn it on, and it generates 30 facial images, all male or all female, which you rate on a 1–9 beauty scale. The program then "breeds" the top-rated faces with one of the others to create two digital offspring, which replace the lowest-rated faces in the pool. By rating round after round of new faces, you create an ever more beautiful population. The game ends when you award some visage a perfect 10. (If you have access to the Web, you can take part in a collective face-breeding experiment by visiting http://www-psych.nmsu.edu/~vic/faceprints/.)

For Johnston, the real fun starts after the judging is finished. By collecting people's ideal faces and comparing them to average faces, he can measure the distance between fantasy and reality. As a rule, he finds that an ideal female has a higher forehead than an average one, as well as fuller lips, a shorter jaw and a smaller chin and nose. Indeed, the ideal 25-year-old woman, as configured by participants in a 1993 study, had a 14-year-old's abundant lips and an 11-year-old's delicate jaw. Because her lower face was so small, she also had relatively prominent eyes and cheekbones.

The participants in that study were all college kids from New Mexico, but researchers have since shown that British and Japanese students express the same bias. And if there are lingering doubts about the depth of that bias, Johnston's latest findings should dispel them. In a forthcoming study, he reports that male volunteers not only consciously prefer women with small lower faces but show marked rises in brain activity when looking at pictures of them. And though Johnston has yet to publish specs on the ideal male, his unpublished findings suggest that a big jaw, a strong chin and an imposing brow are as prized in a man's face as their opposites are in a woman's.

Few of us ever develop the heart-melting proportions of a FacePrints fantasy. And if it's any consolation, beauty is not an all-or-nothing proposition. Madonna became a sex symbol despite her strong nose, and Melanie Griffith's strong jaw hasn't kept her out of the movies. Still, special things have a way of happening to people who approximate the ideal. We pay them huge fees to stand on windblown bluffs and stare into the distance. And past studies have found that square-jawed males not only start having sex earlier than their peers but attain higher rank in the military.

None of this surprises evolutionary psychologists. They note that the facial features we obsess over are precisely the ones that diverge in males and females during puberty, as floods of sex hormones wash us into adulthood. And they reason that hormonal abundance would have been a good clue to mate value in the hunter-gatherer world where our preferences evolved. The tiny jaw that men favor in women is essentially a monument to estrogen – and obliquely, to fertility. No one claims that jaws reveal a woman's odds of getting pregnant. But like breasts, they imply that she could.

Likewise, the heavy lower face that women favor in men is a visible record of the surge in androgens (testosterone and other male sex hormones) that turns small boys into 200-pound spear-throwers. An oversized jaw is biologically expensive, for the androgens required to produce it tend to comprise the immune system. But from a female's perspective, that should make jaw size all the more revealing. Evolutionists think of androgen-based features as "honest advertisements" of disease resistance. If a male can afford them without falling sick, the thinking goes, he must have a superior immune system in the first place.

No one has tracked the immune responses of men with different jawlines to see if these predictions bear out (Thornhill has proposed a study that would involve comparing volunteers' responses to a vaccine). Nor is it clear whether penis size figures into these equations. Despite what everyone thinks he knows on the subject, scientists haven't determined that women have consistent preferences one way or the other.

Our faces are our signatures, but when it comes to raw sex appeal, a nice chin is no match for a perfectly sculpted torso – especially from a man's perspective. Studies from around the world have found that while both sexes value appearance, men place more stock in it than women. And if there are social reasons for that imbalance, there are also biological ones. Just about any male over 14 can produce sperm, but a woman's ability to bear children depends on her age and hormone levels. Female fertility declines by two thirds between the ages of 20 and 44, and it's spent by 54. So while both sexes may eyeball potential partners, says Donald Symons, an anthropologist at the University of California in Santa Barbara, "a larger proportion of a woman's mate value can be detected from visual cues." Mounting evidence suggests there is no better cue than the relative contours of her waist and hips.

Before puberty and after menopause, females have essentially the same waistlines as males. But during puberty, while boys are amassing the bone and muscle of paleolithic hunters, a typical girl gains nearly 35 pounds of so-called reproductive fat around the hips and thighs. Those pounds contain roughly the 80,000 calories need to sustain a pregnancy, and the curves they create provide a gauge of reproductive potential. "You have to get very close to see the details of a woman's face," says Devendra Singh, the University of Texas psychologist. "But you can see the shape of her body from 500 feet, and it says more about mate value."

Almost anything that interferes with fertility – obesity, malnutrition, pregnancy, menopause – changes a woman's shape. Healthy, fertile women typically have waist-hip ratios of .6 to .8, meaning their waists are 60 to 80 percent the size of their hips, whatever their actual weight. To take one familiar example, a 36-25-36 figure would have a WHR of .7. Many women outside this range are healthy and capable of having children, of course. But as researchers in the Netherlands discovered in a 1993 study, even a slight increase in waist size relative to hip size can signal reproductive problems. Among 500 women who were attempting in vitro fertilization, the odds of conceiving during any given cycle declined by 30 percent with every 10 percent increase in WHR. In other words, a woman with a WHR of .9 was nearly a third less likely to get pregnant than one with a WHR of .8, regardless of her age or weight. From an evolutionary perspective, it's hard to imagine men not responding to such a revealing signal. And as Singh has shown repeatedly, they do.

Defining a universal standard of body beauty once seemed a fool's dream; common sense said that if spindly Twiggy and Rubens's girthy *Three Graces* could all excite admiration, then nearly anyone could. But if our ideals of size change from one time and place to the next, our taste in shapes is amazingly stable. A low waist-hip ratio is one of the few features that a long, lean Barbie doll shares with a plump, primitive fertility icon. And Singh's findings suggest that fashion won't change any time soon. In one study, he compiled the measurements of Playboy centerfolds and Miss America winners from 1923 to 1990. Their bodies got measurably leaner over the decades, yet their waist-hip ratios stayed within the narrow range of .68 to .72. (Even Twiggy was no tube; at the peak of her fame in the 1960s, the British model had a WHR of .73).

The same pattern holds when Singh generates line drawings of different female figures and asks male volunteers to rank them for attractiveness, sexiness, health and fertility. He has surveyed men of various backgrounds, nationalities and ages. And whether the judges are 8-year-olds or 85-year-olds, their runaway favorite is a figure of average weight with a .7 WHR. Small wonder that when women were liberated from corsets and bustles, they took up girdles, wide belts and other waist-reducing contraptions. Last year alone, American women's outlays for shape-enhancing garments topped a half-billion dollars.

To some critics, the search for a biology of beauty looks like a thinly veiled political program. "It's the fantasy life of American men being translated into genetics," says poet and social critic Katha Pollitt. "You can look at any feature of modern life and make up a story about why it's genetic." In truth, says Northwestern University anthropologist Micaela di Leonardo, attraction is a complicated social phenomenon, not just a hard-wired response. If attraction were governed by the dictates of baby-making, she says, the men of ancient Greece wouldn't have found young boys so alluring, and gay couples wouldn't crowd modern sidewalks. "People make decisions about sexual and marital partners inside complex networks of friends and relatives," she says. "Human beings cannot be reduced to DNA packets."

Homosexuality is hard to explain as a biological adaptation. So is stamp collecting. But no one claims that human beings are mindless automatons, blindly striving to replicate our genes. We pursue countless passions that have no direct bearing on survival. If we're sometimes attracted to people who can't help us reproduce, that doesn't mean human preferences lack any coherent design. A radio used as a doorstop is still a radio. The beauty mavens' mission – and that of evolutionary psychology in general – is not to explain everything people do but to unmask our biases and make sense of them. "Our minds have evolved to generate pleasurable experiences in response to some things while ignoring other things," says Johnston. "That's why sugar tastes sweet, and that's why we find some people more attractive than others."

The new beauty research does have troubling implications. First, it suggests that we're designed to care about looks, even though looks aren't earned and reveal nothing about character. As writer Ken Siman observes in his new book, "The Beauty Trip," "the kind [of beauty] that inspires awe, lust, and increased jeans sales cannot not be evenly distributed. In a society where everything is supposed to be within reach, this is painful to face." From acne to birth defects, we wear our imperfections as thorns, for we know the world sees them and takes note.

A second implication is that sexual stereotypes are not strictly artificial. At some level, it seems, women are designed to favor dominant males over meek ones, and men are designed to value women for youthful qualities that time quickly steals. Given the slow pace of evolutionary change, our innate preferences aren't likely to fade in the foreseeable future. And if they exist for what were once good biological reasons, that doesn't make them any less nettlesome. "Men often forgo their health, their safety, their spare time and their family life in order to get rank," says Helen Fisher, the Rutgers anthropologist, "because unconsciously, they know that rank wins women." And all too often, those who can trade cynically on their rank do.

But do we have to indulge every appetite that natural selection has preserved in us? Of course not. "I don't know any scientist who seriously thinks you can look to nature for moral guidance," says Thornhill. Even the fashion magazines would provide a better compass.

QUESTIONS

1. Describe the relationship between beauty and averageness in facial features. Is this relationship linear or curvilinear?

2. Why is the evidence from studies of very young children important in understanding whom adults find attractive?

3. According to the article, one of evolution's "goals" was to make women attracted to men, and vice versa. How might this have affected men's and women's preference for facial features? How can this view explain same-sex attraction?

4. How might the same general biological and social mechanisms combine to lead people to find excessive body fat attractive in one culture and unattractive in another?

5. Which of the phenomena discussed in this article are supported by evidence from many different modern cultures? How do opponents of biological theories respond to this type of evidence? Of the many findings discussed in this article, which do you believe makes the strongest evidence in support of some biological basis of beauty?

Ψ CHAPTER 7 Ψ

CLOSE RELATIONSHIPS:
THE NATURE OF INTIMATE RELATIONS

Reading 13: Classic

Some Evidence for Heightened Sexual Attraction Under Conditions of High Anxiety

Donald G. Dutton and Arthur P. Aron

The readings in this section address polar opposite issues in close relationships. Reading 13 below considers why we are attracted to certain people in the first place; Reading 14 following addresses why some marriages will ultimately succeed or fail. The reading below is an excellent example of social psychology at its best. The authors, social psychologists Donald Dutton and Arthur Aron, investigate the possibility that our initial sexual attraction to others may have less to do with the objective qualities they possess than the circumstances in which we first meet them. Specifically, Dutton and Aron predict that people will be more attracted to another person if they meet under emotionally charged conditions than under emotionally neutral conditions. Surprisingly, the kind of emotion felt when meeting doesn't seem to matter; negative emotions may lead to increased attraction as much as positive emotions.

The possibility that interpersonal attraction can be enhanced by strong negative emotions is actually quite old. Two thousand years ago the Greek poet Ovid advised suitors that the ideal place to woo a loved one was during gladiator fights. Although this first century poet did not explain why others would be most attracted to us if approached while they watched two men try to kill one another in hand to hand combat, twentieth century social psychology could offer an explanation. The answer might lie in Schachter and Singer's two-factor theory of emotions, about which you read in Reading 7. Recall that Schachter and Singer believed that strong but ambiguous emotions might be misattributed to other sources. In the next reading, Dutton and Aron argue that in the case of sexual attraction, any strong emotion, even unambiguous negative emotions such as disgust, fear, or hostility, might be confused for feelings of attraction whenever an appropriate object of affection is present.

Ψ

There is a substantial body of indirect evidence suggesting that sexual attractions occur with increased frequency during states of strong emotion. For example, heterosexual love has been observed to be associated both with hate (James, 1910; Suttie, 1935) and with pain (Ellis, 1936). A connection between "aggression" and sexual attractions is supported by Tinbergen's (1954) observations of intermixed courting and aggression behaviors in various animal species, and a series of experiments conducted by Barclay have indicated the existence of a similar phenomenon in human behavior. In one study, Barclay and Haber (1965) arranged for students in one class to be angered by having their professor viciously berate them for having done poorly on a recent test; another class served as a control. Subsequently, both groups were tested for aggressive feelings and sexual arousal. A manipulation check was successful, and the angered group manifested significantly more sexual arousal than did controls ($p < .01$) as measured by explicit sexual content in stories written in response to Thematic Apperception Test (TAT)-like stimuli. Similar results were obtained in two further studies (Barclay, 1969, 1970) in which fraternity and sorority members were angered by the experimenter. The 1970 study employed a female experimenter, which demonstrated that the aggression-sexual arousal link was not specific to male aggression; the 1969 study provided additional support for the hypothesis by using a physiological measure of sexual arousal (acid phosphatase content in urine samples).

Barclay has explained his findings in terms of a special aggression-sexuality link and has cited as support for his position Freud's (1938) argument that prehistoric man had to physically dominate his potential mates and also a study by Clark (1952) in which increased sexual arousal produced by viewing slides of nudes yielded increased aggression in TAT responses. Aron (1970), on the other hand, argued that an aggression-sexuality link exists, but it is only a special case of a more general relationship between emotional arousal of all kinds and sexual attraction. To demonstrate this point, he designed a study in which instead of anger, residual emotion from intense role playing was the independent variable. In this experiment, each of 40 male subjects role played with the same attractive female confederate in either a highly emotional or a minimally emotional situation. Subjects enacting highly emotional roles included significantly more sexual imagery in stories written in response to TAT-like stimuli ($p < .01$) and indicated significantly more desire to kiss the confederate ($p < .05$) than did subjects in the control condition. One possible explanation is suggested by Schachter's theory of emotion (Schachter, 1964; Schachter & Singer, 1962). He argued that environmental cues are used, in certain circumstances, to provide emotional labels for unexplained or ambiguous states of arousal. However, it is notable that much of the above-cited research indicates that a sexual attraction-strong emotion link may occur even when the emotions are unambiguous. Accordingly, taking into account both the Schachter position and findings from sexual attraction research in general, Aron (1970) hypothesized that strong emotions are relabeled as sexual attraction whenever an acceptable object is present, and emotion-producing circumstances do not require the full attention of the individual.

The present series of experiments is designed to test the notion that an attractive female is seen as more attractive by males who encounter her while they experience a strong emotion (fear) than by males not experiencing a strong emotion. Experiment 1 is an attempt to verify this proposed emotion-sexual attraction link in a natural setting. Experiments 2 and 3 are field and laboratory studies which attempt to clarify the results of Experiment 1.

EXPERIMENT 1

Method

Subjects. Subjects were males visiting either of two bridge sites who fit the following criteria: (a) between 18 and 35 years old and (b) unaccompanied by a female companion. Only one member of any group of potential subjects were contacted. A total of 85 subjects were contacted by either a male or a female interviewer.

Site. The experiment was conducted on two bridges over the Capilano River in North Vancouver, British Columbia, Canada. The "experimental" bridge was the Capilano Canyon Suspension Bridge, a five-foot-wide, 450-foot long, bridge constructed of wooden boards attached to wire cables that ran from one side to the other of the Capilano Canyon. The bridge has many arousal-inducing features such as (a) a tendency to tilt, sway, and wobble, creating the impression that one is about to fall over the side; (b) very low handrails of wire cable which contribute to this impression; and (c) a 230-foot drop to rocks and shallow rapids below the bridge. The "control" bridge was a solid wood bridge further upriver. Constructed of heavy cedar, this bridge was only 10 feet above a small, shallow rivulet which ran into the main river, had high handrails, and did not tilt or sway.

Procedure. As subjects crossed either the control or experimental bridge, they were approached by the interviewer.[1]

Female Interviewer. The interviewer explained that she was doing a project for her psychology class on the effects of exposure to scenic attractions on creative expression. She then asked potential subjects if they would fill out a short questionnaire. The questionnaire contained six filler items such as age, education, prior visits to bridge, etc. on the first page. On the second page, subjects were instructed to write a brief, dramatic story based upon a picture of a young woman covering her face with one hand and reaching with the other. The particular TAT item used in the present study was selected for its lack of obvious sexual content, since projective measures of sexual arousal based on explicit sexual stimuli tend to be highly sensitive to individual differences due to sexual defensiveness (Clark and Sensibar, 1955; Eisler, 1968; Leiman and Epstein, 1961; Lubin, 1960). If the subject agreed, the questionnaire was filled out on the bridge.

Stories were later scored for manifest sexual content according to a slightly modified version of the procedure employed by Barclay and Haber (1965). Scores ranged from 1 (no sexual content) to 5 (high sexual content) according to the most sexual reference in the story. Thus, for example, a story with any mention of sexual intercourse received 5 points, but if the most sexual reference was "girl friend," it received a score of 2; "kiss" counted as 3; and "lover," 4.

---

[1] The interviewers were not aware of the experimental hypothesis in order to prevent unintentional differential cueing of subjects in experimental and control groups.

On completion of the questionnaire, the interviewer thanked the subject and offered to explain the experiment in more detail when she had more time. At this point, the interviewer tore the corner off a sheet of paper, wrote down her name and phone number, and invited each subject to call, if he wanted to talk further. Experimental subjects were told that the interviewer's name was Gloria and control subjects, Donna, so that they could easily be classified when they called. On the assumption that curiosity about the experiment should be equal between control and experimental groups, it was felt that differential calling rates might reflect differential attraction to the interviewer.

Male interviewer. The procedure with the male interviewer was identical to that above. Subjects were again supplied with two fictitious names so that if they phoned the interviewer, they could be classified into control or experimental groups.

Results
Check on Arousal Manipulation. Probably the most compelling evidence for arousal on the experimental bridge is to observe people crossing the bridge. Forty percent of subjects observed crossing the bridge walked very slowly and carefully, clasping onto the handrail before taking each step. A questionnaire was administered to 30 males who fit the same criteria as the experimental subjects. Fifteen males on the experimental bridge were asked, "How fearful do you think the average person would be when he crossed this bridge?" The mean rating was 79 on a 100-point scale where 100 was equal to extremely fearful. Fifteen males on the control bridge gave a mean rating of 18 on the same scale ($t = 9.7$, $df = 28$, $p < .001$, two-tailed). In response to the question "How fearful were you while crossing the bridge?" experimental-bridge males gave a rating of 65 and control-bridge males a rating of 3 ($t = 10.6$, $p < .001$, $df = 28$, two-tailed). Hence, it can be concluded that most people are quite anxious on the experimental bridge but not on the control bridge. To prevent suspicion, no checks on the arousal of experimental subjects could be made.

Thematic Apperception Test Responses
Female interviewer. On the experimental bridge, 23 of 33 males who were approached by the female interviewer agreed to fill in the questionnaire. On the control bridge, 22 of 33 agreed. Of the 45 questionnaires completed, 7 were unusable either because they were incomplete or written in a foreign language. The remaining 38 questionnaires (20 experimental and 18 control) had their TAT stories scored for sexual imagery by two scorers who were experienced with TAT scoring. (Although both were familiar with the experimental hypothesis, questionnaires had been coded so that they were blind as to whether any given questionnaire was written by a control or experimental subject.) The interrater reliability was +.87.

Subjects in the experimental group obtained a mean sexual imagery score of 2.47 and those in the control group, a score of 1.41 ($t = 3.19$, $p < .01$, $df = 36$, two-tailed). Thus, the experimental hypothesis was verified by the imagery data.

TABLE 1   BEHAVIORAL RESPONSES AND THEMATIC APPERCEPTION TEST IMAGERY SCORES FOR EACH EXPERIMENTAL GROUP

Interviewer	No. filling in questionnaire	No. accepting phone number	No. phoning	Usable questionnaire	Sexual imagery score
Female					
Control bridge	22/33	16/22	2/16	18	1.41
Experimental bridge	23/33	18/23	9/18	20	2.47
Male					
Control bridge	22/42	6/22	1/6	20	.61
Experimental bridge	23/51	7/23	2/7	20	.80

Male interviewer. Twenty-three out of 51 subjects who were approached on the experimental bridge agreed to fill in the questionnaire. On the control bridge 22 out of 42 agreed. Five of these questionnaires were unusable, leaving 20 usable in both experimental and control groups. These were rated as above. Subjects in the experimental group obtained a mean sexual imagery score of .80 and those in the control group .61 (t = .36, *ns*). Hence, the pattern of result obtained by the female interviewer was not reproduced by the male interviewer.

Behavioral Data

Female interviewer. In the experimental group, 18 of the 23 subjects who agreed to the interview accepted the interviewer's phone number. In the control group, 16 out of 22 accepted (see Table 1). A second measure of sexual attraction was the number of subjects who called the interviewer. In the experimental group 9 out of 18 called, in the control group 2 out of 16 called (x^2 = 5.7, $p < .02$). Taken in conjunction with the sexual imagery data, this finding suggests that subjects in the experimental group were more attracted to the interviewer.

Male interviewer. In the experimental group, 7 out of 23 accepted the interviewer's phone number. In the control group, 6 out of 22 accepted. In the experimental group, 2 subjects called; in the control group, 1 subject called. Again, the pattern of results obtained by the female interviewer was not replicated by the male.

Although the results of this experiment provide prima facie support for an emotion-sexual attraction link, the experiment suffers from interpretative problems that often plague field experiments. The main problem with the study is the possibility of different subject populations on the two bridges. First, the well-advertised suspension bridge is a tourist attraction that may have attracted more out-of-town persons than did the nearby provincial park where the control bridge was located. This difference in subject populations may have affected the results in two ways. The experimental subjects may have been less able to phone the experimenter (if they were in town on a short-term tour) and less likely to hold out the possibility of further liaison with her. If this were the case, the resulting difference due to subject differences would have operated *against* the main hypothesis. Also, this difference in subject populations could not affect the sexual imagery scores unless one assumed the experimental bridge subjects to be more sexually deprived than controls. The results using the male interviewer yielded no significant differences in sexual imagery between experimental and control subjects; however, the possibility still exists that sexual deprivation could have interacted with the presence of the attractive female experimenter to produce the sexual imagery results obtained in this experiment.

Second, differences could exist between experimental and control populations with respect to personality variables. The experimental population might be more predisposed to thrill seeking and therefore more willing to chance phoning a strange female to effect a liaison. Also, present knowledge of personality theory does not allow us to rule out the combination of thrill seeking and greater sexual imagery. Accordingly, a second experiment was carried out in an attempt to rule out any differential subject population explanation for the results of Experiment 1.

EXPERIMENT 2

Method
Subjects. Subjects were 34 males visiting the suspension bridge who fit the same criteria as in Experiment 1.

Procedure. The chief problem of Experiment 2 was choosing a site that would allow contact with aroused and nonaroused members of the same subject population. One possibility was to use as a control group suspension-bridge visitors who had not yet crossed the bridge or who had just gotten out of their cars. Unfortunately, if a substantial percentage of this group subsequently refused to cross the bridge, the self-selecting-subject problem of Experiment 1 would not be circumvented. Alternatively, males who had just crossed the bridge could be used as a control. The problem with this strategy was that this group, having just crossed the bridge, may have felt residual anxiety of elation or both, which would confound the study. To avoid this latter problem, control subjects who had just crossed the bridge and were sitting or walking in a small park were contacted at least 10 minutes after crossing the bridge. This strategy, it was hoped, would rule out residual physiological arousal as a confounding factor. Except that a different female experimenter was used in Experiment 2 and no male interviewer condition was run, all other details of the study were identical to Experiment 1.

Results
... Thematic Apperception Test Responses. In the experimental group, 25 of 34 males who were approached agreed to fill in the questionnaire. In the second group, 25 out of 35 agreed. Of the 50 questionnaires completed, 5 were unusable because they were

incomplete. The remainder (23 experimental and 22 control) were scored for sexual imagery as in Experiment 1. The interrater reliability in Experiment 2 was +.79.

Subjects in the experimental group obtained a mean sexual imagery score of 2.99 and those in the control group, a score of 1.92 ($t = 3.07$, $p < .01$, $df = 36$, two-tailed). Thus the experimental hypothesis was again verified by the imagery data.

Behavioral Data. In the experimental group, 20 of the 25 subjects who agreed to the interview accepted the interviewer's phone number. In the control group, 19 out of 23 accepted. In the experimental group, 13 out of 20 called, while in the control group, 7 out of 23 phoned ($x^2 = 5.89$, $p < .02$). Thus the behavioral result of Experiment 1 was also replicated. ...

GENERAL DISCUSSION

The results of these studies would seem to provide a basis of support for an emotion-sexual attraction link. The Barclay studies (Barclay, 1969, 1970; Barclay and Haber, 1965) have already demonstrated such a link for aggression and sexual arousal, and the present findings seem to suggest that a link may hold for fear as well. Indeed, the present outcome would seem to be particularly satisfying in light of the very strong differences obtained from the relatively small subject populations, and because these results were obtained... outside of the laboratory in a setting in which real-world sexual attractions might be expected to occur. ...

The theoretical implications of these results are twofold. In the first place, they provide additional support in favor of the theoretical positions from which the original hypothesis was derived: the Schachter and Singer (1962) tradition of cognitive labeling of emotions and the Aron (1970) conceptual framework for sexual attraction processes. In the second place, these data seem to be inconsistent with (or at least unpredictable by) standard theories of interpersonal attraction. Both the reinforcement (Byrne, 1969) and the cognitive consistency (Festinger, 1957; Heider, 1958) points of view would seem to predict that a negative emotional state associated with the object would *decrease* her attractiveness; and neither theory would seem to be easily capable of explaining the arousal of a greater sexual emotion in the experimental condition of the present experiments.

Although the present data support the cognitive relabeling approach in general, they are consistent with more than one interpretation of the mechanics of the process. The attribution notions of Nisbett and Valins (1972), self-perception theory (Bem, 1972), and role theory (Sarbin and Allen, 1968) can all provide possible explanations for the anxiety-sexuality link. A further possible explanation is that heightened emotion, instead of being relabeled as sexual, serves merely to disinhibit the expression of preexistent sexual feelings. It is known that inhibition and sexual defensiveness influence sexual content in TAT stories (Clark, 1952), and this alternative cannot be ruled out by the present data. Yet another alternative suggested by Barclay (personal communication, 1971), is that the aggression-sexuality and anxiety-sexuality links may be independent phenomena and not necessarily subcases of a general emotion-sexuality link.

REFERENCES

ARON, A. (1970) *Relationship variables in human heterosexual attraction.* Unpublished doctoral dissertation, University of Toronto.

BARCLAY, A. M. (1969). The effect of hostility on physiological and fantasy responses. *Journal of Personality, 37,* 651-667.

BARCLAY, A.M. (1970). The effect of female aggressiveness on aggressive and sexual fantasies. *Journal of Projective Techniques and Personality Assessment, 34,* 19-26.

BARCLAY, A.M., AND HABER, R.N. (1965). The relation of aggressive to sexual motivation. *Journal of Personality, 33,* 462-475.

BEM, D. (1972). Self-perception theory. In L. Berkowitz (Ed.) *Advances in experimental social psychology.* Vol. 6. New York: Academic Press.

BYRNE, D. (1969). Attitudes and attraction. In L. Berkowitz (Ed.) *Advances in experimental social psychology,* Vol. 4. New York: Academic Press.

CLARK, R.A. (1952). The projective measurement of experimentally induced levels of sexual motivation. *Journal of Experimental Psychology, 44,* 391-399.

CLARK, R.A., AND SENSIBAR, M.R. (1955). The relationship between symbolic and manifest projections of sexuality with some incidental correlates. *Journal of Abnormal Social Psychology, 50,* 327-334.

EISLER, R.M. (1968). Thematic expression of sexual conflict under varying stimulus conditions. *Journal of Consulting and Clinical Psychology, 32,* 216-220.

ELLIS, H. (1936). *Studies in the Psychology of Sex.* New York: Random House.

FESTINGER, L. (1957). *A theory of cognitive dissonance.* Evanston, IL: Row, Peterson.

FREUD, S. (1938). *Basic writings.* New York: Modern Library.

HEIDER, F. (1958). *The psychology of interpersonal relations.* New York: Wiley.

James, W. (1910). *The principles of psychology.* Vol. 2. New York: Holt.

KELLY, J. (1967). Attribution theory in social psychology. In D. Levine (Ed.), *Nebraska Symposium on Motivation.* Lincoln: University of Nebraska Press, 1967.

LEIMAN, A.H., AND EPSTEIN, S. (1961). Thematic sexual responses as related to sexual drive and guilt. *Journal of Abnormal and Social Psychology, 63,* 169-175.

LUBIN, B. (1960). Some effects of set and stimulus properties on T.A.T. stories. *Journal of Projective Techniques, 24,* 11-16.

MURRAY, H.A. (1943). *Thematic Apperception Test manual.* Cambridge, MA: Harvard University Press.

NISBETT, R., AND VALINS, S. (1972). *Perceiving the causes of one's own behavior.* New York: General Learning Press.

SARBIN, T.R., AND ALLEN, V.L. (1968). *Role theory: Handbook of social psychology.* Reading, MA: Addison-Wesley.

SCHACHTER, S. (1959). *The psychology of affiliation.* Stanford, CA: Stanford University Press.

SCHACHTER, S. (1964). The interaction of cognitive and physiological determinants of emotional state. In L. Berkowitz (Ed.), *Advances in experimental social psychology.* Vol. 1. New York: Academic Press.

SCHACHTER, S., AND SINGER, J.E. Cognitive, social and physiological components of the emotional state. *Psychological Review,* 1962, 69, 379-399.

SUTTIE, I.D. (1935). *The origins of love and hate.* London: Kegan Paul.

TINBERGEN, N. (1954). The origin and evolution of courtship and threat display. In J.S. Huxley, A.C. Hardy, and E.B. Ford (Eds.), *Evolution as a process*. London: Allen and Unwin.

QUESTIONS

1. Which type of data – the TAT scores or the returned phone calls--do you believe is more compelling evidence that participants in the experimental condition were more sexually attracted to the female confederate?

2. Why did the confederates use different names in the different conditions? Are there any potential problems with this strategy?

3. The authors suggest two ways in which experimental participants in study 1 may have differed from control participants but are much less concerned about the possibility that they live further away than that they may be more thrill seeking. Why is the latter potential difference more concerning than the former?

4. Which of the following aspects of experimental design was lacking in study 1 but present in study 2: random selection, random assignment, experimental realism, control of potential demand characteristics, control of potential reactance?

5. The authors believe that their results are inconsistent with reinforcement and cognitive consistency theories of attraction. Do you agree? Can you think of a way to reconcile either of these theories with the data presented in these studies?

Reading 14: Contemporary

What Makes Marriage Work?

John Gottman

Whereas the last reading focused on the beginnings of relationships, this next readings focuses on their endings. Unfortunately, relationship breakups are increasingly common in America today. More than half of couples who marry will divorce, many before they even reach their seventh anniversary. For researchers in the area of close relationships, predicting which relationships will continue and which are likely to break up is an important goal. In this next reading, John Gottman discusses what he believes to be among the most important factors affecting whether a relationship is headed towards dissolution: conflict style.

After years of research and hundreds of interviews, Gottman has discovered that how couples resolve conflict is an important indicator of how likely they are to stay together. Many people believe that any conflict will harm a relationship, but Gottman argues that this is incorrect He believes that conflict is inevitable in any relationship, and that conflict often brings people closer together rather than further apart. In the following article, Gottman describes what he believes to be three healthy styles of conflict resolution. He then describes what happens to couples who don't resolve conflicts in a healthy way. Although Gottman's research focuses on married couples, his advice is likely to be equally important for people in less committed relationships.

$$\Psi$$

If you are worried about the future of your marriage or relationship, you have plenty of company. There's no denying that this is a frightening time for couples. More than half of all first marriages end in divorce; 60 percent of second marriages fail. What makes the numbers even more disturbing is that no one seems to understand why our marriages have become so fragile.

In pursuit of the truth about what tears a marriage apart or binds it together, I have found that much of the conventional wisdom – even among marital therapists – is either misguided or dead wrong. For example, some marital patterns that even professionals often take as a sign of a problem – such as having intense fights or avoiding conflict altogether – I have found can signify highly successful adjustments that will keep a couple together. Fighting, when it airs grievances and complaints, can be one of the healthiest things a couple can do for their relationship. If there's one lesson I've learned in my years of research into marital relationships – having interviewed and studied more than 200 couples over 20 years – it is that a lasting marriage results from a couple's ability to

Source: Gottman, J. , What makes marriage work? in J.Gottman, *Why Marriages Succeed or Fail*. Copyright © 1994 by John Gottman. Reprinted with the permission of Simon & Schuster.

resolve the conflicts that are inevitable in any relationship. Many couples tend to equate a low level of conflict with happiness and believe the claim "we never fight" is a sign of marital health. But I believe we grow in our relationships by reconciling our differences. That's how we become more loving people and truly experience the fruits of marriage.

Although there are other dimensions that are telling about a union, the intensity of argument seems to bring out a marriage's true colors. To classify a marriage, in my lab at the University of Washington in Seattle, I look at the frequency of fights, the facial expressions and physiological responses (such as pulse rate and amount of sweating) of both partners during their confrontations, as well as what they say to each other and in what tone of voice they interact verbally.

But there's much more to a successful relationship than knowing how to fight well. Not all stable couples resolve conflicts in the same way, nor do they mean the same thing by "resolving" their conflict. In fact, I have found that there are three different styles of problem solving into which healthy marriages tend to settle.

- *Validating.* Couples compromise often and calmly work out their problems to mutual satisfaction as they arise.
- *Volatile.* Conflict erupts often, resulting in passionate disputes.
- *Conflict-avoiding.* Couples agree to disagree, rarely confronting their differences head-on.

Previously, many psychologists might have considered conflict-avoiding and volatile marriages to be destructive. But my research suggests that all three styles are equally stable and bode equally well for the marriage's future.

"HEALTHY" MARRIAGE STYLES

One of the first things to go in a marriage is politeness. As laughter and validation disappear, criticism and pain well up. Your attempts to get communication back on track seem useless, and partners become lost in hostile and negative thoughts and feelings. Yet here's the surprise: There are couples whose fights are as deafening as thunder yet who have long-lasting, happy relationships.

The following three newly married couples accurately illustrate the three distinct styles of marriage.

Bert and Betty, both 30, both came from families that weren't very communicative, and they were determined to make communication a priority in their relationship. Although they squabbled occasionally, they usually addressed their differences before their anger boiled over. Rather than engaging in shouting matches, they dealt with their disagreements by having "conferences" in which each aired his or her perspective. Usually, they were able to arrive at a compromise.

Max, 40, and Anita, 25, admitted that they quarreled far more than the average couple. They also tended to interrupt each other and defend their own point of view rather than listen to what their partner was expressing. Eventually, however, they would reach some sort of accord. Despite their frequent tension, however, they seemed to take much delight in each other.

Joe, 29, and Sheila, 27, said they thought alike about almost everything and felt "an instant comfort" from the start. Although they spent a good deal of time apart, they still enjoyed each other's company and fought very rarely. When tension did arise, both considered solo jogging more helpful in soothing the waters than talking things out or arguing.

Not surprisingly, Bert and Betty were still happily married four years after I'd first interviewed them. However, so were Max and Anita, as well as Joe and Sheila. Marriages like Bert and Betty's, though, which emphasize communication and compromise, have long been held up as the ideal. Even when discussing a hot topic, they display a lot of ease and calm, and have a keen ability to listen to and understand each other's emotions.

That's why I call such couples "validators": In the midst of disagreement they still let their partners know that they consider his or her emotions valid, even if they don't agree with them. This expression of mutual respect tends to limit the number of arguments couples need to have.

Anita and Max take a different approach to squabbling than do Bert and Betty, yet their marriage remained just as solid over time. How can people who seem to thrive on skirmishes live happily together? The truth is that not every couple who fights this frequently has a stable marriage. But we call those who do "volatile." Such couples fight on a grand scale and have an even grander time making up.

More than the other types, volatile couples see themselves as equals. They are independent sorts who believe that marriage should emphasize and strengthen their individuality. Indeed, they are very open with each other about their feelings – both positive and negative. These marriages tend to be passionate and exciting, as if the marital punch has been spiked with danger.

Moving from a volatile to an avoidant style of marriage, like Joe and Sheila's, is like leaving the tumult of a hurricane for the placid waters of a summer lake. Not much seems to happen in this type of marriage. A more accurate name for them is "conflict minimizers," because they make light of their differences rather than resolving them. This type of successful coupling flies in the face of conventional wisdom that links marital stability to skillful "talking things out."

It may well be that these different types of couples could glean a lot from each other's approach – for example, the volatile couple learning to ignore some conflicts and the avoidant one learning how to compromise. But the prognosis for these three types of marriage is quite positive – they are each healthy adaptations to living intimately with another human being.

THE ECOLOGY OF MARRIAGE

The balance between negativity and positivity appears to be the key dynamic in what amounts to the emotional ecology of every marriage. There seems to be some kind of thermostat operating in healthy marriages that regulates this balance. For example, when partners get contemptuous, they correct it with lots of positivity – not necessarily right away, but sometime soon.

What really separates contended couples from those in deep marital misery is a healthy balance between their positive and negative feelings and actions toward each other.

Volatile couples, for example, stick together by balancing their frequent arguments with a lot of love and passion. But by balance I do not mean a 50–50 equilibrium. As part of my research I carefully charted the amount of time couples spend fighting versus interacting positively – touching, smiling, paying compliments, laughing, etc. Across the board I found there was a very specific ratio that exists between the amount of positivity and negativity in a stable marriage, whether it is marked by validation, volatility, or conflict avoidance.

That magic ratio is 5 to 1. As long as there is five times as much positive feeling and interaction between husband and wife as there is negative, the marriage was likely to be stable over time. In contrast, those couples who were heading for divorce were doing far too little on the positive side to compensate for growing negativity between them.

WARNING SIGNS: THE FOUR HORSEMEN

If you are in the middle of a troubled marriage, it can seem that your predicament is nearly impossible to sort out. But in fact unhappy marriages do resemble each other in one overriding way: they followed the same, *specific*, downward spiral before coming to a sad end.

Being able to predict what emotions and reactions lead a couple into trouble is crucial to improving a marriage's chances. By pinpointing how marriages destabilize, I believe couples will be able to find their way back to the happiness they felt when their marital adventure began.

The first cascade a couple hits as they tumble down the marital rapids is comprised of the "Four Horsemen" – four disastrous ways of interacting that sabotage your attempts to communicate with your partner. As these behaviors become more and more entrenched, husband and wife focus increasingly on the escalating sense of negativity and tension in their marriage. Eventually they become deaf to each other's efforts at peacemaking. As each new horseman arrives, he paves the way for the next, each insidiously overriding a marriage that started out full of promise.

THE FIRST HORSEMAN: CRITICISM

When Eric and Pamela married fresh out of college, it soon became clear that they had different notions of what frugality meant. Pamela found herself complaining about Eric's spending habits, yet as time passed she found that her comments did not lead to any change on her husband's part. Rather, something potentially damaging to their marriage soon began occurring: instead of complaining about his actions, she began to criticize *him*.

On the surface, there may not seem to be much difference between complaining and criticizing. But criticizing involves attacking someone's *personality* or character rather than a specific *behavior*, usually with blame. When Pamela said things like "You always think about yourself," she assaulted Eric, not just his actions, and blamed him for being selfish.

Since few couples can completely avoid criticizing each other now and then, the first horseman often takes up long-term residence even in relatively healthy marriages. One reason is that criticizing is just a short hop beyond complaining, which is actually one of the healthiest activities that can occur in a marriage. Expressing anger and disagreement makes the marriage stronger in the long run than suppressing the complaint.

The trouble begins when you feel that your complaints go unheeded and your spouse repeats the offending habits. Over time, it becomes more and more likely that your complaints will pick up steam. With each successive complaint you're likely to throw in your inventory of prior, unresolved grievances. Eventually you begin blaming your partner and being critical of his or her personality rather than of a specific deed.

One common type of criticism is to bring up a long list of complaints. I call this "kitchen sinking": you throw in every negative thing you can think of. Another form is to accuse your partner of betraying you, of being untrustworthy: "I trusted you to balance the checkbook and you let me down! Your recklessness amazes me." In contrast, complaints don't necessarily finger the spouse as a culprit; they are more a direct expression of one's own dissatisfaction with a particular situation.

Criticisms also tend to be generalizations. A telltale sign that you've slipped from complaining to criticizing is if global phrases like "you never" or "you always" start punctuating your exchanges:

Complaint: "We don't go out as much as I'd like to."

Criticism: "You never take me anywhere."

Being critical can begin innocently enough and is often the expression of pent-up, unresolved anger. It may be one of those natural self-destruct mechanisms inherent in all relationships. Problems occur when criticism becomes so pervasive that it corrodes the marriage. When that happens it heralds the arrival of the next horseman that can drag you toward marital difficulty.

THE SECOND HORSEMAN: CONTEMPT

By their first anniversary, Eric and Pamela still hadn't resolved their financial differences. Unfortunately, their fights were becoming more frequent and personal. Pamela was feeling disgusted with Eric. In the heat of one particularly nasty argument, she found herself shrieking: "Why are you so irresponsible?" Fed up and insulted, Eric retorted, "Oh, shut up. You're just a cheapskate. I don't know how I ended up with you anyway." The second horseman – contempt – had entered the scene.

What separates contempt from criticism is the intention to insult and psychologically abuse your partner. With your words and body language, you're lobbing insults right into the heart of your partner's sense of self. Fueling these contemptuous actions are negative thoughts about the partner – he or she is stupid, incompetent, a fool. In direct or subtle fashion, that message gets across along with the criticism.

When this happened, they ceased being able to remember why they had fallen in love in the first place. As a consequence, they rarely complimented each other anymore or expressed mutual admiration or attraction. The focal point of their relationship became abusiveness.

What Pamela and Eric experienced is hardly uncommon. When contempt begins to overwhelm your relationship, you tend to forget your partner's positive qualities, at least while you're feeling upset. You can't remember a single positive quality or act. This immediate decay of admiration is an important reason why contempt ought to be banned from marital interactions.

Recognizing when you or your spouse is expressing contempt is fairly easy. Among the most common signs are:

- *Insults and name-calling*
- *Hostile humor*
- *Mockery*
- *Body language* – including sneering, rolling your eyes, curling your upper lip.

It is easy to feel overly critical at times, and it is human to state criticism in a contemptuous way now and then, even in the best relationships. Yet if abusiveness seems to be a problem in your relationship, the best way to neutralize it is to stop seeing arguments with your spouse as a way to retaliate or exhibit your superior moral stance. Rather, your relationship will improve if you approach your spouse with precise complaints rather than attacking your partner's personality or character.

THE THIRD HORSEMAN: DEFENSIVENESS

Once contempt entered their home, Eric and Pamela's marriage went from bad to worse. When either of them acted contemptuously, the other responded defensively, which just made matters worse. Now they both felt victimized by the other – and neither was willing to take responsibility for setting things right. In effect, they both constantly pleaded innocent.

The fact that defensiveness is an understandable reaction to feeling besieged is one reason it is so destructive – the "victim" doesn't see anything wrong with being defensive. But defensive phrases, and the attitude they express, tend to escalate a conflict rather than resolve anything. If you are being defensive, you are adding to your marital troubles. Familiarize yourself with the signs of defensiveness so you can recognize them for what they truly are:

- *Denying Responsibility.* No matter what your partner charges, you insist in no uncertain terms that you are not to blame.
- *Making Excuses.* You claim that external circumstances beyond your control forced you to act in a certain way.
- *Disagreeing with Negative Mind-Reading.* Sometimes your spouse will make assumptions about your private feelings, behavior, or motives (in phrases such as "You think it's a waste of time" or "I know how you hate it"). When this "mind-reading" is delivered in a negative manner, it may trigger defensiveness in you.
- *Cross-Complaining.* You meet your partner's complaint (or criticism) with an immediate complaint of your own, totally ignoring what your partner has said.
- *Repeating Yourself.* Rather than attempting to understand the spouse's point of view, couples who specialize in this technique simply repeat their own position to each other again and again. Both think they are right and that trying to understand the other's perspective is a waste of time.

The first step toward breaking out of defensiveness is to no longer see your partner's words as an attack but as information that is being strongly expressed. Try to understand and empathize with your partner. This is admittedly hard to do when you feel under siege, but it is possible and its effects are miraculous. If you are genuinely open and receptive when your partner is expecting a defensive response, he or she is less likely to criticize you or react contemptuously when disagreements arise.

THE FOURTH HORSEMAN: STONEWALLING

Exhausted and overwhelmed by Pamela's attacks, Eric eventually stopped responding, even defensively, to her accusations. Their marriage went from being marred by poor communication to being virtually destroyed by none. Once Eric stopped listening to Pamela, their relationship became extraordinarily difficult to repair. Instead of arguing about specific issues, every confrontation degenerated into Pamela screaming at Eric that he was shutting her out: "You never say anything. You just sit there. It's like talking to a brick wall."

Stonewalling often happens while a couple is in the process of talking things out. The stonewaller just removes himself by turning into a stone wall. Usually someone who is listening reacts to what the speaker is saying, looks at the speaker, and says things like "Uh huh" or "Hmmm" to indicate he is tracking. But the stonewaller abandons these messages, replacing them with stony silence.

Stonewallers do not seem to realize that it is a very powerful act: It conveys disapproval, icy distance, and smugness. It is very upsetting to speak to a stonewalling listener. This is especially true when a man stonewalls a woman. Most men don't get physiologically aroused when their wives stonewall them, but wives' heart rates go up dramatically when their husbands stonewall them.

The fourth horseman need not mark the end of a relationship. But if your interactions have deteriorated to this extent you are at great risk of catapulting even farther down the marital cascade – becoming so overwhelmed by the negativity in your relationship that you end up divorced, separated, or living lonely, parallel lives in the same home. Once the fourth horseman becomes a regular resident, it takes a good deal of hard work and soul-searching to save the marriage.

The four horsemen are not the end of the line. It is only after they turn a relationship sour that the ultimate danger arises: Partners seize on powerful thoughts and beliefs about their spouses that cement their negativity. Only if these inner thoughts go unchallenged are you likely to topple down the final marital cascade, one that leads to distance and isolation. However, if you learn to recognize what is happening to your once-happy marriage, you can still develop the tools you need to regain control of it.

QUESTIONS

1. What three conflict styles does Gottman believe can characterize a healthy marriage? Prior to reading this article, would you have thought that these three styles were equally healthy?

2. How does complaining differ from criticizing? When is a marriage partner likely to switch from one to the other?

3. How does contempt differ from criticizing? What are the common signs of contempt?

4. Is a relationship in which couples express more negativity always more unstable than a relationship in which couples express less negativity? Why or why not?

5. Describe how a person in a healthy relationship might respond to his or her spouse's criticism? How would a person whose relationship was in the third stage of dissolution (i.e., characterized by the "third horseman") respond? How would a person whose relationship was in the fourth stage of dissolution respond?

Ψ

PART V

HELPING AND HURTING

OTHERS

Ψ Ψ

Ψ CHAPTER 8 Ψ

PROSOCIAL BEHAVIOR

Reading 15: Classic

Models and Helping: Naturalistic Studies in Aiding Behavior

James H. Bryan and Mary Ann Test

In 1962, many people were shocked to learn that a woman named Kitty Genovese had been pursued and slowly killed outside her apartment. Most shocking was that her long, fatal ordeal occurred in full view of more than thirty neighbors, not one of whom lifted a finger to help her until it was too late.

Alarmed by the event, social psychologists began a wave of studies aimed at understanding when people do and do not help others. Armed with a social psychological perspective suggesting that situational factors, and not dispositional factors, are most important in determining whether a person in need will receive help, this research led to many interesting findings.

In this next article, social psychologists James Bryan and Mary Test describe research showing that people will be more likely to give help if they have recently seen another person doing so. Their methodological approach was simple yet elegant. This article begins with an overview of some previous research, which leads them to believe that modeling will increase helpful behavior. Next they describe in detail two studies in which they observed the modeling effect, and finally discuss the implications of their research.

Ψ

Recently, concern has been evidenced regarding the determinants and correlates of altruistic behavior, those acts wherein individuals share or sacrifice a presumed positive reinforcer for no apparent social or material gain. Studies addressed to these behaviors have explored both individual differences in the tendency to be altruistic and the situational determinants of such responses. Gore and Rotter (1963) found that students at a southern Negro college were more likely to volunteer for a social protest movement if they perceived sources of reinforcement as internally rather than externally guided. Subjects high on internal control were more likely to volunteer as freedom riders, marchers, or petition signers than subjects who perceived others as primary agents of reinforcement. Experimental evidence has been generated supporting the often-made

Source: Bryan, J.H., and Test, M.A. (1967). Models and helping: Naturalistic studies in aiding behavior. *Journal of Personality and Social Psychology, 6,* 400-407. Copyright © 1967 by the American Psychological Association. Reprinted with permission.

assumption that guilt may serve as a stimulus to altruistic activity. Darlington and Macker (1966) found that subjects led to believe that they had harmed another through incompetent performances on the experimental tasks (three paper-and-pencil tests) were more willing than control subjects to donate blood to a local hospital. ... Midlarsky and Bryan (1967) found that children exposed to treatment conditions designed to produce empathy were more willing to donate M&M candies than subjects given control conditions, while Handlon and Gross (1959), Ugurel-Semin (1952), Wright (1942), and Midlarsky and Bryan have found sharing to be positively correlated with age among school-age children. Lastly, Berkowitz and Friedman (1967) have demonstrated that adolescents of the working class and the bureaucratic middle class are less affected in their helping behaviors by interpersonal attraction than adolescents of the entrepreneur middle class.

Three hypotheses have emerged regarding the situational determinants of self-sacrificing behaviors. One suggests that individuals behave in an altruistic fashion because of compliance to a norm of reciprocity. That is, individuals are aware of the social debts and credits established between them, and expect that ultimately the mutual exchange of goods and services will balance (Gouldner, 1960). Berkowitz and Daniels (1964) have suggested that individuals might show a generalization of such obligatory feelings and thus aid others who had not previously assisted them.

A second hypothesis was put forth by Berkowitz and his colleagues (Berkowitz, 1966; Berkowitz & Daniels, 1963; Berkowitz, Klanderman, & Harris, 1964; Daniels & Berkowitz, 1963) who have postulated the social responsibility norm. They have contended that dependency on others evokes helping responses even under conditions where the possibility of external rewards for the helper are remote. Using supervisor's ratings of an unknown and absent other to produce dependency, and a box-construction task as the dependent variable, considerable support has been generated for the suggestion that dependency increases helping.

A third major determinant of helping may be the presence of helping (or nonhelping) models. While attention to the effects of models has generally been directed toward antisocial behaviors (cf. Bandura & Walters, 1963; Freed, Chandler, Mouton, & Blake, 1955; Lefkowitz, Blake, & Mouton, 1955), some recent evidence suggests that observation of self-sacrificing models may lead to subsequent succorant behavior by children. For example, Rosenhan and White (1967) have demonstrated that children are more likely to donate highly valued gift certificates to residents of a fictitious orphanage if they have seen an adult do so. Hartup and Coates[1] found that nursery school children who have been exposed to a self-sacrificing peer were more likely to be altruistic than children not so exposed. Test and Bryan[2] found that female college students were more likely to render aid to another in computing arithmetic problems if they saw other people so doing.

---

[1] W.W. Hartup and B. Coates. *Imitation of peers as a function of reinforcement from the peer group and rewardingness of the model.* Unpublished manuscript, 1966.

[2] M.A. Test and J.H. Bryan. *Dependency, models and reciprocity.* Unpublished manuscript, 1966.

The present series of experiments was designed to test the effects of models in natural settings on subject samples other than college or high school students, and in contexts other than a schoolroom or university setting. The [two] experiments reported are concerned with the impact of observing helping models upon subsequent helping behaviors. ...

EXPERIMENT I: LADY IN DISTRESS: A FLAT TIRE STUDY

Few studies have been concerned with the effects of models upon adults, and fewer still with the impact of prosocial models upon them (Wheeler, 1966). Those that have been concerned with such behaviors have invariably employed college students as subjects. For example, Rosenbaum and Blake (1955) and Rosenbaum (1956) have found that college students exposed to a model who volunteered, upon the personal request of the experimenter, to participate in an experiment would be more likely to consent than subjects not exposed to such a model or than subjects who observed a model refuse to cooperate. Pressures toward conformity in these experiments were great, however, as the request was made directly by the experimenter and in the presence of a large number of other students.

Test and Bryan found that the observation of helping models significantly increased the subsequent offers of aid by observers. However, in that study, subjects were given the task of solving arithmetic problems and then rating their difficulty, a task ordinarily requiring autonomous efforts. Furthermore, the experiment was conducted within a university setting, a context where independence of thought is often stressed. The effects of the model may have been simply to increase the subjects' faith that assisting others was allowed. While questionnaire data of the study did not support this interpretation, such effects could not be ruled out entirely. Thus, it is possible that the model impact was simply a propriety-defining activity which reduced the inhibitions associated with such helping behavior.

In general, then, investigations of modeling that employ adults as subjects and that demand self-sacrifice on the part of subjects are limited in number, exploit strong pressures toward conformity, and rely upon college students as subjects. The present experiment was designed to assess the impact of models upon subsequent spontaneous offers of help in other than a university setting.

Method

The standard condition consisted of an undergraduate female stationed by a 1964 Ford Mustang (control car) with a flat left-rear tire. An inflated tire was leaned upon the left side of the auto. The girl, the flat tire, and the inflated tire were conspicuous to the passing traffic.

In the model condition, a 1965 Oldsmobile was located approximately 1/4 mile from the control car. The car was raised by jack under the left rear bumper, and a girl was watching a male changing the flat tire.

In the no-model condition, the model was absent; thus, only the control car was visible to the passing traffic.

The cars were located in a predominantly residential section in Los Angeles, California. They were placed in such a manner that no intersection separated the model from the control car. No turnoffs were thus available to the passing traffic. Further, opposite flows of traffic were divided by a separator such that the first U turn available to the traffic going in the opposite direction of the control car would be after exposure to the model condition.

The experiment was conducted on two successive Saturdays between the hours of 1:45 and 5:50 P.M. Each treatment condition lasted for the time required for 1000 vehicles to pass the control car. While private automobiles and trucks, motorscooters, and motorcycles were tallied as vehicles, commercial trucks, taxis, and buses were not. Vehicle count was made by a fourth member of the experiment who stood approximately 100 feet from the control car hidden from the passing motorists. On the first Saturday, the model condition was run first and lasted from 1:45 to 3:15 P.M. In order to exploit changing traffic patterns and to keep the time intervals equal across treatment conditions, the control car was moved several blocks and placed on the opposite side of the street for the no-model condition. The time of the no-model treatment was 4:00 to 5:00 P.M. On the following Saturday, counterbalancing the order and the location of treatment conditions was accomplished. That is, the no-model condition was run initially and the control car was placed in the same location that it had been placed on the previous Saturday during the model condition. The time of the no-model condition was 2:00 to 3:30 P.M. For the model condition, the control car was placed in that locale where it had been previously during the no-model condition. The time of the model condition was 4:30 to 5:30 P.M.

Individuals who had stopped to offer help were told by the young lady that she had already phoned an auto club and that help was imminent. Those who nonetheless insisted on helping her were told the nature of the experiment.

Results

The dependent variable was the number of cars that stopped and from which at least one individual offered help to the stooge by the control car. Of the 4000 passing vehicles, 93 stopped. With the model car absent, 35 vehicles stopped; with the model present, 58 halted. The difference between the conditions was statistically significant (c^2 = 5.53, corrected for continuity, df = 1, $p < .02$, two-tailed). Virtually all offers of aid were from men rather than women drivers.

The time of day had little impact upon the offering of aid. Fifty vehicles stopped during the early part of the afternoon; 43 during the later hours. Likewise, differences in help offers were not great between successive Saturdays, as 45 offers of aid were made on the first Saturday, 48 on the second Saturday.

The results of the present study support the hypothesis that helping behaviors can be significantly increased through the observation of others' helpfulness. However, other plausible hypotheses exist which may account for the findings. It is possible to account for the differences in treatment effects by differences in sympathy arousal. That is, in the model condition, the motorist observed a woman who had had some difficulty. Such observations may have elicited sympathy and may have served as a reminder to the driver of his own social responsibilities.

Another explanation of the findings revolves around traffic slowdown. It is possible that the imposition of the model condition served to reduce traffic speed, thus making subsequent stopping to help a less hazardous undertaking. While the time taken for 1000 autos to pass the control car was virtually identical in the model and no-model condition and thus not supportive of such an explanation, the "slowdown" hypothesis cannot be eliminated. Assuming the model effect to be real, one might still argue that it was not a norm of helping that was facilitated by the model, but rather that inhibitions against picking up helpless young ladies were reduced. That is, within the model condition, the passing motorists may have observed a tempted other and thus felt less constrained themselves regarding similar efforts. Indeed, the insistence of some people to help in spite of the imminent arrival of other aiders suggested the operation of motives other than simply helping. Indeed, while the authors did not index the frequency of pick-up attempts, it was clear that a rather large number were evidenced.

Because of the number of alternative explanations, the evidence supporting the hypothesis that the observation of helpers per se will increase subsequent aiding is weak. Experiment II was designed to test further the prediction that the perception of another's altruistic activity would elicit similar behavior on the part of the observer.

EXPERIMENT II: COINS IN THE KETTLE

The investigation was conducted on December 14th between the hours of 10:00 A.M. and 5:00 P.M. The subjects were shoppers at a large department store in Princeton, New Jersey. Observations made on the previous day indicated that the shoppers were overwhelmingly Caucasian females.

A Salvation Army kettle was placed on the sidewalk in front of the main entrance to the store. Two females, both in experimenter's employ, alternatively manned the kettle for periods of 25 minutes. One solicitor was a Negro, the other a Caucasian. Each wore a Salvation Army cape and hat. Although allowed to ring the Salvation Army bell, they were not permitted to make any verbal plea or to maintain eye contact with the passing shoppers, except to thank any contributor for his donation.

The model condition (M) was produced as follows: Once every minute on the minute, a male dressed as a white-collar worker would approach the kettle from within the store and contribute 5 cents. As the model donated, he started a stopwatch and walked from the kettle toward a parking lot as if searching for someone. He then returned to the store. The following 20-second period constituted the duration of the treatment condition.

Following a subsequent lapse of 20 seconds, the next 20-second period defined the no-model condition (NM). Within any one minute, therefore, both M and NM treatments occurred. There were 365 occasions of each treatment.

It should be noted that it was possible that some subjects in the NM condition observed the contribution of the model or a donor affected by the model. If that hypothesis is correct, however, the effects of such incidents would be to reduce rather than enhance the differences between treatments.

Results

The dependent variable was the number of people who independently donated to the Salvation Army. People obviously acquainted, as for example, man and wife, were construed as one potential donating unit. In such conditions, if both members of a couple contributed, they were counted as a single donor.

Since there were no differences in model effects for the Negro or Caucasian solicitor, data obtained from each were combined. The total number of contributors under the NM condition was 43; under the M condition, 69. Assuming that the chance distribution of donations would be equal across the two conditions, a chi-square analysis was performed. The chi-square equaled 6.01 ($p < .01$)[3]

In spite of precautions concerning the elimination of correlated observations within a treatment condition, it was possible for subjects in any one observational period to influence one another. Such influence may have been mediated through acquaintances not eliminated by our procedures or the observations of others as well as the model donating. A more conservative analysis of the data, insuring independent observation, was therefore made. Instead of comparing treatments by analyzing the number of donors, the analysis used, as the dependent variable, the number of observation periods in which there was a contribution, that is, those periods in which more than one donation occurred were scored identically to those in which only a single contribution was received. Occasions of donations equaled 60 in the M treatment, 43 in the NM condition. The chi-square equaled 2.89 ($p < .05$).

The results of Experiment II further support the hypothesis that observation of altruistic activity will increase such behavior among observers. But the matter is not yet entirely clear, for when the observer saw the model donate he saw two things: first, the actual donation, and second, the polite and potentially reinforcing interaction that occurred between the donor and solicitor. Conceivably, the observation of an altruistic model, per se, who was not socially reinforced for his behavior, would have little or no effect on an observer. ...

DISCUSSION

The results of [these] [two] experiments clearly replicate those of Test and Bryan and extend the findings over a variety of subject populations, settings, and tasks. The results hold for college students, motorists, and shoppers; in the university laboratory, city streets, and shopping centers; and when helping is indexed by aiding others solve

---

[3] All chi-square analyses were corrected for continuity and all tests of significance were one-tailed.

arithmetic problems, changing flat tires, or donating money to the Salvation Army. The findings then are quite consistent: the presence of helping models significantly increases subsequent altruistic behavior.

That generosity breeds generosity is interesting in light of the recent concern with helping behaviors in emergency contexts. Darley and Latané[4] and Latané and Darley[5] have found that subjects are less inclined to act quickly in emergency situations when in the presence of other potential helpers. Whether faced with a medical emergency (a simulated epileptic seizure) or a dangerous natural event (simulated fire), the rapidity with which students sought to aid was reduced by the presence of others. These findings have been interpreted in three ways: as reflecting the subjects' willingness to diffuse responsibility (others will aid); as reflecting their diffusion of blame (others didn't aid either); or as reflecting conformity to the nonpanicked stooges. It is clear that the results of [these] experiments in the present series do not follow that which might be predicted by the diffusion concepts. A giving model apparently does not lend credibility to the belief that others than the self will make the necessary sacrifices. The helping other did not strengthen the observer's willingness to diffuse his social obligations, but rather stimulated greater social responsibility. In light of these results, the delayed reaction exhibited by the subjects tested by Darley and Latané might be best attributable to conformity behavior. As they have suggested, subjects faced with a unique and stressful situation may have been either reassured by the presence of calm others or fearful of acting stupid or cowardly. Additionally, it is possible that diffusion of responsibility is only associated with anxiety-inducing situations. The current data fail to indicate that such diffusion occurs in nonstressful situations which demand fulfillment of social obligations.

While it appears clear that the behavior of the motorists and shoppers was not dictated by a variety of situational and social pressures usually associated with the study of modeling in adults or experiment in academic settings (Orne, 1962), the mechanisms underlying the effects are not obvious. While the presence of the model in the flat-tire study may have reminded the motorists as to the social responsibility norm, a hypothesis does not appear reasonable in accounting for the results in the coins-in-the-kettle [study]. The bell-ringing Salvation Army worker, with kettle and self placed squarely in the pathway of the oncoming pedestrian, would seem to be reminder enough of one's obligation toward charity. A priori, it would not appear necessary to superimpose upon that scene the donating other for purposes of cognitive curing (Wheeler, 1966).

One hypothesis to account for the model effect is that the observer is given more information regarding the consequences of such donation behavior.... It is possible that the model serves to communicate to the potential donor relevant information concerning the consequences of his act. That is, the model may demonstrate that an approach to the solicitor does not involve an unwanted interpersonal interaction (e.g., lectures on religion).

A second hypothesis to account for the data pertains to the shame-provoking capacities of the model. It is reasonable to assume that most people feel that they are, by

---

[4] J. Darley and B. Latané. *Diffusion of responsibility in emergency situations*. Unpublished manuscript, 1966.
[5] B. Latané and J. Darley. *Group inhibition of bystander intervention in emergencies*. Unpublished manuscript, 1966.

and large, benevolent and charitable. Furthermore, it is likely that such a self-image is rarely challenged: first because charitable acts are not frequently required; second, at least in the street scenes employed in the current series of studies, solicitations are made in the context of many nongiving others. That is, a multitude of negative models – of noncharitable others – surround the solicitations in the current series of studies. Indeed, the contexts are such that most people are not helping; many more cars pass than stop to offer aid to the lady in distress; and there are many more people who refuse to put coins in the kettle than those who do. However, the witnessing of a donor, an individual who not only recognizes his social responsibility but in fact acts upon it, may produce a greater challenge to the good-self image of the observer. Acts rather than thoughts may be required of the observer in order to maintain the self-image of benevolence and charity. If such is the case, then the model characteristics most effective in producing prosocial behavior by socialized adults would be those directed toward shame or guilt production (e.g., donations from the poor), rather than those reflecting potential reinforcement power (e.g., donations from the high-status).

Whatever the mechanism underlying the model effect, it does appear quite clear that prosocial behavior can be elicited through the observation of benign others.

REFERENCES

BANDURA, A., & WALTERS, R. H. (1963). *Social learning and personality development*. New York: Holt, Rinehart & Winston.

BERKOWITZ, L. (1966). A laboratory investigation of social class and national differences in helping behavior. *International Journal of Psychology, 1*, 231–240.

BERKOWITZ, L., & DANIELS, L. (1963). Responsibility and dependency. *Journal of Abnormal and Social Psychology, 66*, 429–436.

BERKOWITZ, L., & DANIELS, L. (1964). Affecting the salience of the social responsibility norm: Effects of past help on the response to dependency relationships. *Journal of Abnormal and Social Psychology, 68*, 275–281.

BERKOWITZ, L., & FRIEDMAN, P. (1967). Some social class differences in helping behavior. *Journal of Personality and Social Psychology, 5*, 217–225.

BERKOWITZ, L., KLANDERMAN, S. B., & HARRIS, R. (1964). Effects of experimenter awareness and sex of subject and experimenter on reactions to dependency relationships. *Sociometry, 27*, 327–337.

DANIELS, L., & BERKOWITZ, L. (1963). Liking and response to dependency relationships. *Human Relations, 16*, 141–148.

DARLINGTON, R. B., & MACKER, C. E. (1966). Displacement of guilt-produced altruistic behavior. *Journal of Personality and Social Psychology, 4*, 442–443.

FREED, A., CHANDLER, P., MOUTON, J., & BLAKE, R. (1955). Stimulus and background factors in sign violation. *Journal of Personality, 23*, 449.

GORE, P. M., & ROTTER, J. B. (1963). A personality correlate of social action. *Journal of Personality, 31*, 58–64.

GOULDNER, A. (1960). The norm of reciprocity: A preliminary statement. *American Sociological Review, 25*, 161–178.

HANDLON, B. J., & GROSS, P. (1959). The development of sharing behavior. *Journal of Abnormal and Social Psychology, 59*, 425–428.

LEFKOWITZ, M., BLAKE, R., & MOUTON, J. (1955). Status factors in pedestrian violation of traffic signals. *Journal of Abnormal and Social Psychology, 51*, 704–706.

MIDLARSKY, E., & BRYAN, J. H. (1967). Training charity in children. *Journal of Abnormal and Social Psychology, 5*, 408–415.

ROSENBAUM, M. (1956). The effect of stimulus and background factors on the volunteering response. *Journal of Abnormal and Social Psychology, 53*, 118–121.

ROSENBAUM, M. & BLAKE, R. (1955). Volunteering as a function of field structure. *Journal of Abnormal and Social Psychology, 50*, 193–196.

ROSENHAN, D., & WHITE, G. M. (1967). Observation and rehearsal as determinants of prosocial behavior. *Journal of Personality and Social Psychology, 5*, 424–431.

UGUREL-SEMIN, R. Moral behavior and moral judgment of children. (1952). *Journal of Abnormal and Social Psychology, 47*, 463–474.

WHEELER, L. (1966). Toward a theory of behavioral contagion. *Psychological Review, 73*, 179–192.

Wright, B. A. (1942). Altruism in children and perceived conduct of others. *Journal of Abnormal and Social Psychology, 37*, 218–233.

QUESTIONS

1. What two norms do the authors suggest might encourage people to help others in need? Could both norms operate at the same time?

2. What third factor do the authors suggest will influence helping behavior? Do they cite previous empirical evidence to support this prediction? What is the authors' goal in this research?

3. Who are the subjects in the first experiment? In what two conditions did they participate?

4. What was the major finding in each of these studies? Which of the three factors influencing altruistic behavior, discussed at the beginning of the article, can explain the results of the first study? Which can explain the results of both studies?

5. What three explanations have been suggested to explain Darley and Latané's findings? Which of these explanations do the two current studies support?

Reading 16: Contemporary

Cities with Heart

Robert V. Levine

Most of us are familiar with the stereotype that people in big cities are not as friendly or helpful as people in small cities. Looking at statistics of crime and violence, it's clear that hurtful behaviors are indeed more common in larger cities. But what about helpful behaviors? Do indices of helpful behavior show a similar pattern, with small towns being more helpful than larger cities? Or is it the case that big cities have more helpful as well as more hurtful people? Psychologist Robert Levine set out to answer this question.

In thirty-six small, medium, and large cities spread across the United States, Levine and his colleagues set about to measure the helpfulness of city residents. In all, six areas were measured, ranging from per capita donations to the United Way, to helping retrieve a stranger's dropped pen. The results of this study were sometimes surprising and sometimes not. For example, if people have ever told you that New York City was one of the least friendly places in the United States, they are, according to Levine, correct. However, Levine, a native of New York City, does not believe that the residents of such places are themselves less dispositionally helpful, only that they find themselves in an environment that discourages helpful behavior.

Ψ

Thomas Wolfe once wrote that city people "have no manners, no courtesy, no consideration for the rights of others, and no humanity." Here in post–Rodney King America, most of us would agree that urban residents see more than their share of human nature's nastier side. Ample evidence demonstrates that the rates of crime and violence rise with population density.

But what of the benevolent side of city people? While growing up in New York City, I was taught that big cities simply have more of everything, both good and bad. Of course, there were more criminals. But I was assured that beneath the seemingly harsh exteriors, you would find as many compassionate hearts as in any small town.

Over the past two years, my research group – students Todd Martinez, Garry Brase, Kerry Sorenson, and other volunteers – spent much of their summer vacations traveling nationwide conducting these experiments. We compared the frequency of helpful acts in various places to answer two basic questions. First, how does overall helping compare from one city and region to another? Second, which characteristics of communities best predict how helpful residents are toward strangers?

Source: Levine, R. V. (1993, October). Cities with heart. *American Demographics*, 46–54. Copyright © 1993 by American Demographics. Reprinted with permission.

WHERE DO PEOPLE HELP?

The team conducted six different experiments in 36 cities of various sizes in all four regions of the country:

Dropped a Pen
Walking at a moderate pace, the researcher approached a solitary pedestrian passing in the opposite direction. When 15 to 20 feet away, the researcher reached into his pocket, "accidentally" dropped his pen behind him, and continued walking. Helping was scored on a five-point scale, ranging from no help offered to picking up the pen and running back to hand it to the researcher.

Helping a Blind Person across the street
Researchers dressed in dark glasses and carrying white canes acted the role of blind persons needing help crossing the street. Just before the light turned green, they stepped up to the corner, held out their cane, and waited for help. A trial was terminated after 60 seconds or when the light turned red, whichever came first. Helping was measured on a two-point scale: helped or did not help.

A Hurt Leg
Walking with a heavy limp and wearing a large, clearly visible leg brace, researchers "accidentally" dropped and then unsuccessfully struggled to reach down for a pile of magazines as they came within 20 feet of a passing pedestrian. Helping was scored on a three-point scale ranging from no help to picking up the magazines and asking to be of further assistance.

Change for a Quarter
With a quarter in full view, researchers approached pedestrians passing in the opposite direction and asked politely if they could make change. Responses were scored on a four-point scale ranging from totally ignoring the request to stopping to check for change.

Lost Letter
A neat handwritten note reading, "I found this next to your car," was placed on a stamped envelope addressed to the researcher's home. The envelope was then left on the windshield of a randomly selected car parked at a meter in a main shopping area. The response rate was measured by the share of letters that later arrived because people were helpful enough to mail them.

United Way Contributions
As a general measure of charitable contributions, we looked at 1990 per capita contributions to United Way campaigns in each city.

The researchers conducted the experiments in downtown areas on clear summer days during primary business hours, targeting a relatively equal number of able-bodied men

Helping Behavior

Disregard for strangers seems to increase with population density and environmental stress.

(36 cities ranked by overall score for helping behavior, population density rank, environmental stress rank, and pace of life rank)

	Overall Helping Rank	Lowest Population Density	Least Environmental Stress	Fastest Pace of Life
1	Rochester, NY	Bakersfield, CA	East Lansing, MI	Boston, MA
2	East Lansing, MI	Fresno, CA	Indianapolis, IN	Buffalo, NY
3	Nashville, TN	Santa Barbara, CA	Worcester, MA	New York, NY
4	Memphis, TN	Shreveport, LA	Atlanta, GA	Salt Lake City, UT
5	Houston, TX	Chattanooga, TN	Buffalo, NY	Columbus, OH
6	Chattanooga, TN	Knoxville, TN	Memphis, TN	Worcester, MA
7	Knoxville, TN	Nashville, TN	San Francisco, CA	Providence, RI
8	Canton, OH	East Lansing, MI	Shreveport, LA	Springfield, MA
9	Kansas City, MO	Sacramento, CA	Springfield, MA	Rochester, NY
10	Indianapolis, IN	Kansas City, MO	Boston, MA	Kansas City, MO
11	St. Louis, MO	Rochester, NY	Kansas City, MO	St. Louis, MO
12	Louisville, KY	Columbus, OH	Nashville, TN	Houston, TX
13	Columbus, OH	Canton, OH	Providence, RI	Paterson, NJ
14	Detroit, MI	Indianapolis, IN	Rochester, NY	Bakersfield, CA
15	Santa Barbara, CA	Louisville, KY	Chicago, IL	Atlanta, GA
16	Dallas, TX	Memphis, TN	Louisville, KY	Detroit, MI
17	Worcester, MA	St. Louis, MO	Paterson, NJ	Youngstown, OH
18	Springfield, MA	Worcester, MA	Chattanooga, TN	Indianapolis, IN
19	San Diego, CA	Youngstown, OH	Columbus, OH	Chicago, IL
20	San Jose, CA	Springfield, MA	Dallas, TX	Philadelphia, PA
21	Atlanta, GA	Atlanta, GA	Knoxville, TN	Louisville, KY
22	Bakersfield, CA	Dallas, TX	Salt Lake City, UT	Canton, OH
23	Buffalo, NY	San Diego, CA	Detroit, MI	Knoxville, TN
24	Salt Lake City, UT	Houston, TX	Houston, TX	San Francisco, CA
25	Boston, MA	Salt Lake City, UT	Los Angeles, CA	Chattanooga, TN
26	Shreveport, LA	Buffalo, NY	Philadelphia, PA	Dallas, TX
27	Providence, RI	Providence, RI	San Jose, CA	Nashville, TN
28	Philadelphia, PA	Detroit, MI	Bakersfield, CA	San Diego, CA
29	Youngstown, OH	San Jose, CA	Fresno, CA	East Lansing, MI
30	Chicago, IL	Philadelphia, PA	New York, NY	Fresno, CA
31	San Francisco, CA	Boston, MA	Sacramento, CA	Memphis, TN
32	Sacramento, CA	San Francisco, CA	San Diego, CA	San Jose, CA
33	Fresno, CA	Los Angeles, CA	St. Louis, MO	Shreveport, LA
34	Los Angeles, CA	Paterson, NJ	Santa Barbara, CA*	Sacramento, CA
35	Paterson, NJ	Chicago, IL	Canton, OH*	Los Angeles, CA
36	New York, NY	New York, NY	Youngstown, OH*	Santa Barbara, CA*

Note: Boxes denote ties.

*data not available

Source: Environmental stress rank is based on Zero Population Growth, Environmental Stress Index, 1991; and author's research.

Towns With Pity

Overall Helping Rank	Dropped Pen	Hurt Leg	Make Change	Blind Person	Lost Letter	United Way
1	Rochester, NY	Springfield, MA	Chattanooga, TN	Louisville, KY	Kansas City, MO	San Diego, CA	Rochester, NY
2	East Lansing, MI	Santa Barbara, CA	Fresno, CA	Houston, TX	Knoxville, TN	Detroit, MI	Chattanooga, TN
3	Nashville, TN	East Lansing, MI	Nashville, TN	Knoxville, TN	Rochester, NY	East Lansing, MI	Columbus, OH
4	Memphis, TN	Louisville, KY	Sacramento, CA	Canton, OH	Bakersfield, CA	Indianapolis, IN	Indianapolis, IN
5	Houston, TX	San Francisco, CA	Shreveport, LA	Detroit, MI	Dallas, TX	Worcester, MA	St. Louis, MO
6	Chattanooga, TN	Memphis, TN	Memphis, TN	East Lansing, MI	Nashville, TN	Knoxville, TN	Kansas City, MO
7	Knoxville, TN	Dallas, TX	San Diego, CA	Boston, MA	Chicago, IL	Canton, OH	Philadelphia, PA
8	Canton, OH	Houston, TX	Providence, RI	Nashville, TN	Columbus, OH	Columbus, OH	Dallas, TX
9	Kansas City, MO	Salt Lake City, UT	San Jose, CA	Worcester, MA	East Lansing, MI	San Francisco, CA	Nashville, TN
10	Indianapolis, IN	Bakersfield, CA	Canton, OH	Santa Barbara, CA	Indianapolis, IN	San Jose, CA	Boston, MA
11	St. Louis, MO	Detroit, MI	Kansas City, MO	Buffalo, NY	St. Louis, MO	Chattanooga, TN	Springfield, MA
12	Louisville, KY	Canton, OH	Atlanta, GA	Kansas City, MO	Memphis, TN	Rochester, NY	Canton, OH
13	Columbus, OH	Knoxville, TN	Houston, TX	Rochester, NY	Buffalo, NY	Salt Lake City, UT	Atlanta, GA
14	Detroit, MI	Nashville, TN	Paterson, NJ	San Jose, CA	Houston, TX	St. Louis, MO	Worcester, MA
15	Santa Barbara, CA	St. Louis, MO	St. Louis, MO	Indianapolis, IN	Atlanta, GA	Los Angeles, CA	Louisville, KY
16	Dallas, TX	Indianapolis, IN	Bakersfield, CA	Chattanooga, TN	New York, NY	Louisville, KY	Memphis, TN
17	Worcester, MA	San Diego, CA	Youngstown, OH	Memphis, TN	Santa Barbara, CA	Memphis, TN	Buffalo, NY
18	Springfield, MA	Worcester, MA	Rochester, NY	Bakersfield, CA	Louisville, KY	Santa Barbara, CA	Detroit, MI

19	San Diego, CA	Atlanta, GA	Santa Barbara, CA	Salt Lake City, UT	Canton, OH	Youngstown, OH	Houston, TX
20	San Jose, CA	Rochester, NY	Detroit, MI	Columbus, OH	Philadelphia, PA	Houston, TX	Knoxville, TN
21	Atlanta, GA	Fresno, CA	East Lansing, MI	Springfield, IL	Shreveport, LA	Sacramento, CA	San Jose, CA
22	Bakersfield, CA	Paterson, NJ	Salt Lake City, UT	St. Louis, MO	Providence, RI	Buffalo, NY	East Lansing, MI
23	Buffalo, NY	Kansas City, MO	Dallas, TX	Fresno, CA	Detroit, MI	Dallas, TX	Chicago, IL
24	Salt Lake City, UT	Los Angeles, CA	Springfield, IL	Shreveport, IL	Los Angeles, CA	Kansas City, MO	San Francisco, CA
25	Boston, MA	Sacramento, CA	Boston, MA	Youngstown, OH	San Jose, CA	Nashville, TN	Providence, RI
26	Shreveport, LA	Shreveport, LA	Worcester, MA	Dallas, TX	Worcester, MA	New York, NY	Santa Barbara, CA
27	Providence, RI	Chattanooga, TN	Chicago, IL	Los Angeles, CA	Chattanooga, TN	Springfield, IL	Youngstown, OH
28	Philadelphia, PA	Columbus, OH	Indianapolis, IN	Philadelphia, PA	San Francisco, CA	Philadelphia, PA	San Diego, CA
29	Youngstown, OH	Boston, MA	Columbus, OH	Atlanta, GA	Youngstown, OH	Chicago, IL	New York, NY
30	Chicago, IL	Philadelphia, PA	Knoxville, TN	San Diego, CA	Boston, MA	Providence, RI	Los Angeles, CA
31	San Francisco, CA	Providence, RI	Buffalo, NY	Chicago, IL	Fresno, CA	Atlanta, GA	Sacramento, CA
32	Sacramento, CA	San Jose, CA	Louisville, KY	Providence, RI	Paterson, NJ	Boston, MA	Salt Lake City, UT
33	Fresno, CA	Youngstown, OH	Philadelphia, PA	San Francisco, CA	Sacramento, CA	Paterson, NJ	Shreveport, LA
34	Los Angeles, CA	Buffalo, NY	San Francisco, CA	Sacramento, CA	San Diego, CA	Shreveport, LA	Paterson, NJ
35	Paterson, NJ	New York, NY	New York, NY	New York, NY	Springfield, MA	Bakersfield, CA	Bakersfield, CA
36	New York, NY	Chicago, IL	Los Angeles, CA	Paterson, NJ	Salt Lake City, UT	Fresno, CA	Fresno, CA

Note: See text for explanation of individual helping tests. Boxes denote ties.
Source: 1990 per capita contributions to the United Way campaigns in each city; and author's research.

and women pedestrians. They conducted 379 trials of the blind-person episode; approached approximately 700 people in each of the dropped-pen, hurt-leg, and asking-for-change episodes; and left a total of 1,032 "lost" letters.

NEW YORK, NEW YORK

New York State is home to both the most and least helpful of the 36 cities. Rochester ranks first, closely followed by a group of small and medium-sized cities in the South and Midwest. New York City ranks last.

Generally speaking, the study did not find much difference from city to city. At the extremes, however, the differences are dramatic. In the dropped-pen situation, a stranger would have lost more than three times as many pens in Chicago as in Springfield, Massachusetts. Nearly 80 percent of passersby checked their pockets for change in first-place Louisville, compared with 11 percent in last-place Paterson, New Jersey. Fresno came in dead last on two measures, returning only half (53 percent) as many letters as did San Diego (100 percent). Also, Fresno's per capita contribution to United Way is less than one-tenth that of front-runner Rochester.

Why are people so much less helpful in some places than in others? Studies have shown that urban dwellers are more likely than rural people to do each other harm. Our results indicate that they are also less likely to do them good. This unwillingness to help increases with the degree of "cityness." In other words, density drives strangers apart.

"Cities give not the human senses room enough," wrote Ralph Waldo Emerson. Urban theorists have long argued that crowding brings out our worst nature, and these data support the notion. Places with lower population densities are far more likely to offer help, particularly in situations that call for face-to-face, spontaneous responses such as a dropped pen, a hurt leg, or the need for change. Research shows that squeezing many people into a small space leads to feelings of alienation, anonymity, and social isolation. At the same time, feelings of guilt, shame, and social commitment tend to decline. Ultimately, people feel less responsible for their behavior toward others – especially strangers.

Population density has direct psychological effects on people. It also leads to stressful conditions that can take a toll on helping behavior. For example, people are less helpful in cities that have higher costs of living. These high costs are, in turn, related to population density, because the laws of supply and demand drive up the prices of land and other resources when they are limited.

High concentrations of people also produce stress on the environment. We compared our findings with Zero Population Growth's Environmental Stress Index, which rates the environmental quality of cities. As predicted, people were less helpful in environmentally stressed-out cities.

Stressful situations and their consequent behaviors ultimately sustain one another. Violent crime results from stressful conditions but is itself a source of urban stress. Ultimately, inaction becomes the norm. Big cities see more of the worst and less of the best of human nature.

One characteristic that does not affect helping behavior is the general pace of life. In a previous study of the same cities, we looked at four indicators of the pace of life: walking speed, work speed, speaking speed, and clock and watch accuracy. Since helping people essentially demands a sacrifice of time, people who live in cities where time is at a premium would presumably be less helpful.

Yet there is no consistent relationship between a city's pace of life and its helpfulness. Some cities fit the expected pattern. New York, for example, has the third-fastest pace of life and is the least helpful place. But Rochester has the ninth-fastest pace, and its people are most helpful. Laid-back Los Angeles, the slowest city, is also one of the least helpful, ranking 34th.

Todd Martinez, who gathered data in both New York City and (pre–Rodney King situation) Los Angeles, was acutely aware of the differences between the two cities. "I hated doing L.A. People looked at me but just didn't seem to want to bother," he says. "For a few trials, I was acting the hurt-leg episode on a narrow sidewalk with just enough space for a person to squeeze by. After I dropped my magazines, one man walked up very close to me, checked out the situation, and then sidestepped around me without a word.

"Los Angeles was the only city that I worked where I found myself getting frustrated and angry when people didn't help. In New York, for some reason, I never took it personally. People looked like they were too busy to help. It was as if they saw me, but didn't really notice me or anything else around them."

To real-life strangers in need, of course, thoughts are less important than actions. The bottom line is that a stranger's prospects are just as bleak in New York as in Los Angeles. People either find the time to help or they don't.

ROCHESTER'S SECOND WIN

More than 50 years ago, sociologist Robert Angell combined a series of statistics from the 1940 census to assess the 'moral integration' of 43 U.S. cities. Angell measured the degree to which citizens were willing to sacrifice their own private interests for the public good ("Welfare Effort Index") and the frequency with which people violated one another's person and property ("Crime Index"). Angell's methods are not comparable with the current study, but to our astonishment, Rochester also ranked number one on Angell's moral integration index in 1940.

Harry Reis, a psychology professor at the University of Rochester who grew up in New York City, is "not the least bit surprised" by the performance of his adopted home. "I like to describe Rochester as a nice place to live – in both the best and the mildest sense of the word," he says. "It's very traditional and not always very innovative. But it's a town where the social fabric hasn't deteriorated as much as in other places. Unlike New York City, people here don't laugh when you speak of ideals like 'family values.' They take their norms of social responsibility seriously."

Even when people do help in New York City, their altruism sometimes takes a hard edge. On the lost-letter measure, many of the envelopes we received from people had been opened. In almost all cases, the finder had resealed the envelope or mailed the letter in a new one. Sometimes they even attached notes, usually apologizing for opening the letter. Only from New York City, however, did we receive an envelope with its entire side ripped and left open. On the back of the letter, the "helper" had scribbled, in Spanish, a very nasty accusation about the researcher's mother. Below that, he or she added in straightforward English: "F-- you." It is fascinating to imagine this angry New Yorker, perhaps cursing while walking to the mailbox, yet feeling compelled by the norm of social responsibility to assist a stranger. Ironically, this rudely returned letter added to New York's helpfulness score.

While growing up in New York City, I was taught by loving, caring people to ignore the cries of strangers. I learned to walk around people stretched unconscious on sidewalks, because I was told that they just need to "sleep it off." I learned to ignore screams from fighting couples: "they don't want your help." And I was warned to disregard the ramblings of mentally disturbed street people because "you never know how they'll react." The ultimate message: "Don't get involved."

Do our data prove that urbanites are less caring people? Perhaps not. For one thing, no comparable data from small towns exist to show that people there are more helpful than are urbanites. Furthermore, city dwellers we talked with claimed over and over that they care deeply about the needs of strangers, but that the realities of city living prohibit them from reaching out. Many are simply afraid to make contact with strangers. Some are concerned that others might not want unsolicited help. They claim that the stranger might be afraid of outside contact or, in some cases, that it would be patronizing or insulting to offer them help. People speak with nostalgia about the past, when they thought nothing of picking up hitchhikers or arranging a square meal for a hungry stranger. Many express frustration – even anger – that life today deprives them of the satisfaction of feeling like good Samaritans.

To some degree, these may be the rationalizations of unwilling helpers trying to preserve a benevolent self-image. But the evidence, in fact, indicates that helping is affected less by people's inherent nature than by the environment. Studies reveal that seemingly minor changes in a situation can drastically affect helping behavior. In particular, the size of the place where one was raised has less to do with how helpful one is than does the size of one's current home. In other words, small-town natives and urbanites are both less likely to offer help in urban areas.

The future of urban helping may not be as bleak as it seems. Just as the environment can inhibit helping behavior, researchers are currently exploring ways to modify the environment to encourage it. Experiments have found that increasing the level of personal responsibility people feel in a situation increases the likelihood they will help. It also helps to make people feel guilty when they don't help others.

A little more than a century ago, John Habberton wrote: "Nowhere in the world are there more charitable hearts with plenty of money behind them than in large cities, yet nowhere else is there more suffering." The current status of helping activity in our cities is dismal. But helping, like language and other human skills, is a learned behavior.

Research indicates that children who are exposed to altruistic models on television tend to follow suit. Just think how much good it could do them to see positive role models in real life.

QUESTIONS

1. List briefly the six areas the author of this article measured. Which tests required people to help a person they had never seen before?

2. Which city was found to be the most helpful? Did this city finish first in any individual categories?

3. What is the relationship between population density and helping behaviors? How does the author explain this?

4. Some researchers have suggested that people in a hurry are less likely to help others. Was this true in the current study?

5. Does this article suggest that people living in urban areas are less helpful than people in rural areas? Does it suggest that people living in the same city who grew up in an urban area will be less helpful than people who grew up in a rural area?

Ψ CHAPTER 9 Ψ

AGGRESSION

Reading 17: Classic

Weapons as Aggression-Eliciting Stimuli

Leonard Berkowitz and Anthony LePage

The issue of aggression is especially important today in the United States, where more people are murdered each year than in the rest of the industrialized world combined. Because of the enormous social importance of reducing violence, the study of aggression has received considerable attention by psychologists in many disciplines.

For example, personality psychologists have tried to identify traits that explain why some people are more aggressive than others. Surprisingly, this approach has not been very successful. Case studies of even the most violent figures often reveal them to be very ordinary people.

By now you can probably anticipate what kinds of approaches social psychologists have taken to understand aggression. Instead of focusing on the individual, they look for factors in the social environment that can predispose any person to behave aggressively. In this next article, Leonard Berkowitz, the most prominent figure in the social psychological study of aggression, argues that the mere presence of aggressive cues can cause people to behave aggressively. This empirical research report begins by reviewing previous studies and by generating specific hypotheses to be tested in the study. The authors then explain the procedures they used in order to test the hypotheses, and they describe their results. Finally, they provide their final summary in a closing discussion, arguing that the presence of guns can have potentially deadly consequences.

Ψ

Human behavior is often goal directed, guided by strategies and influenced by ego defenses and strivings for cognitive consistency. There clearly are situations, however, in which these purposive considerations are relatively unimportant regulators of action. Habitual behavior patterns become dominant on these occasions, and the person responds relatively automatically to the stimuli impinging upon him. Any really complete psychological system must deal with these stimulus-elicited, impulsive reactions as well as with more complex behavior patterns. More than this, we should also be able to specify

Source: Berkowitz, L., & LePage, A. (1967). Weapons as aggression-eliciting stimuli. *Journal of Personality and Social Psychology, 7,* 202–207. Copyright © 1967 American Psychological Asssociation. Reprinted with permission.

the conditions under which the various behavior determinants increase or decrease in importance.

The senior author has long contended that many aggressive actions are controlled by the stimulus properties of the available targets rather than by anticipations of ends that might be served (Berkowitz, 1962, 1964, 1965). Perhaps because strong emotion results in an increased utilization of only the central cues in the immediate situation (Easterbrook, 1959; Walters & Parke, 1964), anger arousal can lead to impulsive aggressive responses which, for a short time at least, may be relatively free of cognitively mediated inhibitions against aggression or, for that matter, purposes and strategic considerations.[1] This impulsive action is not necessarily pushed out by the anger, however. Berkowitz has suggested that appropriate cues must be present in the situation if aggressive responses are actually to occur. While there is still considerable uncertainty as to just what characteristics define aggressive cue properties, the association of a stimulus with aggression evidently can enhance the aggressive cue value of this stimulus. But whatever its exact genesis, the cue (which may be either in the external environment or represented internally) presumably elicits the aggressive response. Anger (or any other conjectured aggressive "drive") increases the person's reactivity to the cue, possibly energizes the response, and may lower the likelihood of competing reactions, but is not necessary for the production of aggressive behavior.[2]

A variety of observations can be cited in support of this reasoning (cf. Berkowitz, 1965). Thus, the senior author has proposed that some of the effects of observed violence can readily be understood in terms of stimulus-elicited aggression. According to several Wisconsin experiments, observed aggression is particularly likely to produce strong attacks against anger instigators who are associated with the victim of the witnessed violence (Berkowitz & Geen, 1966, 1967; Geen & Berkowitz, 1966). The frustrater's association with the observed victim presumably enhances his cue value for aggression, causing him to evoke stronger attacks from the person who is ready to act aggressively.

More direct evidence for the present formulation can be found in a study conducted by Lowe (1965). His subjects, in being required to learn a concept, either aggressive or [neutral] words, spoke either 20 aggressive or 20 neutral words aloud. Following this "learning task," each subject was to give a peer in an adjacent room an electric shock whenever this person made a mistake in his learning problem. Allowed to vary the intensity of the shocks they administered over a 10-point continuum, the subjects who had uttered the aggressive words gave shocks of significantly greater intensity than did the subjects who had spoken the neutral words. The aggressive words had evidently evoked implicit aggressive responses from the subjects, even though they had not been angered beforehand, which then led to the stronger attacks upon the target person in the next room when he supposedly made errors.

---

[1] Cognitive processes can play a part even in impulsive behavior, most notably by influencing the stimulus qualities (or meaning) of the objects in the situation. As only one illustration, in several experiments by the senior author (cf. Berkowitz, 1965) the name applied to the available target person affected the magnitude of the attacks directed against this individual by angered subjects.

[2] Buss (1961) has advanced a somewhat similar conception of the functioning of anger.

Cultural learning shared by many members of a society can also associate external objects with aggression and thus affect the objects' aggressive cue value. Weapons are a prime example. For many men (and probably women as well) in our society, these objects are closely associated with aggression. Assuming that the weapons do not produce inhibitions that are stronger than the evoked aggressive reactions (as would be the case, e.g., if the weapons were labeled as morally "bad"), the presence of the aggressive objects should generally lead to more intense attacks upon an available target than would occur in the presence of a neutral object.

The present experiment was designed to test this latter hypothesis. At one level, of course, the findings contribute to the current debate as to the desirability of restricting sales of firearms. Many arguments have been raised for such a restriction. Thus, according to recent statistics, Texas communities having virtually no prohibitions against firearms have a much higher homicide rate than other American cities possessing stringent firearm regulations, and J. Edgar Hoover has maintained in *Time* magazine that the availability of firearms is an important factor in murders (Anonymous, 1966). The experiment reported here seeks to determine how this influence may come about. The availability of weapons obviously makes it easier for a person who wants to commit murder to do so. But, in addition, we ask whether weapons can serve as aggression-eliciting stimuli, causing an angered individual to display stronger violence than he would have shown in the absence of such weapons. Social significance aside, and at a more general theoretical level, this research also attempts to demonstrate that situational stimuli can exert "automatic" control over socially relevant human actions.

METHOD

Subjects

The subjects were 100 male undergraduates enrolled in the introductory psychology course at the University of Wisconsin who volunteered for the experiment (without knowing its nature) in order to earn points counting toward their final grade. Thirty-nine other subjects had also been run, but were discarded because they suspected the experimenter's confederate (21), reported receiving fewer electric shocks than were actually given them (7), had not attended to information given them about the procedure (9), or were run while there was equipment malfunctioning (2).

Procedure

General Design. Seven experimental conditions were established, six organized in a 2 x 3 factorial design, with the seventh group serving essentially as a control. Of the men in the factorial design, half were made to be angry with the confederate, while the other subjects received a friendlier treatment from him. All of the subjects were then given an opportunity to administer electric shocks to the confederate, but for two-thirds of the men there were weapons lying on the table near the shock apparatus. Half of these people were informed the weapons belonged to the confederate in order to test the hypothesis that aggressive stimuli which also were associated with the anger instigator would evoke the strongest aggressive reaction from the subjects. The other people seeing the weapons were told the weapons had been left there by a previous experimenter. There was nothing on the table except the shock key when the last third of the subjects in both the angered and nonangered conditions gave the shocks. Finally, the seventh group consisted of angered men who gave shocks when there were two badminton racquets and shuttlecocks lying near the shock key. This condition sought to determine whether the presence of any object near the shock apparatus would reduce inhibitions against aggression, even if the object was not connected with aggressive behavior.

Experimental Manipulations. When each subject arrived in the laboratory, he was informed that two men were required for the experiment and that he would have to wait for the second subject to appear. After a 5-minute wait, the experimenter, acting annoyed, indicated that they had to begin because of his other commitments. He said he would have to look around outside to see if he could find another person who might serve as a substitute for the missing subject. In a few minutes the experimenter returned with the confederate. Depending upon the condition, this person was introduced as either a psychology student who had been about to sign up for another experiment or as a student who had been running another study.

The subject and confederate were told the experiment was a study of physiological reactions to stress. The stress would be created by mild electric shocks, and the subjects could withdraw, the experimenter said, if they objected to these shocks. (No subjects left.) Each person would have to solve a problem knowing that his performance would be evaluated by his partner. The "evaluations" would be in the form of electric shocks, with one shock signifying a very good rating and 10 shocks meaning the performance was judged as very bad. The men were then told what their problems were. The subject's task was to list ideas a publicity agent might employ in order to better a popular singer's record sales and public image. The other person (the confederate) had to think of things a used-car dealer might do in order to increase sales. The two were given 5 minutes to write their answers, and the papers were then collected by the experimenter who supposedly would exchange them.

Following this, the two were placed in separate rooms, supposedly so that they would not influence each other's galvanic skin response (GSR) reactions. The shock electrodes were placed on the subject's right forearm, and GSR electrodes were attached to fingers on his left hand, with wires trailing from the electrodes to the next room. The subject was told he would be the first to receive electric shocks as the evaluation of his problem solution. The experimenter left the subject's room saying he was going to turn on the GSR apparatus, went to the room containing the shock machine and the waiting confederate, and only then looked at the schedule indicating whether the subject was to be angered or not. He informed the confederate how many shocks the subject was to receive, and 30 seconds later the subject was given seven shocks (angered condition) or one shock (nonangered group). The experimenter then went back to the subject, while the confederate quickly arranged the table holding the shock key in the manner appropriate for the subject's condition. Upon entering the subject's room, the experimenter asked him how many shocks he had received and provided the subject with a brief questionnaire on which he was to rate his mood. As soon as this was completed, the subject was taken to the room holding the shock machine. Here the experimenter told the subject it was his turn to evaluate his partner's work. For one group in both the angered and nonangered conditions the shock key was alone on the table (no-object groups). For two other groups in each of these angered and nonangered conditions, however, a 12-gauge shotgun and a .38-caliber revolver were lying on the table near the key (aggressive-weapon conditions). One group in both the angered and nonangered conditions was informed the weapons belonged to the subject's partner. The subjects given this treatment had been told earlier that their partner was a student who had been conducting an experiment.[3] They now were reminded of this, and the experimenter said the weapons were being used in some way by this person in his research (associated-weapons condition); the guns were to be disregarded. The other men were told simply the weapons "belong to someone else" who "must have been doing an experiment in here" (unassociated-weapons group), and they too were asked to disregard the guns. For the last treatment, one group of angered men found two badminton racquets and shuttlecocks lying on the table near the shock key, and these people were also told the equipment belonged to someone else (badminton-racquets group).

Immediately after this information was provided, the experimenter showed the subject what was supposedly his partner's answer to his assigned problem. The subject was reminded that he was to give the partner shocks as his evaluation and was informed that this was the last time shocks would be administered in the study. A second copy of the mood questionnaire was then completed by the subject after he had delivered the shocks. Following this, the subject was asked a number of oral questions about the experiment, including what, if any, suspicions he had. (No doubts were voiced about the presence of the weapons.) At the conclusion of this interview the experiment was explained, and the subject was asked not to talk about the study.

Dependent Variables

As in nearly all the experiments conducted in the senior author's program, the number of shocks given by the subjects serves as the primary aggression measure. However, we also report here findings obtained with the total duration of each subject's shocks, recorded in thousandths of a minute. Attention is also given to each subject's rating of his mood, first immediately after receiving the partner's evaluation and again immediately after administering shocks to the partner. These ratings were made on a series of 10 13-point bipolar scales with an adjective at each end, such as "calm-tense" and "angry–not angry."

---

[3] This information evidently was the major source of suspicion; some of the subjects doubted that a student running an experiment would be used as a subject in another study, even if he was only an undergraduate. This information was provided only in the associated-weapons conditions, in order to connect the guns with the partner and consequently this ground for suspicion was not present in the unassociated-weapons groups.

TABLE 1   ANALYSIS OF VARIANCE RESULTS; FOR NUMBER OF SHOCKS GIVEN BY SUBJECTS IN FACTORIAL DESIGN

Source	df	MS	F
No. shocks received (A)	1	182.04	104.62*
Weapons association (B)	2	1.90	1.09
A x B	2	8.73	5.02*
Error	84	1.74	

$*p < .01.$

RESULTS

Effectiveness of Arousal Treatment

Analyses of variance of the responses to each of the mood scales following the receipt of the partner's evaluation indicate the prior-shock treatment succeeded in creating differences in anger arousal. The subjects getting seven shocks rated themselves as being significantly angrier than the subjects receiving only one shock ($F = 20.65$, $p < .01$). There were no reliable differences among the groups within any one arousal level. Interestingly enough, the only other mood scale to yield a significant effect was the scale "sad-happy." The aroused–seven-shocks men reported a significantly stronger felt sadness than the men getting one shock ($F = 4.63$, $p > .05$).

Aggression toward Partner

A preliminary analysis of variance of the shock data for the six groups in the 3 X 2 factorial design yielded the findings shown in Table 1. As is indicated by the significant interaction, the presence of the weapons significantly affected the number of shocks given by the subject when the subject had received seven shocks. A Duncan multiple-range test was then made of the differences among the seven conditions means, using the

TABLE 2   MEAN NUMBER OF SHOCKS GIVEN IN EACH CONDITION

	SHOCKS RECEIVED	
Condition	1	7
Associated weapons	2.60_a	6.07_d
Unassociated weapons	2.20_a	56.7_{cd}
No object	3.07	4.67_{bc}
Badminton racquets	--	4.60_b

Note: Cells having a common subscript are not significantly differen7t at the .05 level by Duncan multiple-range test. There were 10 subjects in the seven-shocks-received-badminton-racquets group and 15 subjects in each of the other conditions.

TABLE 3   MEAN TOTAL DURATION OF SHOCKS GIVEN IN EACH CONDITION

| | SHOCKS RECEIVED | |
Condition	1	7
Associated weapons	17.93_c	46.93_a
Unassociated weapons	17.33_c	39.47_{ab}
No object	24.47_{bc}	34.80_{ab}
Badminton racquets	--	34.90_{ab}

Note: The duration scores are in thousandths of a minute. Cells having a common subscript are not significantly different at the .05 level by Duncan multiple-range test. There were 10 subjects in the seven-shocks-received-badminton-racquet group and 15 subjects in each of the other conditions.

error variance from a seven-group one-way analysis of variance in the error term. The mean number of shocks administered in each experimental condition and the Duncan test results are given in Table 2. The hypothesis guiding the present study receives good support. The strongly provoked men delivered more frequent electrical attacks upon their tormentor in the presence of a weapon than when nonaggressive objects (the badminton racquets and shuttlecocks) were present or when only the shock key was on the table. The angered subjects gave the greatest number of shocks in the presence of the weapons associated with the anger instigator, as predicted, but this group was not reliably different from the angered–unassociated-weapons conditions. Both of these groups expressing aggression in the presence of weapons were significantly more aggressive than the angered–neutral-object condition, but only the associated-weapons condition differed significantly from the angered–no–object group.

Some support for the present reasoning is also provided by the shock-duration data summarized in Table 3. (We might note here, before beginning, that the results with duration scores – and this has been a consistent finding in the present research program – are less clear-cut than the findings with number of shocks given.) The results indicate that the presence of weapons resulted in a decreased number of attacks upon the partner, although not significantly so, when the subjects had received only one shock beforehand. The condition differences are in the opposite direction, however, for the men given the stronger provocation. Consequently, even though there are no reliable differences among the groups in this angered condition, the angered men administering shocks in the presence of weapons gave significantly longer shocks than the nonangered men also giving shocks with guns lying on the table. The angered–neutral-object and angered–no-object groups, on the other hand, did not differ from the nonangered–no-object condition.

Mood Changes

Analyses of covariance were conducted on each of the mood scales, with the mood ratings made immediately after the subjects received their partners' evaluation held constant in order to determine if there were condition differences in mood changes following the giving of shocks to the partner. Duncan range tests of the adjusted condition means yielded negative results, suggesting that the attacks on the partner did not produce any systematic condition differences. In the case of the felt anger ratings, there were very high correlations between the ratings given before and after the shock administration, with the Pearson rs ranging from .89 in the angered–unassociated-weapons group to .99 in each of the three unangered conditions. The subjects could have felt constrained to repeat their initial responses.

DISCUSSION

Common sense, as well as a good deal of personality theorizing, both influenced to some extent by an egocentric view of human behavior as being caused almost exclusively by motives within the individual, generally neglect the type of weapons effect demonstrated in the present study. If a person holding a gun fires it, we are told either that he wanted to do so (consciously or unconsciously) or that he pulled the trigger "accidentally." The findings summarized suggest yet another possibility: The presence of the weapon might have elicited an intense aggressive reaction from the person with the gun, assuming his inhibitions against aggression were relatively weak at the moment. Indeed, it is altogether conceivable that many hostile acts which supposedly stem from unconscious motivation really arise because of the operation of aggressive cues. Not realizing how these situational stimuli might elicit aggressive behavior, and not detecting the presence of these cues, the observer tends to locate the source of the action in some conjectured underlying, perhaps repressed, motive. Similarly if he is a Skinnerian rather than a dynamically oriented clinician, he might also neglect the operation of aggression-eliciting stimuli by invoking the concept of operant behavior, and thus sidestep the issue altogether. The sources of the hostile action, for him, too, rest within the individual, with the behavior only steered or permitted by discriminative stimuli.

Alternative explanations must be ruled out, however, before the present thesis can be regarded as confirmed. One obvious possibility is that the subjects in the weapons condition reacted to the demand characteristics of the situation as they saw them and exhibited the kind of behavior they thought was required of them. ("These guns on the table mean I'm supposed to be aggressive, so I'll give many shocks.") Several considerations appear to negate this explanation. First, there are the subjects' own verbal reports. None of the subjects voiced any suspicions of the weapons and, furthermore, when they were queried generally denied that the weapons had any effect on them. But even those subjects who did express any doubts about the experiment typically acted like the other subjects. Thus, the eight nonangered-weapons subjects who had been rejected gave only 2.50 shocks on the average, while the 18 angered–no-object or neutral-object men who had been discarded had a mean of 4.50 shocks. The 12 angered-weapon subjects who had been rejected, by contrast, delivered an average of 5.83 shocks to their partner. These latter people were evidently also influenced by the presence of weapons.

Setting all this aside, moreover, it is not altogether certain from the notion of demand characteristics that only the angered subjects would be inclined to act in conformity with the experimenter's supposed demands. The nonangered men in the weapons group did not display a heightened number of attacks on their partner. Would this have been predicted beforehand by researchers interested in demand characteristics? The last finding raises one final observation. Recent unpublished research by Allen and Bragg indicates that awareness of the experimenter's purpose does not necessarily result in an increased display of the behavior the experimenter supposedly desires. Dealing with one kind of socially disapproved action (conformity), Allen and Bragg demonstrated that high levels of experimentally induced awareness of the experimenter's interests generally produced a decreased level of the relevant behavior. Thus, if the subjects in our study had known the experimenter was interested in observing their *aggressive* behavior, they might well have given fewer, rather than more, shocks, since giving shocks is also socially disapproved. This type of phenomenon was also not observed in the weapons conditions.

Nevertheless, any one experiment cannot possibly definitely exclude all of the alternative explanations. Scientific hypotheses are only probability statements, and further research is needed to heighten the likelihood that the present reasoning is correct.

REFERENCES

ANONYMOUS. (1966). A gun-toting nation. *Time*, August 12.

BERKOWITZ, L. (1962). *Aggression: A social psychological analysis*. New York: McGraw-Hill.

BERKOWITZ, L. (1964). Aggressive cues in aggressive behavior and hostility catharsis. *Psychological Review, 71,* 104–122.

BERKOWITZ, L. (1965). The concept of aggressive drive: Some additional considerations. In L. Berkowitz (Ed.), *Advances in experimental social psychology.* Vol. 2. New York: Academic Press, 301–329.

BERKOWITZ, L., & GEEN, R. G. (1966). Film violence and the cue properties of available targets. *Journal of Personality and Social Psychology, 3,* 525–530.

BERKOWITZ, L., & GEEN, R. G. (1967). Stimulus qualities of the target of aggression: A further study. *Journal of Personality and Social Psychology, 5,* 364–368.

BUSS, A. (1961). *The psychology of aggression.* New York: Wiley.

EASTERBROOK, J. A. (1959). The effect of emotion on cue utilization and the organization of behavior. *Psychological Review, 66,* 183–201.

GEEN, R. G., & BERKOWITZ, L. (1966). Name-mediated aggressive cue properties. *Journal of Personality, 34,* 456–465.

LOEW, C. A. (1965). *Acquisition of a hostile attitude and its relationship to aggressive behavior.* Unpublished doctoral dissertation, State University of Iowa.

WALTERS, R. H., & PARKE, R. D. (1964). Social motivation, dependency, and susceptibility to social influence. In L. Berkowitz (Ed.), *Advances in experimental social psychology.* Vol. 1. New York: Academic Press, 231–276.

QUESTIONS

1. Briefly describe the stimulus-elicited aggression theory as it is described at the beginning of this article. What role, if any, does anger play in this type of aggression?

2. How did the emotional reactions of the subjects who received seven shocks differ from those who received one shock? Did their different emotional reactions influence the number of shocks they later gave to the confederate?

3. Did the presence of weapons influence the number of shocks given by subjects who had received one shock? Did it influence the number given by subjects who had received seven shocks?

4. What relationship was found in this study among aggressive cues, anger, and aggression? Did either anger or aggressive cues always lead to aggression?

5. Does the demand characteristics alternative explanation for the results, raised at the end of the article, seem plausible to you? Can you think of a way of carrying out a similar study in which demand characteristics could be ruled out entirely?

Reading 18: Contemporary

Bullying or Peer Abuse at School

Dan Olweus

Social psychologists distinguish between two types of consequences that the social environment can have on behavior. These are sometimes referred to as proximal effects and distal effects. Proximal effects have an immediate and direct impact on behavior. Distal effects have a delayed but pervasive impact on behavior. For example, in the previous reading, Berkowitz and LePage argued that the mere presence of a gun in a situation would increase people's aggressiveness in that situation. Because the presence of a gun has an effect immediately but only in that particular situation, it is said to be a proximal cause of aggression. On the other hand, it has been argued that children who watch large amounts of violence on television are more likely to be globally violent for the rest of their lives. If television violence does cause people to be more aggressive later in life and in many situations, then television viewing is said to be a distal cause of aggression.

In this next reading, psychologist Dan Olweus discusses the problem of aggression at school, or bullying. Olweus's main concern is understanding the early influences that may lead some children to become bullies. For example, he argues that the parents of children who bully tend to be less warm and less involved with their children. Olweus begins by arguing that bullying is a pervasive phenomenon that has not been adequately addressed. He then goes on to dispel some of the common myths about bullying, such as the myth that bullying is the result of competition for grades among children. Finally, he describes an intervention that he believes is successful in promoting peace on the school playground.

Ψ

"For two years, Johnny, a quiet 13-year-old, was a human plaything for some of his classmates. The teenagers badgered Johnny for money, forced him to swallow weeds and drink milk mixed with detergent, beat him up in the rest room and tied a string around his neck, leading him around as a 'pet.' When Johnny's torturers were interrogated about the bullying, they said they pursued their victim because it was fun."[1] Bullying among schoolchildren is certainly a very old and well-known phenomenon. Though many people

Source: Olweus, D. (1995, December). Bullying or peer abuse at school: Facts and intervention. *Current Directions in Psychological Science, 4,* 196–200. Copyright © by Dan Olweus. Reprinted by permission of Blackwell Publishers.
[1] Newspaper clipping, quoted in D. Olweus, *Bullying at school: What we know and what we can do* (Blackwell, Cambridge, MA and Oxford, England, 1993), p. 7.

are acquainted with the problem, it was not until fairly recently – in the early 1970s – that it became the object of systematic research.[2] For a number of years, these efforts were largely confined to Scandinavia. In the 1980s and early 1990s, however, bullying among schoolchildren began to attract attention also in other countries, such as Great Britain, Japan, the Netherlands, Australia, Canada, and the United States. In my definition, a student is being bullied or victimized when he or she is exposed, repeatedly and over time, to negative actions on the part of one or more other students. Negative actions can include physical contact, words, making faces or dirty gestures, and intentional exclusion from a group. An additional criterion of bullying is an imbalance in strength (an asymmetric power relationship): The student who is exposed to the negative actions has difficulty defending himself or herself.

SOME PREVALENCE DATA

On the basis of surveys of more than 150,000 Norwegian and Swedish students with my Bully/Victim Questionnaire, I estimated that in the autumn of 1983, some 15% of the students in Grade 1 through 9 (roughly corresponding to ages 7 through 16) in Scandinavia were involved in bully-victim problems with some regularity.[3] Approximately 9% of the students surveyed were victims, and 7% bullied other students. Very likely, these figures underestimate the number of students involved in these problems during a whole year.

Bullying is thus a considerable problem in Scandinavian schools, a problem that affects a very large number of students. Recent data (in large measure collected with my Bully/Victim Questionnaire) from a number of other countries, including the United States,[4] indicate that this problem certainly exists also outside Scandinavia and with similar or even higher prevalence rates.[5] Applying the Scandinavian percentages to the school population in the United States would yield an estimate (conservatively) that some 5 million students in Grades 1 through 9 are involved in bully-victim problems during a school year.

There are many more boys than girls who bully other students, and boys are also somewhat more often victims of bullying. However, there occurs a good deal of bullying among girls as well, but girls typically use more subtle and indirect ways of bullying. Also, boys often bully girls, and older students often bully younger ones. There is a good deal

---

[2] D. Olweus, *Hackkycklingar och oversittare: Forkning om skolmobbnig* (Almquist & Wicksell, Stockholm, Sweden, 1973); D. Olweus, *Aggression in the schools: Bullies and whipping boys* (Hemisphere Press, Washington, DC, 1978).
[3] Olweus, note 1.
[4] D. Perry, S.J. Kusel, and L.C. Perry, Victims of peer aggression, *Developmental Psychology, 24*, 807–814 (1988); D. Schwartz, K. Dodge, and J. Coie, The emergence of chronic peer victimization in boys' play groups, *Child Development, 64*, 1755–1772 (1993).
[5] For references, see D. Olweus, Annotation: Bullying at school: Basic facts and effects of a school based intervention program, *Journal of Child Psychology and Psychiatry, 35*, 1171–1190 (1994); D. Farrington, Understanding and preventing bullying, in *Crime and justice: A review of research*, Vol. 17, M. Tonry, Ed. (University of Chicago Press, Chicago, 1993).

of evidence to indicate that the behavior patterns involved in bully-victim problems are fairly stable over time.[6] Being a bully or a victim is something that is likely to continue for substantial periods of time unless systematic efforts are made to change the situation.

THREE COMMON MYTHS ABOUT BULLYING

Several common assumptions about the causes of bullying have received no support from empirical data. They include the hypotheses that bullying is a consequence of (a) large class or school size, (b) competition for grades and failure in school, and (c) differences in appearance (e.g., it is believed that students who are fat, are red haired, use glasses, or speak with an unusual dialect are particularly likely to become victims of bullying).

Because the empirical data do not support these hypotheses, one must look for other factors to find the origins of bully-victim problems. The research evidence collected so far suggests clearly that personality characteristics (i.e., typical reaction patterns, discussed in the next section), in combination with physical strength or weakness in the case of boys, are very important in the development of these problems in individual students. At the same time, other factors, such as teachers' attitudes, behavior, and routines, play a major role in determining the extent to which the problems will manifest themselves in a classroom or a school.

CHARACTERISTICS OF TYPICAL VICTIMS AND BULLIES

Briefly, the typical victims are more anxious and insecure than students in general. They are often cautious, sensitive, and quiet. Victims suffer from low self-esteem; they have a negative view of themselves and their situation. If they are boys they are likely to be physically weaker than boys in general. I have labeled this type of victim the *passive* or *submissive victim*, as opposed to the far less common provocative victim.[2,3] It seems that the behavior and attitude of passive victims are a signal that they are insecure and worthless individuals who will not retaliate if they are attacked or insulted. In a nutshell, the typical victims are characterized by an anxious and submissive reaction pattern combined (in the case of boys) with physical weakness.

In a follow-up study, I found that the former victims of bullying at school tended to be more depressed and had lower self-esteem at age 23 than their nonvictimized peers.[7] The results also clearly suggested that this was a consequence of the earlier, persistent victimization, which thus had left its scars on their minds.

---

[6] D. Olweus, Stability of aggressive reaction patterns in males: A review, *Psychological Bulletin, 86*, 852–875 (1979); D. Olweus, Aggression and peer acceptance in adolescent boys: Two short-term longitudinal studies of ratings, *Child Development, 48*, 1301–1313 (1977); Olweus (1978), note 2.

[7] D. Olweus, Victimization by peers: Antecedents and long-term outcomes, in *Social withdrawal, inhibition, and shyness in childhood*, K.H. Rubin and J.B. Assendorf, Eds. (Erlbaum, Hillsdale, NJ, 1993).

A distinctive characteristic of typical bullies is their aggression toward peers, implied in the definition of a bully. But bullies tend to be aggressive also toward adults, both teachers and parents. They are often characterized by impulsivity and strong needs to dominate other people. They have little empathy with victims of bullying. If they are boys, they are likely to be physically stronger than boys in general, and the victims in particular.

In several studies, and using various methods, I have tested the common assumption that bullies are basically insecure individuals under a tough surface. The empirical results did not support this hypothesis and pointed in fact in the opposite direction: The bullies had unusually little anxiety and insecurity, or were roughly average on such dimensions.

In summary, the typical bullies can be described as having an aggressive reaction pattern combined (in the case of boys) with physical strength. I have identified four child-rearing factors that are likely to be particularly important for the development of such a reaction pattern (in boys):[8] the basic emotional attitude of the primary caretaker(s) toward the child during early years (i.e., indifference, lack of warmth and involvement); permissiveness for aggressive behavior by the child (inadequate limit setting); use of power-assertive disciplinary techniques, such as physical punishment; and the temperament of the child (active, hotheaded).

As regards the possible psychological sources underlying bullying behavior, the pattern of empirical findings suggests at least three, partly interrelated motives (in particular in boys, who have been studied more extensively than girls). First, the bullies have strong needs for power and dominance; they seem to enjoy being in control and subduing other people. Second, in light of the family conditions under which many of them have been reared,[8] it is natural to assume that they have developed a certain degree of hostility toward the environment; as a result of such feelings and impulses, they may derive satisfaction from inflicting injury and suffering upon other individuals. Finally, there is clearly an instrumental component to their behavior. Bullies often coerce their victims to provide them with money, cigarettes, beer, and other things of value. In addition, it is obvious that bullying behavior is in many situations rewarded with prestige.

Bullying can also be viewed as a component of a more generally antisocial and rule-breaking (conduct-disordered) behavior pattern. In my follow-up studies, I have found strong support for this view. Approximately 35% to 40% of boys who were characterized as bullies in Grades 6 through 9 had been convicted of at least three officially registered crimes by the age of 24. In contrast, this was true of only 10% of the boys not classified as bullies. Thus, as young adults, the former school bullies had a fourfold increase in relatively serious, recidivist criminality.

---

[8] D. Olweus, Familial and temperamental determinants of aggressive behavior in adolescent boys: A causal analysis, *Developmental Psychology, 16*, 644–660 (1980); see also R. Loeber and M. Stouthamer-Loeber, Family factors as correlates and predictors of conduct problems and juvenile delinquency, in *Crime and justice: A review of research*, Vol. 7, M. Tonry and N. Morris, Eds. (University of Chicago Press, Chicago, 1986).

EFFECTS OF A SCHOOL-BASED INTERVENTION PROGRAM

Against this background, it is appropriate to describe briefly the effects of the intervention program that I developed and evaluated in connection with a nationwide campaign against bully-victim problems in Norwegian schools.

Evaluation of the effects of the intervention program was based on data from approximately 2,500 students originally belonging to 112 classes in Grades 4 through 7 (modal ages: 11-14) in 42 primary and secondary/junior high schools in Bergen, Norway. The subjects of the study were followed over a period of 2.5 years. Because it was not possible to use a strictly experimental setup, a quasi-experimental design (usually called a selection cohorts design) was chosen, contrasting age-equivalent groups who had or had not been exposed to the intervention program.[9] The main findings of the analyses can be summarized as follows:[3,9]

- There were marked reductions – by 50% or more – in bully-victim problems for the periods studied, with 8 and 20 months of intervention, respectively. By and large, the results applied to both boys and girls, and to students from all grades studied.
- There were also clear reductions in general antisocial behavior, such as vandalism, fighting, pilfering, drunkenness, and truancy.
- Various aspects of the social climate of the classroom registered marked improvement: improved order and discipline, more positive social relationships, and a more positive attitude to schoolwork and the school. At the same time, there was an increase in student satisfaction with school life.
- The intervention program not only affected already existing victimization problems; it also had a primary preventive effect in that it reduced considerably the number (and percentage) of new victims.

After a detailed analysis of the quality of the data and possible alternative interpretations of the findings, I concluded that it was very difficult to explain the results obtained as a consequence of (a) underreporting by the students, (b) gradual changes in the students' attitudes to bully-victim problems, (c) repeated measurement, or (d) concomitant changes in other factors, including general time trends. All in all, the changes in bully-victim problems and related behavior patterns were likely to be mainly a consequence of the intervention program and not of some other irrelevant factor. Self-reports, which were used in most of these analyses, are probably the best data source for the purposes of such studies.[10] At the same time, largely parallel results were obtained for

---

[9] For methodological details, see D. Olweus, Bully/victim problems among schoolchildren: Basic facts and effects of a school based intervention program, in *The development and treatment of childhood aggression*, D. Pepler and K.H. Rubin, Eds. (Erlbaum, Hillsdale, NJ, 1991); D. Olweus and F.D. Alsaker, Assessing change in a cohort longitudinal study with hierarchical data, in *Problems and methods in longitudinal research*, D. Magnusson, L.R. Bergman, G. Rudinger, and B. Törestad, Eds. (Cambridge University Press, New York, 1991).

[10] For a brief discussion of the validity of such self-report data, see Olweus, note 5, p. 1174, footnote.

two peer-rating variables and for teacher ratings of bully-victim problems at the class level; for the teacher data, however, the effects were somewhat weaker.

The reported effects of the intervention program must be considered quite positive, in particular because many previous attempts to systematically reduce aggressive and antisocial behavior in preadolescents and adolescents have been relatively unsuccessful. The importance of the results is accentuated by the fact that the prevalence of violence and other antisocial behavior in most industrialized societies has increased disturbingly in recent decades. In the Scandinavian countries, for instance, various forms of officially registered criminality, including criminal violence, have increased by 300% to 600% since the 1950s or 1960s. Similar changes have occurred in most Western, industrialized societies, including the United States.

BASIC PRINCIPLES

The intervention program is built on a limited set of key principles derived chiefly from research on the development and modification of the implicated problem behaviors, in particular, aggressive behavior. It is thus important to try to create a school (and, ideally, also a home) environment characterized by warmth, positive interest, and involvement from adults, on one hand, and firm limits to unacceptable behavior, on the other. Also, when limits and rules are violated, nonhostile, nonphysical sanctions should be applied consistently. Implied in the latter two principles is also a certain degree of monitoring and surveillance of the students' activities in and out of school.[11] Finally, adults both at school and at home should act as authorities, at least in some respects.

These principles have been translated into a number of specific measures to be implemented at the school, class, and individual levels. Table 1 lists the core components that are considered, on the basis of statistical analyses and experience with the program, to be particularly important.[12] With regard to implementation and execution, the program is mainly based on utilization of the existing social environment: teachers and other school personnel, students, and parents. Non-mental health professionals thus play a major role in the desired restructuring of the social environment. Experts such as school psychologists, counselors, and social workers serve important functions planning and coordinating, counseling teachers and parents (groups), and handling relatively serious cases.

Possible reasons for the effectiveness of this nontraditional intervention approach have been discussed in some detail.[13] They include changes in the opportunity and reward structures for bullying behavior (resulting in fewer opportunities and rewards for

---

[11] G.R. Patterson, Performance Models for antisocial boys, *American Psychologist, 41*, 432-444 (1986).

[12] The package constituting the intervention program consists of the Bully/Victim Questionnaire (can be ordered from the author, will be published by Blackwell in 1996), a 20-min video cassette showing scenes from the everyday lives of two bullied children (with English subtitles; can be ordered from the author), and the book *Bullying at school: What we know and what we can do,* note 1.

[13] D. Olweus, Bullying among schoolchildren: Intervention and prevention, in *Aggression and violence throughout the life span,* R.D. Peters, R.J. McMahon, and V.L. Quincy, Eds. (Sage, Newbury Park, CA, 1992).

TABLE 1   OVERVIEW OF THE CORE INTERVENTION PROGRAM

General prerequisites	
+ +	Awareness and involvement on the part of adults
Measures at the school level	
+ +	Questionnaire survey
+ +	School conference day
+ +	Better supervision during recess and lunch time
+	Formation of coordinating group
+	Meeting between staff and parents (PTA) meeting
Measures at the class level	
+ +	Class rules against bullying
+ +	Regular class meetings with students
Measures at the individual level	
+ +	Serious talks with bullies and victims
+ +	Serious talks with parents of involved students
+	Teacher and parent use of imagination

Note: + + indicates a core component; + indicates a highly desirable component.

bullying). Also, bully-victim problems can be an excellent entry point for dealing with a variety of problems that plague today's schools. Furthermore, one can view the program from the perspective of planned organizational change (with quite specific goals) and in this way link it with the current lively work on school effectiveness and school improvement.

This antibullying program is now in use or in the process of being implemented in a considerable number of schools in Europe and North America. Though there have so far been few research-based attempts to evaluate the effects of the program, unsystematic information and reports indicate that the general approach is well received by the adults in the school society and that the program (with or without cultural adaptations or additions of culture-specific components) works well under varying conditions, including ethnic diversity. In addition to the study in Bergen, there has been a recent large-scale evaluation of an implementation containing most of the core elements of the program.[14] This evaluation based on 23 schools (with a good deal of ethnic diversity) in Sheffield, United Kingdom, used a research design similar to that of the Bergen study and likewise showed results that were quite positive (though fewer behavioral aspects were studied). It can be argued that the success and possible generalizability of the program across the cultures is not really surprising, because the existing evidence seems to indicate that the factors and principles affecting the development and modification of aggressive, antisocial behavior are fairly similar across cultural contexts, at least within the Western, industrialized part of the world.

---

[14] P.K. Smith and S. Sharp, *School bullying: Insights and perspectives* (Routledge, London, 1994).

FINAL WORDS

The basic message of these findings is quite clear: With a suitable intervention program, it is definitely possible to reduce dramatically bully-victim problems in school as well as related problem behaviors. This antibullying program can be implemented with relatively simple means and without major costs; it is primarily a question of changing attitudes, behavior, and routines in school life. Introduction of the program is likely to have a number of other positive effects as well.

QUESTIONS

1. According to Olweus's data, what percentage of grade-school students bully others? What percentage are the victims of bullying? Considering his research methods, are these numbers likely to be overestimations, underestimations, or accurate?

2. Is there any truth to the notion that overweight children who wear glasses are the most likely to be the victims of bullying? What physical attributes are characteristics of victims?

3. Compare the self-esteem and insecurity of bullies and nonbullies. What parenting styles increase the likelihood that a child will bully others?

4. What does Olweus believe to be the appropriate form of punishment for bullying? What evidence suggests that combating bullying in school may have important benefits for the entire society?

5. Do you believe that problems with bullying should be dealt with by parents or by the schools? Defend your answer with evidence cited in this reading.

Ψ

PART VI

FORMULATING
PERSPECTIVES
ON THE WORLD

$\Psi \ \Psi$

Ψ CHAPTER 10 Ψ

ATTITUDES:
APPRAISING OUR SOCIAL WORLDS

Reading 19: Classic

Cognitive Consequences of Forced Compliance

Leon Festinger and James M. Carlsmith

The following reading reports one of the most influential studies in social psychology: Leon Festinger and James Carlsmith's first empirical demonstration of a phenomenon they termed cognitive dissonance. This theory explains what happens to a person's attitude if they perform a behavior that is inconsistent with that attitude. In this report the authors examined attitudes about a boring task after performing a behavior that is inconsistent with that attitude (telling a classmate that the task was interesting and intriguing). Described in this context cognitive dissonance may not seem that important. But when you notice that attitude change following counterattitudinal behavior is centrally relevant to numerous issues in health (e.g., beliefs that smoking causes cancer after smoking a first cigarette, or attitudes towards safe sex after a night of unsafe sex), parenting (e.g., attitudes towards doing chores after being paid to do them), education (e.g., attitudes towards reading after being given a gold star for turning in a book report), and consumer behavior (e.g., attitudes towards a new car after spending more money on it than planned), you'll begin to appreciate why this study was so influential.

The theory of cognitive dissonance was itself dissonant with the dominant paradigm in psychology at the time. The prevailing behaviorism, with its emphases on classical and operant conditioning, did not believe psychologists should concern themselves with mental phenomenon but only observable behavior. Cognitive dissonance broke with this tradition by speculating in detail about how people think about their own behavior. Moreover, dissonance not only considered behavior and thought but also people's motivations for thinking about their behavior, making it a very complete and thoroughly modern theory. Rarely in psychology has such a thorough and widely applicable theory been described as simply and elegantly as cognitive dissonance is here.

You will notice some abbreviations in this article that were once commonly used but are today almost never used. Participants were then referred to as "subjects" or more simply as "S." Similarly the experimenter was referred to as "E."

Ψ

Source: Festinger, L. ,and Carlsmith, J.M. (1959). Cognitive consequences of forced compliance. *Journal of Abnormal and Social Psychology, 58*, 203-210.

What happens to a person's private opinion if he is forced to do or say something contrary to that opinion?...

Let us consider a person who privately holds opinion "X" but has, as a result of pressure brought to bear on him, publicly stated that he believes "not X."

1) This person has two cognitions which, psychologically, do not fit together: one of these is the knowledge that he believes "X," the other is the knowledge that he has publicly stated that he believes "not X." If no factors other than his private opinion are considered, it would follow, at least in our culture, that if he believes "X" he would publicly state "X." Hence his cognition of his private belief is dissonant with his cognition concerning his actual public statement.

2) Similarly, the knowledge that he has said "not X" is consonant with (does fit together with) those cognitive elements corresponding to the reasons, pressures, promises of rewards and/or threats of punishment which induced him to say "not X."

3) In evaluating the total magnitude of dissonance, one must take account of both dissonances and consonances. Let us think of the sum of all the dissonances involving some particular cognition as "D" and the sum of all the consonances as "C." Then we might think of the total magnitude of dissonance as being a function of "D" divided by "D" plus "C."

   Let us then see what can be said about the total magnitude of dissonance in a person created by the knowledge that he said "not X" and really believes "X." With everything else held constant, this total magnitude of dissonance would decrease as the number and importance of the pressures which induced him to say "not X" increased.

   Thus, if the overt behavior was brought about by, say, offers of reward or threats of punishment, the magnitude of dissonance is maximal if these promised rewards or threatened punishments were just barely sufficient to induce the person to say "not X." From this point on, as the promised rewards or threatened punishment become larger, the magnitude of dissonance becomes smaller.

4) One way in which the dissonance can be reduced is for the person to change his private opinion so as to bring it into correspondence with what he has said. One would consequently expect to observe such opinion change after a person has been forced or induced to say something contrary to his private opinion. Furthermore, since the pressure to reduce dissonance will be a function of the magnitude of the dissonance, the observed opinion change should be greatest when the pressure used to elicit the overt behavior is just sufficient to do it.

The present experiment was designed to test this derivation under controlled, laboratory conditions. In the experiment we varied the amount of reward used to force persons to make a statement contrary to their private views. The prediction (from 3 and 4 above) is that the larger the reward given to the subject, the smaller will be the subsequent opinion change.

PROCEDURE

Seventy-one male students in the introductory psychology course at Stanford University were used in the experiment. In this course, students are required to spend a certain number of hours as subjects (Ss) in experiments. They choose among the available experiments by signing their names on a sheet posted on the bulletin board which states the nature of the experiment. The present experiment was listed as a two-hour experiment dealing with "Measures of Performance."

During the first week of the course, when the requirement of serving in experiments was announced and explained to the students, the instructor also told them about a study that the psychology department was conducting. He explained that, since they were required to serve in experiments, the department was conducting a study to evaluate these experiments in order to be able to improve them in the future. They were told that a sample of students would be interviewed after having served as Ss. They were urged to cooperate in these interviews by being completely frank and honest. The importance of this announcement will become clear shortly. It enabled us to measure the opinions of our Ss in a context not directly connected with our experiment and in which we could reasonably expect frank and honest expressions of opinion.

When the S arrived for the experiment on "Measures of Performance" he had to wait for a few minutes in the secretary's office. The experimenter (E) then came in, introduced himself to the S and, together, they walked into the laboratory room where the E said:

> This experiment usually takes a little over an hour but, of course, we had to schedule it for two hours. Since we have that extra time, the introductory psychology people asked if they could interview some of our subjects. [Offhand and conversationally.] Did they announce that in class? I gather that they're interviewing some people who have been in experiments. I don't know much about it. Anyhow, they may want to interview you when you're through here.

With no further introduction or explanation the S was shown the first task, which involved putting 12 spools onto a tray, emptying the tray, refilling it with spools, and so on. He was told to use one hand and to work at his own speed. He did this for one-half hour. The E then removed the tray and spools and placed in front of the S a board containing 48 square pegs. His task was to turn each peg a quarter turn clockwise, then another quarter turn, and so on. He was told again to use one hand and to work at his own speed. The S worked at this task for another half hour.

While the S was working on these tasks, the E sat, with a stop watch in his hand, busily making notations on a sheet of paper. He did so in order to make it convincing that this was what the E was interested in and that these tasks and how the S worked on them, was the total experiment. From our point of view the experiment had hardly started. The hour which the S spent working on the repetitive, monotonous tasks was intended to provide, for each S uniformly, an experience about which he would have a somewhat negative opinion.

After the half hour on the second task was over, the *E* conspicuously set the stop watch back to zero, put it away, pushed his chair back, lit a cigarette, and said:

> O.K. Well, that's all we have in the experiment itself. I'd like to explain what this has been all about so you'll have some idea of why you were doing this. [*E* pauses.] Well, the way the experiment is set up is this. There are actually two groups in the experiment. In one, the group you were in, we bring the subject in and give him essentially no introduction to the experiment. That is, all we tell him is what he needs to know in order to do the tasks, and he has no idea of what the experiment is all about, or what it's going to be like, or anything like that. But in the other group, we have a student that we've hired that works for us regularly, and what I do is take him into the next room where the subject is waiting – the same room you were waiting in before – and I introduce him as if he had just finished being a subject in the experiment. That is, I say: "This is so-and-so, who's just finished the experiment, and I've asked him to tell you a little of what it's about before you start." The fellow who works for us then, in conversation with the next subject, makes these points: [The *E* then produced a sheet headed "For Group B" which had written on it: It was very enjoyable, I had a lot of fun, I enjoyed myself, it was very interesting, it was intriguing, it was exciting. The *E* showed this to the *S* and then proceeded with his false explanation of the purpose of the experiment.] Now, of course, we have this student do this, because if the experimenter does it, it doesn't look as realistic, and what we're interested in doing is comparing how these two groups do on the experiment – the one with the previous expectation about the experiment, and the other, like yourself, with essentially none.

Up to this point the procedure was identical for *Ss* in all conditions. From this point on they diverged somewhat. Three conditions were run, Control, One Dollar, and Twenty Dollars, as follows:

Control Condition

The *E* continued:

> Is that fairly clear? [Pause.] Look, that fellow [looks at watch] I was telling you about from the introductory psychology class said he would get here a couple of minutes from now. Would you mind waiting to see if he wants to talk to you? Fine. Why don't we go into the other room to wait? [The *E* left the *S* in the secretary's office for four minutes. He then returned and said:] O.K. Let's check and see if he does want to talk to you.

One and Twenty Dollar Conditions

The E continued:

> Is that fairly clear how it is set up and what we're trying to do? [Pause.] Now, I also have a sort of strange thing to ask you. The thing is this. [Long pause, some confusion

and uncertainty in the following, with a degree of embarrassment on the part of the E. The manner of the E contrasted strongly with the preceding unhesitant and assured false explanation of the experiment. The point was to make it seem to the S that this was the first time the E had done this and that he felt unsure of himself.] The fellow who normally does this for us couldn't do it today – he just phoned in, and something or other came up for him – so we've been looking around for someone that we could hire to do it for us. You see, we've got another subject waiting [looks at watch] who is supposed to be in that other condition. Now Professor ___, who is in charge of this experiment, suggested that perhaps we could take a chance on your doing it for us. I'll tell you what we had in mind: the thing is, if you could do it for us now, then of course you would know how to do it, and if something like this should ever come up again, that is, the regular fellow couldn't make it, and we had a subject scheduled, it would be very reassuring to us to know that we had somebody else we could call on who knew how to do it. So, if you would be willing to do this for us, we'd like to hire you to do it now and then be on call in the future, if something like this should ever happen again. We can pay you a dollar (twenty dollars) for doing this for us, that is, for doing it now and then being on call. Do you think you could do that for us?

If the S hesitated, the E said things like, "It will only take a few minutes," "The regular person is pretty reliable; this is the first time he has missed," or "If we needed you we could phone you a day or two in advance; if you couldn't make it, of course, we wouldn't expect you to come." After the S agreed to do it, the E gave him the previously mentioned sheet of paper headed "For Group B" and asked him to read it through again. The E then paid the S one dollar (twenty dollars), made out a hand-written receipt form, and asked the S to sign it. He then said:

O.K., the way we'll do it is this. As I said, the next subject should be here by now. I think the next one is a girl. I'll take you into the next room and introduce you to her, saying that you've just finished the experiment and that we've asked you to tell her a little about it. And what we want you to do is just sit down and get into a conversation with her and try to get across the points on that sheet of paper. I'll leave you alone and come back after a couple of minutes. O.K.?

The E then took the S into the secretary's office where he had previously waited and where the next S was waiting (The secretary had left the office.) He introduced the girl and the S to one another saying that the S had just finished the experiment and would tell her something about it. He then left saying he would return in a couple of minutes. The girl, an undergraduate hired for this role, said little until the S made some positive remarks about the experiment and then said that she was surprised because a friend of hers had taken the experiment the week before and had told her that it was boring and that she ought to try to get out of it. Most Ss responded by saying something like "Oh, no, it's really very interesting. I'm sure you'll enjoy it." The girl, after this listened quietly, accepting and agreeing to everything the S told her. The discussion between the S and the girl was recorded on a hidden tape recorder.

After two minutes the E returned, asked the girl to go into the experimental room, thanked the S for talking to the girl, wrote down his phone number to continue the fiction that we might call on him again in the future and then said: "Look, could we check and see if that fellow from introductory psychology wants to talk to you?"

From this point on, the procedure for all three conditions was once more identical. As the *E* and the *S* started to walk to the office where the interviewer was, the *E* said: "Thanks very much for working on those tasks for us. I hope you did enjoy it. Most of our subjects tell us afterward that they found it quite interesting. You get a chance to see how you react to the tasks and so forth." This short persuasive communication was made in all conditions in exactly the same way. The reason for doing it, theoretically, was to make it easier for anyone who wanted to persuade himself that the tasks had been, indeed, enjoyable.

When they arrived at the interviewer's office, the *E* asked the interviewer whether or not he wanted to talk to the *S*. The interviewer said yes, the *E* shook hands with the *S*, said good-bye, and left. The interviewer, of course, was always kept in complete ignorance of which condition the *S* was in. The interview consisted of four questions, on each of which the *S* was first encouraged to talk about the matter and was then asked to rate his opinion or reaction on an 11-point scale. The questions are as follows:

1) Were the tasks interesting and enjoyable?
2) Did the experiment give you an opportunity to learn about your own ability to perform these tasks?
3) From what you know about the experiment and the tasks involved in it, would you say the experiment was measuring anything important? That is, do you think the results may have scientific value?
4) Would you have any desire to participate in another similar experiment?

As may be seen, the questions varied in how directly relevant they were to what the *S* had told the girl. This point will be discussed further in connection with the results.

At the close of the interview the *S* was asked what he thought the experiment was about and following this, was asked directly whether or not he was suspicious of anything and, if so, what he was suspicious of. When the interview was over, the interviewer brought the *S* back to the experimental room where the *E* was waiting together with the girl who had posed as the waiting *S*. (In the control condition, of course, the girl was not there.) the true purpose of the experiment was then explained to the *S* in detail, and the reasons for each of the various steps in the experiment were explained carefully in relation to the true purpose. All experimental *Ss* in both One Dollar and Twenty Dollar conditions were asked, after this explanation, to return the money they had been given. All *Ss*, without exception, were quite willing to return the money.

RESULTS

The major results of the experiment are summarized in Table 1 which lists, separately for each of the three experimental conditions, the average rating which the *Ss* gave at the end of each question on the interview.

**TABLE 1   AVERAGE RATINGS ON INTERVIEW QUESTIONS
FOR EACH CONDITION**

Question on Interview	Experimental Conditions		
	Control (N = 20)	One Dollar (N = 20)	Twenty Dollars (N = 20)
How enjoyable tasks were (rated from −5 to +5)	−.45	+1.35	−.05
How much they learned (rated from 0 to 10)	3.08	2.80	3.15
Scientific importance (rated from 0 to 10)	5.60	6.45	5.18
Participate in similar exp. (rated from −5 to +5)	−.62	+1.20	−.25

We will discuss each of the questions on the interview separately, because they were intended to measure different things. One other point before we proceed to examine the data. In all the comparisons, the Control condition should be regarded as a baseline from which to evaluate the results in the other two conditions. The Control condition gives us, essentially, the reactions of Ss to the tasks and their opinions about the experiment as falsely explained to them, without the experimental introduction of dissonance. The data from the other conditions may be viewed, in a sense, as changes from this baseline.

How Enjoyable the Tasks Were

The average ratings on this question, presented in the first row of figures in Table 1, are the results most important to the experiment. These results are the ones most directly relevant to the specific dissonance which was experimentally created. It will be recalled that the tasks were purposely arranged to be rather boring and monotonous. And, indeed, in the Control condition the average rating was -.45, somewhat on the negative side of the neutral point.

In the other two conditions, however, the Ss told someone that these tasks were interesting and enjoyable. The resulting dissonance could, of course, most directly be reduced by persuading themselves that the tasks were, indeed, interesting and enjoyable. In the One Dollar condition, since the magnitude of dissonance was high, the pressure to reduce this dissonance would also be high. In this condition, the average rating was 1.35, considerably on the positive side and significantly different from the Control condition at the .02 level[1] ($t = 2.48$).

In the Twenty Dollar condition, where less dissonance was created experimentally because of the greater importance of the consonant relations, there is correspondingly less evidence of dissonance reduction. The average rating in this condition is only -.05,

---

[1] All statistical tests referred to in this paper are two-tailed.

slightly and not significantly higher than the Control condition. The difference between the One Dollar and Twenty Dollar conditions is significant at the .03 level ($t = 2.22$). In short, when an S was induced, by offer of reward, to say something contrary to his private opinion, this private opinion tended to change so as to correspond more closely with what he had said. The greater the reward offered (beyond what was necessary to elicit the behavior) the smaller was the effect.

Desire to Participate in a Similar Experiment

The results from this question are shown in the last row of Table 1. This question is less directly related to the dissonance that was experimentally created for the Ss. Certainly, the more interesting and enjoyable they felt the tasks were, the greater would be their desire to participate in a similar experiment. But other factors would enter also. Hence, one would expect the results on this question to be very similar to the results on "how enjoyable the tasks were" but weaker. Actually, the result, as may be seen in the table, are in exactly the same direction , and the magnitude of the mean differences is fully as large as on the first question. The variability is greater, however, and the differences do not yield high levels of statistical significance. The difference between the One Dollar condition ($+1.20$) and the Control condition ($-.62$) is significant at the .08 level ($t = 1.78$). The difference between the One Dollar condition and the Twenty Dollar condition ($-.25$) reaches only the .15 level of significance ($t = 1.46$).

The Scientific Importance of the Experiment

This question was included because there was a chance that differences might emerge. There are, after all, other ways in which the experimentally created dissonance could be reduced. For example, one way would be for the S to magnify for himself the value of the reward he obtained. This, however, was unlikely in this experiment because money was used for the reward and it is undoubtedly difficult to convince oneself that one dollar is more than it really is. There is another possible way, however, the Ss were given a very good reason, in addition to being paid, for saying what they did to the waiting girl. The Ss were told it was necessary for the experiment. The dissonance could, consequently, be reduced by magnifying the importance of this cognition. The more scientifically important they considered the experiment to be, the less was the total magnitude of dissonance. It is possible, then, that the results on this questions, shown in the third row of figures in Table 1, might reflect dissonance reduction.

The results are weakly in line with what one would expect if the dissonance were somewhat reduced in this manner. The One Dollar condition is higher than the other two. The difference between the One and Twenty Dollar conditions reaches the .08 level of significance on a two-tailed test ($t = 1.79$). The difference between the One Dollar and Control conditions is not impressive at all ($t = 1.21$). The result that the Twenty Dollar condition is actually lower than the Control condition is undoubtedly a matter of chance ($t = 0.58$).

How Much They Learned From the Experiment

The results on this question are shown in the second row of figures in Table 1. The question was included because, as far as we could see, it had nothing to do with the dissonance that was experimentally created and could not be used for dissonance reduction. One would then expect no differences at all among the three conditions. We felt it was important to show that the effect was not a completely general one but was specific to the content of the dissonance which was created. As can be readily seen in Table 1, there are only negligible differences among conditions. The highest t value for any of these differences is only 0.48.

SUMMARY

Recently, Festinger (1957) has proposed a theory concerning cognitive dissonance. Two derivations from this theory are tested here. These are:

1) If a person is induced to do or say something which is contrary to his private opinion, there will be a tendency for him to change his opinion so as to bring it into correspondence with what he has done or said.
2) The larger the pressure used to elicit the overt behavior (beyond the minimum needed to elicit it) the weaker will be the above-mentioned tendency.

A laboratory experiment was designed to test these derivations. Subjects were subjected to a boring experience and then paid to tell someone that the experience had been interesting and enjoyable. The amount of money paid the subject was varied. The private opinions of the subjects concerning the experiences were then determined.

The results strongly corroborate the theory that was tested.

REFERENCE

FESTINGER, L. (1957). *A theory of cognitive dissonance*. Evanston, IL: Row Peterson.

QUESTIONS

1. Why did the experimenters ask subjects to rate how much they learned from the study? What was the significance of this question?

2. The authors believe that total dissonance is a function of dissonance plus (or perhaps minus) consonance. Which of these two quantities did the experimental manipulation influence?

3. The authors hoped that one dollar would provide the theoretically important "barely sufficient" motivation to lie. Do the results of the study suggest that the authors were successful in providing that precise level of motivation?

4. What predictions would the theory of operant conditioning make for participants in the one and twenty dollar conditions? Were these predictions supported here?

5. The authors believe that the offer of twenty dollars affected participants' response to questions about the study by reducing their total dissonance. Can you think of any alternative explanations for these findings?

Reading 20: Contemporary

Toward an Understanding of the Motivation Underlying Dissonance Effects: Is the Production of Aversive Consequences Necessary?

Eddie Harmon-Jones

The contemporary reading we have selected for the area of attitudes is unique for this book in that the theory it argues for is the same as the theory argued for in the previous classic reading. This does not mean, however, that the original formulation of cognitive dissonance has remained unchallenged in the forty years separating the publication of the two readings. As Harmon-Jones points out at the beginning of this reading, new formulations of and alternative explanations for cognitive dissonance began to appear shortly after Festinger and Carlsmith's 1959 seminal paper was published (reprinted in Reading 19). Among the more influential of these were self-perception theory, self-affirmation theory, and the aversive-consequences revision. These newer theories have won many supporters in the past two decades. Recently, however, supporters of the original theory have been mounting a counter attack. The next reading is part of this very new movement to return to the original formulation of cognitive dissonance.

At issue in this reading is the question of whether people will change their attitude after counter-attitudinal behavior only if their behavior has foreseeable aversive consequences. Recall that Festinger and Carlsmith argued that attitude change occurs any time we engage in counter-attitudinal behavior as the result of a need to see one's own actions and attitudes as being consistent. If instead attitude change occurs only if our behavior is expected to have negative consequences for ourselves or another, then something other than the need to see oneself as being consistent must be operating. Perhaps the important need is that others see us as being consistent or that we see ourselves as being good people (as was argued by self-affirmation theory). In this reading, Harmon-Jones argues that attitude change does occur in the absence of any foreseeable negative consequence and, thus, that Festinger was right in suggesting that the important motive underlying dissonance is a need to see oneself as being consistent.

In the 1960s, researchers began to challenge the original theory of cognitive dissonance and proposed that *cognitive discrepancy*... was not the cause of the cognitive and behavioral changes that were observed in experiments testing dissonance theory. Several revisions

Source: Harmon-Jones, E. (1998). Toward an understanding of the motivation underlying dissonance effects: Is the production of aversive consequences necessary? In Harmon-Jones, E., and Mills, J., *Cognitive Dissonance: Progress on a Pivotal Theory in Social Psychology*. Washington: American Psychological Association, 71-99. Copyright © 1998 by the American Psychological Association. Reprinted by permission.

to the original theory emerged (Aronson, 1969; Collins, 1969; Cooper and Worchel, 1970). One of the most prevalent revisions posited, in contrast to the original theory of dissonance, that cognitive discrepancy was not necessary or sufficient to generate the cognitive and behavioral changes. This revision, which I refer to as the *aversive-consequences* revision, posited that feeling personally responsible for the production of foreseeable aversive consequences was necessary and sufficient to cause these effects (Cooper and Fazio, 1984). Addressing whether the production of aversive consequences is necessary to create dissonance is one of the most fundamental and important questions for dissonance theory and research – it concerns the underlying motivational force driving dissonance effects. In the present chapter, I provide a brief overview of the original version of the theory of cognitive dissonance (see Festinger, 1957... for a more complete description) and the aversive-consequences revision. I then review evidence obtained in a variety of experimental paradigms that indicates that the production of aversive consequences is not necessary to create dissonance effects and that cognitive discrepancy, as defined by the original theory, is sufficient to cause dissonance effects. I conclude by proposing an extension of the original theory that assists in understanding the function of dissonance processes.

THE ORIGINAL VERSION

The original statement of cognitive dissonance theory (Festinger, 1957) proposed that discrepancy between cognitions creates a negative affective state that motivates individuals to attempt to reduce or eliminate the discrepancy between cognitions... . Several paradigms have been used to test predictions derived from dissonance theory. In each of these paradigms, the availability of the cognitions that serve to make the entire set of relevant cognitions more or less discrepant is manipulated. In the induced-compliance paradigm, participants are induced to act contrary to an attitude, and if they are provided few consonant cognitions (few reasons or little justification) for doing so, they are hypothesized to experience dissonance and reduce it, usually by changing their attitude to be more consistent with their behavior. In one of the first induced-compliance experiments, Festinger and Carlsmith (1959) paid participants either $1 (low justification) or $20 (high justification) to tell a fellow participant (confederate) that dull and boring tasks were very interesting and to remain on call to do it again in the future. After participants told this to the confederate, they were asked how interesting and enjoyable the tasks were. As predicted, participants given little justification for performing the counterattitudinal behavior rated the tasks as more interesting than did participants given much justification. Festinger and Carlsmith posited that participants provided low justification (just enough justification to say the counterattitudinal statement) experienced dissonance and changed their attitudes because of the inconsistency between their original attitude (they believed that the task was boring) and their behavior (they had said that the task was interesting). Participants provided with high justification, on the other hand, experienced little dissonance, because receiving $20 to perform the behavior justified the behavior or was consonant with the behavior.

In later research (Brehm and Cohen, 1962), dissonance was manipulated by means of perceived choice. Having low choice to behave counterattitudinally is consonant with that behavior whereas having high choice is not. Experiments found that participants who were given high choice, as opposed to low choice, to write counterattitudinal essays changed their attitudes to be more consistent with their behavior.

AVERSIVE-CONSEQUENCES REVISION

Within the decade after the publication of the provocative Festinger and Carlsmith (1959) experiment, researchers offered alternative theoretical and experimental accounts for their results. One alternative account suggested that low-justification participants in the Festinger and Carlsmith experiment changed their attitudes not because of cognitive discrepancy, but because their actions brought about an aversive event (convincing another person to expect boring tasks to be interesting). In one of the first experiments testing this explanation, Cooper and Worchel (1970) replicated and extended the Festinger and Carlsmith study. Cooper and Worchel found that low-justification participants changed their attitudes to be consistent with their behavior when the confederate believed their statement but not when the confederate did not believe their statement.

Using a slightly different procedure, other research has suggested that when the counterattitudinal actions do not cause aversive consequences, attitude change does not occur (e.g., Collins and Hoyt, 1972; Goethals and Cooper, 1975; Hoyt, Henley, and Collins, 1972). In these experiments, participants' counterattitudinal statements were to be shown to persons who could or could not affect a disliked policy. For example, Hoyt et al (1972) gave participants low or high choice to write counterattitudinal essays saying that "toothbrushing is a dangerous, unhealthy habit" (p. 205). Participants were told that the essays would or would not produce the aversive consequences of influencing junior high school students to quit toothbrushing. Hoyt et al. found that only high choice-aversive-consequences participants changed their attitudes. Other experiments have been offered as support for this revision (Cooper and Fazio, 1984; Scher and Cooper, 1989), and this revision has been widely accepted.

According to the aversive-consequences revision, a sufficient cognitive discrepancy is neither necessary nor sufficient to cause dissonance and discrepancy reduction. Instead, feeling personally responsible for the production of foreseeable aversive consequences is necessary and sufficient. Aversive consequences are events that one would not want to occur (Cooper and Fazio, 1984).

Alternative Explanations for the Evidence Produced by the Aversive-Consequences Revision

The aversive-consequences revision is supported by evidence obtained in the induced-compliance paradigm. More specifically, the support for the aversive-consequences revision comes from the absence of measurable attitude change in the conditions in which aversive consequences are not produced. Note that there are numerous explanations for the absence of this attitude-change effect in the no-aversive-consequences conditions, and these alternative explanations must prevent us from concluding that cognitive discrepancy is not necessary or sufficient to create dissonance. First, this is a null effect. It is difficult to draw clear inferences from null effects. A variety of factors could have produced the null effects. Had these past theorists and researchers drawn the conclusion that feeling personally responsible for producing an aversive outcome intensifies dissonance, I would be in complete agreement, for it is likely that feeling personally responsible for such will intensify dissonance and dissonance-produced attitude change. However, these past theorists and researchers did not draw this conclusion but instead proposed that feelings of personal responsibility for aversive outcomes were necessary to produce dissonance effects.

At least two sets of alternative explanations can be offered for the lack of attitude change in the no-aversive-consequences conditions. The first set of alternative explanations argues that the level of dissonance was not large enough to generate dissonance sufficient to produce attitude change and that the addition of the production of aversive consequences was necessary to produce dissonance sufficient to cause attitude change. Several of the past induced-compliance experiments that included a no-aversive-consequences and an aversive-consequences condition used attitudinal issues that were not extremely negative or positive, that is, control-condition participants reported moderately negative or positive attitudes (e.g., Calder, Ross and Insko, 1973; Nel, Hemreich, and Aronson, 1969). Moreover, the lack of extremity might have reflected ambivalence or a mix of positive and negative attitudes toward the issues. Because the attitudes used in past experiments were not extremely positive or negative and might have been held with ambivalence, they were likely not to arouse much dissonance when behavior counter to them occurred. In essence, the magnitude of dissonance aroused may have been too small to generate attitude change.

In the past experiments, the researchers often encouraged participants to generate lengthy counterattitudinal statements. This may increase the likelihood of finding no attitude change in the no-aversive-consequences conditions. Research has shown that the length of the counterattitudinal statement related inversely with the amount of attitude change that occurs (e.g., Rabbie, Brehm, and Cohen, 1959), that is, longer essays are likely to produce less attitude change. This inverse relationship between essay length and attitude change may occur because participants may provide their own justifications and hence more cognitions consonant with the behavior in these lengthy essays. As the number of consonant cognitions increases, the magnitude of dissonance decreases.

In addition, because of the salience of the audiences in these experiments, the participants' attention may have been focused more on the audience and whether they were convinced or could affect a disliked policy than on the nature of their own counterattitudinal actions or their own attitudes. As a result of this, the magnitude of dissonance may have been determined in large part by what the audience did or would do as a result of the counterattitudinal advocacy. Thus, the unconvinced audience, in contrast to the convinced audience, may have reduced the importance of the dissonant cognitions, to the point of making the counterattitudinal action seem trivial. If the perceived importance of dissonant cognitions is low, dissonance may not reach a magnitude that requires reduction.

Another possible explanation is that participants in these past experiments may have been provided too much justification (too many consonant cognitions) for producing the counterattitudinal statement, and the production of aversive consequences may have been necessary to elicit enough dissonance to produce measurable attitude change. This explanation seems very reasonable when one considers the high compliance rates observed in most if not all of this past research. Typically, 100% of the participants have complied with the experimenter's request to write the counterattitudinal statement. As Festinger (1957) has explained, for attitude change to result from dissonance, the person should be offered "*just enough reward or punishment to elicit the overt compliance*" (p. 95, italics in original). Thus, the past experiments on the necessity of aversive consequences may have had inducing forces (the friendliness of the experimenter, the benefits to science) that were so great that little or no dissonance was produced, and the addition of feeling personally responsible for producing aversive consequences may have been necessary to produce sufficient dissonance to cause measurable discrepancy reduction (e.g., attitude change).

Another set of alternative explanations for the lack of attitude change in the no-aversive-consequences conditions argues that dissonance may have been aroused in participants in the no-aversive-consequences conditions of the past experiments but was not detected. The sole method of detecting dissonance in the experiments testing the aversive-consequences model against the original version of the theory has been assessment of attitude change. Because no assessments of dissonance were obtained in experiments testing the aversive consequences model, it is impossible to know whether dissonance was aroused in the no-aversive-consequences conditions. The only conclusion that can safely be drawn is that measurable attitude change did not occur. On the other hand, attitude change may have occurred in the no-aversive-consequences conditions but may have been small, and it would not have been detected if one had only 10-12 persons per condition, as was done in much of the past research (e.g., Calder et al., 1973; Cooper and Worchel, 1970). In addition, the dissonance may have been reduced in a route other than attitude change. Persons whose counterattitudinal actions had no undesired effects may have reduced dissonance by reducing the importance (Simon, Greenberg, and Brehm, 1995) or the perceived effectiveness (Scheier and Carver, 1980) of the counterattitudinal behavior.

It is unlikely that one of these possible alternative explanations accounts for all of the nonsignificant effects that have been found in the past no-aversive-consequences conditions. However, given the number of plausible alternative explanations for the null effects produced in the past experiments that had been used to support the aversive-consequences revision, my colleagues and I thought it was premature to abandon the original version of the theory.

Induced-Compliance Experimental Results Inconsistent With the Aversive-Consequences Revision

All of the research on the aversive-consequences revision has been conducted using the induced-compliance paradigm, which is the focal paradigm in which predictions derived from dissonance theory and its revisions have been tested. My colleagues and I have conducted several induced-compliance experiments to test the hypothesis that feeling personally responsible for producing aversive consequences is not necessary to produce dissonance and that cognitive discrepancy is sufficient to produce dissonance even in the induced-compliance paradigm. In conducting these experiments, we created a situation in which participants would write counterattitudinal statements but not produce aversive consequences. We designed the experiments so that conditions present in previous induced-compliance experiments that might have prevented attitude change from occurring were not present. We took special care to ensure that the inducing force was "just barely sufficient to induce the person" to behave counter attitudinally. (Festinger and Carlsmith, 1959, p. 204), to reduce the number of consonant cognitions to a bare minimum, so that the dissonance aroused after the action would be at high levels. In addition, we had participants write short counterattitudinal statements about objects toward which they held attitudes that were highly salient, strongly negative (or positive), simple, and not ambivalent. Also, in some of the experiments, we assessed negative affect and arousal, to provide measures of dissonance.

In each experiment, under the guise of an experiment on recall, participants were exposed to a stimulus, were given low or high choice to write a counterattitudinal statement about that stimulus, threw away the statement they wrote, and then completed questionnaires that assessed their attitudes toward the stimulus. We assured participants that their counterattitudinal statements and their responses to the questionnaires would be made in private and would be anonymous. We did so to create a situation in which the counterattitudinal behavior would not lead to aversive consequences, because, as Cooper and Fazio (1984) argued, "making a statement contrary to one's attitude while in solitude does not have the potential for bringing about an aversive event" (p. 232). We predicted that participants provided high choice for engaging in the counterattitudinal behavior would change their attitudes to be more consistent with their behavior, whereas participants provided low choice would not.

Dissonance and a Bitter Beverage. In Experiment One (Harmon-Jones, Brehm, Greenberg, Simon, and Nelson, 1996), the experimenter told participants that he was interested in factors that affect the recall of characteristics of products and that at this point in his research, he was seeing how writing a sentence evaluating a product would affect recall of the characteristics of the product. He told participants that he would have them drink a beverage and that they would be asked to recall characteristics of it. He also informed participants that he was using a variety of drinks, that he would not know what type of drink they would receive, and that they should not let him know what type of drink they received. He also explained that all of their responses would be anonymous and that he would not see their responses to questionnaires but that an assistant would enter them into a computer.

Then the experimenter gave the participant a cup covered with a lid. The cup contained 4 ounces of fruit-punch-flavored Kool-Aid. The Kool-Aid was mixed either with the amount of sugar suggested on the package (one cup per two quarts), to create a pleasant-tasting drink, or with two teaspoons of white vinegar (no sugar), to create an unpleasant-tasting drink. Because the experimenter was unaware of whether participants were given a pleasant- or an unpleasant-tasting drink, he was unaware of whether participants experienced dissonance.

After the participant drank some of the beverage, the experimenter returned to the participant's cubicle and induced the choice manipulation. He told participants in the low-choice condition that they were randomly assigned to write a statement saying they liked the beverage. He told participants in the high-choice condition that they could write a statement saying they liked or disliked the beverage and that it was their choice. The experimenter explained that he needed some more persons to write that they liked the beverage, and he asked the participant if she or he would write that she or he liked the beverage. Once the experimenter gained compliance from the participant, he reminded her or him that it was her or his choice.

The experimenter then asked both low-choice and high-choice participants to write one sentence saying they liked the beverage. He also told participants that he did not "need the sheet of paper you will write your sentence on; we just need for you to go through the process of writing the sentence. So when you are done, just wad it up and throw it in the wastebasket." He did this to ensure that the participants perceived that they had anonymity and that there would be no consequences to their behavior. The experimenter then left the participants alone to write the sentence.

After the participant discarded the sentence, the experimenter gave the participant an envelope and said that previous research had indicated that the characteristics a person recalls about a product may be affected by whether they liked the product and that to take this into account, he needed them to answer a questionnaire that assessed their thoughts about the drink. The questionnaire assessed how much the drink was liked. The experimenter left the participant alone to answer this questionnaire. After the participant finished with this questionnaire, the experimenter had the participant complete a questionnaire that assessed the effectiveness of the manipulation of choice. After assessing suspicion, ensuring that participants perceived their questionnaires and statements to be anonymous, and debriefing, the experimenter collected the participants' statements from the trash can, to assess whether participants complied with the request to write the counterattitudinal statement, and placed the statement with the participants' questionnaires.

Approximately 15% of the participants did not write counterattitudinal statements. This effect suggests that we had designed a situation in which there was just enough but not too much external justification to write the counterattitudinal statement. Results indicated that unpleasant-tasting drink-high-choice participants reported more positive attitudes toward the drink than did unpleasant-tasting drink-low choice participants. This effect was significant when both compliers and noncompliers were included in the analysis. Thus, the results of the first experiment suggested that dissonance can be created in induced-compliance situations void of aversive consequences.

Dissonance, Boring Passages, and Electrodermal Activity. To increase confidence that the results obtained in Experiment One were valid, my colleagues and I attempted to conceptually replicate the effects by means of a different manipulation of choice and a different attitudinal object. Using the same procedures as used in the first experiment, we had participants read a boring passage and gave them low or high choice, by means of written instructions, to write a statement saying that the passage was interesting. Thus, in this experiment, we had only two conditions: low choice and high choice. Because choice was induced by means of written instructions, the experimenter was unaware of when dissonance was expected. Results from Experiment Two replicated those of Experiment One, showing that high choice participants rated the boring passage as more interesting than did low-choice participants (Harmon-Jones et al., 1996).

In Experiment Three (Harmon-Jones et all, 1996), we measured non-specific skin conductance responses (NS-SCRs) that occurred in the three minutes after the writing of the counterattitudinal statement but before the assessment of attitude. Previous research has indicated that increased NS-SCRs are associated with increased sympathetic nervous system activity, which is increased during emotional arousal. If our experimental procedure evoked dissonance, we would observe increased NS-SCRs. Results indicated that participants given high choice to write the counterattitudinal statement evidenced more NS-SCRs and reported that the passage was more interesting than did participants given low choice to write the statement.

SUMMARY

... The results from these experiments support the original theory of dissonance and are inconsistent with the aversive-consequences revision. These experiments are important because they show that dissonance arousal, dissonance affect, and dissonance-producing attitude change can occur in situations in which a sufficient cognitive discrepancy is present but feeling personally responsible for the production of aversive consequences is not present. The present evidence convincingly demonstrates that dissonance effects can be generated by a cognitive discrepancy that does not produce aversive consequences. Indeed, these results suggest that the original version of the theory was abandoned prematurely. ...

REFERENCES

ARONSON, E. (1969). The theory of cognitive dissonance: A current perspective. In L. Berkowitz (Ed.), *Advances in experimental social psychology* (Vol. 4, pp. 1-34). New York: Academic Press.

BREHM, J.W., AND COHEN, A.R. (1962). *Explorations in cognitive dissonance.* New York: Wiley.

CALDER, B.J., ROSS, M., AND INSKO, C.A. (1973). Attitude change and attitude attribution: Effects of incentive, choice, and consequences. *Journal of Personality and Social Psychology, 25,* 84-99.

COLLINS, B.E. (1969). The effect of monetary inducements on the amount of attitude change produced by forced compliance. In A.C. Elms (Ed.), *Role playing, reward, and attitude change* (pp. 209-223). New York: Van Nostrand Reinhold.

COLLINS, B.E., AND HOYT, M.F. (1972). Personal responsibility-for-consequences: An integration and extension of the "forced compliance" literature. *Journal of Experimental Social Psychology, 8,* 558-593.

COOPER, J., AND FAZIO, R.H. (1984). A new look at dissonance theory. In L. Berkowitz (Ed.), *Advances in experimental social psychology* (Vol. 17, pp. 229-264). Orlando, FL: Academic Press.

COOPER, J., AND WORSCHEL, S. (1970). Role of undesired consequences in arousing cognitive dissonance. *Journal of Personality and Social Psychology 16,* 199-206.

FESTINGER, L. (1957). *A theory of cognitive dissonance.* Evanston, IL: Row, Peterson.

Festinger, L., and Carlsmith, H.M. (1959). Cognitive consequences of forced compliance. *Journal of Abnormal and Social Psychology, 58,* 203-210.

GOETHALS, G.R., AND COOPER, J. (1985). When dissonance is reduced: The timing of self-justificatory attitude change. *Journal of Personality and Social Psychology, 32,* 361-367.

HARMON-JONES, E., BREHM, J.W., GREENBERG, J., SIMON, L. AND NELSON, D.E. (1996). Evidence that the production of aversive consequences is not necessary to create cognitive dissonance. *Journal of Personality and Social Psychology, 70,* 5-16.

HOYT, M.F., HENLEY, M.D., AND COLLINS, B.E. (1972). Studies in forced compliance: Confluence of choice and consequence on attitude change. *Journal of Personality and Social Psychology, 23,* 205-210.

NEL, E., HELMREICH, R., AND ARONSON, E. (1969). Opinion change in the advocate as a function of the persuasibility of his audience: A clarification of the meaning of dissonance. *Journal of Personality and Social Psychology, 12,* 117-124.

RABBIE, J.M., BREHM, J.W., AND COHEN, A.R. (1959). Verbalization and reactions to cognitive dissonance. *Journal of Personality, 27,* 407-417.

SCHEIER, M.F., AND CARVER, C.S. (1980). Private and public self-attention, resistance to change, and dissonance reduction. *Journal of Personality and Social Psychology, 39,* 390-405.

SCHER, S.J., AND COOPER, J. (1989). Motivational basis of dissonance: The singular role of behavioral consequences. *Journal of Personality and Social Psychology, 56,* 899-906.

SIMON, L., GREENBERG, J., AND BREHM, J.W. (1995). Trivialization: The forgotten mode of dissonance reduction. *Journal of Personality and Social Psychology, 68,* 247-260.

QUESTIONS

1. According to the aversive-consequences revision of cognitive dissonance, why did participants in the $1 condition of Festinger and Carlsmith's 1959 study change their attitude toward the boring task?

2. What additional independent variable did Hoyt and colleagues' include in their "toothbrushing is dangerous" study to test the aversive-consequences theory of dissonance? Why does Harmon-Jones not accept their results?

3. In Harmon-Jones and colleagues second study the choice manipulation was affected by a written rather than a spoken instruction. What is the benefit of this technique?

4. Why does Harmon-Jones believe that the NS-SCRs data support the original formulation over the aversive-consequences revision of dissonance? If NS-SCRs measure negative emotions, why doesn't this support the aversive-consequences theory?

5. If the original formulation of dissonance is correct, why did participants in Hoyt's study change their attitude most if they believed their essay would be read by junior high school students?

PERSUASION:
CHANGING ATTITUDES

Reading 21: Classic

The Elaboration Likelihood Model of Persuasion

Richard E. Petty and John T. Cacioppo

Like Reading 9, the next reading has also risen to classic status in a very short time. Prior to Richard Petty and John Cacioppo's Elaboration Likelihood Model (ELM for short), many findings in the area of persuasion were almost impossible to understand. Decades of research had simply failed to show consistent effects. In some studies more intelligent people were less persuaded by a message but in other studies they were more persuaded. In some studies an attractive spokesperson (or "source" because that person is the source of the message) was more persuasive but not in other studies. Even the very same message was persuasive to participants in one situation or study but not in another. In sum, when trying to understand the persuasiveness of various sources, messages, and targets, the one consistent finding was inconsistency.

The importance of Petty and Cacioppo's work was to organize and make sense of these many seemingly contradictory findings. The following reading is an excerpt from one of the first published formulations of the ELM. In it Petty and Cacioppo describe three of the central postulates of ELM, focusing on cognitive elaboration. The term elaboration in the model refers to people's thoughts about, or elaborations on, issues relevant to the arguments they have heard. Elaboration following very strong messages may lead to people thinking of even new reasons to accept the message (i.e., persuasion); elaboration following weak messages will probably lead to people rejecting the message (i.e., no persuasion). As described in this reading, elaboration is the key to understanding when a source or message will be persuasive and when a target will be persuaded.

Ψ

POSTULATE 1: SEEKING CORRECTNESS

Our first postulate and an important guiding principle in the ELM agrees with Festinger's (1950) statement that:

People are motivated to hold correct attitudes.

Source: Petty, R.E., and Cacioppo, J.T. (1986). The elaboration likelihood model of persuasion. In L. Berkowitz (Ed.), *Advances in Experimental Social Psychology* (Vol. 19). New York: Academic Press. Copyright © 1986 by Academic Press. Reprinted by permission of the publisher.

Incorrect attitudes are generally maladaptive and can have deleterious behavioral, affective, and cognitive consequences. If a person believes that certain objects, people, or issues are "good" when they are in fact "bad," a number of incorrect behavioral decisions and subsequent disappointments may follow. As Festinger (1954) noted, the implication of such a drive is that "we would expect to observe behavior on the part of persons which enables them to ascertain whether or not their opinions are correct" (p. 118). In his influential theory of social comparison processes, Festinger (1954) focused on how people evaluated the correctness of their opinions by comparing them to the opinions of others. In Section IX.B we address how the ELM accounts for attitude changes induced by exposure to the opinions of varying numbers of other people. But first we need to outline our other postulates.

POSTULATE 2: VARIATIONS IN ELABORATION

Postulate 2 states that:

> Although people want to hold correct attitudes, the amount and nature of issue-relevant elaboration in which people are willing or able to engage to evaluate a message vary with individual and situational factors.

By *elaboration* in a persuasion context, we mean the extent to which a person thinks about the issue-relevant arguments contained in a message. When conditions foster people's motivation and ability to engage in issue-relevant thinking, the "elaboration likelihood" is said to be high. This means that people are likely to attend to the appeal; attempt to access relevant associations, images, and experiences from memory; scrutinize and elaborate upon the externally provided message arguments in light of the associations available from memory; draw inferences about the merits of the arguments for a recommendation based upon their analysis; and consequently derive an overall evaluation of, or attitude toward, the recommendation. This conceptualization suggests that when the elaboration likelihood is high, there should be evidence for the allocation of considerable cognitive resources to the advocacy. Issue-relevant elaboration will typically result in the new arguments, or one's personal translations of them, being integrated into the underlying belief structure (schema) for the attitude object (Cacioppo and Petty, 1984a). As we will note shortly, sometimes this issue-relevant elaboration proceeds in a relatively objective manner and is governed mostly by the strength of the issue-relevant arguments presented, but at other times this elaboration is more biased and may be guided mostly by the person's initial attitude.

Of course, people are not motivated nor are they able to scrutinize carefully every message that they receive (cf. McGuire's 1969, "lazy organism"), and it would not be adaptive for them to do so. As Miller, Maruyama, Beaber, and Valone (1976) noted, "It may be irrational to scrutinize the plethora of counterattitudinal messages received daily. To the extent that one possesses only a limited amount of information processing time and capacity, such scrutiny would disengage the thought processes from the exigencies of daily life" (p. 623). Current research in cognitive and social psychology provides strong support for the view that at times people engage in "controlled," "deep," "systematic," and/or "effortful" analyses of stimuli, and at other times the analyses are better characterized as "automatic," "shallow," "heuristic," and/or "mindless" (for further discussion, see Craik, 1979; Eagly and Chaiken, 1984; Kahneman, Slovic, and Tversky, 1982; Langer, 1978; and Schneider and Shiffrin, 1977).

A. The Elaboration Continuum

One can view the extent of elaboration received by a message as a continuum going from no thought about the issue-relevant information presented to complete elaboration of every argument and complete integration of these elaborations into the person's attitude schema. The likelihood of elaboration will be determined by a person's motivation and ability to evaluate the communication presented (see Figure 1, page 221). In an earlier review of the attitude change literature (Petty and Cacioppo, 1981a), we suggested that the many theories of attitude change could be roughly placed along this elaboration continuum. At the high end of this continuum are theoretical orientations such as inoculation theory (McGuire, 1964), cognitive response theory (Greenwald, 1968; Petty, Ostrom, and Brock, 1981), information integration theory (Anderson, 1981), and the theory of reasoned action (Ajzen and Fishbein, 1980; Fishbein, 1980), which all assume that people typically attempt to carefully evaluate (though not always successfully) the information presented in a message and integrate this information into a coherent position. Researchers within this tradition have emphasized the need to examine what kinds of arguments are persuasive and how variables affect the comprehension, elaboration, learning, integration, and retention of issue-relevant information (McGuire, 1985).

Other persuasion theories do not place much credence on the arguments in a message or issue-relevant thinking. Instead, they focus on how simple affective processes influence attitudes or on how people can employ various rules or inferences to judge their own attitudes or the acceptability of an attitudinal position. Although in most laboratory studies of attitude change subjects will have some motivation and/or ability to form at least a reasonable opinion either by scrutinizing arguments or making an inference about the acceptability of the recommendation based on cues in the context, there are circumstances in which neither arguments nor acceptance cues are present. For example, when subjects are exposed to nonsense syllables, (Staats and Staats, 1957) or polygons (Kunst-Wilson and Zajonc, 1980), no elaboration of arguments is possible because no arguments are presented, and validity cues may be irrelevant because there is no explicit "advocacy" to judge. Theories such as classical conditioning (Staats and Staats, 1958) and mere exposure (Zajonc, 1968, 1980), which describe evaluations of objects changing as a result of rather primitive affective and associational processes, are especially relevant under these circumstances. Although these theories have been tested and applied primarily in situations where no explicit "advocacy" is presented, they also should be applicable to situations in which an issue position is advocated, but people have virtually no ability and/or motivation to consider it. In these situations, attitudes may still be changed if the attitude object is associated with a relatively strong positive or negative affective one, or a weaker cue is continually paired with the attitude object.

If no strong affective cues are presented, it is still possible for people to form a "reasonable" attitude without relying on scrutiny of the issue-relevant arguments presented by relying on various persuasion rules or inferences that may be either rather simple or relatively complex. For example, according to self-perception theory (Bem, 1972), people may come to like or dislike an object as a result of a simple inference based on their own behavior (e.g., if I bought it, I must like it). According to the heuristic model of persuasion (Chaiken, 1980; Eagly and Chaiken, 1984), people may evaluate messages by employing various rules that they have learned on the basis of past experience (e.g., people agree with people they like). Social judgment theory (Sherif and Sherif, 1967) proposes that people are contrasted and rejected if they appear too discrepant (fall in the latitude of rejection), but are assimilated and accepted if they appear closer to one's initial position (fall in the latitude of acceptance; Pallak, Mueller, Dollar, and Pallak, 1972).

In addition to the relatively simply acceptance/rejection rules proposed by the preceding models, attitude change may be affected by more complex reasoning processes, such as those based on balance theory (Heider, 1946; Insko, 1984) or certain attributional principles (e.g., Kelley, 1967; Eagly, Wood, and Chaiken, 1978). Importantly, even reliance on more complex inferences obviates the need for careful scrutiny of the issue-relevant arguments in a message. In other words, each of these processes (e.g., self-perception, assimilation, balance) is postulated to be sufficient to account for attitude change without requiring a personal evaluation of the issue-relevant arguments. In sum, we have proposed that when either motivation or ability to process issue-relevant arguments is low, attitudes may be changed by associating an issue position with various affective cues, or people may attempt to form a reasonable opinion position by making an inference about the likely correctness or desirability of a particular attitude position based on cues such as message discrepancy, one's own behavior, and the characteristics of the message source.

B. Developmental Trends in Elaboration

Interestingly, the attitude change processes that we have just described form an elaboration continuum which likely coincides with the manner in which attitude change processes develop through adulthood. Specifically, the very young child probably has relatively little motivation to think about the true merits of people, objects, and issues, and even less ability to do so. Thus, attitudes may be affected primarily by what feels good or bad. As children mature, they become more motivated to express correct opinions on certain issues, but their ability to scrutinize issue-relevant arguments may still be poor due to lack of knowledge. Therefore, they may be particularly reliant on certain cognitive rules based on personal experience such as "My mother knows what's right," or "If I play with it, I must like it." Consistent with this reasoning, children have been shown to be more susceptible to appeals based on behavioral cues and self-perceptions than issue-relevant argumentation (e.g., Miller, Brickman, and Bolen, 1975).

Finally, as people move into adulthood, interests become more focused and the consequences of holding correct opinions on certain issues increase. In addition, as people's acquired knowledge and cognitive skills grow, this renders them more able to critically analyze issue-relevant information on certain topics and makes them less reliant than children on certain primitive heuristics (cf. Ross, 1981). As we noted earlier, of course, although people may have the requisite ability and motivation to scrutinize certain attitude issues, they will lack motivation and ability on others. Thus, simple inferences and affective cues may still produce attitude change in adults.

In sum, one's initial evaluations are likely to be largely hedonistic since, lacking the motivation and/or ability to consider issue-relevant arguments, attitudes will be based primarily on positive and negative affective cues associated with the attitude object. As development proceeds, some attitudes may be formed on the basis of simple inferences, decision rules, and social attachments. Finally, the formation and change of some attitudes become very thoughtful processes in which issue-relevant information is carefully scrutinized and evaluated in terms of existing knowledge. Importantly, our sequence of the developmental stages of influence is consistent with other developmental models of judgment. For example, in discussing the development of moral standards, Kohlberg (1963) identifies three developmental levels, At the first level (preconventional), moral evaluations are based primarily on the affective consequences of an act. At level two (conventional), evaluations of acts are based primarily on socially accepted rules and laws. Finally, at level three (postconventional), an evaluation of an act is based on a person's idiosyncratic but well-articulated moral code. The parallels to our stages of influence are obvious.

Although we have argued that there is a continuum of message elaboration ranging from none to complete, and that different attitude change processes may operate along the continuum, it is also important to note that these different theoretical processes can be viewed as specifying just two qualitatively distinct routes to persuasion. The first route, which we have called the "central route," occurs when motivation and ability to scrutinize issue-relevant arguments are relatively high. The second, or "peripheral route," occurs when motivation and/or ability are relatively low and attitudes are determined by positive or negative cues in the persuasion context which either become directly associated with the message position or permit a simple inference as to the validity of the message. In short, even though one can view message elaboration as a continuum, we can distinguish persuasion that is primarily a result of issue-relevant argumentation from persuasion that is primarily a result of some cue in the persuasion context that permits attitude change without argument scrutiny. In fact, we will find it useful elsewhere in this article to talk about the elaboration likelihood continuum by referring to the prototypical processes operative at each extreme.

POSTULATE 3: ARGUMENTS, CUES, AND ELABORATION

Much of our discussion so far is summarized in the next postulate.

> Variables can affect the amount and direction of attitude change by (A) serving as persuasive arguments, (B) serving as peripheral cues, and/or (C) affecting the extent or direction of issue and argument elaboration.

In subsequent sections we discuss how many of the typical source, message, recipient, channel, and context variables manipulated in the accumulated persuasion research can be understood in terms of the three-part categorization above, but first we need to define and operationalize the constructs.

A. Argument/Message Quality

One of the least researched and understood questions in the psychology of persuasion is "What makes an argument persuasive?" As we noted earlier, literally thousands of studies and scores of theories have addressed the question of how some extramessage factor (e.g., source credibility, repetition) affects the acceptance of a particular argument, but little is known about what makes a particular argument (or message) persuasive in isolation. In fact, the typical persuasion experiment employs only one message and examines how some extramessage factor affects acceptance of the message conclusion. Furthermore, studies that do include more than one message often do so for purposes of generalizability across topics, not because the messages are proposed to differ in some theoretically meaningful way (e.g., Hovland and Weiss, 1951). There are, of course, notable exceptions to our generalization. For example, a few studies have manipulated the comprehensibility or complexity of a message (e.g., Eagly, 1974; Eagly and Warren, 1975; Regan and Cheng, 1973), mostly to test McGuire's (1968) information processing model, but even these studies were not aimed at uncovering the underlying characteristics of persuasive arguments. Perhaps the most relevant research to date is that in which subjects are asked to rate arguments along various dimensions (e.g., validity, novelty) in order to determine what qualities make an argument persuasive (see Vinokur and Burnstein, 1974), but this kind of research is rare and in its infancy. After over 40 years of work on persuasion in experimental social psychology, Fishbein and Ajzen (1981) could accurately state that "the general neglect of the information contained in a message... is probably the most serious problem in communication and persuasion research" (p. 359).

In the ELM, arguments are viewed as bits of information contained in a communication that are relevant to a person's subjective determination of the true merits of an advocated position. Because people hold attitudes for many different reasons (Katz, 1960), people will invariably differ in the kinds of information they feel are central to the merits of any position (Snyder and DeBono, 1985). Nevertheless, for purposes of testing the ELM, it is necessary to specify arguments that the vast majority of a specifiable population finds compelling rather than specious. In our research on the ELM, we have postponed the question of what specific qualities make arguments persuasive by defining argument quality in an empirical manner. In developing arguments for a topic, we begin by generating a large number of arguments, both intuitively compelling and specious ones, in favor of some issue (e.g., raising tuition). Then, members of the appropriate subject population are given these arguments to rate for persuasiveness. Based on these scores we select arguments with high and low ratings to comprise at least one "strong" and one "weak" message. Subsequently, other subjects are given one of these messages and are told to think about and evaluate it carefully. Following examination of the message, subjects complete a "thought-listing measure" (Brock, 1967; Greenwald, 1968), in which they are instructed to record the thoughts elicited by the message. These thoughts are then coded as to whether they are favorable, unfavorable, or neutral toward the position advocated (see Cacioppo and Petty, 1981c; Cacioppo, Harkins, and Petty, 1981, for further discussion of the thought-listing procedure). We define a "strong message" as one containing arguments (e.g., we should raise tuition so that more books can be purchased for the library) such that when subjects are *instructed* to think about the message, the thoughts that they generate are predominantly favorable. Importantly, for positive attitude change to occur, the thoughts should be more favorable than those available prior to message exposure. On the other hand, we define a "weak message" as one containing arguments (e.g., we should raise tuition so that more trees and shrubs can be planted on campus) such that when subjects are instructed to think about them, the thoughts that they generate are predominantly unfavorable. For negative change (boomerang) to occur, the thoughts should be more unfavorable than those available prior to message exposure.

Once the messages meet the criterion of eliciting the appropriate profile thoughts, they are checked for other characteristics. First, a panel of subjects rates the messages for overall believability. Our goal is to develop arguments that are strong and weak, but that do not strain credulity. (This is not to say that our arguments are necessarily veridical – just reasonable plausible to our subjects.) Next, people from the relevant subject pool rate the messages for comprehensibility, complexity, and familiarity. Again, our goal is to develop strong and weak messages that are roughly equivalent in their novelty and in our subjects' ability to understand them. The top panel of Figure 1 depicts the results of a hypothetical study in which some extramessage "treatment" has no effect on persuasion. In this study, only the quality of the message arguments determined the extent of attitude change. We will compare this simple result with the other possibilities depicted in Figure 1 in the remainder of this article.

B. Peripheral Cues

According to the Elaboration Likelihood Model, one way to influence attitudes is by varying the quality of the arguments in a persuasive message. Another possibility, however, is that a simple cue in the persuasion context affects attitudes in the absence of argument processing. As we noted earlier, some cues will do this because they trigger relatively primitive affective states that become associated with the attitude object.

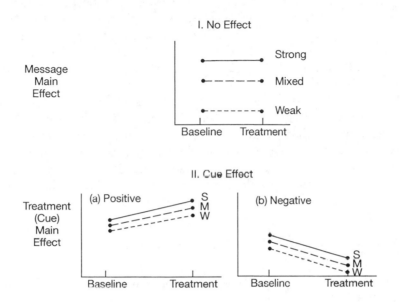

Figure 1

Impact of variables on attitude change according to the ELM. Under conditions of high elaboration likelihood, attitudes are affected mostly by argument quality (I). Under conditions of low elaboration likelihood, attitudes are affected mostly by peripheral cues (II).

Various reinforcing (e.g., food; Janis, Kaye, and Kirschner, 1965) and punishing (e.g., electric shock; Zanna, Kiesler, and Pilkonis, 1970) stimuli have proved effective in this regard. Other cues work, however, because they invoke guiding rules (e.g., balance; Heider, 1946) or inferences (e.g., self-perception; Bem, 1972)

Since cues are postulated to affect attitude change without affecting argument processing, it is possible to test manipulations as potential cues by presenting them to subjects with the advocated position only (i.e., without accompanying persuasive arguments), as in prestige suggestion (see Asch, 1948). If the manipulation is a potential cue, it should have the ability to affect attitudes in the absence of any arguments. Alternatively, one could present an incomprehensible message (e.g., in a foreign language) on some topic along with the potential cue (e.g., speed of speech; Miller *et al.*, 1976). Subjects could be asked to rate, for example, how likely it is that the speaker is convincing. Again, if the cue is operative, it should be capable of affecting judgments even if there are no arguments to process. Finally, a simple procedure might involve merely describing various potential cues to subjects (e.g., a message with 1 vs. 10

arguments; a message from an attractive vs. an unattractive source) and asking them which would more likely be acceptable and/or persuasive. These procedures would not, of course, indicate *why* a cue was effective (e.g., were the judgments due to affective association or the invocation of a simple decision rule?), nor would they eliminate the possibility that more thoughtful processes were involved (e.g., subjects might attempt to generate arguments consistent with the position; cf., Burnstin, Vinokur, and Trope, 1973). However, these procedures would indicate whether or not a manipulation has the *potential* to serve as a peripheral cue.

Panel II in Figure 1 presents the results of a hypothetical study in which strong, weak, and mixed argument messages were presented along with a treatment that served as a peripheral cue. Note that in the pure case of cue processing, the cue affects all three kinds of message equally. Since cues are most likely to operate when subjects are either unmotivated or unable to process issue-relevant arguments... the data show a strong effect for the cue treatment, but little effect for argument quality. In the left half of Panel II the cue is positive, and in the right half the cue is negative.

REFERENCES

AJZEN, I., AND FISHBEIN, M. (1980) *Understanding attitudes and predicting social behavior*. Englewood Cliffs, NJ: Prentice-Hall.

ANDERSON, N. (1981) Integration theory applied to cognitive responses and attitudes. In R. Petty, T. Ostrom, and T. Brock (Eds.), *Cognitive responses in persuasion*. Hillsdale, NJ: Erlbaum.

ASCH, S. (1948). The doctrine of suggestion, prestige, and imitation in social psychology. *Psychological Review, 55*, 250-276.

BEM, D.J. (1972). Self-perception theory. In L. Berkowitz (Ed.), *Advances in experimental social psychology* (Vol. 6), New York: Academic Press.

BROCK, T.C. (1967), Communication discrepancy and intent to persuade as determinants of counterargument production. *Journal of Experimental Social Psychology, 3*, 269-309.

BURNSTEIN, E., VINOKUR, A. AND TROPE, Y. (1973). Interpersonal comparison versus persuasive argumentation: A more direct test of alternative explanation for group induced shifts in individual choice. *Journal of Experimental Social Psychology, 9*, 236-245.

CACIOPPO, J.T., HARKINS, S.G., AND PETTY, R.E. (1981) The nature of attitudes and cognitive responses and their relationships to behavior. In R. Petty, T.Ostrom, and T. Brock (Eds.), *Cognitive responses in persuasion*. Hillsdale, NJ: Erlbaum.

CACIOPPO, J.T., AND PETTY, R.E. (1981c). Social psychological procedures for cognitive response assessment: The thought listing technique. In T. Merluzzi, C. Glass, and M. Genest (Eds.), *Cognitive assessment*. New York: Guilford.

CACIOPPO, J.T., AND PETTY, R.E. (1984c). The Elaboration Likelihood Model. *Advances in Consumer Research, 11*, 673-675.

CHAIKEN, S. (1980). Heuristic versus systematic information processing and the use of source versus message cues in persuasion. *Journal of Personality and Social Psychology, 39*, 752-756.

CRAIK, F.I.M. (1979). Human Memory. *Annual Review of Psychology, 30*, 63-102.

EAGLY, A.H. (1974) Comprehensibility of persuasive arguments as a determinant of opinion change. *Journal of Personality and Social Psychology, 29*, 758-773.

EAGLY, A.H., AND WARREN, R. (1976). Intelligence, comprehension, and opinion change. *Journal of Personality*, *44*, 226-242.

EAGLY, A.H., WOOD, W., AND CHAIKEN, S. (1978). Causal inferences about communicators and their effect on opinion change. *Journal of Personality and Social Psychology, 36*, 424-435.

FESTINGER, L. (1950). Informal social communication. *Psychological Review, 57*, 271-282.

FESTINGER, L. (1954). A theory of social comparison processes. *Human Relations, 7*, 117-140.

FESTINGER, L. (1957). *A theory of cognitive dissonance*. Stanford, CA: Stanford University Press.

FESTINGER, L. AND MACOBY, N. (1964). On resistance to persuasive communications. *Journal of Abnormal and Social Psychology, 68*, 359-366.

FISHBEIN, M. (1980) A theory of reasoned action: Some applications and implications. In H. Howe and M. Page (Eds.), *Nebraska symposium on motivation*, 1979. Lincoln: University of Nebraska Press.

FISHBEIN, M. AND AJZEN, I. (1981). Acceptance, yielding and impact: Cognitive processes in persuasion. In R. Petty, T. Ostrom, and T. Brock (Eds.), *Cognitive responses in persuasion*. Hillsdale, NJ: Erlbaum.

GREENWALD, A.G. (1968). Cognitive learning, cognitive response to persuasion, and attitude change. In A. Greenwald, T. Brock, and T. Ostrom (Eds.), *Psychological foundations of attitudes* (pp. 148-170). New York: Academic Press.

HEIDER, F. (1946). Attitudes and cognitive organization. *Journal of Psychology, 21*, 107-112.

HOVLAND, C.I. AND WEISS, W. (1951). The influence of source credibility on communication effectiveness. *Public Opinion Quarterly, 15*, 635-650.

INSKO, C.A. (1984). Balance theory, the Jordan paradigm, and the Wiest tetrahedron. In L. Berkowitz (Ed.), *Advances in experimental social psychology* (Vol. 18), New York: Academic Press.

JANIS, I.L., KAYE, D., AND KIRSCHNER, P. (1965). Facilitating effects of "eating while reading" on responsiveness to persuasive communications. *Journal of Personality and Social Psychology, 1*, 181-186.

KAHNEMAN, D., SLOVIC, P., AND TVERSKY, A. (Eds.) (1982). *Judgment under uncertainty: Heuristics and biases*. London and New York: Cambridge University Press.

KATZ, D. (1960). The functional approach to the study of attitudes. *Public Opinion Quarterly, 24*, 163-204.

KELLEY, H.H. (1967). Attribution theory in social psychology. In D. Levine (Ed.), *Nebraska symposium on motivation* (Vol. 15). Lincoln: University of Nebraska Press.

KOHLBERG, L. (1963). The development of children's orientations toward a moral order. I. Sequence in the development of moral thought. *Vita Humana, 6*, 11-33.

KUNST-WILSON, W.R., AND ZAJONC, R.B. (1980). Affective discrimination of stimuli that cannot be recognized. *Science, 207*, 557-558.

McGUIRE, W.J. (1964). Inducing resistance to persuasion: Some contemporary approaches. In L. Berkowitz (Ed.), *Advances in experimental social psychology* (Vol. 1). New York: Academic Press.

McGUIRE, W.J. (1968). Personality and attitude change: An information-processing theory. In A. Greenwald, T. Brock, and T. Ostrom (Eds.), *Psychological foundations of attitudes*. New York: Academic Press.

McGUIRE, W.J. (1969). The nature of attitudes and attitude change. In G. Lindzey and E. Aronson (Eds.), *The handbook of social psychology* (2nd ed., Vol. 3). Reading, MA: Addison-Wesley.

McGUIRE, W.J. (1985). Attitudes and attitude change. In G. Lindzey and E. Aronson (Eds.), *Handbook of social psychology* (3rd ed., Vol. 2). New York: Random House.

MILLER ,N., MARUYAMA, G., BEABER, R., AND VALONE, K. (1976). Speed of speech and persuasion. *Journal of Personality and Social Psychology, 34*, 615-625.

MILLER, R.L., BRICKMAN, P., AND BOLEN, D. (1975). Attribution versus persuasion as a means for modifying behavior. *Journal of Personality and Social Psychology, 31*, 430-441.

PALLAK, M.S., MUELLER, M., DOLLAR, K., AND PALLAK, J. (1972). Effect of commitment on responsiveness to an extreme consonant communication. *Journal of Personality and Social Psychology, 23*, 429-436.

PETTY, R.E., AND CACIOPPO, J.T. (1981a). *Attitudes and persuasion: Classic and contemporary approaches.* Dubuque, IA: Wm. C. Brown.

PETTY, R.E., OSTROM, T.M., AND BROCK, T.C. (Eds) (1981). *Cognitive approaches in persuasion.* Hillsdale, NJ: Erlbaum.

REGAN, D.T., AND CHENG, J.B. (1973). Distraction and attitude change: A resolution. *Journal of Experimental Social Psychology, 9*, 138-147.

ROSS, L. (1981). The "intuitive scientist" formulation and its developmental implications. In J.H. Flavell and L. Ross (Eds.), *Social cognitive development: Frontiers and possible futures.* London and New York: Cambridge University Press.

SCHNEIDER, W., AND SHIFFRIN, R.M. (1977). Controlled and automatic human information processing: I. Detection, search, and attention. *Psychological Review, 84*, 1-66.

SHERIF, M., AND SHERIF, C.W. (1967). Attitude as the individual's own categoreis: The social judgment-involvement approach to attitude and attitude change. In C.W. Sherif and M. Sherif (Eds.), *Attitude, ego-involvement, and change.* New York: Wiley.

SNYDER, M., AND DEBONO, K.G. (1985). Appeals to image and claims about quality: Understanding the psychology of advertising. *Journal of Personality and Social Psychology, 49*, 586-597.

STAATS, A.W., AND STAATS, C.K. (1958). Attitudes established by classical conditioning. *Journal of Abnormal and Social Psychology, 57*, 37-40.

STAATS, C.K., AND STAATS, A.W. (1957). Meaning established by classical conditioning. *Journal of Experimental Psychology, 54*, 74-80.

VINOKUR, A., AND BURNSTEIN, E. (1974). The effects of partially shared persuasive arguments on group-induced shifts: A group problem solving approach. *Journal of Personality and Social Psychology, 29*, 305-315.

ZAJONC, R.B. (1968). Attitudinal effects of mere exposure. *Journal of Personality and Social Psychology Monograph Supplement. 9*, 1-27.

ZAJONC, R.B. (1980). Feeling and thinking: Preferences need no inferences. *American Psychologist, 35*, 151-175.

ZAJONC, R.B., AND MARKUS, H. (1982). Affective and cognitive factors in preferences. *Journal of Consumer Research, 9*, 123-131.

ZANNA, M.P., KIESLER, C.A., AND PILKONIS, P.A. (1970). Positive and negative attitudinal affect established by classical conditioning. *Journal of Personality and Social Psychology, 14*, 321-328.

QUESTIONS

1. According to ELM, why might a weak argument be persuasive in the peripheral route but have the reverse effect, or boomerang effect, in the central route?

2. According to the model discussed here, how would persuasion differ in the following two cases: (a) the issue is important but very too complicated to follow and (b) the issue is easy to understand but not important or interesting?

3. If the attractiveness of a spokesperson acted as a pure peripheral cue, would it influence people only if the spokesperson made strong arguments, only if the spokesperson made weak arguments, or both?

4. What psychological feature does Festinger's theory of social comparison share with ELM?

5. In what way is the likelihood of elaboration a continuum? In what way is it a dichotomy, being either low or high?

Reading 22: Contemporary

A Social Psychological Perspective on the Role of Knowledge about AIDS in AIDS Prevention

Marie Helweg-Larsen and Barry E. Collins

This next reading is a good example of the relevance of social psychology to modern social problems. A wide range of professionals in other fields have made use in particular of social psychological theories of persuasion to aid them in their work. While some professionals use these theories strictly for their own benefit (e.g., people who create more persuasive advertisements to get more of our consumer dollars), others have found ways to benefit the larger society as well. The following is an example of the latter type.

Many people consider AIDS to be among the largest crises facing the world today. Although treatments for AIDS have improved dramatically in the past 10 years, there is still no cure for AIDS. Furthermore, treatments to slow down the progress of the disease are so expensive that only the most wealthy citizens in the most wealthy nations can receive these treatments. Because of these limitations in treatment efforts, it is important to find ways of preventing the spread of the disease. Fortunately there are some very simple ways to accomplish this, such as using condoms. Unfortunately, as Helweg-Larsen and Collins reveal in this reading, very few people seem to be following these simple rules of behavior. For example, have you had unprotected sex since first learning that doing so could kill you? If you have to admit that you have, you are by no means alone. Why do so many people ignore AIDS prevention advice? Is there a better way to encourage safe sex practices? Helweg-Larsen and Collins think that the answers to these questions may lie in three social psychological theories: the elaboration likelihood model, the theory of planned behavior, and cognitive dissonance.

Ψ

Widespread ignorance regarding the transmission of HIV in the mid to late 1980s was, at once, a source of despair and optimism. It was discouraging that people knew so little about HIV prevention. At the same time, one could hope that an attack on the ignorance might amount to an attack on the virus itself. Today, many health educators still believe that ignorance is at the root of the spread of the disease and continue to focus on knowledge as a central causal variable in AIDS preventions. Many AIDS interventions are based on the idea that giving people the facts about transmission of HIV will lead to

Source: Helweg-Larsen, M., and Collins, B.E. (1997). A social psychological perspective on the role of knowledge about AIDS in AIDS prevention. *Current Directions in Psychological Science, 6,* 23-26. Copyright © 1997 by Marie Helweg-Larsen and Barry E. Collins. Reprinted by permission of Blackwell Publishers.

positive attitudes toward preventive behaviors (and ultimately behavior change). In fact, some educational programs measure their success by assessing how much people learn about AIDS rather than by assessing people's changes in attitudes or behavior per se (e.g., Farley, Pomputious, Sabella, Helgerson, and Hadler, 1991; Ganz and Greenberg, 1990).

There are a number of philosophical and practical reasons for using information-based approaches to changing health-related behavior. The idea that people will change their behavior when they are informed about the logic of doing so is consistent with the Western worldview, which places individualism, enlightenment, and reason at the center of its value system. Knowledge-based behavior change is, in theory, internalized. Thus, the new behaviors will last longer, display a greater resistance to extinction, and generalize across more situations than will new behaviors arising from other forms of social influence (e.g., reward, coercion, and compliance with authority figures). Behaviors based on these other influences may be relatively situation specific and require surveillance for compliance.

Subscribing to an information-based view, many psychologists (and non-psychologists) believe that knowledge about disease processes is a fundamental variable in any prevention theory or intervention program. Teaching the facts is seen as essential to changing attitudes or behaviors. For example, the author of one health psychology textbook argued that "health information is the first necessary component and a key ingredient in any attempt to bring about health behavior" (DiMatteo, 1991, p. 88). Similarly, the term "AIDS knowledge" is frequently used synonymously with the term "AIDS prevention" in the public-health literature in general and the AIDS prevention literature in particular.

Unfortunately, the evidence that sex education leads to changes in behaviors intended to prevent AIDS or pregnancy is disappointing. Similarly, the many research efforts aimed specifically at examining the relation between knowledge about AIDS (including how AIDS is transmitted) and preventive behaviors suggest overwhelmingly that this relation is weak or nonexistent. A review of global perspectives on AIDS (Mann, Tarantola, and Netter, 1992) concluded that "the failure of information to lead reliably, regularly, or predictably to behavior change has been documented repeatedly in varying cultures and contexts and underscores the need for a comprehensive approach to prevention" (p. 330). Surprisingly, some of the researchers who themselves have found no effects of knowledge about AIDS on AIDS-related attitudes or behaviors nevertheless have made recommendations suggesting that counselors, physicians, and other health care professionals ought to provide more information about AIDS, develop educational programs, and provide sex education (Freeman et al., 1980). Our point is not that people might not benefit from or need such information (e.g., education might help reduce the stigma against persons with AIDS). Rather, we are saying that disease-related information about AIDS seems not to be an important cause of change in sexual behavior.

Surveys indicate that the absolute level of knowledge about AIDS, transmission routes, and preventive behaviors is quite high in some populations even while the frequency of behavior that increase the risk of contamination remains high – a fact that would preclude a strong relationship between knowledge and preventive behaviors. For example, in one study of injection drug users, participants were randomly assigned to an

AIDS education group, an AIDS education group with optional HIV testing, or a wait-list control group (Calsyn, Saxon, Freeman, and Whittaker, 1992). Four months after the intervention, a structured interview could not detect any differences between the groups in either their knowledge about AIDS or their frequency of engaging in risky behaviors. Additionally, the injection drug users were very well informed about AIDS. Between 97% and 99% correctly identified routes of contracting HIV and knew that condoms would prevent its transmission. High absolute levels of knowledge about AIDS have also been found in heterosexual adolescents (e.g., DiClemente, Forrest, Mickler, and Principal Site Investigators, 1990) and gay men (e.g., Aspinwall, Kemeny, Taylor, Schneider, and Dudley, 1991). Thus, one might simply look to these high levels of knowledge to conclude that knowing the facts about AIDS is not sufficient to cause people to change their behavior. If it were, very few people in these populations would be engaging in risky behaviors.

One of the most common reactions to a failure to find a relationship between knowing the facts about AIDS and engaging in risky behaviors is to conclude that information is a necessary, but not a sufficient, condition for behavior change (see J.D. Fisher and Fisher, 1992, for a review). However, as we discuss next, the route to changes in behaviors related to risk of contracting HIV does not (or does not always) pass through the acquisition of knowledge about AIDS.

SOCIAL PSYCHOLOGICAL THEORIES

Within social psychology, a wealth of research on persuasion and attitude change provides clues as to (a) why and under what circumstances information per se does not necessarily lead to behavior change and (b) why uninformed people nevertheless change their attitudes or behaviors. It is not our purpose to review the literature on persuasion and attitude change here, but we provide three illustrations.

First, consider the elaboration likelihood model of attitude change (Petty and Cacioppo, 1986). In this model, it is not knowledge per se but cognitive reactions to knowledge that cause changes in attitude and behavior. The model proposes that one cannot judge how effective a message is simply by examining the information learned – one must know how the recipient of the message reacts to that knowledge. Thus, the message may be ineffective if the person sees the information as irrelevant (e.g., "I'm young and have a strong immune system, so I need not worry") or reacts negatively rather than positively (e.g., "Condoms are too much trouble, and they make me think of death and disease"). Positive reactions, which are key to an effective message, may result from superficial cues in the message (the peripheral route to persuasions) rather than from elaborate, in-depth, thoughtful analysis of the issues (the central route to persuasion). However, research shows that peripheral routes to persuasion (such as having a famous actress promote condom use) result in attitudes that are relatively temporary, are susceptible to change, and have little impact on behavior. If the central route to persuasion does result in attitude change, such change may be relatively enduring, but the person may not have the necessary skills or self-worth to carry the belief into action (Petty, Gleicher, and Jarvis, 1993).

Ajzen's (1988) theory of planned behavior provides a second example in which increased knowledge may or may not produce behavior change. The theory of planned behavior – an extension of Ajzen and Fishbein's (1980) theory of reasoned action – suggests that a behavior follows from intention, which in turn follows from a person's attitude toward the behavior, the perceived options of other people (norms), and perceived control over the behavior (see W.A. Fisher, Fisher, and Rye, 1995, for an application of the theory of reasoned action to AIDS-related behavior). Based on this theory, one would predict that behavior change can be produced without attitude change if new norms can be created (e.g., "I'll start bleaching my needles, not because I personally believe it's important but because everyone wants me to") or if perceived control over the behavior changes (e.g., "Now that I can easily get condoms in vending machines in the restroom, I'll begin using them"). In sum, the theory of planned behavior and the theory of reasoned action suggest that a change in norms or perceived control might reduce the frequency of risky behaviors even if people do not learn more about AIDS.

Cognitive dissonance theory (Festinger, 1957) is a third example of a social psychological theory that suggests a mechanism for attitude and behavior change in which learning a message is not relevant. According to this theory, cognitive dissonance may be evoked when a person holds inconsistent attitudes or acts inconsistently with held attitudes. To reduce the resulting discomfort, the person is motivated to change an inconsistent behavior or attitude so as to eliminate the inconsistency. Using this paradigm, Stone, Aronson, Crain and Winslow (1994) had students develop and videotape a persuasive speech about condom use and also asked the students to think about their own past inconsistent condom use. That is, cognitive dissonance was aroused by reminding students that they were being hypocritical (promoting use even though they had not used condoms consistently in the past). This cognitive dissonance in turn increased students' resolve to use condoms in the future, and more students in this condition (compared with three control conditions) bought condoms following the experiment. The important point here is that the change in intentions (and behaviors) occurred after an apparent inconsistency became clear, not because of new information.

In sum, then, many social psychological theories provide sound theoretical reasons for why information at times does not lead to learning, attitude change, or behavior change, and why attitude and behavior change may occur without new knowledge.

NEGATIVE CONSEQUENCES OF KNOWLEDGE ABOUT AIDS

Some people might argue that even if providing the facts about AIDS is not sufficient (or necessary) to change behaviors, it certainly could not hurt for people to learn more about AIDS as long as the education does not detract from other intervention methods. But in some cases, knowledge about AIDS may inhibit preventive behaviors, such as use of condoms. For example, one study (Berrenberg et al., 1993) measured the degree to which college students felt overwhelmed and irritated by information about AIDS and desired to avoid additional information (called "degree of AIDS information saturation"). The authors found that students with a high level of AIDS information saturation rated AIDS information that was provided as less valuable, less clear, and less disturbing than did students with a lower level of AIDS saturation. The students with a high level of AIDS information saturation also reported fewer intentions to change high-risk behavior. This study hints at the possibility that there may be negative consequences of repeatedly telling people what they already know.

Health educators who believe that rational people make rational choices once they have all the information might create interventions in which they teach individuals to use disease information to persuade their partners to use condoms. However, this approach may be problematic for several related reasons. First, the failure to use condoms is more often related to concerns regarding how one appears to other people than to lack of information about the benefits of using condoms (Leary, Tchividjian, and Kraxberger, 1994). That is, people are embarrassed to buy condoms, are embarrassed about introducing the issue to their partners, and worry about the impression they give to their partners (Helweg-Larsen and Collins, 1994). Knowing the rational reasons for using a condom may not overcome these interpersonal concerns. Second, given the powerful images associated with AIDS (e.g., being gay promiscuous, or "unclean"), AIDS might be exactly the reason one should not use to convince one's partner to use a condom. Research on attitudes and classical conditioning suggests that one should avoid linking a desired behavior (e.g., using condoms) with an image or word (AIDS) that, rightly or wrongly, carries negative connotations.

Third, there is also emerging empirical evidence that introducing disease information in a sexual situation might in fact have adverse effects on a potential partner's perception of a person trying to make a good impression (Collins and Karney, 1995). In one study, students who read a scenario about a college student who mentioned to his or her partner that he or she was "worried about AIDS" judged the student as nice (responsible, sincere, clean, and conscientious) but also unexciting (dull, boring, bland, uninteresting, weak, and passive). Even when these effects were controlled statistically (the effects of the nice and exciting dimensions were statistically removed), college students still perceived a person revealing concern about AIDS to his or her partner to be promiscuous, a poor long-term romantic prospect, and less sexually attractive and less heterosexual than a person who did not mention concern about AIDS.

In sum, providing the facts about disease processes might have negative consequences under certain circumstances, especially if the recipients feel they are already overloaded with such information or if they use (or are taught to use) such information to persuade their partners to use condoms or take other precautionary measures.

CONCLUSION

Not only is knowledge about AIDS an unreliable predictor of attitudes or behavior, but the focus on knowledge-based approaches to behavior change might distract health educators from targeting other factors leading to risky sexual behavior – factors that predict risky behaviors better than does knowledge about AIDS. This is not to say that knowledge might not be important for purposes other than changing attitudes or behaviors. It is to say that researchers should consider a broad array of theories of behavior change, including those that do not focus on information as a determinant of such change. In addition, several social psychological theories of attitude change provide excellent information about when providing factual information is most likely to lead to changes in attitudes or behaviors. In the midst of the AIDS crisis, it is essential that specialists and non-specialists alike become aware that knowledge is not sufficient, is not always necessary, and may in certain circumstances do more harm than good.

Acknowledgments – We thank James Shepperd and David Boninger for providing helpful comments on an earlier draft of this article. This work was supported by a California State Doctoral AIDS Research Training Grant (TG-LA022) awarded through the UCLA School of Publish Health to the first author.

REFERENCES

AJZEN, I. (1988). *Attitudes, personality, and behavior.* Chicago: Dorsey Press

AJZEN, I., AND FISHBEIN, M. (1980) *Understanding attitudes and predicting social behavior.* Englewood Cliffs, NJ: Prentice Hall

ASPINWALL, L.G., KEMENY, M.E., TAYLOR, S.E., SCHNEIDER, S.G., AND DUDLEY, J.P. (1991) Psychosocial predictors of gay men's AIDS risk-reduction behavior. *Health Psychology, 10,* 432-444.

BERRENBERG, J.L., DOUGHERTY, K.L., ERIKSON, M.S., LOWE, J.L., PACOT, D.M., AND ROUSSEAU, C.N.S. (1993, April). *Saturation in AIDS education: Can we still make a difference?* Paper presented at the annual meeting of the Rocky Mountain and Western Psychological Associations, Phoenix, AZ.

CALSYN, D.A., SAXON, A.J., FREEMAN, G., AND WHITTAKER, S. (1992). Ineffectiveness of AIDS education and HIV antibody testing in reducing high-risk behavior among injection drug users. *American Journal of Public Health, 82,* 573-575.

COLLINS, B.E., AND KARNEY, B.P. (1995). *Behavior change and impression management: The case of safer sex.* Unpublished manuscript, University of California, Los Angeles.

DiCLEMENTE, R.J., FORREST, K.A., MICKLER, S., AND PRINCIPAL SITE INVESTIGATORS. (1990). College students' knowledge and attitudes about AIDS and changes in HIV-preventive behaviors. *AIDS Education and Prevention, 2,* 201-212.

DiMATTEO, M.R. (1991) *The psychology of health, illness, and medical care.* (Pacific Grove, CA: Brooks/Cole.

FARLEY, T.A., POMPUTIUS, P.F., SABELLA, W. HELGERSON, S.D., AND HADLER, J.L. (1991) Evaluation of the effect of school-based education on adolescents' AIDS knowledge and attitudes. *Connecticut Medicine, 55,* 15-18.

FESTINGER, L. (1957) *A theory of cognitive dissonance.* Evanston, IL: Row, Peterson.

FISHER, J.D., AND FISHER, W.A. (1992). Changing AIDS-risk behavior. *Psychological Bulletin, 111,* 455-474.

FISHER, W.A., FISHER, J.D., AND RYE, B.J. (1995). Understanding and promoting AIDS-preventive behavior: Insights from the theory of reasoned action. *Health Psychology 14*, 255-264.

FREEMAN, E.W., RICKELS, K., HUGGINS, G.R., MUDD, E.H., GARCIA, C.R., AND DICKENS, H.O. (1980). Adolescent contraceptive use: Comparisons of male and female attitudes and information. *American Journal of Public Health, 70*. 790-797.

GANZ, W., AND GREENBERG, B.S. (1990). The role of informative television programs in the battle against AIDS. *Health Communication, 2*, 199-215.

HELWEG-LARSON, M., AND COLLINS, B.E. (1994). The UCLA Multidimensional Condom Attitudes Scale: Documenting the complex determinants of condom use in college students. *Health Psychology, 13*, 224-237.

LEARY, M.R., TCHIVIDJIAN, L.R., AND KRAXBERGER, B.E. (1994). Self-presentation can be hazardous to your health: Impression management and health risk. *Health Psychology, 13*, 461-470.

MANN, J.M., TARANTOLA, D.J.M., AND NETTER, T.W. (Eds.). (1992). *AIDS in the world.* Cambridge, MA: Harvard University Press.

PETTY, R.E., AND CACIOPPO, J.T. (1986). *Communication and persuasion: Central and peripheral routes to attitude change.* New York: Springer-Verlag.

PETTY, R.E., GLEICHER, F., AND JARVIS, W.B.G. (1993). Persuasion theory and AIDS prevention. In J.B. Pryor and J.D. Reeder (Eds.), *The social psychology of HIV infection* (pp. 155-182). Hillsdale, NJ: Erlbaum.

STONE, J., ARONSON, E., CRAIN, A.L., AND WINSLOW, M.P. (1994). Inducing hypocrisy as a means of encouraging young adults to use condoms. *Personality and Social Psychology Bulletin, 20*, 116-128.

QUESTIONS

1. According to the Elaboration Likelihood Model of persuasion, why might AIDS prevention ads featuring celebrity spokespeople fail to achieve lasting attitude change?

2. According to the theory of planned behavior, why might even the best informative brochure about AIDS prevention fail to produce any change in behavior?

3. Which of the three social psychological theories persuasion reviewed in this article can best explain why embarrassment often prevents condom use?

4. Helweg-Larsen and Collins review evidence that creating cognitive dissonance may increase condom use. Suggest another strategy based on cognitive dissonance theory (described in Reading 19) to increase condom use.

5. Helweg-Larsen and Collins suggest unfortunate consequences of the way AIDS information is currently distributed: classical conditioned negative attitudes towards condoms and negative stereotypes about people concerned about AIDS. Suggest education programs that would be less likely to create these two problems.

Ψ

PART VII
SOCIAL INFLUENCE

Ψ Ψ

Ψ CHAPTER 12 Ψ

CONFORMITY, COMPLIANCE, AND OBEDIENCE: FOLLOWING THE LEAD OF OTHERS

Reading 23: Classic

Behavioral Study of Obedience

Stanley Milgram

At the close of World War II, the world was stunned and horrified to learn about the systematic murder of Jews and other ethnic minorities in the Nazi death camps. People found it difficult to believe that a government could devise a scheme so cruel and inhumane. But more importantly, people wondered at a citizenry that could carry out such obviously immoral orders.

This event was the inspiration behind what is probably the most famous (and infamous) study in social psychology: Stanley Milgram's "behavioral study of obedience." The study is famous for conclusively demonstrating what Arendt called the "banality of evil." People could, indeed wanted to, believe that what happened in Nazi Germany was a unique event, that such blind obedience was due to a highly unusual mixture of social elements. They argued that certainly something like that could never happen in an open democracy such as the United States. Milgram's studies make this belief untenable.

Milgram's study is infamous for what many believe was the unethical treatment of participants. All subjects experienced considerable stress, and many left the study with the realization that they were capable of administering dangerous shocks to a total stranger. In his defense, Milgram points out that neither he, his students at Yale, nor his colleagues in the field expected the type of behavior that they subsequently observed. Keep this in mind as you read this account of his experiment.

Ψ

Obedience is as basic an element in the structure of social life as one can point to. Some system of authority is a requirement of all communal living, and it is only the man dwelling in isolation who is not forced to respond, through defiance or submission, to the commands of others. Obedience, as a determinant of behavior, is of particular relevance to our time. It has been reliably established that from 1933-45 millions of innocent persons were systematically slaughtered on command. Gas chambers were built, death camps were guarded, daily quotas of corpses were produced with the same efficiency as

Source: Milgram, S. (1963). Behavioral study of obedience. *Journal of Abnormal and Social Psychology, 67*, 371–378. Reprinted by permission of Alexandra Milgram, who controls all rights.

the manufacture of appliances. These inhumane policies may have originated in the mind of a single person, but they could only be carried out on a massive scale if a very large number of persons obeyed orders.

Obedience is the psychological mechanism that links individual action to political purpose. It is the dispositional cement that binds men to systems of authority. Facts of recent history and observation in daily life suggest that for many persons obedience may be a deeply ingrained behavior tendency, indeed, a prepotent impulse overriding training in ethics, sympathy, and moral conduct. C. P. Snow (1961) points to its importance when he writes:

> When you think of the long and gloomy history of man, you will find more hideous crimes have been committed in the name of obedience than have ever been committed in the name of rebellion. If you doubt that, read William Shirer's "Rise and Fall of the Third Reich." The German Officer Corps were brought up in the most rigorous code of obedience ... in the name of obedience they were party to, and assisted in, the most wicked large scale actions in the history of the world [p. 24].

While the particular form of obedience dealt with in the present study has its antecedents in these episodes, it must not be thought all obedience entails acts of aggression against others. Obedience serves numerous productive functions. Indeed, the very life of society is predicated on its existence. Obedience may be ennobling and educative and refer to acts of charity and kindness, as well as to destruction.

General Procedure

A procedure was devised which seems useful as a tool for studying obedience (Milgram, 1961). It consists of ordering a naive subject to administer electric shock to a victim. A simulated shock generator is used, with 30 clearly marked voltage levels that range from 15 to 450 volts. The instrument bears verbal designations that range from Slight Shock to Danger: Severe Shock. The responses of the victim, who is a trained confederate of the experimenter, are standardized. The orders to administer shocks are given to the naive subject in the context of a "learning experiment" ostensibly set up to study the effects of punishment on memory. As the experiment proceeds the naive subject is commanded to administer increasingly more intense shocks to the victim, even to the point of reaching the level marked Danger: Severe Shock. Internal resistances become stronger, and at a certain point the subject refuses to go on with the experiment. Behavior prior to this rupture is considered "obedience," in that the subject complies with the commands of the experimenter. The point of rupture is the act of disobedience. A quantitative value is assigned to the subject's performance based on the maximum intensity shock he is willing to administer before he refuses to participate further. Thus for any particular subject and for any particular experimental condition the degree of obedience may be specified with a numerical value. The crux of the study is to systematically vary the factors believed to alter the degree of obedience to the experimental commands.

The technique allows important variables to be manipulated at several points in the experiment. One may vary aspects of the source of command, content and form of command, instrumentalities for its execution, target object, general social setting, etc. The problem, therefore, is not one of designing increasingly more numerous experimental conditions, but of selecting those that best illuminate the process of obedience from the sociopsychological standpoint...

METHOD

Subjects

The subjects were 40 males between the ages of 20 and 50, drawn from New Haven and the surrounding communities. Subjects were obtained by a newspaper advertisement and direct mail solicitation. Those who responded to the appeal believed they were to participate in a study of memory and learning at Yale University. A wide range of occupations is represented in the sample. Typical subjects were postal clerks, high school teachers, salesmen, engineers, and laborers. Subjects ranged in educational level from one who had not finished elementary school, to those who had doctoral and other professional degrees. They were paid $4.50 for their participation in the experiment. However, subjects were told that payment was simply for coming to the laboratory, and that the money was theirs no matter what happened after they arrived. Table 1 shows the proportion of age and occupational types assigned to the experimental condition.

Personnel and Locale

The experiment was conducted on the grounds of Yale University in the elegant interaction laboratory. (This detail is relevant to the perceived legitimacy of the experiment. In further variations, the experiment was dissociated from the university,

TABLE 1   DISTRIBUTION OF AGE AND OCCUPATIONAL TYPES IN THE EXPERIMENT

Occupations	20-29 Years n	30-39 Years n	40-50 Years n	Percentage of total (Occupations)
Workers, skilled and unskilled	4	5	6	37.5
Sales, business, and white-collar	3	6	7	40.0
Professional	1	5	3	22.5
Percentage of total (Age)	20	40	40	

Note: Total $N = 40$.

with consequences for performance.) The role of experimenter was played by a 31-year-old high school teacher of biology. His manner was impassive, and his appearance somewhat stern throughout the experiment. He was dressed in a gray technician's coat. The victim was played by a 47-year-old accountant, trained for the role; he was of Irish-American stock, whom most observers found mild-mannered and likable.

Procedure

One naive subject and one victim (an accomplice) performed in each experiment. A pretext had to be devised that would justify the administration of electric shock by the naive subject. This was effectively accomplished by the cover story. After a general introduction on the presumed relation between punishment and learning, subjects were told:

> But actually, we know very little about the effect of punishment on learning, because almost no truly scientific studies have been made of it in human beings.
>
> For instance, we don't know how much punishment is best for learning – and we don't know how much difference it makes as to who is giving the punishment, whether an adult learns best from a younger or an older person than himself – or many things of that sort.
>
> So in this study we are bringing together a number of adults of different occupations and ages. And we're asking some of them to be teachers and some of them to be learners.
>
> We want to find out just what effect different people have on each other as teachers and learners, and also what effect punishment will have on learning in this situation.
>
> Therefore, I'm going to ask one of you to be the teacher here tonight and the other one to be the learner.
>
> Does either of you have a preference?

Subjects then drew slips of paper from a hat to determine who would be the teacher and who would be the learner in the experiment. The drawing was rigged so that the naive subject was always the teacher and the accomplice always the learner. (Both slips contained the word "Teacher.") Immediately after the drawing, the teacher and learner were taken to an adjacent room and the learner was strapped into an "electric chair" apparatus.

The experimenter explained that the straps were to prevent excessive movement while the learner was being shocked. The effect was to make it impossible for him to escape from the situation. An electrode was attached to the learner's wrist, and electrode paste was applied "to avoid blisters and burns." Subjects were told that the electrode was attached to the shock generator in the adjoining room.

In order to improve credibility the experimenter declared, in response to a question by the learner: "Although the shocks can be extremely painful, they cause no permanent tissue damage."

Learning Task. The lesson administered by the subject was a paired-associate learning task. The subject read a series of word pairs to the learner, and then read the first word of the pair along with four terms. The learner was to indicate which of the four terms had originally been paired with the first word. He communicated his answer by pressing one of four switches in front of him, which in turn lit up one of four numbered quadrants in an answer box located atop the shock generator.

Shock Generator. The instrument panel consists of 30 lever switches set in a horizontal line. Each switch is clearly labeled with a voltage designation that ranges from 15 to 450 volts. There is a 15-volt increment from one switch to the next going from left to right. In addition, the following verbal designations are clearly indicated for groups of four switches going from left to right: Slight Shock, Moderate Shock, Strong Shock, Very Strong Shock, Intense Shock, Extreme Intensity Shock, Danger: Severe Shock. (Two switches after this last designation are simply marked XXX.)

Upon depressing a switch: a pilot light corresponding to each switch is illuminated in bright red; an electric buzzing is heard; and electric blue light, labeled "voltage energizer," flashes; the dial on the voltage meter swings to the right; various relay clicks are sounded.

The upper left-hand corner of the generator is labeled Shock Generator, Type ZLB, Dyson Instrument Company, Waltham, Mass. Output 15 Volts–450 Volts.

Details of the instrument were carefully handled to insure an appearance of authenticity. The panel was engraved by precision industrial engravers, and all components were of high quality. No subject in the experiment suspected that the instrument was merely a simulated shock generator.

Sample Shock. Each naive subject is given a sample shock on the shock generator, prior to beginning his run as teacher. This shock is always 45 volts, and is applied by pressing the third switch of the generator. The shock is applied to the wrist of the naive subject, and has its source in a 45-volt battery wired into the generator. This further convinces the subject of the authenticity of the generator.

Shock Instructions. The subject is told to administer a shock to the learner each time he gives a wrong response. Moreover – and this is the key command – the subject is instructed to "move one level higher on the shock generator each time the learner flashes a wrong answer." He is also instructed to announce the voltage level before administering a shock. This serves to continually remind subjects of the increasing intensity of shocks administered to the learner.

Preliminary and Regular Run. Pretests revealed that the procedure of reading words and administering shocks requires some practice before it can be handled smoothly. Therefore, immediately preceding the regular run, the teacher is given a preliminary series of 10 words to read to the learner. There are 3 neutral words in the practice series (i.e., words that the learner answers correctly), so that shocks are administered for 7 of the words, with the maximum shock at 105 volts (moderate shock). Almost all subjects master the procedure by the time the preliminary run is over.

Subjects are then presented with a second list, and are told that the procedure is the same as for the first list; the experimenter adds, however:

> When you get to the bottom of the list, repeat it over again, and continue giving shocks, until the learner has learned all the pairs correctly.

The experimenter instructs the subject to:

> start from 15 volts and increase the shock level one step each time the learner gives a wrong answer.

Feedback from the Victim. In all conditions the learner gives a predetermined set of responses to the word pair test, based on a schedule of approximately three wrong answers to one correct answer. In the present experimental condition no vocal response or other sign of protest is heard from the learner until Shock Level 300 is reached. When the 300-volt shock is administered, the learner pounds on the wall of the room in which he is bound to the electric chair. The pounding can be heard by the subject. From this point on, the learner's answers no longer appear on the four-way panel.

At this juncture, subjects ordinarily turn to the experimenter for guidance. The experimenter instructs the subject to treat the absence of a response as a wrong answer, and to shock the subject according to the usual schedule. He advised the subjects to allow 5–10 seconds before considering no response as a wrong answer, and to increase the shock level one step each time the learner fails to respond correctly. The learner's pounding is repeated after the 315–volt shock is administered; afterwards he is not heard from, nor do his answers reappear on the four-way signal box.

Experimenter Feedback. At various points in the experiment the subject may turn to the experimenter for advice on whether he should continue to administer shocks. Or he may indicate that he does not wish to go on. It is important to standardize the experimenter's responses to these inquires and reactions.

If the subject indicated his unwillingness to go on the experimenter responded with a sequence of "prods," using as many as necessary to bring the subject into line.

> Prod 1: Please continue, or Please go on.
> Prod 2: The experiment requires that you continue.
> Prod 3: It is absolutely essential that you continue.
> Prod 4: You have no other choice, you must go on.

The prods were always made in sequence: Only if Prod 1 had been unsuccessful, could Prod 2 be used. If the subject refused to obey the experimenter after Prod 4, the experiment was terminated. The experimenter's tone of voice was at all times firm, but not impolite. The sequence was begun anew on each occasion that the subject balked or showed reluctance to follow orders.

Special prods. If the subject asked if the learner was liable to suffer permanent physical injury, the experimenter said:

Although the shocks may be painful, there is no permanent tissue damage, so please go on. [Followed by Prods 2, 3, and 4 if necessary.]

If the subject said that the learner did not want to go on, the experimenter replied:

Whether the learner likes it or not, you must go on until he has learned all the word pairs correctly. So please go on. [Followed by Prods 2, 3, and 4 if necessary.]

Dependent Measures

The primary dependent measure for any subject is the maximum shock he administers before he refuses to go any further. In principle this may vary from 0 (for a subject who refuses to administer even the first shock) to 30 (for a subject who administers the highest shock on the generator). A subject who breaks off the experiment at any point prior to administering the thirtieth shock level is termed a *defiant* subject. One who complies with experimental commands fully, and proceeds to administer all shock levels commanded, is termed an *obedient* subject.

Further Records. With few exceptions experimental sessions were recorded on magnetic tape. Occasional photographs were taken through one-way mirrors. Notes were kept on any unusual behavior occurring during the course of the experiments. On occasion, additional observers were directed to write objective descriptions of the subjects' behavior. The latency and duration of shocks were measured by accurate timing devices.

Interview and Dehoax. Following the experiment, subjects were interviewed; open-ended questions, projective measures, and attitude scales were employed. After the interview, procedures were undertaken to assure that the subject would leave the laboratory in a state of well-being. A friendly reconciliation was arranged between the subject and the victim, and an effort was made to reduce any tensions that arose as a results of the experiment.

RESULTS

Preliminary Notions

Before giving an account of the experimental results, it is instructive to consider how persons predict others will perform when commanded to administer powerful shocks to another person. Fourteen Yale seniors, all psychology majors, were provided with a detailed description of the experimental situation. They were asked to reflect carefully on it, and to predict the behavior of 100 hypothetical subjects. More specifically, they were instructed to plot the distribution of obedience of "100 Americans of diverse occupations, and ranging in age from 20 to 50 years," who were placed in the experimental situation.

There was considerable agreement among the respondents on the expected behavior of hypothetical subjects. All respondents predicted that only an insignificant minority would go through to the end of the shock series. (The estimates ranged from 0 to 3%; i.e, the most "pessimistic" member of the class predicted that of 100 persons, 3 would continue through to the most potent shock available on the shock generator – 450 volts.) The class mean was 1.2%. The question was also posed informally to colleagues of the author, and the most general feeling was that few if any subjects would go beyond the designation Very Strong Shock.

Result of Experiment I

Subjects Accept Situation. With few exceptions, subjects were convinced of the reality of the experimental situation, that they were administering shocks to another person, and the most potent shocks were extremely painful. In the postexperimental interview subjects were asked: "How painful to the learner were the last few shocks that you administered to him?" Subjects were instructed to indicate their answers on a printed 14-point scale ranging from "Not at all painful" to "Extremely painful." The modal response was 14 (Extremely painful) with the mean at 13.42.

Signs of Extreme Tension. Many subjects showed signs of nervousness in the experimental situation, and especially upon administering the more powerful shocks. In a large number of cases the degree of tension reached extremes that are rarely seen in sociopsychological laboratory studies. Subjects were observed to sweat, tremble, stutter, bite their lips, groan, and dig their fingernails into their flesh. These were characteristic rather than exceptional responses to the experiment.

One sign of tension was the regular occurrence of nervous laughing fits. Fourteen of the 40 subjects showed definite signs of nervous laughter and smiling. The laughter seemed entirely out of place, even bizarre. Full-blown, uncontrollable seizures were observed for 3 subjects. On one occasion we observed a seizure so violently convulsive that it was necessary to call a halt to the experiment. The subject, a 46-year-old encyclopedia salesman, was seriously embarrassed by his untoward and uncontrollable behavior. In the postexperimental interviews subjects took pains to point out that they were not sadistic types, and that the laughter did not mean they enjoyed shocking the victim.

Distribution of Scores. It had been conjectured that persons would not, in general agree to administer shocks beyond the level designated as Very Strong Shock. The distribution of maximum shocks for this experiment is shown in Table 2. The obtained distribution of scores deviates radically from the prediction.

TABLE 2   DISTRIBUTION OF BREAKOFF POINTS

Verbal Designation and Voltage Indication	Number of Subjects for Whom This Was Maximum Shock
Slight Shock	0
15	0
30	0
45	0
60	
Moderate Shock	
75	0
90	0
105	0
120	0
Strong Shock	
135	0
150	0
165	0
180	
Very Strong Shock	
195	0
210	0
225	0
240	0
Intense Shock	
255	0
270	0
285	0
300	5
Extreme Intensity Shock	
315	4
330	2
345	1
360	1
Danger: Severe Shock	
375	1
390	0
405	0
420	0
XXX	
435	0
450	26

Upon command of the experimenter, each of the 40 subjects went beyond the expected breakoff point. No subject stopped prior to administering Shock Level 20. (At this level – 300 volts – the victim kicks on the wall and no longer provides answers to the teacher's multiple-choice questions.)

Of the 40 subjects, 5 refused to obey the experimental commands beyond the 300-volt level. Four more subjects administered one further shock, and then refused to go on. Two broke off at the 330-volt level, and 1 each at 345, 360, and 375 volts. Thus a total of 14 subjects defied the experimenter. It is instructive to reprint their remarks at the point of defiance, as transcribed from the tape recordings:

> [0124] I think he's trying to communicate, he's knocking. ... Well it's not fair to shock the guy ... these are terrific volts. I don't think this is very humane. ... Oh, I can't go on with this; no, this isn't right. It's a hell of an experiment. The guy is suffering in there. No, I don't want to go on. This is crazy. [Subject refused to administer more shocks.]
>
> [0123] He's banging in there. I'm gonna chicken out. I'd like to continue, but I can't do that to a man. ... I'm sorry I can't do that to a man I'll hurt his heart. You take your check. ... No really, I couldn't do it.

These subjects were frequently in a highly agitated and even angered state. Sometimes, verbal protest was at a minimum, and the subject simply got up from his chair in front of the shock generator, and indicated that he wished to leave the laboratory.

Of the 40 subjects, 26 obeyed the orders of the experimenter to the end, proceeding to punish the victim until they reached the most potent shock available on the shock generator. At that point, the experimenter called a halt to the session. (The maximum shock is labeled 450 volts, and is two steps beyond the designation: Danger: Severe Shock.) Although obedient subjects continued to administer shocks, they often did so under extreme stress. Some expressed reluctance to administer shocks beyond the 300-volt level, and displayed fears similar to those who defied the experimenter; yet they obeyed.

After the maximum shocks had been delivered, and the experimenter called a halt to the proceedings, many obedient subjects heaved sighs of relief, mopped their brows, rubbed their fingers over their eyes, or nervously fumbled cigarettes. Some shook their heads, apparently in regret. Some subjects had remained calm throughout the experiment, and displayed only minimal signs of tension from beginning to end.

DISCUSSION

The experiment yielded two findings that were surprising. The first finding concerns the sheer strength of obedient tendencies manifested in this situation. Subjects have learned from childhood that it is a fundamental breach of moral conduct to hurt another person against his will. Yet, 26 subjects abandon this tenet in following the instructions of an authority who has no special powers to enforce his commands. To disobey would bring no material loss to the subject; no punishment would ensue. It is clear from the remarks and outward behavior of many participants that in punishing the victim they are often acting against their own values. Subjects often expressed deep disapproval of shocking a man in the face of his objections, and others denounced it as stupid and senseless. Yet the majority complied with the experimental commands. This outcome was surprising from two perspectives: first, from the standpoint of predictions made in the questionnaire described earlier. (Here, however, it is possible that the remoteness of the respondents from the actual situation, and the difficulty of conveying to them the concrete details of the experiment, could account for the serious underestimation of obedience.)

But the results were also unexpected to persons who observed the experiment in progress, through one-way mirrors. Observers often uttered expressions of disbelief upon seeing a subject administer more powerful shocks to the victim. These persons had a full acquaintance with the details of the situation, and yet systematically underestimated the amount of obedience that subjects would display.

The second unanticipated effect was the extraordinary tension generated by the procedures. One might suppose that a subject would simply break off or continue as his conscience dictated. Yet, this is very far from what happened. There were striking reactions of tension and emotional strain. One observer related:

> I observed a mature and initially poised businessman enter the laboratory smiling and confident. Within 20 minutes he was reduced to a twitching, stuttering wreck, who was rapidly approaching a point of nervous collapse. He constantly pulled on his earlobe, and twisted his hands. At one point he pushed his fist into his forehead and muttered: "Oh God, let's stop it." And yet he continued to respond to every word of the experimenter, and obeyed to the end.

Any understanding of the phenomenon of obedience must rest on an analysis of the particular conditions in which it occurs. The following features of the experiment go some distance in explaining the high amount of obedience observed in the situation.

1. The experiment is sponsored by and takes place on the grounds of an institution of unimpeachable reputation, Yale University. It may be reasonably presumed that the personnel are competent and reputable. The importance of this background authority is now being studied by conducting a series of experiments outside of New Haven, and without any visible ties to the university.

2. The experiment is, on the face of it, designed to attain a worthy purpose – advancement of knowledge about learning and memory. Obedience occurs not as an end in itself, but as an instrumental element in a situation that the subject construes as significant, and meaningful. He may not be able to see its full significance, but he may properly assume that the experimenter does.

3. The subject perceives that the victim has voluntarily submitted to the authority system of the experimenter. He is not (at first) an unwilling captive impressed for involuntary service. He has taken the trouble to come to the laboratory

presumably to aid the experimental research. That he later becomes an involuntary subject does not alter the fact that, initially, he consented to participate without qualification. Thus he has in some degree incurred an obligation toward the experimenter.

4. The subject, too, has entered the experiment voluntarily, and perceives himself under obligation to aid the experimenter. He has made a commitment, and to disrupt the experiment is a repudiation of this initial promise of aid.

5. Certain features of the procedure strengthen the subject's sense of obligation to the experimenter. For one, he has been paid for coming to the laboratory. In part this is canceled out by the experimenter's statement that:

> Of course, as in all experiments, the money is yours simply for coming to the laboratory. From this point on, no matter that happens, the money is yours.[1]

6. From the subject's standpoint, the fact that he is the teacher and the other man the learner is purely a chance consequence (it is determined by drawing lots) and he, the subject, ran the same risk as the other man in being assigned the role of learner. Since the assignment of positions in the experiment was achieved by fair means, the learner is deprived of any basis of complaint on this count. (A similar situation obtains in Army units, in which – in the absence of volunteers – a particularly dangerous mission may be assigned by drawing lots, and the unlucky soldier is expected to bear his misfortune with sportsmanship.)

7. There is, at best, ambiguity with regard to the prerogatives of a psychologist and the corresponding rights of his subject. There is a vagueness of expectation concerning what a psychologist may require of his subject and when he is overstepping acceptable limits. Moreover, the experiment occurs in a closed setting, and thus provides no opportunity for the subject to remove these ambiguities by discussion with others. There are few standards that seem directly applicable to the situation, which is a novel one for most subjects.

8. The subjects are assured that the shocks administered to the subject are "painful but not dangerous." Thus they assume that the discomfort caused the victim is momentary, while the scientific gains resulting from the experiment are enduring.

9. Through Shock Level 20 the victim continues to provide answers on the signal box. The subject may construe this as a sign that the victim is still willing to "play the game." It is only after Shock Level 20 that the victim repudiates the rules completely, refusing to answer further.

These features help to explain the high amount of obedience obtained in this experiment. Many of the arguments raised need not remain matters of speculation, but

---

[1] Forty-three subjects, undergraduates at Yale University, were run in the experiment without payment. The results are very similar to those obtained with paid subjects.

can be reduced to testable propositions to be confirmed or disproved by further experiments.[2]

The following features of the experiment concern the nature of the conflict which the subjects faces.

10. The subject is placed in a position in which he must respond to the competing demands of two persons: the experimenter and the victim. The conflict must be resolved by meeting the demands of one or the other; satisfaction of the victim and the experimenter are mutually exclusive. Moreover, the resolution must take the form of a highly visible action, that of continuing to shock the victim or breaking off the experiment. Thus the subject is forced into a public conflict that does not permit any completely satisfactory solution.

11. While the demands of the experimenter carry the weight of scientific authority, the demands of the victim spring from his personal experience of pain and suffering. The two claims need not be regarded as equally pressing and legitimate. The experimenter seeks an abstract scientific datum; the victim cries out for relief from physical suffering caused by the subject's actions.

12. The experiment gives the subject little time for reflection. The conflict comes on rapidly. It is only minutes after the subject has been seated before the shock generator that the victim begins his protests. Moreover, the subject perceives that he has gone through but two-thirds of the shock levels at the time the subject's first protests are heard. Thus he understands that the conflict will have a persistent aspect to it, and may well become more intense as increasingly more powerful shocks are required. The rapidity with which the conflict descends on the subject, and his realization that it is predictably recurrent, may well be sources of tension to him.

13. At a more general level, the conflict stems from the oppositions: first, the disposition not to harm other people, and second, the tendency to obey those whom we perceive to be legitimate authorities.

REFERENCES

BUSS, A. H. (1961). *The psychology of aggression*. New York: Wiley.
MILGRAM S. (1961) Dynamics of obedience. Washington: *National Science Foundation*, 25 January. (Mimeo)
SNOW, C. P. (1961) Either-or. *Progressive*, (Feb.), 24.

---

[2] A series of recently completed experiments employing the obedience paradigm is reported in Milgram (1964).

QUESTIONS

1. How does Milgram view obedience? Does he believe obedience is, in general, good or bad?

2. Briefly describe the subjects in this experiment. Do you consider them to be relatively representative of people in the United States?

3. Did subjects in this experiment believe in the authenticity of the shock generator? What steps were taken to insure their acceptance?

4. What percentage of subjects gave "very strong shocks"? What percentage gave "extreme intensity shocks"? What percentage gave the highest shocks of 450 volts?

5. If this study were conducted today on your campus, what percentage of students do you think would administer the 450-volt shock? Compare your prediction with those of Yale students at the time the experiment was conducted.

Reading 24: Contemporary

Commitment and Consistency

Robert B. Cialdini

In the previous reading, Stanley Milgram discussed when and why people obey others' orders. Yet explicit orders are only one form of social influence. For example, Milgram's research cannot explain why we go along with the request of merchandisers to buy their products. This form of persuasion is much more subtle than that studied by Milgram.

The next reading is an excerpt from social psychologist Robert Cialdini's fascinating book on social influence. In the chapter from which this reading was excerpted, Cialdini discusses what has been called "the hobgoblin of little minds": foolish consistency. A foolish consistency is the tendency to avoid rethinking decisions once they have been made, even when doing so would clearly be to one's advantage. Why do people remain committed to past decisions? And how do advertisers and manufacturers use commitment to their advantage? Cialdini answers these questions, and more.

Ψ

A study done by a pair of Canadian psychologists (Knox & Inkster, 1968) uncovered something fascinating about people at the racetrack: Just after placing bets they are more confident of their horses' chances of winning than they are immediately before laying down the bets. Of course, nothing about the horse's chances actually shifts; it's the same horse, on the same track, in the same field; but in the minds of those bettors, its prospects improve significantly once that ticket is purchased. Although a bit puzzling at first glance, the reason for the dramatic change has to do with a common weapon of social influence. Like the other weapons of influence, this one lies deep within us, directing our actions with quiet power. It is, quite simply, our nearly obsessive desire to be (and to appear) consistent with what we have already done. *Once we make a choice or take a stand, we will encounter personal and interpersonal pressures to behave consistently with that commitment.* Those pressures will cause us to respond in ways that justify our earlier decision. We simply convince ourselves that we have made the right choice and, no doubt, feel better about our decision.

For evidence, let's examine the story of my neighbor Sara and her live-in boyfriend, Tim. After they met, they dated for a while, even after Tim lost his job, and eventually moved in together. Things were never perfect for Sara: She wanted Tim to marry her and

Source: Cialdini, R.B. (1993). *Influence: Science and practice (3rd ed.).* New York: Harper Collins. Copyright © 1993 by Allyn & Bacon. Reprinted by permission of the publisher.

to stop his heavy drinking; Tim resisted both ideas. After an especially difficult period of conflict, Sara broke off the relationship and Tim moved out. At the same time, an old boyfriend of Sara's called her. They started seeing each other socially and quickly became engaged and made wedding plans. They had gone so far as to set a date and issue invitations when Tim called. He had repented and wanted to move back in. When Sara told him her marriage plans, he begged her to change her mind; he wanted to be together with her as before. Sara refused, saying she didn't want to live like that again. Tim even offered to marry her, but she still said she preferred the other boyfriend. Finally, Tim volunteered to quit drinking if she would only relent. Feeling that under those conditions Tim had the edge, Sara decided to break her engagement, cancel the wedding, retract the invitations, and let Tim move back in with her.

Within a month, Tim informed Sara that he didn't think he needed to stop drinking after all. A month later, he decided that they should "wait and see" before getting married. Two years have since passed; Tim and Sara continue to live together exactly as before. Tim still drinks, and there are still no marriage plans, yet Sara is more devoted to him than she ever was. She says that being forced to choose taught her that Tim really is number one in her heart. So, after choosing Tim over her other boyfriend, Sara became happier, even though the conditions under which she had made her choice have never been fulfilled. Obviously, horse-race bettors are not alone in their willingness to believe in the correctness of a difficult choice once made. Indeed, we all fool ourselves from time to time in order to keep our thoughts and beliefs consistent with what we have already done or decided (Conway & Ross, 1984; Goethals & Reckman, 1973; Rosenfeld, Kennedy, & Giacalone, 1986).

WHIRRING ALONG

Psychologists have long understood the power of the consistency principle to direct human action. Prominent theorists such as Leon Festinger (1957), Fritz Heider (1946), and Theodore Newcomb (1953) have viewed the desire for consistency as a central motivator of behavior. Is this tendency to be consistent really strong enough to compel us to do what we ordinarily would not want to do? There is no question about it. The drive to be (and look) consistent constitutes a highly potent weapon of social influence, often causing us to act in ways that are clearly contrary to our own best interest.

Consider what happened when researchers staged thefts on a New York City beach to see if onlookers would risk personal harm to halt the crime. In the study, an accomplice of the researchers would put a beach blanket down five feet from the blanket of a randomly chosen individual – the experimental subject. After several minutes of relaxing on the blanket and listening to music from a portable radio, the accomplice would stand up and leave the blanket to stroll down the beach. Soon, thereafter, a researcher, pretending to be a thief, would approach, grab the radio, and try to hurry away with it. As you might guess, under normal conditions, subjects were very reluctant to put themselves in harm's way by challenging the thief – only four people did so in the 20 times that the theft was staged. But when the same procedure was tried another 20 times with a slight twist, the results were drastically different. In these incidents, before leaving the blanket, the accomplice would simply ask the subject to please "watch my things," something everyone agreed to do. Now, propelled by the rule for consistency, 19 of the 20 subjects became virtual vigilantes, running after and stopping the thief, demanding an explanation, often restraining the thief physically or snatching the radio away (Moriarty, 1975).

To understand why consistency is so powerful a motive, we should recognize that, in most circumstances, consistency is valued and adaptive. Inconsistency is commonly thought to be an undesirable personality trait (Allgeier, Byrne, Brooks, & Revnes, 1979; Asch, 1946). The person whose beliefs, words, and deeds don't match is seen as confused, two-faced, even mentally ill. On the other side, a high degree of consistency is normally associated with personal and intellectual strength. It is the heart of logic, rationality, stability, and honesty. A quote attributed to the great British chemist, Michael Faraday, suggests the extent to which being consistent is approved – sometimes more than being right. When asked after a lecture if he meant to imply that a hated academic rival was always wrong, Faraday glowered at the questioner and replied, "He's not that consistent."

Certainly, then, good personal consistency is highly valued in our culture – and well it should be. Most of the time we will be better off if our approach to things is well laced with consistency. Without it our lives would be difficult, erratic, and disjointed.

The Quick Fix

Since it is so typically in our best interests to be consistent, we fall into the habit of being automatically consistent even in situations where it is not the sensible way to be. When it occurs unthinkingly, consistency can be disastrous. Nonetheless, even blind consistency has its attractions.

First, like most other forms of automatic responding, it offers a shortcut through the complexities of modern life. Once we have made up our minds about issues, stubborn consistency allows us a very appealing luxury: We don't have to think hard about the issues anymore. We don't really have to sift through the blizzard of information we encounter every day to identify relevant facts; we don't have to expend the mental energy to weigh the pros and cons; we don't have to make any further tough decisions. Instead, all we have to do when confronted with the issues is turn on our consistency tape, *whirr*, and we know just what to believe, say, or do. We need only believe, say, or do whatever is consistent with our earlier decision.

The allure of such a luxury is not to be minimized. It allows us a convenient, relatively effortless, and efficient method for dealing with the complexities of daily life that make severe demands on our mental energies and capacities. It is not hard to understand, then, why automatic consistency is a difficult reaction to curb. It offers us a way to evade the rigors of continuing thought. With our consistency tapes operating, we can go about our business happily excused from having to think too much. As Sir Joshua Reynolds noted, "There is no expedient to which a man will not resort to avoid the real labor of thinking."...

If, as it appears, automatic consistency functions as a shield against thought, it should not be surprising that such consistency can also be exploited by those who would prefer that we respond to their requests without thinking. For the profiteers, whose interest will be served by an unthinking, mechanical reaction to their requests, our tendency for automatic consistency is a gold mine. So clever are they at arranging to have us play our consistency tapes when it profits them that we seldom realize that we have been taken. In fine jujitsu fashion, they structure their interactions with us so that our own need to be consistent leads directly to their benefit.

Certain large toy manufacturers use just such an approach to reduce a problem created by seasonal buying patterns. Of course, the boom time for toy companies occurs before and during the Christmas holiday season. Their problem is that toy sales then go into a terrible slump for the next couple of months. Their customers have already spent the amount in their toy budgets and are stiffly resistant to their children's pleas for more.

So the toy manufacturers are faced with a dilemma: how to keep sales high during the peak season and, at the same time, retain a healthy demand for toys in the immediately following months. Their difficulty certainly doesn't lie in motivating kids to want more toys after Christmas. The problem lies in motivating postholiday spent-out parents to buy another plaything for their already toy-glutted children. What could the toy companies possibly do to produce that unlikely behavior? Some have tried greatly increased advertising campaigns, others have reduced prices during the slack period, but neither of those standard sales devices has proved successful. Both tactics are costly, and have been ineffective in increasing sales to desired levels. Parents are simply not in a toy-buying mood, and the influences of advertising or reduced expense are not enough to shake that stony resistance.

Certain large toy manufacturers, however, think they have found a solution. It's an ingenious one, involving no more than a normal advertising expense and an understanding of the powerful pull of the need for consistency. My first hint of the way the toy companies' strategy worked came after I fell for it and then, in true patsy form, fell for it again.

It was January, and I was in the town's largest toy store. After purchasing all too many gifts there for my son a month before, I had sworn not to enter that place or any like it for a long, long time. Yet there I was, not only in the diabolic place but also in the process of buying my son another expensive toy – a big, electric road-race set. In front of the road-race display I happened to meet a former neighbor who was buying his son the same toy. The odd thing was that we almost never saw each other anymore. In fact, the last time had been a year earlier in the same store when we were both buying our sons an expensive post-Christmas gift – that time a robot that walked, talked, and laid waste. We laughed about our strange pattern of seeing each other only once a year at the same time, in the same place, while doing the same thing. Later that day, I mentioned the coincidence to a friend who, it turned out, had once worked in the toy business.

"No coincidence," he said knowingly.

"What do you mean, 'No coincidence'?"

"Look," he said, "let me ask you a couple of questions about the road-race set you bought this year. First, did you promise your son that he'd get one for Christmas?"

"Well, yes I did. Christopher had seen a bunch of ads for them on the Saturday morning cartoon shows and said that was what he wanted for Christmas. I saw a couple of ads myself and it looked like fun; so I said OK."

"Strike one," he announced. "Now for my second question. When you went to buy one, did you find all the stores sold out?"

"That's right, I did! The stores said they'd ordered some but didn't know when they'd get any more in. So I had to buy Christopher some other toys to make up for the road-race set. But how did you know?"

"Strike two," he said. "Just let me ask one more question. Didn't this same sort of thing happen the year before with the robot toy?"

"Wait a minute...you're right. That's just what happened. This is incredible. How did you know?"

"No psychic powers; I just happen to know how several of the big toy companies jack up their January and February sales. They start prior to Christmas with attractive TV ads for certain special toys. The kids, naturally, want what they see and extract Christmas promises for these items from their parents. Now here's where the genius of the companies' plan comes in: They *undersupply* the stores with the toys they've gotten the parents to promise. Most parents find those toys sold out and are forced to substitute other toys of equal value. The toy manufacturers, of course, make a point of supplying the stores with plenty of these substitutes. Then, after Christmas, the companies start running the ads again for the other, special toys. That juices up the kids to want those toys more than ever. They go running to their parents whining, 'You promised, you promised,' and the adults go trudging off to the store to live up dutifully to their words."

"Where," I said, beginning to seethe now, "they meet other parents they haven't seen for a year, falling for the same trick, right?"

"Right. Uh, where are you going?"

"I'm going to take the road-race set right back to the store." I was so angry I was nearly shouting.

"Wait. Think for a minute first. Why did you buy it this morning?"

"Because I didn't want to let Christopher down and because I wanted to teach him that promises are to be lived up to."

"Well, has any of that changed? Look, if you take his toy away now, he won't understand why. He'll just know that his father broke a promise to him. Is that what you want?"

"No," I said, sighing, "I guess not. So, you're telling me that the toy companies doubled their profits on me for the past two years, and I never knew it; and now that I do, I'm still trapped – by my own words. So, what you're really telling me is, 'Strike three.'"

He nodded, 'And you're out.'

COMMITMENT IS THE KEY

Once we realize that the power of consistency is formidable in directing human action, an important practical question immediately arises: How is that force engaged? What produces the click that activates the *whirr* of the powerful consistency tape? Social psychologists think they know the answer: commitment. If I can get you to make a commitment (that is, to take a stand, to go on record), I will have set the stage for your automatic and ill-considered consistency with that earlier commitment. Once a stand is taken, there is a natural tendency to behave in ways that are stubbornly consistent with the stand.

As we've already seen, social psychologists are not the only ones who understand the connection between commitment and consistency. Commitment strategies are aimed at us by compliance professionals of nearly every sort. Each of the strategies is intended to get us to take some action or make some statement that will trap us into later compliance through consistency pressures. Procedures designed to create commitment take various forms. Some are bluntly straightforward; others are among the most subtle compliance tactics we will encounter. On the blunt side, consider the approach of Jack Stanko, used-car sales manager for an Albuquerque auto dealership. While leading a session called "Used Car Merchandising" at a National Auto Dealers Association convention in San Francisco, he advised 100 sales-hungry dealers as follows: "Put 'em on paper. Get the customer's OK on paper. Get the money up front. Control 'em. Control the deal. Ask 'em if they would buy the car right now if the price is right. Pin 'em down" (Rubinstein, 1985). Obviously, Mr. Stanko – an expert in these matters – believes that the way to customer compliance is through their commitments, thereby to "control 'em" for profit.

Commitment practices involving substantially more finesse can be just as effective. For instance, suppose you wanted to increase the number of people in your area who would agree to go door-to-door collecting donations for your favorite charity. You would be wise to study the approach taken by social psychologist Steven J. Sherman. He simply called a sample of Bloomington, Indiana, residents as part of a survey he was taking and asked them to predict what they would say if asked to spend three hours collecting money for the American Cancer Society. Of course, not wanting to seem uncharitable to the survey-taker or to themselves, many of these people said that they would volunteer. The consequence of this subtle commitment procedure was a 700 percent increase in volunteers when, a few days later, a representative of the American Cancer Society did call and ask for neighborhood canvassers (Sherman, 1980). Using the same strategy, but this time asking Columbus, Ohio, residents to predict whether they would vote on Election Day, other researchers have been able to increase significantly the turnout in a U.S. presidential election among those called (Greenwald, Carnot, Beach, & Young, 1987).

Perhaps an even more crafty commitment technique has been developed by telephone solicitors for charity. Have you noticed that callers asking you to contribute to some cause or another these days seem to begin things by inquiring about your current health and well-being? "Hello, Mr./Ms. Targetperson?," they say. "How are you feeling this evening?," or "How are you doing today?" The caller's intent with this sort of introduction is not merely to seem friendly and caring. It is to get you to respond – as you normally do to such polite, superficial inquiries – with a polite, superficial comment of your own: "Just fine" or "Real good" or "I'm doing great, thanks." Once you have publicly stated that all is well, it becomes much easier for the solicitor to corner you into aiding those for whom all is not well: "I'm glad to hear that, because I'm calling to ask if you'd be willing to make a donation to help out the unfortunate victims of..."

The theory behind this tactic is that people who have just asserted that they are doing/feeling fine – even as a routine part of a sociable exchange – will consequently find it awkward to appear stingy in the context of their own admittedly favored circumstances. If all this sounds a bit far-fetched, consider the findings of consumer researcher Daniel Howard (1990), who put the theory to test. Residents of Dallas, Texas, were called on the phone and asked if they would agree to allow a representative of the Hunger Relief Committee to come to their homes to sell them cookies, the proceeds from which would be used to supply meals for the needy. When tried alone, that request (labeled the standard solicitation approach) produced only 18 percent agreement. However, if the caller initially asked, "How are you feeling this evening?" and waited for a reply before proceeding with the standard approach, several noteworthy things happened. First, of the 120 individuals called, most (108) gave the customary favorable reply ("Good," "Fine," "Real well," etc.) Second, 32 percent of the people who got the How-are-you-feeling-tonight question agreed to receive the cookie seller at their homes, nearly twice the success rate of the standard solicitation approach. Third, true to the consistency principle, almost everyone (89 percent) who agreed to such a visit did in fact make a cookie purchase when contacted at home.

To make sure that this tactic doesn't generate its successes simply because a solicitor who uses it seems more concerned and courteous than one who doesn't, Howard conducted another study. This time callers began either with the question, "How are you feeling this evening?" (and waited for a response before proceeding) or with the statement "I hope you are feeling well this evening" and then proceeded to the standard solicitation approach. Despite the fact that the caller started each type of interaction with a warm and friendly comment, the How-are-you-feeling technique was by far superior to its rival (33 percent versus 15 percent compliance), because only it drew an exploitable public commitment from its targets. Note that the commitment was able to get twice as much compliance from these targets even though at the time it occurred it must have seemed to them an altogether inconsequential reply to an altogether superficial question – yet another fine example of social jujitsu at work.

REFERENCES

ALLGEIER, A.R., BYRNE, D., BROOKS, B., & REVNES, D. (1979). The waffle phenomenon: Negative evaluations of those who shift attitudinally. *Journal of Applied Social Psychology, 9,* 170–182.

ASCH, S. (1946). Forming impressions of personality. *Journal of Abnormal and Social Psychology, 41,* 259–290.

CONWAY M., & ROSS, M. (1984). Getting what you want by revising what you had. *Journal of Personality and Social Psychology, 47,* 738–748.

FESTINGER, L. (1957). *A theory of cognitive dissonance.* Stanford: Stanford University Press.

GOETHALS, G.R., & RECKMAN, R.F. (1973). The perception of consistency in attitudes. *Journal of Experimental Social Psychology, 9,* 491–501.

GREENWALD, A.F., CARNOT, C.G., BEACH, R., & YOUNG, B. (1987). Increasing voting behavior by asking people if they expect to vote. *Journal of Applied Psychology, 72,* 315–318.

HEIDER, F. (1946). Attitudes and cognitive organization. *Journal of Psychology, 21,* 107–112.

HOWARD, D.J. (1990). The influence of verbal responses to common greetings on compliance behavior: The foot-in-the-mouth effect. *Journal of Applied Social Psychology, 20,* 1185–1196.

KNOX, R.E., & INKSTER, J.A. (1968). Postdecisional dissonance at post time. *Journal of Personality and Social Psychology, 8,* 319–323.

MORIARTY, T. (1975). Crime, commitment, and the responsive bystander. *Journal of Personality and Social Psychology, 31,* 370–376.

NEWCOMB, T. (1953). An approach to the study of communicative acts. *Psychological Review, 60,* 393–404.

ROSENFELD, P., KENNEDY, J.G., & GIACALONE, R.A. (1986). Decision-making: A demonstration of the postdecision dissonance effect. *Journal of Social Psychology, 126,* 663–665.

RUBINSTEIN, S. (1985, January 30). What they teach used car salesmen. *San Francisco Chronicle.*

SHERMAN, S.J. (1980). On the self-erasing nature of errors of prediction. *Journal of Personality and Social Psychology, 39,* 211–221.

QUESTIONS

1. What does gamblers' increased confidence after placing a bet have to do with Sara's forgiving her boyfriend Tim?

2. Do you think Sara's commitment to Tim is the result of wanting to appear consistent to others? Do you think her commitment is caused by mental laziness?

3. What are the two main benefits of consistency? What is the difference between a foolish consistency and an intelligent consistency?

4. What kind of consistency forced Cialdini not to return the race-car set even after he discovered that he had been tricked? What advice would you give parents to help them avoid buying twice as many toys as they would like?

5. Do you agree that it is somewhat illogical for people to chase after someone who appears to be stealing goods that they had promised to watch? Why or why not?

Ψ CHAPTER 13 Ψ

LAW AND ORDER: THE LEGAL SYSTEM

Reading 25: Classic

Reconstruction of Automobile Destruction: An Example of the Interaction Between Language and Memory

Elizabeth F. Loftus and John C. Palmer

Social psychology has a long record of conducting research guided by important social issues. Members of the research community continually adapt their research to address new questions as they emerge. One such area of growing importance over the past decade has been the American legal system. In recent years many people have been shocked by jury verdicts that seemed improbable, successful law suits that seemed frivolous, systemic corruption in the people and institutions entrusted to carry out justice, and controversial changes in rules governing police policy. Additionally we have often been divided over such controversies as whether to trust the memories of young children or of people who claim to have repressed memories for many years. These controversies have given rise to hundreds of studies applying principles of social psychology to dozens of questions about the American legal system.

The two readings in this section address potential biases in eyewitness memory. This first reading was somewhat ahead of its time by investigating this currently hot topic more than 25 years ago. In the first of the two studies described in this reading, Elizabeth Loftus and John Palmer set out to demonstrate empirically a phenomenon that had already been recognized by the Supreme Court: the influence of an eyewitness's testimony by leading questions. Having demonstrated the phenomenon in Study 1, the authors attempt in Study 2 to suggest why it occurs. They propose that an eyewitness who has been asked leading questions may simultaneous hold two memories of an event -- one accurate memory and one false memory -- and not be able to tell them apart.

Ψ

How accurately do we remember the details of a complex event, like a traffic accident, that has happened in our presence? More specifically, how well do we do when asked to estimate some numerical quantity such as how long the accident took, how fast the cars

Source: Loftus, E.F., and Palmer, J.C. (1974). Reconstruction of automobile destruction: An example of the interaction between language and memory. *Journal of Verbal Learning and Verbal Behavior 13,* 585-589. Copyright © 1974 by Academic Press. Reprinted by permission of the publisher.

were traveling, or how much time elapsed between the sounding of a horn and the moment of collision?

It is well documented that most people are markedly inaccurate in reporting such numerical details as time, speed, and distance (Bird, 1927; Whipple, 1909). For example, most people have difficulty estimating the duration of an event, with some research indicating that the tendency is to overestimate the duration of events which are complex (Block, 1974; Marshall, 1969; Ornstein, 1969). The judgment of speed is especially difficult, and practically every automobile accident results in huge variations from one witness to another as to how fast a vehicle was actually traveling (Gardner, 1933). In one test administered to Air Force personnel who knew in advance that they would be questioned about the speed of a moving automobile, estimates ranged from 10 to 50 mph. The car they watched was actually going only 12 mph (Marshall, 1969, p. 23).

Given the inaccuracies in estimates of speed, it seems likely that there are variables which are potentially powerful in terms of influencing these estimates. The present research was conducted to investigate one such variable, namely, the phrasing of the question used to elicit the speed judgment. Some questions are clearly more suggestive than others. This fact of life has resulted in the legal concept of a leading question and in legal rules indicating when leading questions are allowed (*Supreme Court Reporter*, 1973). A leading question is simply one that, either by its form or content, suggests to the witness what answer is desired or leads him to the desired answer.

In the present study, subjects were shown films of traffic accidents and then they answered questions about the accident. The subjects were interrogated about the speed of the vehicles in one of several ways. For example, some subjects were asked, "About how fast were the cars going when they hit each other?" while others were asked, "About how fast were the cars going when they smashed into each other?" As Fillmore (1971) and Bransford and McCarrell (in press) have noted, *hit* and *smashed* may involve specification of differential rates of movement. Furthermore, the two verbs may also involve differential specification of the likely consequences of the events to which they are referring. The impact of the accident is apparently gentler for *hit* than for *smashed*.

EXPERIMENT 1

Method

Forty-five students participated in groups of various sizes. Seven films were show, each depicting a traffic accident. These films were segments from longer driver's education films borrowed from the Evergreen Safety Council and the Seattle Police Department. The length of the film segments ranged from five to thirty seconds. Following each film, the subjects received a questionnaire asking them first to "give an account of the accident you have just seen," and then to answer a series of specific questions about the accident.

The critical question was the one that interrogated the subject about the speed of the vehicles involved in the collision. Nine subjects were asked, "About how fast were the cards going when they hit each other?" Equal numbers of the remaining subjects were

**TABLE 1   SPEED ESTIMATES FOR THE VERBS
USED IN EXPERMENT I**

Verb	Mean speed estimate
Smashed	40.8
Collided	39.3
Bumped	38.1
Hit	34.0
Contacted	31.8

interrogated with the verbs *smashed, collided, bumped,* and *contacted* in place of *hit.* The entire experiment lasted about an hour and a half. A different ordering of the films was presented to each group of subjects.

Results

Table 1 presents the mean speed estimates for the various verbs. Following the procedures outlined by Clark (1973), an analysis of variance was performed with verbs as a fixed effect, and subjects and films as random effects, yielding a significant quasi F ratio $F'(5,55) = 4.65, p < .005$.

Some information about the accuracy of subjects' estimates can be obtained from our data. Four of the seven films were staged crashes; the original purpose of these films was to illustrate what can happen to human beings when cars collide at various speeds. One collision took place at 20 mph, one at 30, and two at 40. The mean estimates of speed for these four films were: 37.7, 36.2, 39.7, and 36.1 mph, respectively. In agreement with previous work, people are not very good at judging how fast a vehicle was actually traveling.

Discussion

The results of this experiment indicate that the form of a question (in this case, changes in a single word) can markedly and systematically affect a witness's answer to that question. The actual speed of the vehicles controlled little variance in the subject reporting, while the phrasing of the question controlled considerable variance.

Two interpretations of this finding are possible. First, it is possible that the differential speed estimates result merely from response-bias factors. A subject is uncertain whether to say 30 mph or 40 mph, for example, and the verb *smashed* biases his response towards the higher estimate. A second interpretation is that the question form causes a change in the subject's memory representation of the accident. The verb *smashed* may change a subject's memory such that he "sees" the accident as being more severe than it actually was. If this is the case, we might expect subjects to "remember" other details that did not actually occur, but are commensurate with an accident occurring at higher speeds. The second experiment was designed to provide additional insights into the origin of the differential speed estimates.

EXPERIMENT II

Method

One hundred and fifty students participated in this experiment, in groups of various sizes. A film depicting a multiple car accident was shown, followed by a questionnaire. The film lasted less than 1 min; the accident in the film lasted 4 sec. At the end of the film, the subjects received a questionnaire asking them first to describe the accident in their own words, and then to answer a series of questions about the accident. The critical question was the one that interrogated the subject about the speed of the vehicles. Fifty subjects were asked, "About how fast were the cars going when they smashed into each other?" Fifty subjects were asked, "About how fast were the cars going when they hit each other?" Fifty subjects were not interrogated about vehicular speed.

One week later, the subjects returned and without viewing the film again they answered a series of questions about the accident. The critical question here was, "Did you see any broken glass?" which the subjects answered by checking "yes" or "no." This question was embedded in a list totaling 10 questions, and it appeared in a random position in the list. There was no broken glass in the accident, but since broken glass is commensurate with accidents occurring at high speed, we expected that the subjects who had been asked the *smashed* question might more often say "yes" to this critical question.

Results

The mean estimate of speed for subjects interrogated with *smashed* was 10.46 mph; with *hit* the estimate was 8.00 mph. These means are significantly different, $t(98) = 2.00, p < .05$.

Table 2 presents the distribution of "yes" and "no" responses for the *smashed*, *hit*, and control subjects. An independence chi-square test on these responses was significant beyond the .025 level, $x^2(2) = 7.76$. The important result in Table 2 is that the probability of saying "yes," P(Y), to the question about broken glass is .32 when the verb *smashed* is used, and .14 with *hit*. Thus smashed leads both to more "yes" responses and to higher speed estimates. It appears to be the case that the effect of the verb is mediated at least in part by the speed estimate. The question now arises: Is *smashed* doing anything else besides increasing the estimate of speed? To answer this, the function relating P(Y) to speed estimate was calculated separately for *smashed* and *hit*. If the speed estimate is the only way in which effect of verb is mediated, then for a given speed estimate, P(Y) should be independent of verb. Table 3 shows that this is not the case. P(Y) is lower for *hit* than for *smashed*; the difference between the two verbs ranges from .03 for estimates of 1-5 mph to .18 for estimates of 6-10 mph. The average difference between the two curves is about .12. Whereas the unconditioned difference of .18 between the *smashed* and *hit* conditions is attenuated, it is by no means eliminated when the estimate of speed is controlled for. It thus appears that the verb *smashed* has other effects besides that of simply increasing the estimate of speed. One possibility will be discussed in the next section.

TABLE 2
DISTRIBUTION OF "YES" AND "NO"
RESPONSES TO THE QUESTION, "DID YOU SEE
ANY BROKEN GLASS?"

Response	Verb Condition		
	Smashed	Hit	Control
Yes	16	7	6
No	34	43	44

DISCUSSION

To reiterate, we have first of all provided an additional demonstration of something that has been known for some time, namely, that the way a question is asked can enormously influence the answer that is given. In this instance, the question, "About how fast were the cars going when they smashed into each other?" led to higher estimates of speed than the same question asked with the verb *smashed* replaced by *hit*. Furthermore, this seemingly small change had consequences for how the questions are answered a week after the original event occurred.

As a framework for discussing these results, we would like to propose that two kinds of information go into one's memory for some complex occurrence. The first is information gleaned during the perception of the original event; the second is external information supplied after the fact. Over time, information from these two sources may be integrated in such a way that we are unable to tell from which source some specific detail is recalled. All we have is one "memory."

Discussing the present experiments in these terms, we propose that the subject first forms some representation of the accident he has witnessed. The experimenter then, while asking, "About how fast were the cars going when they smashed into each other?" supplies a piece of external information, namely, that the cars did indeed smash into each

TABLE 3
PROBABILITY OF SAYING "YES" TO, "DID
YOU SEE ANY BROKEN GLASS?" CONDITIONALIZED
ON SPEED ESTIMATES

Verb Condition	Speed estimate (mph)			
	1-5	6-10	11-15	16-20
Smashed	.09	.27	.41	.62
Hit	.06	.09	.25	.50

other. When these two pieces of information are integrated, the subject has a memory of an accident that was more severe than in fact it was. Since broken glass is commensurate with a severe accident, the subject is more likely to think that broken glass was present.

There is some connection between the present work and earlier work on the influence of verbal labels in memory for visually presented form of stimuli. A classic study in psychology showed that when subjects are asked to reproduce a visually presented form, their drawings tend to err in the direction of a more familiar object suggested by a verbal label initially associated with the to-be remembered form (Carmichael, Hogan, and Walter, 1932). More recently, Daniel (1972) showed that recognition memory, as well as reproductive memory, was similarly affected by verbal labels, and he concluded that the verbal label causes a shift in the memory strength of forms which are better representatives of the label.

When the experimenter asks the subject, "About how fast were the cars going when they smashed into each other?", he is effectively labeling the accident a smash. Extrapolating the conclusions of Daniel to this situation, it is natural to conclude that the label, smash, causes a shift in the memory representation of the accident in the direction of being more similar to a representation suggested by the verbal label.

REFERENCES

BIRD, C. The influence of the press upon the accuracy of report. *Journal of Abnormal and Social Psychology*, 1927, 22, 123-129.

BLOCK, R.A. Memory and the experience of duration in retrospect. *Memory and Cognition*, 1972, 2, 153-160.

BRANSFORD, J.D., AND MCCARRELL, N.S. A sketch of a cognitive approach to comprehension: Some thoughts about understanding what it means to comprehend. In D. PALERMO AND W. WEIMER (Eds.), *Cognition and the symbolic processes*. Washington, D.C.: V.H. Winston and Co., in press.

CARMICHAEL, L., HOGAN, H.P., AND WALTER, A.A. An experimental study of the effect of language on the reproduction of visually perceived form. *Journal of Experimental Psychology*, 1932, 15, 73-86.

CLARK, H..H. The language-as-fixed-effect fallacy: A critique of language statistics in psychological research. *Journal of Verbal Learning and Verbal Behavior*, 1973, 12, 335-359.

DANIEL, T.C. Nature of the effect of verbal labels on recognition memory for form. *Journal of Experimental Psychology*, 1972, 96, 152-157.

FILLMORE, C.J. Types of lexical information. In D.D. Steinberg and L.A. Jakobovitz (Eds.), *Semantics: An interdisciplinary reader in philosophy, linguistics, and psychology*. Cambridge: Cambridge University Press, 1971.

GARDNER, D.S. The perception and memory of witnesses. *Cornell Law Quarterly*, 1933, 8, 391-409.

MARSHALL, J. *Law and psychology in conflict*. New York: Anchor Books, 1969.

ORNSTEIN, R.E. *On the experience of time*. Harmondsworth. Middlesex. England: Penguin, 1969.

WHIPPLE, G.M. The observer as reporter: A survey of the psychology of testimony. *Psychological Bulletin*, 1909, 6, 153-170.

Supreme Court Reporter, 1973, 3: Rules of Evidence for United States Courts and Magistrates.

QUESTIONS

1. In the first study, were participants' estimates of the speed of cars in accidents more influenced by the actual speed or by leading questions?

2. Think about the suggested speed of the five verbs used in the first experiment: bumped, collided, contacted, hit, and smashed. The authors focus their attention on the effects of the two verbs "hit" and "smashed;" did the other three verbs lead to the kinds of speed estimates you would have expected?

3. Why did the authors wait one week in experiment two between asking participants to estimate the speed of the cars in the accident and asking them whether they saw glass at the accident scene?

4. The authors believe that their results are due to participants confusing their two memories of the car accident: the actual memory and the false memory suggested by leading questions. Can you suggest an alternative explanation for their findings?

5. In the second study, participants who heard the verb "hit" were no more likely to falsely recall seeing glass than those in the control condition. Can the authors two-memory explanation explain why this verb did not lead to false memories in this study?

Reading 26: Contemporary

Eyewitness Suggestibility

D. Stephen Lindsay

During a trial, the second most powerful evidence that a prosecuting attorney could introduce to convince a jury of a defendant's guilt is the testimony of an eyewitness (admission of guilt by the defendant is the most powerful evidence). But is it wise for jurors to place so much emphasis on the testimony (or lack of testimony) of eyewitnesses? How reliable are they?

Most people assume that anyone willing to testify as an eyewitness must surely have a reasonably clear memory of the events in question. Yet a great deal of recent research on memory suggests that it is far more fallible than previously believed. The previous reading showed that eyewitnesses can be biased by leading questions. This next reading considers a second source of bias that can affect eyewitnesses' memories: post-event information. For example, if a police officer suggests to eyewitnesses a detail that they, in fact, did not notice (e.g., that the perpetrator was 6'2"), it is sometimes possible that the witnesses will later "remember" seeing that detail. In other words, police may sometimes implant new memories where they did not previously exist.

In the following reading, Stephen Lindsay argues that post-event information can distort memory, although this bias may not be as common as some believe it to be. He then turns to a consideration of why this occurs. Interestingly, he concludes that previous authors, including the authors of the previous reading Loftus and Palmer, were mistaken in supporting the source monitoring hypothesis.

Ψ

The attorney faces the witness with a somber and resolute gaze and asks, "Please describe for the court the events of the afternoon of Wednesday, June 3, 1992." Like many everyday tasks, providing a detailed and accurate answer to this question demands bewilderingly complex cognitive processes and skills. One of the many sources of difficulty is that during the lengthy interval between seeing an event and testifying about it in court, witnesses are often exposed to many different sources of information about the event: information implied in questions posed by police and lawyers, media reports, and statements made by other witnesses, among other sources. Some of this information may be inaccurate. What effect does such misleading postevent information (MPI) have on eyewitnesses' ability to provide accurate testimony?

Source: Lindsay, D.S. (1993, June). Eyewitness suggestibility. *Current Directions in Psychological Science, 2,* 86-89. Copyright © 1993 by D. Stephen Lindsay. Reprinted by permission of Blackwell Publishers.

We owe the modern renaissance of this line of inquiry to work by Loftus and colleagues.[1] Loftus's basic procedure consists of three phases: In Phase 1, subjects view an event; in Phase 2, they receive verbal information about the event (with or without misleading suggestions about certain "critical" details); and in Phase 3, they take a memory test that includes questions about the critical details. For example, subjects in one study watched a slide show that depicted an automobile accident; some subjects were later given a misleading suggestion concerning what kind of traffic sign had marked a particular intersection (e.g., some subjects saw a stop sign at this intersection but were later misinformed that it was a yield sign). At test, subjects were given a two-alternative, forced-choice recognition test, with instructions to indicate which item in each pair they had seen in the initial slide show. Most of the test items consisted of an event detail paired with a new distractor, but the critical test items consisted of an event detail paired with the corresponding suggested detail (e.g., stop sign vs. yield sign). On the critical test items, subjects who had received MPI were dramatically less accurate than control subjects.

This *misinformation effect* is very robust and has been replicated using a variety of procedures (including naturalistic staged crimes) in labs around the world.[4] It is also often a large effect: Differences of 20% to 30% between performance on misled and control items are not unusual. And it is a very famous effect: Most introductory psychology textbooks include a brief (and uncritical) summary of Loftus's major findings, and most cast them in Loftus's theoretical terms.

According to Loftus's "overwriting" hypothesis (aka "destructive updating" or "mentalmorphosis"), when the MPI is presented, it may be added to the preexisting memory record of witnessing the event in such a way that the new information destroys and replaces memory representations with which it conflicts. This theoretical account of the misinformation effect has two important implications. First, it holds that MPI can irreparably destroy the memory trace of event details. Second, it implies that the MPI becomes an integral part of the memory of witnessing the event itself, such that when subjects later remember what was suggested to them, they will experience it as remembering witnessing that thing in the event. Both of these claims have been challenged.

MEMORY IMPAIRMENT

In 1985, McCloskey and Zaragoza published a powerful critique of purported demonstrations of memory impairment in the misinformation effect.[2] Previous theorists had already argued against Loftus's overwriting hypothesis and in favor of a *coexistence*

---

[1] For a historical review, see S.J. Ceci and M.Bruck, The suggestibility of the child witness: A historical review and synthesis, *Psychological Bulletin* (in press). For a review of Loftus' work, see E. Loftus, When a lie becomes memory's truth: Memory distortion after exposure to misinformation, *Current Directions in Psychological Science, 1,* 121-123) (1992).

[2] M. McCloskey and M. Zaragoza, Misleading postevent information and memory for events: Arguments and evidence against memory impairment hypotheses, *Journal of Experimental Psychology: General, 114,* 1–16 (1985).

hypothesis, according to which memory for the MPI does not destroy memory for the original event detail but instead impairs people's ability to retrieve the original memory.[3] McCloskey and Zaragoza went beyond this position and argued that the methods used could not even address the question of whether MPI impairs ability to remember event details, because a variety of demand characteristics and response biases could lead subjects to perform more poorly on misled items than on control items even if there were no memory impairment effect. For example, subjects who remember the event detail might nonetheless base their test responses on the suggested detail in order to play along with the perceived desires of the experimenter.

In addition to critiquing previous studies, McCloskey and Zaragoza reported new studies that used a modified test to eliminate demand characteristics and response biases. On the critical test items in the modified test, subjects choose between the event detail (e.g., stop sign) and a new item not presented in either the event or the MPI (e.g., caution sign). McCloskey and Zaragoza argued that if MPI impairs memory for the event detail, then MPI should lower performance on the modified test. In six experiments, MPI had no effect on subjects' ability to discriminate between the event detail and a new distractor.

McCloskey and Zaragoza's arguments and evidence suggested that what had long been viewed as a dramatic memory phenomenon with important practical implications was merely an artifact of demand characteristics and inappropriate testing methods. This critique had a galvanizing effect on applied memory researchers, producing a flood of new studies. Although a number of researchers have recently reported support for the hypothesis that MPI impairs ability to remember event details, the issue has remained controversial.[4]

SOURCE-MONITORING CONFUSIONS

Whereas most of the controversy in this area has revolved around the memory impairment issue (i.e., whether MPI impairs ability to remember what was witnessed), Marcia Johnson and I have focused on the question of whether misled subjects sometimes genuinely believe they remember seeing suggested details in the event itself.[5] From a forensic point of view, the possibility that witnesses can come to believe they had witnessed things that were merely suggested to them may be more ominous than the possibility that suggestions can impair memory for what was witnessed.

---

[3] See, e.g., D.A. Bekerian and J.M. Bowers, Eyewitness testimony: Were we misled? *Journal of Experimental Psychology: Learning, Memory, and Cognition, 9,* 139–145 (1983).

[4] For evidence of memory impairment among adults tested with the modified test, as well as a review of the memory impairment debate, see R.F. Belli, P.D. Windshitl, T.T. McCarthy, and S.E. Winfrey, Detecting memory impairment with a modified test procedure: Manipulating retention interval with centrally presented event items, *Journal of Experimental Psychology: Learning, Memory, and Cognition, 18,* 356–367 (1992).

[5] For a review of the relationship between source monitoring and eyewitness testimony, see D.S. Lindsay, Memory source monitoring and eyewitness testimony, in *Adult Eyewitness Testimony,* D.F. Ross, J.D. Read, and M.P. Toglia, Eds. (Cambridge University Press, New York, in press).

Do misled subjects ever "remember" seeing something that was only verbally suggested to them? Johnson and I argued that subjects do sometimes experience such source-monitoring confusions. Every autobiographical memory has a source, defined by the conditions under which that memory was acquired (where and when the event occurred, in what media and through what modalities it was apprehended, etc.). We argued that memories do not have abstract "tags" or "labels" that specify their sources. Rather, memories include various kinds of information, such as records of the perceptual qualities of an experience, and the sources of event memories are identified via decision-making processes performed when the events are recollected. People sometimes struggle consciously to identify the source of a recollection, but more often make such attributions without conscious awareness of any decision making.

A source-monitoring error occurs when a memory derived from one source is misattributed to another source (e.g., you recall something you heard Kathy say, and mistakenly remember the speaker as Liz). The likelihood of source misattributions varies with the amount and nature of the source-specific information in the memory record, the discriminability of the potential sources, and the stringency of the decision processes and criteria used during remembering. Thus, for example, you are more likely to mistakenly remember Liz saying something you actually heard from Kathy if the memory record is vague than if it is clear, if the two people are similar to one another than if they are dissimilar, or if the source attribution is made quickly and automatically than if it is made with careful deliberation.

One implication of these ideas is that eyewitnesses may misidentify memories of information presented before the event as memories of things they saw in the event itself, just as they may misidentify memories of postevent suggestions as memories of the event. We have demonstrated that this is indeed the case in a study in which verbal misinformation was presented before subjects viewed the scene about which they were later questioned.[6] At test, subjects often claimed to have seen things in the event that were in fact merely suggested in the information before the visual scene.

Consistent with the idea that the stringency of source-monitoring criteria plays an important role in eyewitness suggestibility, in other experiments we found that a suggestibility effect obtained among subjects tested with a recognition test was eliminated among subjects tested with a source-monitoring test that required them to identify the sources of their memories of each test item. The two tests consisted of the same list of items: Subjects given the recognition test were to respond "yes" to items they remembered seeing in the visual event and "no" to all other items, whereas subjects given the source-monitoring test were to indicate, for each item, whether they remembered seeing that item only in the event, only in the postevent information, in both sources, or in neither. As is typically found, subjects tested with the recognition test often claimed to have seen suggested items in the event. In contrast, subjects tested with the source-monitoring test correctly attributed their memories of suggested details to the postevent information. We viewed these findings as evidence that subjects tested with recognition

---

[6] D. S. Lindsay and M.K. Johnson, The reversed suggestibility effect, *Bulletin of the Psychonomic Society, 27,* 111-113 (1989).

tests sometimes misidentify memories of MPI as memories of the event because they are using lax or inappropriate source-monitoring criteria. The source-monitoring instructions led subjects to use more stringent criteria and thereby correctly attribute memories of suggested details to the postevent information.[7]

More recent research demonstrates that even subjects tested with source-monitoring tests sometimes claim to have seen suggested details in the event, provided conditions make it difficult to discriminate between memories of the event and memories of the MPI.[8] For example, Zaragoza and colleagues have shown that illusory memories of eyewitnessing are more likely to be obtained on a source-monitoring test if subjects are instructed to form visual images of the postevent information when it is presented.

Unfortunately, source-monitoring tests do not altogether eliminate the possibility that demand characteristics might contribute to apparent source-monitoring confusions. Subjects are led to believe that everything in the postevent information was also in the event, and they may wish to show that they paid attention to both the event and the postevent information. This may motivate subjects to claim that they remember things from both sources even if they are aware that they remember them only from the postevent information. Consistent with this account, subjects in these studies very rarely claimed that suggested details had been seen only in the event; rather, when they erred, they claimed that suggested details had been in both the event and the postevent information.

More compelling evidence that subjects sometimes mistake memories of postevent suggestions as memories of the event itself comes from a study using Jacoby's opposition procedure.[8] In this experiment, conditions were set up that the effect of knowingly using memories of the postevent information would be opposite to the effect of genuine memory source confusions. To do this, we correctly informed subjects at test that the postevent information did not include any correct answers to the test questions. Acquisition conditions were manipulated such that remembering the suggestions and their source would be very easy for some subjects and relatively difficult for other subjects. In the easy condition, subjects received the MPI 2 days after viewing the event, minutes before taking the test, and under conditions that differed from those in which they viewed the event. Thus, at test, it would be easy for these subjects to remember the MPI and its source. Subjects in the difficult condition, in contrast, received the MPI minutes after viewing the event, under very similar conditions, 2 days before taking the test. Thus, at the time of the test, it would be relatively difficult for these subjects to differentiate between memories of the event and memories of the postevent narrative.

---

[7] Zaragoza and Koshmider interpreted very similar results from independent research as a demonstration of the role of demand characteristics (i.e., they argued that the source-monitoring test reduced demands to report having seen suggested details). See M.S. Zaragoza and J.W. Koshmider, III, Misled subjects may know more than their performance implies, *Journal of Experimental Psychology: Learning, Memory, and Cognition, 15*, 246–255 (1989).
[8] D.S. Lindsay, Misleading suggestions can impair eyewitnesses' ability to remember event details, Journal of Experimental Psychology: Learning, Memory, and Cognition, 16, 1077–1083 (1990). For a review of Jacoby's development of the opposition procedure, see L.L. Jacoby and C.M. Kelley, A process-dissociation framework for investigating unconscious influences: Freudian slips, projective tests, subliminal perception, and signal detection theory, Current Directions in Psychological Science, 1, 174–179 (1992).

Subjects were given a cued-recall test with six questions: Three concerned details about which MPI had been given, and three were control questions. Before taking the test, subjects were explicitly and emphatically told not to report anything they remembered from the postevent information. Subjects in the easy condition showed no tendency to report suggested details, indicating that subjects tried to avoid reporting information from the postevent information. Nonetheless, subjects in the difficult condition quite often reported the suggested details as things they recalled seeing in the event. Even though subjects were specifically trying to avoid reporting memories of the MPI, they frequently did so.

MEMORY IMPAIRMENT REDUX

The opposition study described above also provided important evidence that MPI can impair subjects' ability to remember event details. Although subjects in the easy condition were able to identify the source of their memories of suggested details (and so did not erroneously report seeing them in the event), the misleading suggestions nonetheless hampered these subjects' ability to report the event details: Correct recall of event details was significantly lower on misled items than on control items. Correct recall of event details was significantly impaired by MPI even among those subjects in the easy condition who never reported any suggested details. Neither differential rates of guessing nor differential response criteria can account for the lower level of recall of event details on misled than control items in the easy condition. This is powerful evidence that misleading suggestions can impair eyewitnesses' ability to remember event details.

SUMMARY AND CONCLUSIONS

Recent research indicates that much of the large and dramatic misinformation effect typically obtained with Loftus's standard procedure is due to aware uses of memory for the postevent information. For example, some subjects may fail to notice the critical detail in the event but remember the MPI; because the postevent information is presented as a reliable source of information, such subjects would quite reasonably rely upon it when tested.

Yet it is clear that subjects do sometimes experience memories of things they read or heard about after the event as recollections of seeing those things in the event. Such source confusions are more likely when the event and the MPI give rise to high similar memory records and when source-monitoring criteria are lax. However, compelling illusory memories of eyewitnessing sometimes occur even when criteria are very stringent – even when subjects are trying to avoid making such errors.

There is also growing evidence that misleading suggestions can impair subjects' ability to remember event details. Current evidence indicates that memory impairment effects are likely to be small and nonreliable when memory is tested with appropriate recognition probes (as in McCloskey and Zaragoza's modified test) but may be considerably larger and more robust when appropriate recall measures are used (as in the opposition test). Debate about the mechanisms that underlie memory impairment effects (e.g., whether MPI degrades memory traces of event details or merely interferes with retrieval) is likely to continue for some time. At present, we can conclude that under some conditions MPI can impair people's ability to remember what they witnessed and can lead them to believe that they witnessed things they did not, but that neither of these effects is as large or robust as earlier research suggested.

QUESTIONS

1. Explain the process by which Loftus believes MPIs distort memory. Why does Lindsay disagree with Loftus's position?

2. What does Lindsay mean by "source-monitoring"? Is this a bias in storing information or recalling information?

3. In what three ways did the easy and difficult conditions differ in Lindsay's test using Jacoby's opposition procedure? Can we tell from this test which of the three differences had the greatest impact of memory?

4. Police normally try to question eyewitnesses immediately after a crime has occurred. What are the pros and cons of this strategy for eyewitness accuracy?

5. In addition to questioning eyewitnesses immediately after an event, police sometimes question them again days later. How might this strategy affect eyewitness accuracy?

Ψ

PART VIII

THE SOCIAL CONTEXT
OF SOCIETY

Ψ Ψ

Ψ CHAPTER 14 Ψ

GROUPS:
JOINING WITH OTHERS

Reading 27: Classic

Social Facilitation

Robert B. Zajonc

This next reading returns to the first topic recognized as following under the purview of social psychology. Recall from Reading 1 that the study most often attributed as being the first in modern social psychology was Normal Triplett's investigation of motor performance under conditions of competition. Triplett observed in his experimental task -- just as in competitive cycling -- most people performed motor tasks faster when competing against another than when working alone. Over the next few decades others extended Triplett's findings into other contexts. It was generally found that tasks were better accomplished if performed with other people rather than alone. Moreover these effects were not limited to competition: performance was enhanced even when the other people merely sat and watched. Because performance was facilitated by the presence of a social audience, this phenomenon became known as social facilitation. Although facilitation effects were the rule in this early work, there were exceptions. Some researchers found that participants performed significantly worse on tasks in front of an audience.

For decades these social facilitation findings were known but not well understood. The following reading by Robert Zajonc (whose last name rhymes with science) brought new life to the study of facilitation effects by proposing a solution to the previous inconsistency with which they were observed. The theory as it is first presented below, which came to be known as the mere presence theory, is yet rough around the edges and had yet to be fully tested. But this reading was important to the field because in it Zajonc pointed in the direction that he and others subsequently followed in elucidating the mechanisms of performance in front of an audience.

Ψ

Most textbook definitions of social psychology involve considerations about the influence of man upon man, or, more generally, on individual upon individual. And most of them, explicitly or implicitly, commit the main efforts of social psychology to the problem of how and why the behavior of one individual affects the behavior of another. The influences of individuals on each others' behavior which are of interest to social psychologists today take on very complex forms. Often they involve vast networks of

Source: Zajonc, R.B. (1965). Social facilitation. *Science, 149*, 269-274. Copyright © by the American Association for the Advancement of Science. Reprinted by permission from the publisher.

interindividual effects, such as one finds in studying the process of group decision-making, competition, or conformity to a group norm. But the fundamental forms of interindividual influence are represented by the oldest experimental paradigm of social psychology: social facilitation. This paradigm, dating back to Triplett's original experiments on pacing and competition, carried out in 1897 (*1*), examines the consequences upon behavior which derive from the sheet presence of other individuals.

Until the late 1930s, interest in social facilitation was quite active, but with the outbreak of World War II it suddenly died. And it is truly regrettable that it died, because the basic questions about social facilitation – its dynamics and its causes – which are in effect the basic questions of social psychology, were never solved. It is with these questions that this article is concerned. I first examine past results in this nearly completely abandoned area of research and then suggest a general hypothesis which might explain them.

Research in the area of social facilitation may be classified in terms of two experimental paradigms: audience effects and co-action effects. The first experimental paradigm involves the observation of behavior when it occurs in the presence of passive spectators. The second examines behavior when it occurs in the presence of other individuals also engaged in the same activity. We shall consider past literature in these two areas separately.

AUDIENCE EFFECTS

Simple motor responses are particularly sensitive to social facilitation effects. In 1925 Travis (*2*) obtained such effects in a study in which he used the pursuit-rotor task. In this task the subject is required to follow a small revolving target by means of a stylus which he holds in his hand. If the stylus is even momentarily off target during a revolution, the revolution counts as an error. First each subject was trained for several consecutive days until his performance reached a stable level. One day after the conclusion of the training the subject was called to the laboratory, given five trials alone, and then ten trials in the presence of from four to eight upperclassmen and graduate students. They had been asked by the experimenter to watch the subject quietly and attentively. Travis found a clear improvement in performance when his subjects were confronted with an audience. Their accuracy on the ten trials before an audience was greater than on any ten previous trials, including those on which they had scored highest.

A considerably greater improvement on performance was recently obtained in a somewhat different setting and on a different task (*3*). Each subject (all were National Guard trainees) was placed in a separate booth. He was seated in front of a panel outfitted with 20 red lamps in a circle. The lamps on this panel light in a clockwise sequence at 12 revolutions per minute. At random intervals one or another light fails to go on in its proper sequence. On the average there are 25 such failures per hour. The subject's task is to signal whenever a light fails to go on. After 20 minutes of intensive training, followed by a short rest, the National Guard trainees monitored the light panels for 125 minutes. Subjects in one group performed their task alone. Subjects in another group were told that from time to time a lieutenant colonel or a master-sergeant would visit them in the booth to observe their performance. These visits actually took place about four times during the experimental session. There was no doubt about the results. The accuracy of the supervised subjects was on the average 34 percent higher than the accuracy of the trainees working in isolation, and toward the end of the experimental session the accuracy of the supervised subjects was more than twice as high as that of the subjects working in isolation. Those expecting to be visited by a superior missed, during the last experimental period, 20 percent of the light failures, while those expecting no such visits missed 64 percent of the failures.

Dashiell, who, in the early 1930's carried out an extensive program of research on social facilitation, also found considerable improvement in performance due to audience effects on such tasks as simple multiplication or word association (4). But, as is the case in many other areas, negative audience effects were also found. In 1933 Pessin asked college students to learn lists of nonsense syllables under two conditions, alone and in the presence of several spectators (5). When confronted with an audience, his subjects required an average of 11.27 trials to learn a seven-item list. When working alone they needed only 9.85 trials. The average number of errors made in the "audience" condition was considerably higher than the number in the "alone" condition. In 1931 Husband found that the presence of spectators interferes with the learning of a finger maze (6), and in 1933 Pessin and Husband (7) confirmed Husband's results. The number of trials which the isolated subjects required for learning the finger maze was 17.1. Subjects confronted with spectators, however, required 19.1 trials. The average number of errors for the isolated subjects was 33.7; the number for those working in the presence of an audience was 40.5.

The results thus far reviewed seem to contradict one another. On a pursuit-rotor task Travis found that the presence of an audience improves performance. The learning of nonsense syllables and maze learning, however, seem to be inhibited by the presence of an audience, as shown by Pessin's experiment. The picture is further complicated by the fact that when Pessin's subjects were asked, several days later, to recall the nonsense syllables they had learned, a reversal was found. The subjects who tried to recall the lists in the presence of spectators did considerably better than those who tried to recall them alone. Why are the learning of nonsense syllables and maze learning inhibited by the presence of spectators? And why, on the other hand, does performance on a pursuit-rotor, word-association, multiplication, or a vigilance task improve in the presence of others?

There is just one, rather subtle, consistency in the above results. It would appear that the emission of well-learned responses is facilitated by the presence of spectators, while the acquisition of new responses is impaired. To put the statement in conventional psychological language, performance is facilitated and learning is impaired by the presence of spectators.

This tentative generalization can be reformulated so that different features of the problem are placed into focus. During the early stages of learning, especially of the type involved in social facilitation studies, the subject's responses are mostly the wrong ones. A person learning a finger maze, or a person learning a list of nonsense syllables, emits more wrong responses than right ones in the early stages of training. Most learning experiments continue until he ceases to make mistakes – until his performance is perfect. It may be said, therefore, that during training it is primarily the wrong responses which are dominant and strong; they are the ones which have the highest probability of occurrence. But after the individual has mastered the task, correct responses necessarily gain ascendancy in his task-relevant behavioral repertoire. Now they are the ones which are more probable – in other words, dominant. Our tentative generalization may now be simplified: audience enhances the emission of dominant responses. If the dominant responses are the correct ones, as is the case upon achieving mastery, the presence of an audience will be of benefit to the individual. But if they are mostly wrong, as is the case in the early stages of learning, then these wrong responses will be enhanced in the presence of an audience, and the emission of correct responses will be postponed or prevented.

There is a class of psychological processes which are known to enhance the emission of dominant responses. They are subsumed under the concepts of drive, arousal, and activation (8). If we could show that the presence of an audience has arousal consequences for the subject, we would be a step further along in trying to arrange the results of social-facilitation experiments into a neater package. But let us first consider another set of experimental findings.

CO-ACTION EFFECTS

... The experiments on social facilitation performed by Floyd Allport in 1920 and continued by Dashiell in 1930 (4, 17), both of whom used human subjects, are the ones best known. Allport's subjects worked either in separate cubicles or sitting around a common table. When working in isolation they did the various tasks at the same time and were monitored by common time signals. Allport did everything possible to reduce the tendency to compete. The subjects were told that the results of their tests would not be compared and would not be shown to other staff members, and that they themselves should refrain from making any such comparisons.

Among the tasks used were the following: chain word association, vowel cancellation, reversible perspective, multiplication, problem solving, and judgments of odors and weights. The results of Allport's experiments are well known: in all but the problem-solving and judgments test, performance was better in groups than in the "alone" condition. How do these results fit our generalization? Word association, multiplication, the cancellation of vowels, and the reversal of the perceived orientation of an ambiguous figure all involve responses which are well established. They are responses which are either very well learned or under a very strong influence of the stimulus as in the word-association task of the reversible-perspective test. The problem-solving test consists of disproving arguments of ancient philosophers. In contrast to the other tests, it does not involve well-learned responses. On the contrary, the probability of wrong (that is, logically incorrect) responses on tasks of this sort is rather high; in other words, wrong responses are dominant. Of interest, however, is the finding that while intellectual work suffered in the group situation, sheet output of words was increased. When working together, Allport's subjects tended consistently to write more. Therefore, the generalization proposed in the previous section can again be applied: if the presence of others raises the probability of dominant responses, and if strong (and many) incorrect response tendencies prevail, then the presence of others can only be detrimental to performance. The results of the judgment tests have little bearing on the present argument, since Allport gives no accuracy figures for evaluating performance. The data reported only show that the presence of others was associated with the avoidance of extreme judgments.

In 1928 Travis (*18*), whose work on the pursuit rotor I have already noted, repeated Allport's chain-word-association experiment. In contrast to Allport's results, Travis found that the presence of others decreased performance. The number of associations given by his subjects was greater when they worked in isolation. It is very significant, however, that Travis used stutterers as his subjects. In a way, stuttering is a manifestation of a struggle between conflicting response tendencies, all of which are strong and all of which compete for expression. The stutterer, momentarily hung up in the middle of a sentence, waits for the correct response to reach full ascendancy. He stammers because other competing tendencies are dominant at that moment. It is reasonable to assume that, to the extent that the verbal habits of a stutterer are characterized by conflicting response tendencies, the presence of others, by enhancing each of these response tendencies, simply heightens his conflict. Performance is thus impaired. ...

THE PRESENCE OF OTHERS AS A SOURCE OF AROUSAL

The results I have discussed thus far lead to one generalization and to one hypothesis. The generalization which organizes these results is that the presence of others, as spectators or as co-actors, enhances the emission of dominant responses. We also know from extensive research literature that arousal, activation, or drive all have as a consequence the enhancement of dominant responses (*22*). We now need to examine the hypothesis that the presence of others increases the individual's general arousal or drive level.

The evidence which bears on the relationship between the presence of others and arousal is, unfortunately, only indirect. But there is some very suggestive evidence in one area of research. One of the more reliable indicators of arousal and drive is the activity of the endocrine systems in general, and of the adrenal cortex in particular. Adrenocortical functions are extremely sensitive to changes in emotional arousal, and it has been known for some time that organisms subjected to prolonged stress are likely to manifest substantial adrenocortical hypertrophy (*23*). Recent work (*24*) has shown that the main biochemical component of the adrenocortical output is hydrocortisone (17-hydroxycorticosterone). Psychiatric patients characterized by anxiety states for instance, show elevated plasma levels of hydrocortisone (*25*). Mason, Brady, and Disman (*26*) have recently trained monkeys to press a lever for food and have given these animals unavoidable electric shocks, all preceded by warning signals. This procedure led to elevated hydrocortisone levels; the levels returned to normal within 1 hour after the end

TABLE 1
BASAL PLASMA CONCENTRATIONS

Subject	Time	Conc. of 17-hydroxycorticosterone in caged monkeys (µg per 100 ml of plasma)	
		In separate rooms	In same room
M-1	9 a.m.	23	34
M-1	3 p.m.	16	27
M-2	9 a.m.	28	34
M-2	3 p.m.	19	23
M-3	9 a.m.	32	38
M-3	3 p.m.	23	31
Mean	9 a.m.	28	35
Mean	3 p.m.	19	27

Basal Plasma concentrations of 17-hydroxycorticosterone in monkeys housed alone (cages in separate rooms), then in a room with other monkeys (cages in same room). [Leiderman and Shapiro (35, p. 7)]

of the experimental session. This "anxiety" reaction can apparently be attenuated if the animal is given repeated doses of reserpine 1 day before the experimental session (27). Sidman's conditional avoidance schedule also results in raising the hydrocortisone levels by a factor of 2 to 4 (26). In this schedule, the animal receives an electric shock every 20 seconds without warning, unless he presses a lever. Each press delays the shock for 20 seconds.

While there is a fair amount of evidence that adrenocortical activity is a reliable symptom of arousal, similar endocrine manifestations were found to be associated with increased population density (28). Crowded mice, for instance, show increased amphetamine toxicity – that is, susceptibility to the excitatory effects of amphetamine – against which they can be protected by the administration of phenobarbital, chlorpromazine, or reserpine (29). Mason and Brady (30) have recently reported that monkeys caged together had considerably higher plasma levels of hydrocortisone than monkeys housed in individual cages. Thiessen (31) found increases in adrenal weights in mice housed in groups of 10 and 20 as compared with mice housed alone. The mere presence of other animals in the same room, but in separate cages, was also found to produce elevated levels of hydrocortisone. Table 1, taken from a report by Mason and Brady (30), shows plasma levels of hydrocortisone for three animals which lived at one time in cages that afforded them the possibility of visual and tactile contact and, at another time, in separate rooms.

Mason and Brady also report urinary levels of hydrocortisone, by days of the week, for five monkeys from their laboratory and for one human hospital patient. These very suggestive figures are reproduced in Table 2 (30). In the monkeys, the low weekend traffic and activity in the laboratory seem to be associated with a clear decrease in hydrocortisone. As for the hospital patient, Mason and Brady report (20, p. 8) "he was confined to a thoracic surgery ward that bustled with activity during the weekdays when

TABLE 2
VARIATIONS IN URINARY CONCENTRATIONS

Subjects	Amounts Excreted (mg/24 hr)								
	Mon.	Tues.	Wed.	Thurs.	Fri.	Sat.	Sun.	Mon.	Tues.
Monkeys	1.88	1.71	1.60	1.52	1.70	1.16	1.17	1.88	
Patient		5.9	6.5	4.5	5.7	3.3	3.9	6.0	5.2

Variations in urinary concentration of hydorcortisone over a 9-day period for five laboratory monkeys and one human hospital patient. [Leiderman and Shapiro (35, p. 8)]

surgery and admissions occurred. On the weekends the patient retired to the nearby Red Cross building, with its quieter and more pleasant environment."

Admittedly, the evidence that the mere presence of others raises the arousal level is indirect and scanty. And, as a matter of fact, some work seems to suggest that there are conditions, such as stress, under which the presence of others may lower the animal's arousal level. Bovard (32), for instance, hypothesized that the presence of another member of the same species may protect the individual under stress by inhibiting the activity of the posterior hypothalamic centers which trigger the pituitary adrenal cortical and sympathetico-adrenal medullary responses to stress. Evidence for Bovard's hypothesis, however, is as indirect as evidence for the one which predicts arousal as a consequence of the presence of others, and even more scanty.

SUMMARY AND CONCLUSION

If one were to draw one practical suggestion from the review of the social-facilitation effects which are summarized in this article he would advise the student to study all alone, preferably in an isolated cubicle, and to arrange to take his examinations in the company of many other students, on stage, and in the presence of a large audience. The results of his examination would be beyond his wildest expectations, provided, of course, he had learned his material quite thoroughly. ...

REFERENCES AND NOTES

1. N TRIPLETT, *Amer. J. Psychol.* 9, 507 (1897).
2. L.E. TRAVIS, J. *Abnormal Soc. Psychol.* 20, 142 (1925).
3. B.O. BERGUM AND D.J. LEHR, *J. Appl. Psychol.* 47, 75 (1963).
4. J.F. DASHIELL, *J. Abnormal Soc. Psychol.* 25, 190 (1930).
5. J. PESSIN, *Amer. J. Psychol.* 45, 263 (1933).

6. R. W. HUSBAND, J. GENET. *Psychol.* 39, 258 (1931. In this task the blindfolded subject traces a maze with his finger.
7. J. PESSIN AND R.W. HUSBAND, *J. Abnormal Soc. Psychol.* 28, 148 (1933).
8. See, for instance, E. Dufy, *Activation and Behavior* (Wiley, New York, 1962); K.W. Spence, *Behavior Theory and Conditioning* (Yale Univ. Press, New Haven, 1956); R.B. Zajonc and B. Nieuwenhuyse, *J. Exp. Psychol.* 67, 276 (1964).
9. E. BAYER, Z. *Psychol.* 112, 1 (1929).
10. C.W. TOLMAN AND G.T. WILSON, *Animal Behavior* 13, 134 (1965).
11. H.F. HARLOW, J. GENET. *Psychol.* 43, 211 (1932).
12. W.T. JAMES, *J. Comp Physiol. Psychol.* 46, 427 (1953): J. Genet. *Psychol.* 96, 1232 (1960); W.T. James and D.J. Cannon, *ibid.*, 87, 225 (1956).
13. S.C. CHEN, *Physiol. Zool.* 10, 420 (1937).
14. P.H;. KLOPFER, *Science* 128, 903 (1958).
15. W.C. ALLEE AND R.H. MASURE, *Physiol. Zool.* 22, 131 (1936).
16. M.J. GATES AND W.C. ALLEE, *J. Comp. Psychol.* 15, 331 (1933).
17. F.H. ALLPORT, *J. Exp. Psychol.* 3, 159 (1920).
18. L.E. TRAVIS, *J. Abnormal Soc. Psychol.* 23, 45 (1928).
19. E. RASMUSSEN, *Acta. Psychol.* 4, 275 (1939).
20. R. ADER AND R. TATUM, *J. Exp. Anal. Behavior* 6, 357 (1963).
21. H. GURNEE, *J. Abnormal Soc. Psychol.* 34, 529 (1939); J.C. Welty, *Physiol. Zool.* 7, 85 (1934).
22. See K.W. Spence, *Behavior Theory and Conditioning* (Yale Univ. Press, New Haven, 1956).
23. H. SELYE, *J. Clin. Endocrin.* 6, 117 (1946).\
24. D.H. NELSON AND L.T. SAMUELS, *ibid.* 12, 519 (1952).
25. E.L. BLISS, A.A. SANDBERG, D.H. NELSON, *J. Clin. Invest.* 32, 9 (1953); F. BOARD, H. PERSKY, D.A. HAMBERG, *Psychosom. Med.* 18, 324 (1956).
26. J.W. MASON, J.V. BRADY, M. SIDMAN, *Endocrinology* 60, 741 (1957).
27. J.W. MASON AND J. V. BRADY, *Science* 124, 983 (1954).
28. D.D. THIESSEN, *Texas Rep. Biol. Med.* 22, 266 (1964).
29. L. LASAGNA AND W.P. MCCANN, *Science* 125, 1241 (1957).
30. J.W. MASON AND J.V. BRADY, in *Psychological Approaches to Social Behavior*, P.H. Leiderman and D. Shapiro, Eds. (Stanford Univ. Press, Stanford, Calif., 1964).
31. D.D. THIESSEN, *J. Comp. Physiol. Psychol.* 57, 412 (1964).
32. E.W. BOVARD, *Psychol. Rev.* 66, 267 (1959).
33. F.H. ALLPORT, *Social Psychology* (Houghton Mifflin, Boston, 1924).
34. J.R. DAVITZ AND D.J. MASON, *J. Comp. Physiol. Psychol.* 48, 149 (1955).
35. P.H. LEIDERMAN AND D. SHAPIRO, Eds. *Psychobiological Approaches to Social Behavior* (Stanford Univ. Press, Stanford, Calif., 1964).
36. The preparation of this article was supported in part by grants Nonr-1224 (34) from the Office of Naval Research and GS-629 from the National Science Foundation.

QUESTIONS

1. Zajonc continues to refer to audience effects as "social facilitation" even though performance is not always enhanced. What then does he say is being facilitated?

2. What role does Zajonc seem to believe andrenocortical activity plays in social facilitation?

3. Allport's early work on social facilitation found that performance on reversible perspective tests was enhanced in groups even though these tasks were unfamiliar to participants, a situation that lead to reduced performance in audience effect studies. How can Zajonc's theory explain this inconsistency?

4. What evidence presented here would seem to indicate that facilitation effects could occur in non-social as well as social situations? Give an example of a non-social event that might produce the same effects.

5. According to the theory presented here, how would your ability to answer the questions above be affected if they were asked to you by your professor during class? Can you explain the notion of "dominant response" in this example?

Reading 28: Contemporary

Group Decision Fiascoes Continue: Space Shuttle Challenger and a Revised Groupthink Framework

Gregory Moorhead, Richard Ference, and Chris P. Neck

The previous reading on social facilitation revitalized research on how people behave in groups. A few years later, Irving Janis expanded the definition of "group behavior" to include how groups think and make decisions. Specifically, he proposed that under certain circumstances groups will develop symptoms of a very unhealthy process of decision making that he termed "groupthink." As Gregory Moorhead and his colleagues explain in this next reading, groups operating under groupthink make predictable decisions, decisions that fail to take into account important information and which, consequently, often have disastrous consequences. Janis' initial work on groupthink was used to explain such infamous decisions as Kennedy's decision to invade Cuba at the Bay of Pigs and Nixon's decision to break into the Democratic National Committee's offices at Watergate. According to the authors of this next reading, groupthink can also explain one of the most tragic events in American history in the second half of the twentieth century: the explosion of the space shuttle Challenger on January 28th, 1986.

In January of 1986 NASA was extremely popular in the eyes of both Congress and the American people. They hadn't lost an astronaut in 20 years and had since put men on the moon, put Skylab into orbit, and developed the highly successful space shuttles. According to Moorhead, this string of successes and the confidence it inspired may be partially to blame for the events of January 28th. Despite strong objections from the scientists and engineers who developed the Challenger's solid rocket boosters, NASA officials decided to launch the shuttle in dangerously cold weather. Although you and your classmates were probably less than 10 years old at the time, most of you will probably never forget the consequences of that decision or the image of billowing smoke and fire that ended the lives of seven Americans.

Ψ

In 1972 a new dimension was added to our understanding of group decision making with the proposal of the groupthink hypothesis by Janis (1972). Janis coined the term "groupthink" to refer to "a mode of thinking that people engage in when they are deeply involved in a cohesive in-group, when the members' striving for unanimity override their motivation to realistically appraise alternative courses of action" (Janis, 1972, p. 8). The hypothesis was supported by his hindsight analysis of several political-military fiascoes

Source: Moorhead, G., Ference, R., and Neck, C.P. (1991). Group decision fiascoes continue: Space Shuttle Challenger and a revised groupthink framework. *Human Relations*, 539-550. Reprinted by permission of Plenum Publishing Corporation.

and successes that are differentiated by the occurrence or non-occurrence of antecedent conditions, groupthink symptoms, and decision making defects.

In a subsequent volume, Janis further explicates the theory and adds an analysis of the Watergate transcripts and various published memoirs and accounts of principals involved, concluding that the Watergate cover-up decision also was a result of groupthink (Janis, 1983). Both volumes propose prescriptions for preventing the occurrence of groupthink, many of which have appeared in popular press, in books on executive decision making, and in management textbooks. Multiple advocacy decision-making procedures have been adopted at the executive levels in many organizations, including the executive branch of the government. One would think that by 1986, 13 years after the publication of a popular book, that its prescriptions might be well ingrained in our management and decision-making styles. Unfortunately, it has not happened.

On January 28, 1986, the space shuttle Challenger was launched from Kennedy Space Center. The temperature that morning was in the mid-20's, well below the previous low temperatures at which the shuttle engines had been tested. Seventy-three seconds after launch, the Challenger exploded, killing all seven astronauts aboard, and becoming the worst disaster in space flight history. The catastrophe shocked the nation, crippled the American space program, and is destined to be remembered as the most tragic national event since the assassination of John F. Kennedy in 1963.

The Presidential Commission that investigated the accident pointed to a flawed decision-making process as a primary contributory cause. The decision was made the night before the launch in the Level I Flight Readiness Review meeting. Due to the work of the Presidential Commission, information concerning that meeting is available for analysis as a group decision possibly susceptible to groupthink.

In this paper, we report the results of our analysis of the Level I Flight Readiness Review meeting as a decision-making situation that displays evidence of groupthink. We review the antecedent conditions, the groupthink symptoms, and the possible decision-making defects, as suggested by Janis (1983). In addition, we take the next and more important step by going beyond the development of another example of groupthink to make recommendations for renewed inquiry into group decision-making processes.

THEORY AND EVIDENCE

The meeting(s) took place throughout the day and evening from 12:36 pm (EST), January 27, 1986 following the decision to not launch the Challenger due to high crosswinds at the launch site. Discussions continued through about 12:00 midnight (EST) via teleconferencing and Telefax systems connecting the Kennedy Space Center in Florida, Morton Thiokol (MTI) in Utah, Johnson Space Center in Houston, and the Marshall Space Flight Center. The Level I Flight Readiness Review is the highest level of review prior to launch. It comprises the highest level of management at the three space centers and at MTI, the private supplier of the solid rocket booster engine.

To briefly state the situation, the MTI engineers recommended not to launch if temperatures of the O-ring seals on the rocket were below 53 degrees Fahrenheit, which was the lowest temperature of any previous flight. Laurence B. Mulloy, manager of the Solid Rocket Booster Project at Marshall Space Flight Center, states:

> The bottom line of that, though, initially was that Thiokol engineering, Bob Lund, who is the Vice President and Director of Engineering, who is here today, recommended that the 51-L [the Challenger] not be launched if the O-ring temperatures predicted at launch time would be lower than any previous launch, and that was 53 degrees. (*Report of the Presidential Commission on the Space Shuttle Accident, 1986*, p. 91-92.).

This recommendation was made at 8:45 pm, January 27, 1986 (*Report of the Presidential Commission on the Space Shuttle Accident, 1986*). Through the ensuing discussions the decision to launch was made.

ANTECEDENT CONDITIONS

The three primary antecedent conditions for the development of groupthink are: a highly cohesive group, leader preference for a certain decision, and insulation of the group from qualified outside opinions. These conditions existed in this situation.

Cohesive Group. The people who made the decision to launch had worked together for many years. They were familiar with each other and had grown through the ranks of the space program. A high degree of *esprit de corps* existed between the members.

Leader Preference. Two top level managers actively promoted their pro-launch opinions in the face of opposition. The commission report states that several managers at space centers and MTI pushed for launch, regardless of the low temperatures.

Insulation from Experts. MTI engineers made their recommendations relatively early in the evening. The top level decision-making group knew of their objections but did not meet with them directly to review their data and concerns. As Roger Boisjoly, a Thiokol engineer, states in his remarks to the Presidential Commission:

> And the bottom line was that the engineering people would not recommend a launch below 53 degrees Fahrenheit. ... From this point on, management formulated the points to base their decision on. There was never one comment in favor, as I have said, of launching by any engineer or other nonmanagement person.... I was not even asked to participate in giving any input to the final decision charts (*Report of the Presidential Commission on the Space Shuttle Accident, 1986*, p. 91-92).

This testimonial indicates that the top decision-making team was insulated from the engineers who possessed the expertise regarding the functioning of the equipment.

Janis identified eight symptoms of groupthink. They are presented here along with evidence from the *Report of the Presidential Commission on the Space Shuttle Accident* (1986).

Invulnerability. When groupthink occurs, most or all of the members of the decision-making group have an illusion of invulnerability that reassures them in the face of obvious dangers. This illusion leads the group to become overly optimistic and willing to take extraordinary risks. It may also cause them to ignore clear warnings of danger.

The solid rocket joint problem that destroyed Challenger was discussed often at flight readiness review meetings prior to flight. However, Commission member Richard Feynman concluded from the testimony that a mentality of overconfidence existed due to the extraordinary record of success of space flights. Every time we send one up it is successful. Involved members may seem to think that on the next one we can lower our standards or take more risks because it always works (*Time*, 1986).

The invulnerability illusion may have built up over time as a result of NASA's own spectacular history. NASA had not lost an astronaut since 1967 when a flash fire in the capsule of Apollo 1 killed three. Since that time NASA had a string of 55 successful missions. They had put a man on the moon, built and launched Skylab and the shuttle, and retrieved defective satellites from orbit. In the minds of most Americans and apparently their own, they could do no wrong.

Rationalization. Victims of groupthink collectively construct rationalizations that discount warnings and other forms of negative feedback. If these signals were taken seriously when presented, the group members would be forced to reconsider their assumptions each time they re-commit themselves to their past decisions.

In the Level I flight readiness meeting when the Challenger was given final launch approval, MTI engineers presented evidence that the joint would fail. Their argument was based on the fact that in the coldest previous launch (air temperature 30 degrees) the joint in question experienced serious erosion and that no data existed as to how the joint would perform at colder temperatures. Flight center officials put forth numerous technical rationalizations faulting MTI's analysis. One of these rationalizations was that the engineer's data were inconclusive. As Mr. Boisjoly emphasized to the Commission:

> I was asked, yes, at that point in time I was asked to quantify my concerns, and I said I couldn't. I couldn't quantify it. I had no data to quantify it, but I did say I knew that it was away from goodness in the current data base. Someone on the net commented that we had soot blow-by on SRM-22 [Flight 61-A, October, 1985] which was launched at 75 degrees. I don't remember who made the comment, but that is where the first comment came in about the disparity between my conclusion and the observed data because SRM-22 [Flight 61-A, October 1985] had blow-by at essentially a room temperature launch. I then said that SRM-15 [Flight 51-C, January 1985] had much more blow-by indication and that it was indeed telling us that lower temperature was a factor. I was asked again for data to support my claim, and I said I have none other than what is being presented (*Report of the Presidential Commission on the Space Shuttle Accident*, 1986, p. 89).

Discussions became twisted (compared to previous meetings) and no one detected it. Under normal conditions, MTI would have to prove the shuttle boosters readiness for launch, instead they found themselves being forced to prove that the boosters were unsafe. Boisjoly's testimony supports this description of the discussion:

This was a meeting where the determination was to launch, and it was up to us to prove beyond a shadow of a doubt that it was not safe to do so. This is in total reverse to what the position usually is in a preflight conversation or a flight readiness review. It is usually exactly the opposite of that (*Report of the Presidential Commission on the Space Shuttle Accident*, 1986, p. 93).

Morality. Group members often believe, without question, in the inherent morality of their position. They tend to ignore the ethical or moral consequences of their decision.

In the Challenger case, this point was raised by a very high level MTI manager, Allan J. McDonald, who tried to stop the launch and said that he would not want to have to defend the decision to launch. He stated to the Commission:

I made the statement that if we're wrong and something goes wrong on this flight, I wouldn't want to have to be the person to stand up in front of board in inquiry and say that I went ahead and told them to go ahead and fly this thing outside what the motor was qualified to (*Report of the Presidential Commission on the Space Shuttle Accident*, 1986, p. 95).

Some members did not hear this statement because it occurred during a break. Three top officials who did hear it ignored it.

Stereotyped Views of Others. Victims of groupthink often have a stereotyped view of the opposition of anyone with a competing opinion. They feel that the opposition is too stupid or too weak to understand or deal effectively with the problem.

Two of the top three NASA officials responsible for the launch displayed this attitude. They felt that they completely understood the nature of the joint problem and never seriously considered the objections raised by the MTI engineers. In fact they denigrated and badgered the opposition and their information and opinions.

Pressure on Dissent. Group members often apply direct pressure to anyone who questions the validity of these arguments supporting a decision or position favored by the majority. These same two officials pressured MTI to change its position after MTI originally recommended that the launch not take place. These two officials pressured MTI personnel to prove that it was not safe to launch, rather than to prove the opposite. As mentioned earlier, this was a total reversal of normal preflight procedures. It was this pressure that top MTI management was responding to when they overruled their engineering staff and recommended launch. As the Commission report states:

At approximately 11 p.m. Eastern Standard Time, the Thiokol/NASA teleconference resumed, the Thiokol management stating that they had reassessed the problem, that the temperature effects were a concern, but that the data was admittedly inconclusive (p. 96).

This seems to indicate the NASA's pressure on these Thiokol officials forced them to change their recommendation from delay to execution of the launch.

Self-Censorship.   Group members tend to censor themselves when they have opinions or ideas that deviate from the apparent group consensus. Janis feels that this reflects each member's inclination to minimize to himself or herself the importance of his or her own doubts and counter-arguments.

The most obvious evidence of self-censorship occurred when a vice president of MTI, who had previously presented information against launch, bowed to pressure from NASA and accepted their rationalizations for launch. He then wrote these up and presented them to NASA as the reasons that MTI had changed its recommendation to launch.

Illusion of Unanimity. Group members falling victim to groupthink share an illusion of unanimity concerning judgments made by members speaking in favor of the majority view. This symptom is caused in part by the preceding one and is aided by the false assumption that any participant who remains silent is in agreement with the majority opinion. The group leader and other members support each other by playing up points of convergence in their thinking at the expense of fully exploring points of divergence that might reveal unsettling problems.

No participant from NASA ever openly agreed with or even took sides with MTI in the discussion. The silence from NASA was probably amplified by the fact that the meeting was a teleconference linking the participants at three different locations. Obviously, body language which might have been evidenced by dissenters was not visible to others who might also have held a dissenting opinion. Thus, silence meant agreement.

Mindguarding. Certain group members assume the role of guarding the minds of others in the group. They attempt to shield the group from adverse information that might destroy the majority view of the facts regarding the appropriateness of the decision.

The top management of Marshall knew that the rocket casings had been ordered redesigned to correct a flaw 5 months previous to this launch. This information and other technical details concerning the history of the joint problem was withheld at the meeting.

DECISION-MAKING DEFECTS

The result of the antecedent conditions and the symptoms of groupthink is a defective decision-making process. Janis discusses several defects in decision making that can result.

Few Alternatives. The group considers only a few alternatives, often only two. No initial survey of all possible alternatives occurs. The Flight Readiness Review team had a launch/no-launch decision to make. These were the only two alternatives considered. Other possible alternatives might have been to delay the launch for further testing, or to delay until the temperatures reached an appropriate level.

No Re-Examination of Alternatives. The group fails to re-examine alternatives that may have been initially discarded based on early unfavorable information. Top NASA officials spent time and effort defending and strengthening their position, rather than examining the MTI position.

Rejecting Expert Opinions. Members make little or no attempt to seek outside experts' opinions. NASA did not seek out other experts who might have some expertise in this area. They assumed that they had all the information.

Rejecting Negative Information. Members tend to focus on supportive information and ignore any data or information that might cast a negative light on their preferred alternative. MTI representatives repeatedly tried to point out errors in the rationale the NASA officials were using to justify the launch. Even after the decision was made, the argument continued until a NASA official told the MTI representative that it was no longer his concern.

No Contingency Plans. Members spent little time discussing the possible consequences of the decision and, therefore, fail to develop contingency plans. There is no documented evidence in the Rogers Commission Report of any discussion of the possible consequences of an incorrect decision.

The major categories and key elements of the groupthink hypothesis have been presented (albeit somewhat briefly) along with evidence from the discussions prior to the launching of the Challenger, as reported in the President's Commission to investigate the accident. The antecedent conditions were present in the decision-making group, even though the group was in several physical locations. The leaders had a preferred solution and engaged in behaviors designed to promote it rather than critically appraise alternatives. These behaviors were evidence of most of the symptoms leading to a defective decision-making process.

DISCUSSION

This situation provides another example of decision making in which the group fell victim to the groupthink syndrome, as have so many previous groups. It illustrates the situation characteristics, the symptoms of group think, and decision-making defects as described by Janis. This situation, however, also illustrates several other aspects of situations that are critical to the development of groupthink that need to be included in a revised formulation of the groupthink model. First, the element of time in influencing the development of groupthink has not received adequate attention. In the decision to launch the space shuttle Challenger, time was a crucial part of the decision-making process. The launch had been delayed once, and the window for another launch was fast closing. The leaders of the decision team were concerned about public and congressional perceptions of the entire space shuttle program and its continued funding and may have felt that further delays of the launch could seriously impact future funding. With the space window fast closing, the decision team was faced with a launch now or seriously damage the program decision. One top level manager's response to Thiokol's initial recommendation to postpone the launch indicates the presence of time pressure:

> With this LCC (Launch Commit Criteria, i.e., do not launch with a temperature greater [sic] than 53 degrees, we may not be able to launch until next April. We need to consider this carefully before we jump to any conclusions. *(Report of the Presidential Commission on the Space Shuttle Accident, 1986, p. 96).*

Time pressure could have played a role in the group choosing to agree and to self-censor their comments. We propose that in certain situations when there is pressure to make a decision quickly, the elements may combine to foster the development of groupthink.

The second revision needs to be in the role of the leadership of the decision-making group In the space shuttle Challenger incident, the leadership of the group varied from a shared type of leadership to a very clear leader in the situation. This may indicate that the leadership role needs to be clearly defined and a style that demands open disclosure of information, points of opposition, complaints, and dissension. We propose the leadership style is a crucial variable that moderates the relationship between the group characteristics and the development of the symptoms. Janis (1983) is a primary form of evidence to support the inclusion of leadership style in the enhanced model. His account of why the *same* group succumbed to groupthink in one decision (Bay of Pigs) and not in another (Cuban Missile Crisis) supports the depiction of leadership style as a moderator variable. In these decisions, the only condition that changed was the leadership style of the President. In other words, the element that seemed to distinguish why groupthink occurred in the Bay of Pigs decision and not in the Cuban Missile Crisis situation is the president's change in his behavior.

These two variables, time and leadership style, are proposed as moderators of the impact of the group characteristics on groupthink symptoms. This relationship is portrayed graphically in Fig. 1. In effect, we propose that the groupthink symptoms result from the group characteristics, as proposed by Janis, but only in the presence of the moderator variables of time and certain leadership styles.

Time, as an important element in the model, is relatively straightforward. When a decision must be made within a very short time frame, pressure on members to agree, to avoid time-consuming arguments and reports from outside experts, and to self-censor themselves may increase. These pressures inevitably cause group members to seek agreement. In Janis's original model, time was included indirectly as a function of the antecedent condition, group cohesion. Janis (1983) argued that time pressures can adversely affect decision quality in two ways. First, it affects the decision makers' mental efficiency and judgment, interfering with their ability to concentrate on complicated discussions, to absorb new information, and to use imagination to anticipate the future consequences of alternative courses of action. Second, time pressure is a source of stress that will have the effect of inducing a policy-making group to become more cohesive and more likely to engage in groupthink.

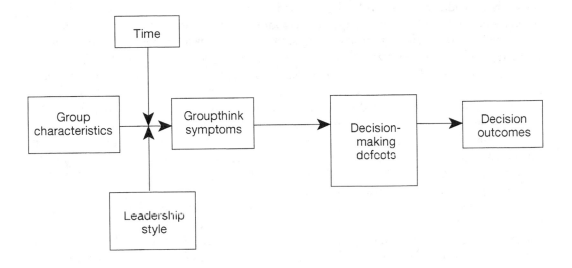

Figure 1
Revised groupthink framework

Leadership style is shown to be a moderator because of the importance it plays in either promoting or avoiding the development of the symptoms of the groupthink. The leader, even though she or he may not promote a preferred solution, may allow or even assist the group seeking agreement by not forcing the group to critically appraise all alternative courses of action. The focus of this leadership variable is on the degree to which the leader allows or promotes discussion and evaluation of alternatives. It is not a matter of simply not making known a preferred solution; the issue is one of stimulation of critical thinking among the group.

IMPACT ON PRESCRIPTIONS FOR PREVENTION

The revised model suggests that more specific prescriptions for prevention of groupthink can be made. First, group members need to be aware of the impact that a short decision time frame has on decision processes. When a decision must be made quickly, there will be more pressure to agree, i.e., discouragement of dissent, self-censorship, avoidance of expert opinion, and assumptions about unanimity. The type of leadership suggested here is not one that sits back and simply does not make known her or his preferred solution. This type of leader must be one that requires all members to speak up with concerns, questions, and new information. The leader must know what some of these concerns are and which members are likely to have serious doubts so that the people with concerns can be called upon to voice them. This type of group leadership does not simply assign the role of devil's advocate and step out of the way. This leader actually plays the role or makes sure that others do. A leader with the required style to avoid groupthink is not a laissez faire leader or non-involved participative leader. This leader is active in directing the activities of the group but does not make known a preferred solution. The group still must develop and evaluate alternative courses of action, but under the direct influence of a strong, demanding leader who forces critical appraisal of all alternatives.

Finally, a combination of the two variables suggests that the leader needs to help members to avoid the problems created by the time elements. For example, the leader may be able to alter an externally imposed time frame for the decision by negotiating an extension or even paying late fees, if necessary. If an extension is not possible, the leader may need to help the group eliminate the effects of time on the decision processes. This can be done by forcing attention to issues rather than time, encouraging dissension and confrontation, and scheduling special sessions to hear reports from outside experts that challenge prevailing views within the group.

Janis presents, in both editions of his book, several recommendations for preventing the occurrence of groupthink. These recommendations focus on the inclusion of outside experts in the decision-making process, all members taking the role of devil's advocate and critically appraising all alternative courses of action, and the leader not expressing a preferred solution. The revised groupthink framework suggests several new prescriptions that may be helpful in preventing further decision fiascoes similar to the decision to launch the space shuttle Challenger.

REFERENCES

Time, Fixing NASA. June 9, 1986.
Janis, I.L. (1983) *Victims of Groupthink*. Boston: Houghton Mifflin.
Janis, I.L. (1983) *Groupthink* (2nd ed., revised. Boston: Houghton Mifflin.
Report of the Presidential Commission on the Space Shuttle Accident. Washington, D.C.: July 1986.

QUESTIONS

1. What three characteristics make some groups prone to groupthink? Which of these were present in the group that decided to launch the Challenger in January 1986?

2. Janis specified eight symptoms that indicate a group is under the influence of groupthink. Based on the evidence given in this reading, how many of these symptoms do you believe were present when the decision to launch was made?

3. The same group that made the disastrous decision to launch on January 28th 1986 had previously made much better decisions (e.g., calling off the launch a few days earlier because of unfavorable conditions). What additional outside factor might have been present on January 27th that contributed to the existence of groupthink on that day?

4. What aspect of NASA's decision-making group do the authors focus on in making their recommendations for change? Can you think of other changes that might effectively reduce the symptoms of groupthink?

5. Does the groupthink perspective presented here suggest that NASA should have fired the people who decided to launch in spite of MTI recommendations? Why or why not?

Ψ CHAPTER 15 Ψ

BUSINESS, ORGANIZATIONS, AND THE ENVIRONMENT: APPLYING SOCIAL PSYCHOLOGY IN A COMPLEX WORLD

Reading 29: Classic

The Social Problems of an Industrial Civilization

Elton Mayo

The industrial revolution greatly improved the economies of many countries. The production of goods increased dramatically with the construction of larger plants employing more people. Unfortunately, the workers in these plants did not always share in the prosperity. Yet conditions in may places continued to improve, and conditions in post–World War I America were somewhat better than they had been several decades earlier. This improvement was due in part to moral and legal concerns. But beyond this, some companies began to realize that by looking out for their workers, they were helping themselves as well.

As it turned out, even for those companies whose motivated self-interest called for it, developing a content and motivated work force was not easily done. Elton Mayo, describing the situation he saw in 1923, realized that the contemporary understanding of what he called "human economics" was woefully insufficient. In the following reading, Mayo describes his first, and possibly the first, attempt by a psychologist to explain the complexities of human economics.

In 1923 Mayo was asked to investigate the problems of turnover in the mule-spinning department of a textile mill. While at first glance the working conditions seemed good enough, the workers were plagued by fatigue and low morale. Even financial incentive schemes had totally failed to improve worker morale or production. The solution that Mayo offered was small and simple; the results were anything but.

Ψ

Economic theory in its human aspect is woefully insufficient; indeed it is absurd. Humanity is not adequately described as a horde of individuals, each actuated by self-interest, each fighting his neighbor for the scarce material of survival. Realization that such theories completely falsify the normal human scene drives us back to study of

Source: Mayo, E. (1946). *The social problems of an industrial civilization* (2nd ed.). Boston: Division of Research, Harvard Business School, 1945. Reprinted by permission of Harvard Business School Publishing Corporation.

particular human situations. *Knowledge-of-acquaintance* of the actual event, intimate understanding of the complexity of human relationships, must precede the formulation of alternatives to current economic abstractions. This is the clinical method, the necessary preliminary to laboratory investigation. Only when clinically tested by successful treatment can a diagnosis be safely developed toward logical elaboration and laboratory experiment.

The first inquiry we undertook ran headlong into an illustration of the insufficiency of the assumption that individual self-interest actually operates as adequate incentive. Rather more than twenty years ago we were asked to discover, if possible, the causes of a high labor turnover in the mule-spinning department of a textile mill near Philadelphia.[1] The general labor situation elsewhere in the plant seemed highly satisfactory; the employers were unusually enlightened and humane; the work was exceedingly well organized in respect of operations and the company was generally regarded as an extremely successful venture. But the president and his director of personnel were much troubled by the situation in the mule-spinning department. Whereas the general labor turnover in other departments was estimated to be approximately 5% or 6% per annum, in the spinning department the turnover was estimated at approximately 250%. That is to say, about 100 men had to be taken on every year in order to keep about 40 working. And the difficulty tended to be most acute when the factory was busily employed and most in need of men.

Several firms of efficiency engineers had been consulted; their firms had instituted altogether four financial incentive schemes. And these schemes had been a total failure; labor turnover had not dropped one point, nor had production improved: it was almost as a last resort that the firm consulted a university. Although other plants in the vicinity had apparently drifted into acceptance of low morale amongst mule spinners as inevitable, the president of this company refused to believe that the situation was beyond remedy.

On a first inspection the conditions of work in the department did not seem to differ in any general respect from conditions elsewhere in the mill. For some time Saturday work had been discontinued throughout the plant, so that the work week was of 50 hours – five days of 10 hours, two shifts of 5 hours each separated by a 45-minute lunch interval. The mule-spinner attendant was known as a piecer; his work involved walking up and down a long alley, perhaps 30 yards or more, on either side of which a machine head was operating spinning frames. These frames moved back and forth stretching yarn taken from the carding machines, twisting it, and rolling it up on cops. The number of frames operated by a machine head varied from 10 to 14. All had to be closely watched; threads constantly broke and had to be pieced together. The number of piecers in an alley, usually two or three, varied according to the kind of yarn being spun. To an observer the work looked monotonous – walking up and down an alley twisting together broken threads. The only variation in work occurred when a machine head was stopped in order to doff or to replace some spools.

---

[1] For a more detailed account of this inquiry, see Elton Mayo, "Revery and Industrial Fatigue," *Personnel Journal*, Vol. III, No. 8, December, 1924, pp. 273-281.

Dr. S. D. Ludlum, professor of neuropsychiatry in the graduate school of medicine in the University of Pennsylvania, was of immense aid to us at this stage as later in the study. He arranged that a registered nurse, one of our group, should be able to relate her small clinic for minor troubles in the plant direct to the Polyclinic Hospital in Philadelphia. Serious cases she referred to the hospital clinicians; minor injuries, a cut or splinter, she could deal with herself. This arrangement seemed to do away with any need for further explanation. Workers gratefully accepted the services of the nurse and, in some instances, the further clinical aid of the hospital. These services were real and understandable. From the first the mule spinners formed a large part of the nurse's regular callers – and either when at work or in the clinic talked to her and to us quite freely. It was of course clearly understood that nothing said to any of us was ever repeated to anyone in the plant.

As the men began to talk to us, the picture of the situation developed quite differently from that obtained at first inspection. We discovered that almost every piecer suffered from foot trouble of one or another kind for which he apparently knew no effective remedy. Many also claimed neuritis in various localities of arms, shoulders, or legs. But above and beyond all this, the striking fact was the uniformly pessimistic nature of the preoccupations of these workers while at work. To this there seemed no exception: their own opinion of their work was low, even lower than the estimate of mule spinning held by other workers in the plant. We discovered also that the job was essentially solitary: there might be three workers in an alley, but the amount of communication between them in a day was almost nil. One might be piecing threads together here; another, 20 yards away. And the doffing process when it took place involved rapid work with a minimum of communication. Some of the men were young – in the twenties, others were in the fifties – all alike claimed that they were too fatigued to enjoy social evenings after work. Occasionally a worker would flare out into apparently unreasonable anger and incontinently leave his job.

The whole group was characterized by a species of strongly held loyalty to the company president. He had been a colonel in the regular United States Army and had seen active service both before and during the First World War. Many of the workers had been in the trenches in France under his immediate command and had the highest opinion of him; they had come with him from his regiment to the textile mill. Perhaps for this reason their pessimistic moods showed no anger against "The Colonel" or "the company." For the most part the individual seemed to be almost melancholic about himself; this mood alternated with spurts of rage against some immediate supervisor.

After some discussion the management permitted us to experiment with rest periods – two of 10 minutes' length in the morning and two again in the afternoon. We arranged these rests so that the work period should be divided thus: 2 hours' work, 10 minutes' rest; 1 1/2 hours' work, 10 minutes' rest; and a final work period of 1 hour and 10 minutes. The actual uninterrupted work period thus diminished in morning and afternoon. In these rest periods the workers were permitted to lie down; we instructed them in the best methods of securing the maximum of muscular relaxation. We encouraged them to sleep for 10 minutes and most of them were able to do so.

We began with one team of piecers, about one-third of the total number, and the results were encouraging from the outset. The men themselves were pleased and interested; they speedily adopted the method of rest we advised. The effect was immediate – symptoms of melancholy preoccupation almost wholly disappeared, the labor turnover came to an end, production was maintained, and the morale generally improved. Such immediate effects could not be attributed to the mere elimination of physical fatigue. This was confirmed by the fact that an almost equivalent improvement showed itself in the work of the other two-thirds of the piecers. These men had discussed the experiment at lunch time with their fellows and were confident that "The Colonel" would extend the system to them if it were found satisfactory. And in the October of that year, 1923, this expectation was fulfilled; the management, pleased with the improved condition of the men and the work, decided to extend the rest period system to include the entire personnel of the spinning department. This made it possible for us to do what we could not do before – to measure the effect of the rest periods upon the productivity of the department.

Until October, 1923, the spinning department had never earned a bonus under one of the incentive systems introduced; in October and for the months recorded thereafter, with one interesting exception, the spinners consistently earned a bonus in addition to their wages. I have elsewhere described the bonus plan[2] and shall not repeat this detail here. Enough to say that, if the production of the department in any month exceeded 75% of a carefully calculated possibility, every spinner was paid an excess percentage of his flat-rate wage equivalent to the average excess percentage of production over 75%. Thus a monthly man-hour efficiency of 80% meant a 5% bonus on his monthly wage to every employee in the department. As said above, no fraction of bonus had ever been earned by the department. We were unable to get figures showing the average productivity of the department before October, 1923, when the experiment proper began; but it was generally admitted by executives and supervisors that production had never been above an approximate 70%.

The period from October, 1923, to mid-February, 1924, inclusive, showed a surprising change. The mental and physical condition of the men continued to improve, and, whereas the financial incentive of the bonus had not operated to stimulate production while they felt fatigued, they were now pleased by the fact that under conditions of work that seemed much easier they were earning bonuses as never before. The system was not, however, altogether satisfactory at this time. The immediate supervisors had never liked the sight of workers lying asleep on sacks while the mules were running; it occurred to one of them that the men should be made to "earn" their rest periods. That is to say, a task was set and, if finished within a given time, the men had their rest. For the most part, the workers had three or four rests every day and the innovation worked well enough. For example, the monthly average of productivity ran as follows:

---

[2] Elton Mayo, "Revery and Industrial Fatigue," loc. cit.

	8	*Efficiency*	*Bonus*
October	1923	79 ½ %	4 ½%
November	"	78 ¾	3 ¾
December	"	82	7
January	1924	78 ¾	3 ¾
February	"	80 1/4	5 ¼

This, for workers who had never before earned a bonus, meant much.

This general condition continued until Friday, February 15, when in response to a heavy demand for goods the supervisor who had introduced the idea of earned rest periods ordered the whole system abandoned. Within five days production fell to a point lower than it had been for months. And on February 22, we found that the old pessimistic preoccupations had returned in full force, thus coinciding almost exactly with the drop in production. The executive officer in charge ordered the resumption of the rest period system on Monday, February 25; this was done, but the idea of earned rest periods was also reinstated even more strongly then before. At this point, the workers gave every symptom of profound discouragement; they professed a belief that the system would be discontinued before long. In spite of this, the daily record for March showed definite improvement, but the general average for the month was back at the old point, 70%.

At this point the president of the company, "The Colonel," took charge. His military service had taught him two important things – one, to care for his men, and, two, not be afraid of making decisions. He called a conference in his office to discuss the remarkable diminution from 80% to 70% in the department's productive efficiency. We were able to point out that in March there had been a recrudescence of absenteeism, an ill that had notably diminished in the October to February period. This meant that the men were taking their rest periods in the form of "missed" days, a proceeding that did not greatly remedy their condition and that produced chaos in the plant. We put it therefore that the question was not whether a certain proportion of their working time was to be given up to rest. We pointed out that they took the rest, whether it was given them or not. We were asking that a less proportion should be thus allotted, but that it should be done systematically. Furthermore, we were able to claim that the whole rest period system had never had a fair trial. In other words, it had not been possible for a worker to know as he entered the factory in the morning that he was assured of his four rests in the day.

In order to test our claim, the president ordered that during the month of April the spinning mules should be shut down for 10 minutes at a time four times a day and that all hands from the floor supervisor down should rest as they had been instructed to do. There was some difficulty in securing the requisite amount of floor space for approximately 40 men to lie down by their machines and in securing sufficient sacking to provide for their comfort. With the exception of the president himself, there were few who believed that this drastic alteration of method could result in increased production. The men themselves believed that 40 minutes lost by 40 men per day during a whole month could not be recovered. They pointed out that the machines could not be "speeded up" and that there was no other way of recovering the lost time. In spite of this general belief, the returns for April showed an improvement on March.[3] The March production-efficiency figure had been 70%, the April figure was 77.5%. This, while it represented a 7.5% gain in the company's rating, was actually a 10% gain. The men had had their rests, the pessimism had again disappeared; simultaneously, their morale had much improved, absenteeism had diminished, and every worker had earned a 2.5% bonus on his wages. In the month of May and thereafter, the president ordered a return to the system of alternating rest periods, with this important difference that each group of three men in an alley was to determine for itself the method of alternation, the understanding being that every worker was to have four such rest periods daily and regularly. In the month of May, the average efficiency of men-hour production was 80.25%. In June it reached the then record high figure of 85%. During the following three months the department maintained its improved capacity: July, 82%; August, 83.5%; September, 86.5%.

It is interesting to observe the difference that an absolute certainty of a minimum number of rest periods made. The months from April to September differed from the preceding months in this respect and they revealed a steady progress. Mondays and Fridays were no longer the worst days in the week. The irregularity reported in May was due to the fact that the spinning mules were constantly "running away from the cards," that is, outdistancing the carding machines which supplied them with spooled yarn. By June, the company had put in two new carding machines, and June was as steadily above 85% as March was below 75%.

The investigation began with a question as to the causes of a very high labor turnover. In the 12 months of experiment there was no labor turnover at all. This does not mean that no worker left the factory – during a period of trade slackness, some were laid off, one at least moved his place of residence and found work elsewhere, another was found to be phthisical and sent to the country. But the former problem of a highly emotional labor turnover ceased to exist. The factory began to hold its mule spinners and no longer had difficulty in maintaining a full complement in times of rushed work. The attitude of management to the innovation was revealed in the fact that the company purchased army cots for the workers to rest upon. When these cots proved unequal to the wear and tear, management installed a bed and mattress at the end of each alley as provision for the workers' adequate rest. And the workers developed the habit of sleeping for the last three rest periods of the day, that late morning rest and both afternoon rests. Experience seemed to show that the benefit was directly proportionate to the completeness of the relaxation – hence the beds. Several years later, the president of the company said publicly that from this time the labor turnover sank to an approximate 5% or 6% per annum and stayed there until the mules were taken out and ring spinning substituted.

At the time when we completed our part in this work, we were sure that we had not wholly discovered the causes of the high labor turnover. We could not even attribute the change to the mere introduction of rest periods; inevitably many other changes had been

---

[3] Ibid.

simultaneously introduced. For example, we had listened carefully and with full attention to anything a worker wished to say, whatever the character of his comment. In addition to this, we – supported by the president – had demonstrated an interest in what was said by the introduction of experimental changes, by instruction in the best methods of relaxation. The Colonel also had demonstrated unmistakably a sincere interest in his workers' welfare; he had lived up to his Army reputation. The supervisor who instituted the earning of rest periods was swept aside by the president and the company – thereby "placing" the company's attitude in the minds of its workers.

But, in addition to this – and we did not see this clearly at the time – the president had effected another important change. He had helped to transform a horde of "solitaries" into a social group. In May, 1924, he placed the control of rest periods squarely in the hands of the workers in an alley with no one to say them nay. This led to consultation, not only between individuals, but between alleys throughout the group – and to a feeling of responsibility directly to the president. And the general social changes effected were astonishing – even in relationships outside the factory. One worker told us with great surprise that he had begun taking his wife to "movies" in the evenings, a thing he had not done for years. Another, equally to his surprise, gave up a habit of spending alcoholic weekends on bootleg liquor. In general the change was complex, and the difficulty of assigning the part played in it by various aspects of the experiment impossible to resolve. We should have liked to experiment further, but this desire – probably wisely in the circumstances – was disallowed. Thus the inquiry left us with many questions unanswered, but it pointed in a direction for further studies, the results of which later proved helpful in reinterpreting the data of this first investigation.

But we had moved onwards. The efficiency experts had not consulted the workers; they regarded workers' statements as exaggerated or due to misconception of the facts and therefore to be ignored. Yet to ignore an important symptom – whatever its character – on supposedly moral grounds is preposterous. The "expert" assumptions of rabble hypothesis and individual self-interest as a basis for diagnosis led nowhere. On the other hand, careful and pedestrian consideration of the worker's situation taken as part of a clinical diagnosis led us to results so surprising that we could at the time only partly explain them.

QUESTIONS

1. What physical difficulties did the mule spinners initially complain of? What other difficulties did they have?

2. Mayo says that humanity is not just a "horde of individuals, each actuated by self-interest, each fighting his neighbor for... survival." How does this study support this supposition?

3. Did the mule spinners work harder when their rest was guaranteed or when they had to earn it? Under which system was absenteeism greater?

4. In what ways does the textile mill in this article follow the bureaucratic model? In what ways does it not?

5. Considering that Mayo introduced only one change in the mule spinning department, why is he not sure what the improved conditions are attributable to?

Reading 30: Contemporary

Ambivalence and Stereotypes Cause Sexual Harassment: A Theory with Implications for Organizational Change

Susan T. Fiske and Peter Glick

Our final reading examines the issue of discrimination in the workplace. This form of discrimination represents a very costly problem: Some estimates suggest that discrimination in the workplace costs U.S. businesses more than $1 billion a year in lost potential earnings.

In this reading, social psychologists Susan Fiske and Peter Glick focus their attention on one form of workplace discrimination: sexual harassment. According to Fiske and Glick, gender-based discrimination is fundamentally different from other types of discrimination. Unlike most mutually antagonistic groups, men and women have many positive as well as negative attitudes about one another. This ambivalence, in conjunction with stereotypes about women and their role in the workplace, too often leads to sexual harassment.

Fiske and Glick begin by describing their theory of ambivalent sexism and explaining how it leads to harassment. Next, they examine some characteristics of the workplace that subtly encourage harassment by activating men's ambivalent stereotypes. Finally, they suggest institutional changes that could help reduce harassment by changing those aspects of office culture that normally support it.

Ψ

Harassment in the workplace results, we argue, from the complex interplay of ambivalent motives and gender stereotyping of women and jobs. The first section of this article describes a theoretical basis for examining men's various motives toward women, highlighting the sources of ambivalence... . This theory of cognitive-motivational interplay then describes the different kinds of harassment that can result. These cognitive-motivational dynamics can be encouraged by certain organizational contexts, described in the next section. Organizational remedies suggested by the theory and by social psychological research are offered in the final section of the paper.

Our purpose here is to identify the psychology of motivation and stereotyping that leads to harassment, as well as the organizational context that supports or undermines this psychology. The identified factors are not exhaustive, nor are all of them necessary in

Source: Fiske, S.T., and Glick, P. (1995). Ambivalence and stereotypes cause sexual harassment. A theory with implications for organizational change. *Journal of Social Issues, 51*, 97-115. Copyright © 1995 by Susan T. Fiske and Peter Glick. Reprinted by permission of Blackwell Publishers.

any given case of harassment, nor is any one of them a sufficient cause of harassment. But in our analysis, these are prominent psychological forces that underlie men's sexual harassment of women.[1]

AMBIVALENT MOTIVATIONS

Sexual harassment reflects common motivations that underlie many men's goals in many of their interactions with women. Traditionally, men's motivational orientation toward women has been deeply ambivalent, reflecting male desires for both dominance and intimacy. As a result, both positive and negative feelings coexist toward women that may lead men to experience certain feelings as subjectively positive even though they encourage behaviors that are problematic for women. Elsewhere, we have validated a scale, the Ambivalent Sexism Inventory, which distinguishes hostile and benevolent sexism (Glick & Fiske, 1994). Hostile sexism refers to sexist antipathy toward women based on an ideology of male dominance, male superiority, and a hostile form of sexuality (in which women are treated merely as sexual objects). Benevolent sexism refers to *subjectively positive*, though sexist, attitudes that include protectiveness toward women, positively valenced stereotypes of women (e.g., nurturance), and a desire for heterosexual intimacy. Both types of sexism have three components, each of which encompass a hostile and a "benevolent" aspect (see Glick & Fiske, 1994, for further evidence and references): (a) *Paternalism* is an orientation toward interacting with women as a father dealing with his children. This orientation encompasses not only attitudes of male superiority and dominance over women, but also a protectiveness toward women as "the weaker sex." (b) *Gender differentiation* is the motivation to make distinctions between the sexes. Gender identity is perhaps the first group-based component of self-identity to be learned (Maccoby, 1988). This aspect of men's identity is a source of self-esteem to the extent that women are viewed as inferior, promoting a competitive attitude toward women (particularly those who enter male domains). Traditional gender roles, however, also promote favorable attitudes toward women as mothers and homemakers (Eagly & Mladinic, 1993). (c) *Heterosexuality* makes relations between men and women uniquely different from other group relationships. Whereas ingroups and outgroups typically maintain stark social boundaries to avoid intimacy (Tajfel, 1982), our most intimate relations are more likely to be across, rather than within, gender lines (Berscheid, Snyder, & Omoto, 1989). Although men's sexual attraction can be the source of extremely positive feelings toward women and be linked to a genuine desire for intimacy, sexual desire is for men who are most likely to harass, also (or primarily) linked to hostility and a desire to dominate women (Bargh & Raymond, 1995; Pryor, Giedd, & Williams, 1995). Dominative paternalism, competitive gender differentiation, and hostile heterosexuality together compose *Hostile Sexism*, whereas protective paternalism, complementary gender differentiation, and heterosexual intimacy motives comprise *Benevolent Sexism*.

---

[1] While we recognize that women can sexually harass men and that within-sex sexual harassment also occurs, we concentrate here on the theoretical analysis of men harassing women.

**TABLE 1   TYPES OF HARASSMENT MOTIVES AND STEREOTYPES
PREDICTED BY AMBIVALENT SEXISM**

Type of Harassment	Primary Motives	Reactions to Rejection	Stereotypes of Women	Stereotypes of Jobs
Earnest	Sexual Intimacy	Depends on attraction and likely success	Sexy	Pink Collar
Hostile	Domination paternalistic and competitive)	Increased harassment	Non-traditional	Blue or white collar
Ambivalent Paternalistic	Paternalism and sexual intimacy	Shift to hostility	Traditional and sexy	Pink collar
Competitive	Gender differentia-tion and sexual intimacy	Shift to hostility	Non-traditional and sexy	Blue or white collar

The ambivalent motives evident in these three components of sexist attitudes imply two potential core types of sexual harassment (see Table 1): an "earnest" (subjectively "benevolent") form motivated by a genuine desire for lasting heterosexual intimacy and a "hostile" form in which sexuality is merely another form of male domination. The earnest form is illustrated by a male pipefitter, truly named Romeo at Jacksonville Shipyard, who made repeated and unwelcome advances to a female welder, who reported that he told her "all the time that he was in love with me, wanted to go out with me" and that his penis "worked like a drill motor" (*Robinson v. Jacksonville Shipyards, Inc.*, 1989, Banks III, 72–81, 173). Here, the harassment is expressed less in ambivalence than in persistence despite clear communications to desist. One might consider it romantic although misguided, but it is harassing in its form and repetition. The hostile form is illustrated by a male shipyard worker commenting:

> Women are only fit company for something that howls....There's nothing worse than having to work around women...[to a female co-worker:] I don't care where you go. You can go flash the sailors if you want to. (Comments by a co-worker, reported by plaintiff Robinson, I:196–202; II: 1–9; *Robinson v. Jacksonville Shipyards, Inc.*)

Upon being remonstrated by an outside observer – "Why do you treat her that way for?" – a worker replied "Well, that's the way you've got to treat them. She hasn't got virgin ears. She's heard it all before." And on another, similar occasion, he advised observers, "Don't look away and laugh [at her discomfort]. Laugh in her face" (*Robinson*, I:196–202; II:1–9). The hostility expresses a desire to dominate, whether in competition between peers over gender differentiation (removing women from men's spheres) or in dominative paternalism from a supervisor to a subordinate (dealing with uppity women).

Benevolent and hostile motives, however, are not mutually exclusive (Glick & Fiske, 1994), suggesting a third, perhaps more common, type – "ambivalent harassment." Ambivalent harassment combines elements of both hostile and benevolent sexism. Depending on which subjectively positive and hostile motivations combine, different subtypes of ambivalent harassment may occur. In one version of ambivalence, the harasser may honestly believe his motives are benevolent ("I desire her, want to love and protect her"), even though his attraction to the woman and his willingness to persist in the face of her refusals are largely the result of, for example, his superior and her subordinate position on the job. This subtype of ambivalent harassment combines overt feelings of protective paternalism and heterosexual intimacy (benevolent sexism) with (possibly covert) motivations of dominative paternalism (hostile sexism).

A second subtype of ambivalent harassment may be a mixture of "benevolent" sexual attraction and a hostile desire to "tame" an independent or competitive woman, thereby combining competitive gender differentiation (hostile sexism) with overt desires for heterosexual intimacy (benevolent sexism). This ambivalent phenomenon is often evident when a few women "invade" a previously all-male environment; for example, the "boy's club" at Jacksonville Shipyards painted "Men Only" on one of the work trailers, as well as sexually hostile graffiti in places where the women would be sure to see it; the men's harassing interactions with the women extended the hostile and exclusionary message, whereas the surface content was the expression of sexual attraction (e.g., crude sexual come-ons).

Ambivalent harassment may be particularly insidious because the man can readily justify his actions to himself as not harassment (Bargh & Raymond, 1995) but something benign (protecting the woman in the first, paternalistic, subtype; "harmless male bonding" in the second, competitive, subtype; and sexual attraction in both). Such justifications may disinhibit behavior in which a man might not otherwise engage, as may prevailing social norms that cast men as the primary initiators of heterosexual romantic relationships (Zillmann & Weaver, 1989).

The motives for harassment are likely to affect how a man reacts to a woman's refusal to accept his sexual advances. For harassment stemming from the *purely hostile* motive to dominate, a woman's refusal, disgust, or fear may simply signal to the harasser that he is achieving his goal of "putting her in her place." In contrast, for a man whose advances stem from an earnest desire for a lasting relationship, persistence may depend on the depth of his positive feelings for the woman and his capacity to absorb rejection. For ambivalent harassers of the paternalistic subtype, the man in a superordinate organizational position may maintain the illusion that even though she refuses now, eventually the woman will reciprocate his attraction. This illusion is likely to persist because many victims of harassment are reluctant directly to confront or emphatically to reject their harasser for fear of retaliation (Fitzgerald, Swan, & Fisher, 1995) and also because men in superordinate positions view their status as adding to their own sexual attractiveness (Gutek, 1985). For those with paternalistic as well as intimacy motivations, then, repeated and unambiguous refusals of their advances may destroy any benevolent feelings toward their female targets and turn their behavior from ambivalent to purely hostile. For ambivalent harassers of the competitive subtype, rejection signals one more arena in which they cannot compete successfully. The rejection is likely to escalate competition into overt hostility. Women who accept workplace sexual advances are in one sense reaffirming the man's sexual identify, thereby diminishing the gender competitive threat. (But these women are unlikely to be evaluated seriously as co-workers; Fiske, Goodwin, Rosen, & Rosenthal, 1994.)

In short, there is sound theoretical basis for examining men's motives toward women, highlighting the sources of ambivalence. The motives suggest different types of harassment, but these types also correspond to different cognitive images or stereotypes of women, described in the next section....

The cognitive-motivational dynamics underlying harassment can be encouraged by certain organizational contexts, described in this section. The occupational groups known as pink, white, and blue collar are highly sex segregated (Gottfredson, 1981). This segregation has important effects on organizational contexts: (a) in contexts with few or no women performing a particular job, the occupational role often takes on a "masculine culture" (Gutek, 1985); (b) the few women who do break into these jobs have a "token" status (Kanter, 1977); (c) men have little history or experience of dealing with women in the job, so they react on the basis of limited information, thereby promoting stereotypes (Fiske & Neuberg, 1990); and (d) dramatic power asymmetries are created between the men and women (Fiske, 1993). All these effects together heighten the probability of sexual harassment.

Masculine Culture

The percentage of men in an occupation has a strong positive correlation to the perceived masculinity and a negative correlation to the perceived femininity of traits required to perform the job (Glick, 1991). In male-dominated jobs, the masculine sex role often "spills over" into the job, fusing masculine gender identity with the work role and culture (Gutek, 1985). For instance, even though leadership studies (Fleishman, 1967) have long emphasized the importance of the stereotypically feminine trait of "consideration" (being expressive and nurturant with subordinates), popular images of a good leader (a traditionally male work role) emphasize only masculine traits (e.g., independence, ambition). The more masculine the job culture (i.e., the stronger the association of masculine traits to the exclusion of feminine traits), the greater is the hostility likely faced by women who enter these occupations. Women in these occupations are seen as disrupting the "masculine camaraderie" that infuses the culture of the occupation.

Although a masculine culture is more the rule than the exception among male-dominated jobs, jobs with similar sex ratios do vary in this regard, with some being viewed as requiring feminine as well as masculine traits (Glick, 1991). Indeed, there may be variation among subspecialties of the same job. Pediatric medicine, for example, is less stereotypically masculine than neurosurgery. Women seeking M.D. degrees may face less hostility if they go into the former, as opposed to the latter, specialty. Jobs that derive their "masculinity" from forms of intelligence that are viewed as uniquely masculine (e.g., engineering) or physical strength requirements (e.g., construction work) are those in which women are most likely to face hostile resistance (Gottfredson, 1981).

Solo Status

The perception of newly integrated women as disruptive comes with even the smallest inroads into these masculinized occupations, the female "token" or "solo." The presence of even a single woman can create heightened self-consciousness about gender roles and work behavior by the male majority. Certain aspects of the male job culture may normally be given no thought (e.g., in blue-collar settings, the prevalence of swearing and dirty jokes; in white-collar setting, business conducted around all-male sports). But the entrance of even more woman may force self-consciousness, and the previously easy-going atmosphere may become tense and uncomfortable for many male workers (Fiske & Ruscher, 1993). This discomfort, of course, is allegedly caused by the female solo, who may then be the target of a hostile backlash and intimidating tests to see whether she will complain about the masculine job culture (e.g., "Let's see if she can take a ribbing like one of the guys"). Such testing often takes the form of sexual harassment.

Solo status also heightens the salience of the token woman's gender and increases the probability that she will be tagged as a particular type of woman. The roles mentioned in the literature (e.g., Kanter, 1977) correspond to our previously described common subtypes of women: Some solo women may be thrust into (or adopt) a traditional role that buys male protection (e.g., the Mother who nurtures the boys in the group, the Mascot or Pet who functions as an admiring and sexless younger sister). Others, however, will be stereotyped as the Seductress, who is cast mainly as a sex object (but who may be able to buy protection from a high-status male, making her off limits to other men). Solo women who refuse to fit into a sex-typed role tend to be seen as more competent, but less agreeable and cooperative co-workers; they face hostility from the group and are often tagged as Iron Maidens (tough, threatening, and unfeminine). All three of these roles, purely traditional, purely sexual, or purely nontraditional, disadvantage the woman so placed. As described earlier, each of these roles elicits different kinds of sexual harassment, unless organizations act to counteract it....

ORGANIZATIONAL REMEDIES

Organizational remedies suggested by the present theory and by existing social psychological research are offered in this, the final section of the paper; these particular ideas follow from the theory, but of course many other interventions may be appropriate. The current notions are described according to the features of organizational context just noted.

Masculine Culture

To the extent that a masculine culture permeates a job and male stereotypes define it, organizations need to reframe people's perceptions of the job category. Job descriptions can minimize gender-associated characteristics as aspects of the job, if they are indeed superfluous. Internally, inhouse recruitment notices, job titles, and stated promotion criteria all communicate whether a job is gender neutral or not. For example, the title "secretary" is more stereotypically female than the title "administrative aide," but the duties could easily be similar. And of course, the actual distribution of the sexes in jobs can provide role models that convey whether "people like me" can do this job.

How people are treated once in the job can encourage or discourage stereotyping and harassment. A professional environment that minimizes sexual joking, presumed intimacy, and inappropriate informality also minimizes sexual harassment (Gutek, 1985). One gender's culture is less likely to dominate, the more professional and task oriented the environment.

Certain aspects of an unprofessional work environment particularly matter to sexual harassment. There is by now ample evidence to indicate that the presence of pornography in the workplace encourages stereotyping and harassment of women (Rudman & Borgida, in press; McKenzie-Mohr & Zanna, 1990). It is not merely the sexual nature of pornography but the fact that it targets women and reduces them to their sexual characteristics that damages the workplace.

Both the company's external advertising campaigns and personnel recruitment are also relevant here. For example, the focus of the lawsuit against Stroh's Beer Company named its "Swedish bikini team" ads as contributing to a sexually harassing discriminatory work environment. And personnel ads can emphasize sexual (attractiveness) and gender-related (demeanor) traits or not. Reducing the hegemony of masculine culture, especially sexualized masculine culture, may well discourage sexual harassment.

Solo Status

The sheer numbers of men and women in a particular job category contribute to the masculine culture associated with it. Clearly, the long-term remedy is to increase the numbers of the underrepresented sex. But the applicant pool may not be immediately available or qualified; turnover may be slow, with the net effect that ratios do not change quickly. In the transition periods, some people will have solo or near-solo status.

The solution to solo structures is to achieve a critical mass of 20% or more, and not fewer than two individuals (Pettigrew & Martin, 1987). As a transitional step, the underrepresented group could be recruited department by department, with critical-mass clusters within each department, before moving on to the next department. However, this could be legally dicey, if groups are ghettoized. The ideal situation is massive and effective recruitment efforts....

CONCLUSION

Our theory of ambivalent motivations and gender stereotypes proposes three core male motivations in interaction with women: paternalism, gender differentiation, and heterosexual attraction. These motives combine to produce four types of harassment: earnest (based on subjectively benevolent motives of sexual intimacy seeking), hostile (either dominative paternalism or competitive gender differentiation), paternalistic ambivalence (combining dominative and protective paternalism and sexual intimacy seeking), and competitive ambivalence (combining competitive gender differentiation and sexual intimacy seeking). Women fitting various subtypes – respectively, sexy, nontraditional, traditional and sexy, and nontraditional and sexy – seem most likely to elicit the corresponding motives and harassment.

We offer this theory in the hope of encouraging more theory-based examination of gender stereotyping and sexual harassment, as also occurs elsewhere in this issue. Theory will allow the development, testing, and application of more coherent causal analyses and less merely descriptive research on these important topics. The theory admittedly is described here without a direct empirical test. Elsewhere, we have developed and validated the Ambivalent Sexism Inventory (Glick & Fiske, 1994), which demonstrates the separate hostile and "benevolent" (i.e., subjectively positive) components of sexism, including paternalism, gender differentiation, and heterosexual attraction. These motives, the parallel stereotypes, and the corresponding harassment provide new ways to conceptualize and investigate how men and women can most constructively and happily relate to each other in the workplace.

REFERENCES

BARGH, J.A., & RAYMOND, P. (1995). The naive misuse of power: Nonconscious sources of sexual harassment. *Journal of Social Issues, 51*, 85–96.

BERSCHEID E., SNYDER, M., & OMOTO, A. (1989). The Relationship Closeness Inventory: Assessing the closeness of interpersonal relationships. *Journal of Personality and Social Psychology, 57*, 792–807.

EAGLY, A.H., & MLADINIC, A. (1993). Are people prejudiced against women? Some answers from research on attitudes, gender stereotypes, and judgments of competence. In W. Stroebe & M. Hewstone (Eds.), *European review of social psychology* (Vol. 5, pp. 1–35). New York: Wiley.

FISKE, S.T. (1993). Controlling other people: The impact of power on stereotyping. *American Psychologist, 48*, 621–628.

FISKE, S.T., GOODWIN, S.A., ROSEN, L.D., & ROSENTHAL, A.M. (1994). *Romantic outcome dependency and the (in)accuracy of impression formation: A case of clouded judgment.* Manuscript submitted for publication.

FISKE, S.T., & NEUBERG, S.L. (1990). A continuum of impression formation, from category-based to individuating processes: Influences of information and motivation on attention and interpretation. In M.P. Zanna (Ed.), *Advances in experimental social psychology* (Vol. 23, pp. 1–74). New York: Academic Press.

FISKE, S.T., & RUSCHER, J.B. (1993). Negative interdependence and prejudice: Whence the affect? In D.M. Mackie & D.L. Hamilton (Eds.), *Affect, cognition, and stereotyping: Interactive processes in group perception* (pp. 239–268). New York: Academic Press.

FITZGERALD, L.F., SWAN, S., & FISCHER, K. (1995). Why didn't she just report him? The psychological and legal implications of women's responses to sexual harassment. *Journal of Social Issues, 51*, 117–138.

FLESICHMAN, E.A. (1967). Performance of assessment based on an empirically derived task taxonomy. *Human Factors, 9*, 349–366.

GLICK, P. (1991). Trait-based and sex-based discrimination in occupational prestige, occupational salary, and hiring. *Sex Roles, 25*, 351–378.

GLICK, P., FISKE, S.T. (1994). *The Ambivalent Sexism Inventory: Differentiating hostile and benevolent sexism.* Manuscript submitted for publication.

GOTTFREDSON, L.S. (1981). Circumscription and compromise: A developmental theory of occupational aspirations. *Journal of Counseling Psychology Monograph, 28,* 545–579.

GUTEK, B.A. (1985). *Sex and the workplace.* San Francisco: Jossey-Bass.

KANTER, R.M. (1977). *Men and women of the corporation.* New York: Basic Books.

MACCOBY, E.E. (1988). Gender as a social category. *Developmental Psychology, 24,* 755–765.

MCKENZIE-MOHR, D., & ZANNA, M.P. (1990). Treating women as sexual objects: Look to the (gender schematic) male who has viewed pornography. *Personality and Social Psychology Bulletin, 16,* 296–308.

PETTIGREW, T.F., & MARTIN, J. (1987). Shaping the organizational context for black American inclusion. *Journal of Social Issues, 43(1),* 41–78.

PRYOR, J.B., GIEDD, J.L., & WILLIAMS, K.B. (1995). A social psychological model for predicting sexual harassment. *Journal of Social Issues, 51,* 69–84.

Robinson v. Jacksonville Shipyards, Inc. (M.D. Fla. 1989; Case No. 86-927). Depositions by Banks, III, 72–81, 173; Robinson, I, 196–202, II, 1–9.

RUDMAN, L.A., & BORGIDA, E. (in press). The afterglow of construct accessibility: The cognitive and behavioral consequences of priming men to view women as sexual objects. *Journal of Experimental Social Psychology.*

TAJFEL, H. (Ed.). (1982). *Social identity and intergroup relations.* London: Cambridge University Press.

ZILLMANN, D., & WEAVER, J.B. (1989). Pornography and men's sexual callousness toward women. In D. Zillmann & J. Bryant (Eds.), *Pornography: Research advances and policy considerations* (pp. 95–125). Hillsdale: Erlbaum.

QUESTIONS

1. Why do Fiske and Glick believe that sexism is fundamentally different from any other form of discrimination?

2. What is "benevolent" sexism? In what sense are the attitudes of benevolent sexism positive? In what sense are they negative?

3. Why do the authors believe that ambivalent harassment may more insidious than other forms of harassment?

4. Why are women unlikely to reject directly and emphatically male colleagues' unwanted sexual advances? How might such a refusal make their situation worse?

5. What does it mean to say that a woman has "solo status"? How does this affect the likelihood that harassment will occur in the workplace? What solution do the authors suggest?